Spinoza & the Origins of Modern Critical Theory

THE BUCKNELL LECTURES IN LITERARY THEORY
General Editors: Michael Payne and Harold Schweizer

The lectures in this series explore some of the fundamental changes in literary studies that have occurred during the past thirty years in response to new work in feminism, Marxism, psychoanalysis, and deconstruction. They assess the impact of these changes and examine specific texts in the light of this new work. Each volume in the series includes a critical assessment of the lecturer's own publications, an interview, and a comprehensive bibliography.

Frank Kermode   *Poetry, Narrative, History*
Terry Eagleton   *The Significance of Theory*
Toril Moi   *Feminist Theory and Simone de Beauvoir*
J. Hillis Miller   *Hawthorne and History*
Christopher Norris *Spinoza and the Origins of Modern Critical Theory*

For my friends in the Red Choir
(Côr Cochion), Cardiff

Spinoza & the Origins of Modern Critical Theory

Christopher Norris

Basil Blackwell

Copyright © Christopher Norris 1991
Introduction © Michael Payne 1991

First published 1991

Basil Blackwell Ltd
108 Cowley Road, Oxford, OX4 1JF, UK

Basil Blackwell, Inc.
3 Cambridge Center
Cambridge, Massachusetts 02142, USA

British Library Cataloguing in Publication Data

A CIP catalogue record for this book is available from the British Library.

Library of Congress Cataloging in Publication Data
Norris, Christopher.
    Spinoza and the origins of modern critical theory / Christopher Norris.
        p.   cm.— (The Bucknell lectures in literary theory)
    Includes bibliographical references and index.
    ISBN 0–631–17557–1   — ISBN 0–631–17558–X (pbk.)
    1. Critical theory.   2. Spinoza, Benedictus de,
        1632–1677–Influence.   I. Title.   II. Series.
    BD175.N67   1991   90–37648
        199'.492—dc20   CIP

Typeset in 11 on 13 pt Plantin
by Photo·graphics, Honiton, Devon
Printed in Great Britain by Billing & Son Ltd, Worcester

Contents

Preface

Fundamental and far-reaching changes in literary studies, often compared to paradigmatic shifts in the sciences, have been taking place during the last thirty years. These changes have included enlarging the literary canon not only to include novels, poems and plays by writers whose race, gender or nationality had marginalized their work but also to include texts by philosophers, psychoanalysts, historians, anthropologists, social and religious thinkers, who previously were studied by critics merely as 'background'. The stance of the critic and student of literature is also now more in question than ever before. In 1951 it was possible for Cleanth Brooks to declare with confidence that the critic's job was to describe and evaluate literary objects, implying the relevance for criticism of the model of scientific objectivity while leaving unasked questions concerning significant issues in scientific theory, such as complementarity, indeterminacy and the use of metaphor. Now the possibility of value-free scepticism is itself in doubt as many feminist, Marxist and psychoanalytic theorists have stressed the inescapability of ideology and the consequent obligation of teachers and students of literature to declare their political, axiological and aesthetic positions in order to make those positions conscious and available for examination. Such expansion and deepening of literary studies has, for many critics, revitalized their field.

Those for whom the theoretical revolution has been regenerative would readily echo, and apply to criticism, Lacan's call to revitalize psychoanalysis: 'I consider it to be an urgent task to disengage from concepts that are being deadened by routine use the meaning that they regain both from a re-examination of their history and from a reflexion on their subjective foundations. That, no doubt, is the teacher's prime function.'

Many practising writers and teachers of literature, however, see recent developments in literary theory as dangerous and anti-humanistic. They would insist that displacement of the centrality of the word, claims for the 'death of the author', emphasis upon gaps and incapacities in language, and indiscriminate opening of the canon threaten to marginalize literature itself. In this view the advance of theory is possible only because of literature's retreat in the face of aggressive moves by Marxism, feminism, deconstruction and psychoanalysis. Furthermore, at a time of militant conservativism and the dominance of corporate values in America and Western Europe, literary theory threatens to diminish further the declining audience for literature and criticism. Theoretical books are difficult to read; they usually assume that their readers possess knowledge that few have who have received a traditional literary education; they often require massive reassessments of language, meaning and the world; they seem to draw their life from suspect branches of other disciplines: professional philosophers usually avoid Derrida; psychoanalysts dismiss Freud as unscientific; Lacan was excommunicated even by the International Psycho-Analytical Association.

The volumes in this series record part of the attempt at Bucknell University to sustain conversation about changes in literary studies, the impact of those changes on literary art and the significance of literary theory for the humanities and human sciences. A generous grant from the Andrew W. Mellon Foundation has made possible a five-year series of visiting lectureships by internationally known participants in the reshaping of literary studies. Each volume includes a comprehensive introduction to the published work of the lecturer, the two Bucknell Lectures, an interview and a comprehensive bibliography.*

* At Professor Norris's request the interview has not been published in this volume, since the main text is a good deal longer than others in the series.

Introduction

In his first book, *William Empson and the Philosophy of Literary Criticism* (1978), Christopher Norris lays the foundation for his later work on deconstruction. He sees Empson, in contrast to the American New Critics, as stressing the continuity of the language of poetry with the language of prose. In overt violation of the New Critical credo, Empson rejects 'the formalist doctrines of discontinuity and poetic autonomy' (WE, 5), reverts to paraphrase as a mode of explanatory criticism, and insists that 'ambiguity is essentially a part of the normal, rational–deductive habits of thought' (WE, 6). Norris observes that the argument for discontinuity put forward by Eliot, Hulme, and Ransom was an effort to teach the poem 'to know its proper place' (WE, 7) in order to separate poetry from philosophy and religion. Thus Hulme dismisses Romanticism as 'spilt religion'; Ransom sees poetry's task as the transformation of passion into 'crisp, objective constructs'; and Eliot, carrying the formalist programme into practice in the ironies and paradoxes of *The Waste Land* and the *Four Quartets*, cuts poetic meaning off from the possibility of reasoned argument. Norris sees Empson's aim in all his books as making 'terms between poetry and the normal conditions of language and commonsense discourse' (WE, 9).

In his opposition to the behaviourist psychology of I. A. Richards, Empson (in Norris's view) has much in common with Stanley Cavell and J. L. Austin. Cavell argues that the critic and the artist share the common project 'not to discount subjectivity, but to include it . . . to master it in exemplary ways'; and Austin demonstrates the existence of 'a peculiar and intimate relation' between 'the emotion and the natural manner of venting it', which is also Empson's central concern in *The Structure of Complex Words* (WE, 12). Norris perceptively finds Empson's preoccupation with pastoral to be fundamental to his critical theory. For Empson, the pastoral attitude involves a pretence of humility and the irony of 'putting the complex into the simple' (WE, 16). Just as the poet 'masters' subjectivity and 'vents' emotion by putting experience into language, so the critic continues that creative process by interpreting the poem in a critical prose that is continuous with the language of the poem. Norris, in turn, as a commentator on Empson, Derrida, de Man, and a host of other theorists and philosophers continues this pastoral attitude. In an exemplary prose style marked by ironic simplicity, Norris compacts and elucidates literary theory and practice, often daring to approach the very edge of what Empson called the 'deep blankness' of inexpressibility, which has become a recurring concern of deconstruction.

Building on his study of Empson, Norris's *Deconstruction: Theory and Practice* (1982) traces the path from structuralism and the New Criticism to philosophical and literary deconstruction. In Allen Tate's and R. P. Blackmur's discontent with the strained 'middle position between imagination and philosophy' (DTP, 14) that New Critics had assigned themselves, Norris finds an important anticipation of the desire to move beyond formalism, although that step was not definitively taken until J. Hillis Miller, Geoffrey Hartman, and Paul de Man became fully responsive to continental theory and emerged as 'the protagonists of deconstruction' in America (DTP, 15). Their Yale colleague W. K. Wimsatt was quick to identify and to denounce as heresy their questioning of the privileged autonomy of poetic form and their declaring a wide range of speculative freedoms for the literary critic. Chief among those freedoms is the opportunity to develop a critical style continuous with the literary texts the interpreter deals with, although this freedom is exercised simultaneously with the welcome assumption of the responsibility to account for the interpreter's own theoretical puzzles and uncertainties within the critical response (or critical text) itself. Such self-reflexivity about the languages and procedures of criticism removes absolute territorial boundaries between poetic and critical texts and between imagination and philosophy.

Norris is quick to point out, however, that these developments in American literary criticism are manifestations of but one mode of deconstruction, which also has a 'more toughly argumentative aspect' (DTP, 17) that can be seen in the work of Jacques Derrida and Paul de Man. Norris's books on Derrida and de Man develop three phases of the argument sketched in *Deconstruction: Theory and*

Practice. First, Norris argues the benefits 'of mutual interrogative exchange' (D, 17) between literature and philosophy, as against arguments for their separation (such as Wimsatt's) or for their identity (such as Rorty's). Second, Norris puts into practice Nietzsche's insight that all philosophy rests on 'a shifting texture of figurative language' (DTP, 58), which philosophers commonly ignore or suppress. Like Nietzsche, Derrida, and de Man, Norris works to reacquaint philosophy with its textuality and to overcome its defensiveness about the presence of metaphor, metonymy, and anthropomorphism in its texts. Third, Norris sustains a powerful argument for the political engagement of deconstruction against, for example, the reservations and open attacks of Eagleton and Lentricchia. In his call for post-Althusserian Marxist theory to recognize the figurative nature of its own formulations, Norris affirms Edward Said's view that 'texts are irreducibly "worldly" in the sense that they take on a circumstantial setting and lead a varied afterlife of meanings and *uses* which place them squarely in the public domain . . . Texts are in and of the world because they lend themselves to strategies of reading whose intent is always part of a struggle for interpretative power' (DTP, 88).

In his study of *Derrida* (1987), Norris interweaves this three-part argument with an elegant statement of the project of deconstruction. Despite its great institutional success in literature departments of American universities, deconstruction prides itself on being marginal to the established concerns of philosophy and criticism. Indeed, Derrida's relentless criticism of institutional practices in the humanities necessitates this sense of difference. Derrida's neologism, *différance*, asserts the differential and deferred processes of meaning in language against authoritarian efforts of reduction and definition. Norris emphasizes, however, Derrida's strategy of working within the language of existing institutions to 'defamiliarize' their habits of thought in order to criticize and destabilize them from within. Derrida's typical deconstructive moves include

the dismantling of conceptual oppositions, the taking apart of hierarchical systems of thought which can then be *reinscribed* within a different order of textual signification. Or again: deconstruction is the vigilant seeking-out of those 'aporias', blindspots or moments of self-contradiction where a text involuntarily betrays the tension between rhetoric and logic, between what it manifestly *means to say* and what it is nonetheless *constrained to mean*. To 'deconstruct' a piece of writing is therefore to operate a kind of strategic reversal, seizing on precisely those unregarded details (casual metaphors, foot-notes, incidental turns of argument) which are always, and necess-arily, passed over by interpreters of a more orthodox persuasion. For it is here, in the margins of the text, that deconstruction discovers those same unsettling forces at work (D, 19).

Norris insists, however, that deconstruction is not an open invitation to interpretive free play, an anti-philosophy, or an attempted break with philosophy. On the contrary, deconstruction is nothing if it is not rooted in the 'prolonged, meticulous encounter' with texts (D, 22). For philosophy this means an end to attempts to keep philosophical texts separate from literature in order to preserve philosophy's self-image as a 'privileged, truth-speaking discourse, immune from the vagaries of writing' (D, 22); and for literature this means an end to the elevation of the poem as a verbal icon ministered to by critical high priests. Although Derrida acknowl-edges that the poet Valéry had already placed philosophy 'not far from poetry' (D, 22) as a branch of literature, thus requiring of its readers a poet's disciplined awareness of language, philosophy is not exclusively, therefore, an 'affair of form' (D, 23). Norris's work as a whole, following the examples of Valéry and Derrida, might be seen as an attempt to keep philosophy conscious of its textuality. Such an attempt, however, while opening literature and philosophy up to mutual interrogation, also involves wrestling with the question (to paraphrase Stanley Cavell) of how literature and philosophy can be and know themselves and still interrogate each other, how they can sustain mutuality without collapsing into sameness.

Especially in his readings of Plato's *Phaedrus*, Derrida shows the anticipatory presence of deconstruction, which is '*always already*' at work, even in those texts that would seem most expressly committed to a "logocentric" order of assumptions' (D, 57). Philosophy cannot know itself without engaging in that patient, attentive deconstruc-tive reading that seizes on those moments in a text 'where something escapes, exceeds or perplexes the sovereignty of logocentric reason' (D, 83). Such reading gives careful attention to the minute details of the text, resisting the apparently ubiquitous preference for the spirit over the letter. Norris traces Derrida's sustained effort to expose deconstructive processes at work in those texts – such as the *Phaedrus*, Saussure's *Course in General Linguistics*, Rousseau's *Essay on the Origin of Languages*, and Lévi-Strauss' 'The Writing Lesson' – that would seem to raise anticipatory defences against deconstruc-tion in their arguments for the priority of speech over writing and for the spirit over the body or the letter of the text. Rather than carrying out his project as a joyfully irresponsible exercise in interpretive free-play, as has sometimes erroneously been claimed, Derrida (Norris stresses) sets out to 'demand a reason for reasonableness itself' (D, 160) and insists, therefore, on keeping the uses of reason's fruits under reason's control. For such a commitment the greatest challenge and clearest need is 'for a mode of thinking that can best exert its critical leverage at those points where rational discourse comes up against the limits of calculability' (D, 162).

Two of the central threads in Norris's argument – that Derridean deconstruction continues the tradition of enlightened critique formulated in Kant and that its commitments are fundamentally ethical and humanistic – are tied effectively together in Norris's discussion of Derrida's 'nuclear criticism'. Derrida has argued in 'No Apocalypse, Not Now' that deconstruction can make a major contribution to thinking within and against the arguments for nuclear deterrence. The nuclear threat has created not only a political stalemate but also a paralysis of reason in part because '"deterrence" is a word for which there exists no adequate *concept*, no place within a system of coherent or intelligibile thinking that would make proper sense of it in any given context' (D, 163). Nuclear politics is beyond usual standards of competence and expertise; the experts'

> knowledge is based on the self-deluding premise that strategies of deterrence (or nuclear war-fighting plans) are matters of applied expertise and rational prevision. But this is to ignore the *rhetorical* dimension of nuclear thinking. . . . Nuclear 'reality' has entered the realm of apocalyptic fantasy. What *counts* . . . is the power to raise the fantasy stakes to a point where rival interpretations are effectively played off the field (D, 164).

Deconstruction can expose the rhetorical status of nuclear politics and the illogicality of nuclear deterrence: planning for the use of nuclear weapons is to admit the uncertainty of nuclear deterrence, and any hint that the use of such weapons is inconceivable undermines the strategy of deterrence. Derrida argues that anti-nuclear protest is not enough. Disarmers must internally dismantle the arguments for nuclear deterrence, showing that its 'logic' is 'either rhetorical-strategic escalation or nothing at all' (D, 168).

Although Frank Lentricchia and Terry Eagleton had already systematically attacked Paul de Man's work as a barrier against oppositional political activity, the revelation in 1987 that de Man had written anti-Semitic articles for the pro-Nazi Belgian newspaper *Le Soir* not only provided antagonists to deconstruction with a powerful polemical weapon but also partly eclipsed Derrida's demonstration of the ethical and political potential in deconstruction. Norris's *Paul de Man: Deconstruction and the Critique of Aesthetic Ideology* (1988) was nearly completed when the texts of those early writings came to light. (Norris considers them, along with responses by friends and detractors of de Man, in a postscript.) If ever there were a pressing occasion to rethink the relationship between the word and the world, poetry and history, text and author, de Man's work as a whole provides it. (Since the publication of Norris's book, other major reactions to de Man's journalism have included Frank Kermode, 'Paul de Man's Abyss', *London Review of Books*, 16 March 1989, pp. 3–7, and Terry Eagleton, 'The Emptying of a Former Self', *TLS*, 26 May 1989, pp. 573–4.) It may of course be objected that violent denunciations of de Man are unjust in comparison, for example, to the less heated responses to the more open collaboration of Martin Heidegger or Herbert von Karajan. Norris, however, shows that when the vicious media campaign to discredit de Man is set aside, there remains 'the fact . . . that de Man went on [from his early writings] to devote the major part of his life's work to a critique of that same seductive mythology that had once so grievously misled his thinking' (PDM, 197).

Like Empson and Derrida, de Man refuses to claim he knows precisely how to distinguish literature from other sorts of language. Indeed, he is at pains to show that all language is tropologically literary, despite attempts in certain modes especially of philosophical discourse to suppress literary kinship. Norris traces through de Man's work the elaboration of two main theses. First, de Man sets out to expose 'the delusory character of any such appeal to *organic* or *naturalizing* metaphors when dealing with questions of poetry, language or representation' (PDM, xii) as those that can be traced from misreadings of Kant through Schiller and Coleridge to the New Critics. Second, he claims that 'our reading of critical texts can best proceed by way of noting those ironic disparities between meaning and intent that seem to characterize all systematic reflection on literary language' (PDM, xii). This second thesis applies with equal force to the language of philosophy. As Norris proceeds with his close reading of de Man's work, he develops further the brilliantly achieved two-sided argument of his study of Derrida by demonstrating the relation between the political significance of that work and the interests of rational critique that constitute the Kantian heritage of deconstruction. Unlike Norris's previous books, however, this one practises a hermeneutics of suspicion in its insistence that de Man's texts '*ought* to be approached with a measure of argued resistance and scepticism' (PDM, xxi). Nevertheless, Norris does not allow his reader to forget the duality of de Man's temperament: on the one hand, his personal warmth and ability to inspire deep loyalty, and on the other, the austerity and often grim impersonality of his writing.

This duality is not simply an incidental aspect of de Man's personality. Central to de Man's project is a deconstructive rethinking of Romantic ideology, which celebrates (as in Hegel's *Aesthetics*) metaphor or symbol as the manifestation of unified genius. Norris observes that 'for Hegel, the symbolic is the highest form of art, the most advanced stage that aesthetic consciousness can reach in its striving for a realm of unified knowledge and perception beyond the antinomies of alienated spirit' (PDM, 29). The Romantic dream invisions the unity of art and nature, poetry and philosophy, imagination and reason, all achieved as an emanation of organic, creative genius. De Man affirms allegory over symbol and metaphor precisely because it refuses to fall under the spell of that dream. The allegorical mode implicitly marks as arbitrary the links between the literal and other layers of meaning. In so doing, allegory resists the seduction of visionary transcendence, 'insisting absolutely on the timebound nature of all understanding and the plain impossibility that language should achieve – as the Romantics desired – a state beyond the antinomies of subject and object, mind and nature, the temporal and the eternal' (PDM, 10). Norris agrees with Lentricchia that another important consequence for de Man of awakening from the Romantic dream is a rejection of revolutionary eschatology. De Man sees Wordsworth's vision of 'The types and symbols of Eternity,/Of first and last, and midst, and without end' (*Prelude*, Book VI, 571–2), and Hölderlin's Titanic mythology of the overthrow of a heroic order, as prime manifestations of the illusion that revolutionary action offers an escape from temporality. In opposition to that illusion, authentic criticism for de Man 'allows the precedence of poetry over politics' (PDM, 9).

Heidegger's readings of Hölderlin provide de Man not only with important refinements in his critique of Romantic ideology but also with a model for his theory of blindness and insight. Norris explains that 'it is Heidegger's interest to think back beyond the history of

Western "metaphysical" thought, from Plato to the present, and give voice to that primordial experience of Being which is glimpsed obscurely in the fragments of the pre-Socratic philosopher-poets, but then progressively concealed or distorted by the claims of merely abstract, conceptual understanding' (PDM, 11–12). In Hölderlin, Heidegger finds 'the poet of poets' who states the essence of poetry, which for Heidegger consists in the power to embody in poetry the absolute presence of Being. In a careful, deconstructive reading of Hölderlin and Heidegger, however, de Man shows that Heidegger's desire to find a precursor poet who can recover the wisdom that philosophy has renounced leads him to misread Hölderlin. Hölderlin *desires* the union of language and the divine ('the Holy be my Word') just as Heidegger does; but all he is able to do is pray for it, expressing his longing for unmediated presence. If de Man is thinking of Romantic radicalism here in terms of his encounter with Nazism, rather than (for example) in terms of the context of a utopian vision from the sixties, then his deconstruction of the mystique of revolution and Romantic historiography might itself be, however unwittingly, a redemptive political and ethical act, a critique of his former collaboration. His theoretical insights occur nonetheless in the recognition not only of Heidegger's but of his own former blindness. Norris rightly stresses, however, that de Man manifests little joyful exuberance in his insights. In contrast to the sparkling performances of close reading in William Empson's or Hillis Miller's books, 'with de Man one always feels the opposite, negative compulsion at work – as if the entire effort of that singular intelligence were devoted to foreclosing, regretfully but firmly, whatever new dimensions of sense the adventurous reader might hope to find' (PDM, 115).

In his most recent book, *Deconstruction and the Interests of Theory* (1988), Norris himself adopts this rhetoric of foreclosure for quite different purposes. Here he gives more scope than in his earlier books to developing the link between Kantian rational critique and emancipatory theoretical discourse. What seems abruptly chastening here is the argument that the interdisciplinary (or 'colonizing drive') in literary theory 'has resulted in a loss of argumentative rigour, a blurring of distinctions between logic and rhetoric, and a generalized notion of "intertextuality" which reduces all language to a mere play of ungrounded narrative or figural representations' (DIT, 9). The consequence of this loss of argumentative rigour is politically more damaging to the oppositional potential in deconstruction than what Eagleton and Lentricchia had seen in their readings of de Man. Norris demonstrates how extreme relativism and nihilism in some modes of postmodernist theory have provided right-wing historians and jurists with a powerful means of discrediting, often with brazen candour, all forms of oppositional thought. Norris develops a closely reasoned argument for rescuing deconstruction from the neo-pragmatism of Richard Rorty and Stanley Fish, on the one hand, and from the decadent postmodernism of Jean-François Lyotard and Jean Baudrillard on the other. Whereas Rorty thinks that philosophy has substituted the quest for knowledge with 'presently valid or workable belief' (DIT, 67), Fish sees meaning as determined by interpretive communities that determine what texts are significant and what interpretations are to be taken seriously. Professionalism for him is the 'inescapable fact of intellectual life' (DIT, 132). Although radically different in tone from these neo-pragmatists, the postmoderns reach similar conclusions: for Lyotard there is no ground for reason and truth outside currently accepted belief, and for Baudrillard 'truth' and 'reality' are indistinguishable from mass-media simulations. More damaging to theory's emancipatory function, because more widely influential, is Foucault's 'equating all forms of knowledge with the exercise of a power whose effects may be located in discourse but whose authority is subject to no kind of rational account' (DIT, 240). Free of such rational critique, discourse inspired by Foucault

> has lent itself to a great variety of uses, all of them in some sense 'radical' but otherwise spanning the political range from New-Right reaction to ultra left activist rhetoric. And this ambivalence can be seen as the result of abandoning that tradition of enlightened critique which has characterized not only Marxist thinking but every attempt to separate truth from ideological illusion (DIT, 242).

Norris convincingly argues that the British historian Jonathan Clark, for example, has appropriated the Foucauldian view that history is always a 'history of the present' and that its discourse is shaped by currently prevailing social and political interests in order to discredit any form of oppositional discourse in politics, economics, or history that does not conform to Thatcherite ideology. (Norris's critique of Clark [DIT, 22–6] was in fact prophetic of Clark's public support of overt moves by the Thatcher government in the summer of 1989 to introduce partisan politics into the teaching of history in British primary and secondary schools.) Norris's point is that critical theory can engage the political, legal, economic, and historical issues of the moment only if it refuses to capitulate to the postmodernist renunciation of the power and means to distinguish reason from rhetoric, knowledge from power. He sees that holding out against the 'relativizing drift' of theory towards political conservatism is essential if truth is to be 'not a product of consensus-belief but the upshot of an ongoing rational debate where consensus values should always be subject to question' (DIT, 26).

Christopher Norris's work has been justly celebrated in Europe, America, and Japan because of its lucid presentation of key issues in contemporary literary theory. There is also in his work a compelling argument for the recovery of deconstruction from the superficial enthusiasm of those who have hastily embraced it. If that recovery is to be successful and the argumentative rigour of Derrida and de Man recognized, the tradition of Enlightenment rational critique must also be reinvigorated. A large portion of the history of literary criticism and theory in this century has been a battle for the Kantian legacy of critique. Norris has made a convincing case that New Criticism's claim to that legacy is illegitimate and that the claim of deconstruction is credible only if deconstruction resists neo-pragmatism and the decadent modes of postmodernism.

Spinoza is important for Norris's project not only because so many recent theorists (such as Althusser, Macherey, and Deleuze) have returned to Spinoza's works, but also because of his rejection of the view that fictions are mere pseudo-statements removed from reason, truth, and ethical action. It is not surprising, therefore, to find Spinoza thinking that religion is the principal cause of human error when its basis is an authority denying reason and invoking revealed truth. Norris concludes his study of Spinoza and the origins of modern critical thought with a sustained examination of the Islamic fundamentalist response to Rushdie's *The Satanic Verses*, a text that resists the easy formalist defence of mere fictionality. Spinoza thoroughly understood the terrible consequences of forging links between fanatical readings of scripture and the intrusion of law into the domain of speculative thought, which results in law becoming a sectarian instrument. Norris demonstrates both the lasting importance of Spinoza's thought for poets and theorists and its vital contribution to the continuing project of Enlightenment thought.

Michael Payne

Author's Preface

The name of Spinoza has not figured much in recent Anglophone literary-critical debate. With the exception of one, fairly short-lived episode – the spell of intensive theorizing that emerged under the sign of Althusserian Marxism – he has enjoyed nothing like the degree of interest accorded to other leading philosophers in the European tradition. Most theorists with a decent working knowledge of post-structuralism or deconstruction could probably give some account of these movements in relation to such strong precursors as Descartes, Kant, Hegel, Nietzsche, Husserl and maybe Heidegger. Of course there is disagreement when it comes to establishing precise lines of descent, or arguing the case for this or that thinker as a source of continuing insights and ideas. But Spinoza figures hardly at all in these various elective genealogies. Among critical theorists – at least in Britain and North America – his writings have been pretty much ignored, save for the occasional reference to him as an out-and-out idealist metaphysician whose thought exemplifies the errors and delusions to which such thinking is chronically prone. Analytical philosophers have had more time for Spinoza, though usually by way of a 'rational reconstruction' which concedes a few salient points of interest in Spinoza's system while consigning what remains – the entire 'metaphysical' doctrine – to the history of outworn ideas.

In what follows I shall suggest that critical theorists have a good deal to learn from Spinoza, not least because they have often been engaged all unwittingly in a rehearsal of the same arguments. For there is a sense in which *every* theoretical activity must presuppose at least some of the basic tenets of Spinoza's thought. These include the idea that theory is capable of providing a better, more adequate conceptual grasp of experiences that would otherwise belong to the realm of pre-reflective 'commonsense' knowledge. To theorize is to take up a critical distance from the data of first-hand subjective understanding, or to claim some superior cognitive standpoint from which to adjudicate in matters of truth and falsehood. For Spinoza, it is the chief virtue of philosophy that it enables the mind to essay this progress beyond the partial, perplexed and contradictory evidence of the senses, giving access to a realm of necessary truths where everything assumes its appointed place in the eternal scheme of things. If it were humanly possible to achieve such absolute knowledge – to transcend our creaturely dependence on the inlets of sensory perception, the fallible workings of memory, imagination, language, and other such sources of 'inadequate ideas' – then we would comprehend everything *sub specie aeternitatis*, or redeemed from the contingent, error-prone nature of mortal understanding. But of course this standpoint can only be envisaged as an ultimate ideal, a regulative notion by which (as he argues) we can and should be guided, but which cannot be attained under the given conditions of human finitude and temporal experience. And it is within the limits imposed by those same conditions that Spinoza carries on his other great project, directed toward a knowledge of actions and events *sub specie durationis*, or as viewed against a background of particular socio-historical circumstances, most immediately those of the seventeenth-century Dutch experiment in liberal democracy whose rise and imminent fall he witnessed at first hand.[1] This is the radical Spinoza more or less unknown to Anglo-American readers, though not – as we shall see – to French philosophers and left-wing intellectuals, many of whom continue to acknowledge his formative influence on their own thinking.

So this book has three main aims. Firstly, it seeks to establish the case that nearly all the great debates in present-day literary theory have their origin in one or another aspect of Spinoza's work. Secondly, it points to a number of specific (mostly French) movements of thought over the past three decades where Spinoza has figured as a major source of theoretical arguments and ideas. And thirdly – most important – it argues that a better understanding of Spinoza's work may help us to perceive some of the fallacies, blindspots, and effects of foreshortened historical perspective that have characterized the discourse of literary theory in its latest 'postmodern' phase. This seems to me a matter of particular urgency since so much current talk has an air of pseudo-sophisticated 'philosophic' import which goes along all too readily with various irrationalist and anti-Enlightenment doctrines. One thing we can learn from Spinoza – especially from his writings on scripture, politics, and history – is the need to distinguish between different orders of truth claim, those that offer arguments (and invite counterarguments) by way of establishing their credentials, and those that trade on some mystified appeal to divine revelation, scriptural authority, or a truth beyond the powers of rational understanding. There is a tendency nowadays – most pronounced among critics of a poststructuralist or postmodernist persuasion – to treat all talk of 'truth' as a regrettable throwback to bad old Enlightenment habits of thought. In the same way, adepts of literary deconstruction often refer breezily to 'logocentrism' or the Western 'metaphysics of presence' as if these (along with 'truth') could henceforth be dispensed with to everyone's obvious benefit, since then we might emerge into a realm of utopian 'freeplay' where the tedious old constraints of consistency, logic, and right reading would no longer exert their tyrannical power. What drops out of sight in these massively simplified accounts is the fact that the critique of scriptural revelation (in Spinoza) or the deconstruction of 'Western metaphysics' (in Derrida) are projects carried through by dint of much argument and rigorous thinking, intellectual achievements of the highest order which still find room for truth, if not for certain (revealed or transcendental) forms of presumptive truth-claim.

I shall have a good deal to say in this book about Spinoza's proleptic contribution to debates in post-structuralism, deconstruction, New Historicism and other present-day schools. For the moment I wish only to advance the more general claim: that by reading him afresh – or maybe for the first time – one achieves a perspective on these recent ideas that makes some of them appear decidedly wrongheaded or devoid of intellectual consequence, while others take on an added measure of historical and philosophic interest. Nietzsche came across Spinoza belatedly – in the summer of 1881 – but his reaction (recorded in a well-known letter to Overbeck) leaves no doubt of his having discovered a kindred spirit.

> Not only is his overall tendency like mine – making knowledge the *most powerful* affect – but in five main points of his doctrine I recognize myself; this most unusual and loneliest thinker is closest to me in precisely these matters: he denies the freedom of the will, teleology, the moral world order, the unegoistic, and evil...[2]

Nietzsche's pleasurable thrill of recognition is one that would leave many commentators cold, although it does find an echo – as we shall see – in the reading proposed by a latter-day Nietzschean like Gilles Deleuze. And Deleuze for his part would have little sympathy with those thinkers in the Anglo-American tradition for whom it is axiomatic that philosophical ideas can be of interest only in so far as they achieve the requisite standards of logical consistency and truth. Thus Stuart Hampshire: 'his (Spinoza's) is an interesting, not implausible, account of freedom of mind, as the detachment from causes in the common order of nature, a detachment that lasts while self-critical thinking lasts'.[3]

Where the commentators divide is in the degree of significance they attach to the passions (or the pressures of historical circumstance) that went into the making of a work like the *Ethics*. For this is famously a text that offers itself – at least to all appearances – as a purely rational-deductive chain of arguments, one through which those passions may have run (so to speak) like wine through ice, leaving no trace behind. 'Emotion recollected in tranquillity' – the Wordsworthian formula best describes those readings that take the *Ethics* more or less as it asks to be taken, discounting any signs of 'mental struggle on the part of the author', or any indication of its 'origin or course of development'.[4] The words are those of Robert A. Duff in his 1903 book *Spinoza's Political and Ethical Philosophy*. But Duff also registers the problems faced by any present-day exegete who respects Spinoza's intentions in this matter and seeks to exclude all reference to 'extraneous' (personal or socio-political) concerns. As he puts it:

[m]orality treated in geometrical fashion, principles of conduct proved by an array of definitions, axioms, postulates, propositions, corollaries, and scholia, do not now exercise the same fascination over the student, as they did in days when mathematics was the one type of exact or demonstrated knowledge. On the contrary, it begets in a modern reader the suspicion of a deductive or *a priori* manipulation of experience, and taints the whole atmosphere of the book.[5]

There are four main lines of response to this problem, as exemplified by recent commentators on Spinoza. One – the predominant Anglo-American line – is to dump a good deal of the seventeenth-century 'metaphysical' baggage, but translate its terms wherever possible into the idiom of present-day linguistic or analytical philosophy.

Stuart Hampshire offers one good example of this approach, and Jonathan Bennett the most extensive treatment overtly geared to the interests of 'rational reconstruction'. The second response is that of readers like Deleuze, for whom (to cite one fairly typical passage) 'the Spinozists are Hölderlin, Kleist and Nietzsche, because they think in terms of speeds and slownesses, of frozen catatonias and accelerated movements, unformed elements, nonsubjectified affects'.[6] In short, Deleuze is already on the path to what he will later call a 'schizo-analytical' reading of Spinoza, one that not merely rejects the demands of conceptual coherence, clarity and rigour laid down by commentators like Hampshire and Bennett, but which sees it as a positive virtue in these texts that they explode such repressive 'Oedipal' ideas in pursuit of a purely libidinal economy of instinct, affect, and 'desiring-production'.[7] I shall have more to say about this curious (indeed thoroughly zany) episode in Spinoza's 'postmodern' reception-history. For the moment I mention it only by way of signalling the sheer diversity of present-day responses to his work.

The third and fourth options are those that will occupy me most in the following chapters. They both have to do with the relation in Spinoza's work between philosophical issues of reason, truth and knowledge on the one hand, and socio-historical or political concerns on the other. This relationship is in turn capable of two very different (but not, as I shall argue, mutually exclusive) readings. One is the approach adopted by theorists like Althusser and Macherey, an approach that starts out from Spinoza's distinction between 'imaginary' (or confused) and 'adequate' (or conceptually valid) ideas, and which then goes on to elaborate that distinction into a full-scale Marxist 'science' of material, historical and ideological conjunctures.[8] The other approach would eschew such high theoreticist ambitions for the sake of determining just what it was, in the immediate context of Spinoza's life and times, that led him not only to think as he did but to cast his thoughts in the form of a treatise constructed *more geometrico*, or after the manner of Euclid's *Elements*.[9] And this takes us back to our earlier question as to whether such a text can really be read at its own professed level of abstract universality.

What emerges from recent historical scholarship – books like Simon Schama's superb study *The Embarrassment of Riches* – is the extent to which these same ideals went along with a progressive or liberal-democratic ideology, one that found its closest philosophical equivalent in the 'left-Cartesian' strain of rational-deductive thought. But at the same time there were forces of social disruption – religious, sectarian, and resurgent monarchist interests – which threatened to destroy this hard-won state of enlightened ecumenical and multi-ethnic coexistence. Schama makes the point with reference to Spinoza's most influential patron, the statesman-philosopher de Witt:

> Such conflicts [i.e. the growing spate of trade-wars, civil altercations etc.] remained obstinately the contentions of power, authority, religion, dynastic amour propre and custom – the very issues that Grotius had deemed inadequate pretexts for the prosecution of a just war . . . At a later date, the more Johan de Witt relied on Cartesian actuarial calculations of diplomatic contingency, the more vulnerable he became to acts of public unreason. [In the end] he was done to death in the aftermath of a judicial travesty perpetrated on his brother. In striving for the best possible principles by which to arrange their relations with other states, the Dutch succeeded only in bringing out the worst in all concerned. The world they were condemned to live in was the world of their public ethics turned upside down.[10]

Hence – it might be argued – the ambivalence encountered so often in Spinoza's works: on the one hand his commitment to a method of reasoning *more geometrico*, his address to an ideal community of readers, a republic of learning beyond all merely partisan opinions and interests; on the other, his enforced recognition of the fact that no such community existed, so that thinking could only serve a practical end in so far as it adjusted to the given conditions of prejudice, unreason, and sectarian strife. In his 'political' writings, therefore, Spinoza took full and detailed account of the various well-documented failures – the upshot (as he saw it) of confused or 'imaginary' ideas, conjoined with the seemingly contingent nature of historical events as viewed *sub specie durationis* – that had characterized all societies to date, from Old Testament to present-day times. And it is precisely in his treatment of these manifold errors – these sources of imaginary 'misrecognition', as Althusserian theory would have it – that Spinoza once again anticipates the interests of modern critical thought.

It will be clear by now that this book is addressed more to students of recent intellectual history – in particular, of French post-structuralism and its various offshoots – than to scholars who have specialized mainly or exclusively in the study of Spinoza's work. Nevertheless I would hope that its arguments stand up in light of the best – and not only the most up-to-date – philosophical commentaries on Spinoza. As usual, I have derived much benefit and stimulus from discussing these issues with my colleagues and friends in Cardiff, especially Robin Attfield, Kate and Andrew Belsey, Carol Bretman, Simon Critchley, Terence Hawkes, Kathy Kerr, Nigel Mapp, Kevin Mills, Peter Sedgwick, Ian Whitehouse and Zouher Zoughbi. Thanks also to Robert Stradling and Scott Newton, for directing my attention to some first-rate historical background material; to Kathy, Nigel and Peter (again) for reading the typescript with exemplary thoroughness and care; and to Michael Payne of Bucknell University who invited me to give the Andrew W. Mellon lectures in Autumn, 1989, and thus got me down to some serious work on what had been, until then, a rather vaguely formulated project. I am especially grateful to Holly Henry and Brenda O'Boyle for taking time off from their studies at Bucknell to compile the Bibliography and Index. Much of the reading and thinking was done during a semester I spent as Visiting Professor at the Graduate Center, City University, New York. My thanks to David Greetham, for inviting me in the first place; to Sam Levin, Angus Fletcher and their colleagues for many hours of fruitful conversation; and to all my students at CUNY for allowing me to bring the discussion back to Spinoza whenever I could. Finally – and all too briefly – let me say how much my work on this book has been helped along by the friendship and sustaining interest of Andrew Benjamin, John Drakakis, Cheryl Fish, Paul Hamilton, Geoffrey Harpham, Tina Krontiris, Dan Latimer, Wendy Lewis and Massimo Verdicchio.

Some portions of this book have appeared previously in the journal *Textual Practice* and the volume *Encyclopaedia of Literature and Criticism*, eds. Martin Coyle, Peter Garside, Malcolm Kelsall and John Peck (1990). I am grateful to the publishers (Routledge) for permission to reprint material from both sources.

Cardiff, August 1990

A Note on Texts

There are several good texts, editions and reprints of the *Ethics* currently available in English translation. By far the best is to be found in Vol. I of *The Collected Works of Spinoza*, edited by Edwin Curley (Princeton, New Jersey: Princeton University Press, 1985). There are also complete texts of the *Ethics* in *Spinoza: Selections*, ed. John Wild (New York: Charles Scribner's, 1958) and Vol. II of *The Chief Works of Benedict de Spinoza*, translated and edited by R. H. M. Elwes (current reprint: New York: Dover, 1951). In any case I have followed the usual scholarly procedure of referring to passages on the system devised by Spinoza himself, i.e. by signalling first the *Part* (I–V) and then the various numbered Propositions, Axioms, Definitions, Corollaries, Notes, or Demonstrations. So the reader should have no difficulty in locating the relevant passage whichever text she or he may be using. Thus for instance: *E* I, A 7 = *Ethics*, Part I, Axiom 7; *E* II, P 40 = *Ethics*, Part II, Proposition 40; *E* IV, P 35, C 2 = *Ethics* Part IV, Proposition 35, Corollary 2; *E* V, P 6 D = *Ethics*, Part V, Proposition 6, Demonstration.

References to other main works of Spinoza are given as follows:

On the Improvement of the Understanding, in R. H. M. Elwes (ed. & trans.), *The Chief Works of Benedict de Spinoza* (New York: Dover, 1951), Vol. II, pp. 3–41. Henceforth referred to as *OIU* with page-numbers in the text.

A Theologico-Political Treatise, in Elwes, *The Chief Works*, Vol. I, pp. 3–266. Henceforth referred to as *TPT* with page-numbers in the text.

A Political Treatise, in Elwes, *The Chief Works*, Vol. I, pp. 279–387. Henceforth referred to as *PT* with page-numbers in the text.

Selected Correspondence, in Elwes, *The Chief Works*, Vol. II, pp. 273–420. Henceforth referred to as *Correspondence* with page-numbers in the text.

For the rest, I have used what seemed the most convenient system of notes and references. Where a work is mentioned several times over in a short space I have given full details in an endnote at the first instance and then used an abbreviated signal (author, title or acronym) with page-number in the text. Otherwise – as in most cases – I have provided a full reference for each passage cited. These entries (one sequence for each chapter) are gathered at the end of the book.

I should have liked to claim that the argument was constructed *more geometrico* on Spinozist principles, falling out as it does (aside from the chapter-breaks) into twenty-one sections of near-identical length. In fact this had more to do with the work-habits induced by reliance on a fairly primitive piece of word-processing equipment. But it strikes me now (and I hope the reader will agree) that this arbitrary discipline can have beneficial effects, at least in so far as it concentrates attention on the argument in hand and discourages lengthy digressions. It is interesting to speculate how the *Ethics* might have differed in structure and style had Spinoza made use of this new technology. One can think of few works on the highest intellectual plane whose mode of composition invites such anachronistic fantasies. Meanwhile, the reader may wish to consult two volumes which offer some assistance in this respect: Jon Wetlesen, *Internal Guide to the Ethics of Spinoza: index to Spinoza's cross-references in the Ethics, rearranged so as to refer from earlier to later statements* (Filosofisk Institutt Universiteit i Oslo, Oslo, 1974) and Michel Guéret, André Robinet and Paul Tombeur, *Spinoza, Ethica: concordances, index, listes de fréquence, tables comparatives* (Publications de CETEDOC, Université catholique de Louvain, Louvain-la-Neuve, 1977).

1 Spinoza *versus* Hegel: the Althusserian Moment

I

Baruch de Spinoza (1632–77) might not seem the most obvious starting-point for anyone concerned with issues in present-day literary criticism. Most Anglophone readers will have a vague knowledge of Spinoza as some kind of pantheist or visionary mystic, a thinker in the high metaphysical tradition for whom God was the ground of all being and the end-point of philosophic wisdom. This impression comes chiefly from the German and English Romantics, among them Novalis, who described him as a 'God-intoxicated' soul, and Coleridge who – among other admiring references – let drop some remarks about Shakespeare as a 'Spinozistic deity', presiding serenely over worlds and characters of his own creating without the least obtrusion of personal interest or motive.[1] Others, who may have read Matthew Arnold's essay on Spinoza, will know that this is one side only in a pattern of extreme antithetical response that in some degree persists down to this day.[2] Arnold starts out by quoting in its entirety the curse of excommunication pronounced upon Spinoza by the Elders of the Portuguese Synagogue at Amsterdam in 1656. It is an appalling document which found numerous echoes in the charges of apostasy, atheism, corrupting influence and so forth that were levelled against him, by Jews and Christians alike, during the next two centuries and more.[3] For the Romantics, conversely, Spinoza was an intellectual hero, a character of supreme, almost saintly disinterest who had opened the way to their own pantheist ideas of God, mind and nature as belonging to a single, indivisible order of harmonious coexistence.

To his opponents 'Spinozism' rapidly became a code-word for that strain of free-thinking rationalist critique which found room for 'God' only as a kind of rhetorical place-filler, disguising what would otherwise amount to a downright atheist creed. From their point of view Spinoza had denied the most fundamental tenets of religious faith. He had rejected, among other things, the divine authority of scripture, the attributes of God as defined in both Jewish and Christian tradition, the existence of human free-will and choice (which he considered just a species of chimerical idea brought about by our simply not grasping the concatenated chains of cause and effect), and – above all – the subjugation of mere human reason to the dictates of revealed religious truth. And indeed, these charges found ample warrant in the content of Spinoza's writings. On the question of scriptural authority he argues that the Old Testament prophets laboured under a double burden: that of their own scientific ignorance (which predisposed them to believe in miracles where some natural explanation would have served much better), and that of having to maintain social order by persuading a fickle, superstitious people to obey God's commands for fear of divine retribution. Thus the prophets 'made more legitimate use of argument in proportion as their knowledge approached more nearly to ordinary knowledge' (*TPT*, p. 159). And again: 'prophetic knowledge is inferior to natural knowledge, which needs no sign, and in itself implies certitude' (*TPT*, p. 28). In short, Spinoza views the Old Testament texts as very largely a product of the need to exact obedience and respect for law from a people who had long been subject to alien rule, and who had not yet arrived at the stage of mature self-government.

Much of what Spinoza has to say in this connection looks forward to present-day thinking about the sociology of belief and the legitimizing power of religious doctrine. More specifically, it anticipates something of the current 'New Historicist' interest in the way that such beliefs may produce a kind of sceptical backlash, a perception on the part of free-thinking intellectuals like Spinoza that perhaps *all* religion is a species of pious fraud, and not just those 'primitive', 'superstitious' or 'pagan' varieties that so plainly demonstrate the workings of priestly guile. Stephen Greenblatt has shown this process at work in a series of essays on the encounter between New World and European cultures in the Elizabethan age of colonial expansion.[4] For the most part the Spanish and English were content to take the standard line, treating the American-Indian religions as mere impostures forced upon a credulous people in order to maintain power in the hands of an elite power-group. But to some minds it seemed that the demystifying process couldn't stop there, and that perhaps Christianity was just another bag of exploitative tricks, used at home to prop up a repressive regime and abroad to justify further imperial adventures. Greenblatt offers some striking examples of how this reflex logic fed back into the discourse of Renaissance 'atheism' or heterodox opinion, giving rise to something like the climate of police-state repression and scandalized rumour-mongering that surrounded Spinoza's writings from the outset. These tactics could always be revived at times of ideological stress, as for instance during the period of anti-Jacobin hysteria provoked by the Napoleonic Wars, when Coleridge and Wordsworth had their famous conversation (duly recorded by a local police informer) about one 'Spy Nozy' and his radical associates.[5] At least it seems clear that Spinoza's writings were open to an interpretation which discounted their overt professions of faith and took them as a thinly-veiled attack on Jewish and Christian religions alike.

The other main charge against Spinoza was that his system amounted to a hard-line determinist creed, one that denied the essential human attributes of free-will and ethical choice. This followed from his argument that such ideas come about only through our partial and distorted understanding of the causes that determine our very last thought and action. The highest point of philosophical wisdom, for Spinoza, was to put such troubling illusions aside and accept that we exist as creatures of finite knowledge and experience within an all-embracing order of causal relations whose nature – could we but grasp it – would finally lay those illusions to rest. Only then might we attain to that state of tranquil self-possession that results from acknowledging our place in the eternal scheme of things and not striving after vain ideals of personal autonomy and freedom.

Such is the argument presented most fully in Spinoza's *Ethics*, a work that sets out to demonstrate the truth of this argument through a system of axioms, definitions, propositions, corollaries, etc. whose model is that of Euclidean geometry. It assumes that knowledge is arrived at by framing 'adequate ideas' whose truth will then be guaranteed by their conforming to the order of causal necessity manifest in every aspect of thought and experience. 'That which is contained in the intellect in representation must necessarily be granted in nature . . . therefore the intellect, in function finite, or in function infinite, must comprehend the attributes of God, and nothing else' (*E* I, P 30). Such is Spinoza's radical monism, his doctrine that subject and object (or mind and nature) must be grasped as two 'attributes' of a single 'substance' whose name is interchangeably God or Nature (*Deus sive Natura*). God is self-caused (*causa sui*), the one and indivisible substance, containing in itself all the modes and attributes that pertain to our bodily or mental experience. The knowledge of God is therefore a knowledge that dispels any notion of the mind as existing in a realm apart from the order of natural or causal necessity. Moreover, it leaves no room for God as conceived in traditional (Judaeo-Christian) terms: an omnipotent deity whose powers transcend all the laws or regularities of nature. If God and Nature are strictly synonymous – if the divine substance is immanent in nature to the point where all such distinctions must at last fall away – then clearly it can make no sense to talk of God's 'freedom' to suspend or abolish natural laws. Hence Spinoza's rationalist critique of the Old Testament prophets and their over-willingness to resort to supernatural or miraculous explanations. Hence also his insistence that the 'intellectual love of God' – the highest form of philosophic wisdom – was so far from conflicting with 'materialist' or scientific interests that these two kinds of knowledge were alternative paths to the same, self-identical truth.

One can therefore understand why Spinoza's work should have gained a following among nature-mystics and pantheists on the one hand, and atheists, radicals and materialist thinkers on the other. From a Spinozist standpoint these differences would amount to nothing more than a shift of terminology or preferential idiom. He reached this conclusion partly through attempting, in an early work, to explicate the principles of Cartesian philosophy *more geometrico*.[6] The result was to convince Spinoza that Descartes had gone wrong by asserting a mind-body dualism – an absolute distinction between *res cogitans* and *res extensa* – which couldn't then be bridged by any amount of sophistical juggling with the categories. (Least of all could the problem be resolved by Descartes' desperate recourse to the pineal gland as the seat of the soul and supposed point of contact between mental and physical realms.) The only way out of this dilemma, he believed, was to adopt a form of psycho-physical parallelism which treated mind and body as alternative attributes, or (in more up-to-date parlance) as falling under two alternative descriptions, both of which would none the less appear *sub specie aeternitatis* as aspects of the one, indivisible substance (call it 'God' or 'Nature'). Thus 'the body cannot determine the mind to thought, neither can the mind determine the body to motion, nor rest, nor anything else, if there be anything else' (*E* III, P 2). To this extent Spinoza found himself compelled to accept a version of the mind-body dualism. But he sought to escape its problematical entailments by arguing (1) that this necessity is owing to our lack of an adequate (i.e. God-like) knowledge of the ultimate unity of mind and matter, (2) that such knowledge can at least be glimpsed at certain moments of privileged insight, achieved through the exercise of critical reason, and (3) that in any case the distinction is metaphysically untenable, since on the one hand bodily impressions only exist as 'ideas' (or modes of apprehension) in the mind, while on the other there is no conceiving of mental activity as apart from its embodiment in this or that mode of physical existence. Thus, according to the *Ethics*, 'substance thinking and substance extended are one and the same substance, comprehended now through one attribute, now through the other' (*E* II, P 7).

This should be sufficient, Spinoza thinks, to persuade us that free-will as normally understood is the merest of delusions, and that genuine freedom consists in the acceptance – the *willing* acceptance – of our having no choice but to recognize this fact. For it then becomes clear 'that a mental decision and a bodily appetite, or determined state, are simultaneous, or rather are one and the same thing, which we call decision, when it is regarded under and explained through the attribute of thought, and a conditioned state, when it is regarded under the attribute of extension, and deduced from the laws of motion and rest' (*E* III, P 2 note). It was possible (just) for some of Spinoza's pious exegetes to present this doctrine as more or less compatible with received ideas of salvation-through-faith, or God's purpose working itself out in mysterious ways. But it struck most people – admirers and opponents alike – as an attack on those two basic precepts (of divine omnipotence and human moral accountability) in the absence of which religion must appear just a bugbear for credulous minds. This impresson was reinforced by Spinoza's arguments (in the *Tractatus Theologico-Politicus*) against any form of fideist belief in miracles, divine interventions etc., as an affront to rational intelligence and a legacy of primitive times when such ideas held sway over an ignorant populace. 'From such a phenomenon (i.e. miracles), and certainly from a result surpassing our understanding, we can gain no knowledge' (*TPT* p. 85). And this because there *is not and cannot be* any ultimate divergence between the laws of nature, as revealed by way of adequate ideas, and the truths of religion as likewise vouchsafed through the 'intellectual love of God'.

If the Christians found reason to execrate his memory, still more so did the scholars and custodians of Jewish tradition, since Spinoza clearly favoured the New over the Old Testament as an altogether more impressive record of critical intelligence at work.[7] Thus Moses 'never used legitimate arguments', falling back instead on mere 'imagination' and forms of mass-persuasive technique, whereas 'the long deductions and arguments of Paul . . . are in no wise written from supernatural revelation' (*TPT*, p. 159). Here as in the *Ethics*, Spinoza is drawing a firm distinction between an *imaginary* realm of confused ideas, sensuous impressions, metaphors mistaken for concepts, and on the other hand a critical discourse that offers good reason for its truth-claims and no longer has to rely on such dubious appeals. The prophets had recourse to fallacious modes of argument, not merely (as Spinoza is careful to add) out of power-seeking motives or a will to deceive, but in order to maintain social cohesion and the rule of law among a people as yet incapable of reasoning clearly on their own account. But this makes it all the more important to criticize scripture from a rational standpoint and not be misled into reading such language as a deliverance of revealed truth. For the Old Testament prophets 'perceived by imagination, and not by sure mental laws' (*TPT*, p. 26). That is to say, they were mistaken in so far as they claimed divine authority for a mode of persuasion necessarily adapted to the limiting conditions of their own time and place. In short, it is 'one thing to understand the meaning of Scripture and the prophets, and quite another thing to understand the meaning of God, or the actual truth' (pp. 170–71). And this distinction is vital since otherwise it might seem that *all* such truth-claims were purely fictitious, mere instruments of power in the hands of a priestly or secular elite.

In fact, as we have seen, Spinoza's protestations weren't enough to prevent his work from being read in exactly this way, that is, as an unqualified attack on every form of religious belief. But in the *Tractatus* he insists (overtly at least) that religion has nothing to fear from the exercise of rational critique so long as we observe the essential distinction between these two kinds or levels of understanding. Since 'the highest power of Scriptural interpretation belongs to every man, the rule for such interpretation should be nothing but the natural light of reason which is common to all – not any supernatural light nor any external authority' (*TPT*, p. 119). And this means, in effect, that the reader has to practise a form of socio-cultural hermeneutics (or *Ideologiekritik*) in order to separate the truth of the scriptures – their rational content – from the various accretions of myth, metaphor and other such 'imaginary' devices.

Spinoza's work laid the basis for developments in biblical scholarship which increasingly stressed this critical dimension and thus led up to the various forms of modern 'demythologizing' approach.[8] One of the reasons why Matthew Arnold so admired Spinoza was his own acquaintance with this tradition (through the so-called 'Higher Criticism' practised by mainly German theologians and hermeneutic theorists), and his sense that Christianity could only be saved – restored to any kind of intellectual dignity or worth – by facing up to the problem of reconciling faith with the dictates of critical method.[9] Arnold's liberalism in this regard turned out to have sharp limits, as when he attacked Bishop Colenso for publishing a book on the Higher Criticism aimed at a popular readership, and thus (in Arnold's view) risking the spread of a sceptical attitude beyond the safe confines of scholarly debate.[10] Here again, it proved difficult to halt the march of enlightened critical reason at a point where any further demystification might threaten the interests of church and state. But there is – as Jonathan Arac has recently argued – a whole dimension of Arnold's thinking that drops out of sight when he is treated as merely one more figure in the line of 'culture and society' ideologues that runs from the later Coleridge to T. S. Eliot, F. R. Leavis and the present-day discipline of English Studies.[11] For Arnold not only registered the impact of these new 'continental' ideas but saw very plainly what effect they would have on disciplines (like literary criticism) which had so far managed to deflect or resist any such radical critique. His frequent evasiveness on the topic – giving rise, among other things, to his notion of 'touchstones' as a timeless, intuitive measure of literary worth, and his belief in a realm of values transcending any mere 'historical estimate' – was no doubt the result of exactly this clear-eyed perception on Arnold's part.[12] And one could venture, moreover, that his reading of Spinoza was decisive in producing an extreme sensitivity to such issues in the realm of interpretive authority and truth. After Arnold, it would fall very largely to literary criticism – a fact well documented in recent studies – to sustain this burden of controversy through various kinds of legitimation-crisis brought on by increasing social, political and ideological pressures.[13]

There are other good reasons for regarding Spinoza as among

the most significant precursors of modern literary criticism. The *Tractatus* marks a break with previous ideas of scriptural exegesis when it insists on the distinction between *truth* as arrived at by the exercise of reason alone and *meaning* as interpreted from literary sources with due regard to matters of style, context, historical background, cultural difference etc.[14] This could be seen as an argument for treating the scriptures – or at least a large portion of them – as fictive or imaginative writings, and therefore as simply not amenable to assessment on rational or truth-seeking grounds. Spinoza made this point with particular emphasis in his quarrel with Maimonides, a heterodox interpreter of the Jewish source-texts who had argued – seemingly to similar effect – that the truths of religion must always be in keeping with the dictates of human reason.[15] But Maimonides, unlike Spinoza, took this to mean that the scriptures should themselves admit of some rational interpretation, thus requiring that the exegete bring great subtlety to bear in extracting truths from a recalcitrant text. He thus set out to prove, in Spinoza's words, that 'each passage in Scripture admits of various, nay, contrary meanings; but that we could never be certain of any particular one till we knew that the passage, as we interpreted it, contained nothing contrary or repugnant to reason. If the literal meaning clashes with reason, though the passage seems in itself perfectly clear, it must be interpreted in some metaphorical sense' (*TPT*, p. 114).

On the face of it there is no great difference between this and Spinoza's position. Both assert the priority of reason over beliefs brought about through miracle, metaphor, analogy or other such dubious means. Both regard truth as a matter of possessing adequate (i.e. rational-deductive) ideas, as opposed to mere 'imaginary' proofs. But Maimonides wants to bring scripture into line with this demand by working (so to speak) on a principle of charity, reading metaphorically where the plain sense goes against reason, and thus discovering the kernel of truth within the shell of mystified belief. For Spinoza, conversely, it is an error to suppose that such language bears any relation to truth, where truth is defined – as it must be for philosophic purposes – in terms of adequate ideas. Thus the upshot of all Maimonides' exegetical subleties is confusion worse confounded through a failure to make this necessary distinction. The scriptures are 'in many places inexplicable, or at best mere subject for guesswork; but . . . such difficulties only arise when we endeavour to follow the meaning of a prophet in matters which cannot be perceived, but only imagined, not in things, whereof the understanding can gain a clear and distinct idea' (*TPT*, p. 112). In such cases, Spinoza argues, we should apply a quite different mode of understanding, one that treats the scriptural text as essentially a *literary* artefact, and not as fit material for selective exegesis on the part of rationalizing scholars. Such efforts have a doubly unfortunate result. On the one hand they compromise the faculty of reason by applying it to passages whose meaning cannot be grasped in these terms, but whose authority they are obliged to defend, thus creating all kinds of multiplied error and confusion. On the other, they bring religion into disrepute by seeking to accommodate such passages to a principle of reason which effectively highlights these confusions, and thus makes it all the more difficult to place any credence in scripture. Hence the urgent need, as Spinoza sees it, to maintain a strict demarcation of realms, with reason allowed its legitimate scope in adjudicating matters of truth, while room is still left for alternative modes of utterance (allegory, metaphor, parable, etc.) whose appeal is to 'imagination' only, but which none the less exert a powerful effect upon minds ill-equipped for the rigours of conceptual thought.

This is why he argues, *contra* Maimonides, that 'the Bible must not be accommodated to reason, nor reason to the Bible' (TPT, p. 195). For only by remarking this distinction can philosophy avoid a head-on collision with the articles of religious faith. Far from wishing to 'overthrow the authority of religion', Spinoza takes it as his chief object 'to prevent the clear and uncorrupted passages [of scripture] from being accommodated to and corrupted by the faulty ones' (p. 154). And the best means of achieving this end is to respect the plain sense wherever possible, eschew all forms of excessive hermeneutical licence, and only then – where need arises – make allowance for the inbuilt fallibility of all such archival sources. This may be a matter of anomalies or downright contradictions in the text, as when Spinoza argues that Moses could not have been sole author of the Pentateuch, since 'in Deuteronomy xxxi. 9, the expression occurs, "and Moses wrote the law", words that cannot be ascribed to Moses, but must be those of some other writer narrating the deeds and writings of Moses' (p. 120). More often it involves his basic interpretive rule: that the scriptures should be taken as meaning *just what they say* – read literally as a source of moral and religious truths – so long as those truths are held quite distinct from the dictates of *a priori* reason. As usual, it is the model of Euclidean geometry that Spinoza takes as his ideal case of a knowledge exempt from all accidents of time and place. To comprehend Euclid's arguments 'we need make no researches concerning the life, the pursuits, or the habits of the author; nor need we enquire in what language, nor when he wrote, nor the vicissitudes of his book, nor how, nor by whose advice it has been received' (p. 113). With the scriptures, however, one is obliged to take account of these complicating factors, since their meaning has been subject firstly to the vagaries of prophetic imagination, and secondly to the manifold errors and obscurities resulting from the process of textual transmission.

Thus Spinoza advocates a critical approach that combines hermeneutics, reception-theory, exegetical close-reading and comparative philology. And the aim of this exercise is not to find ever more subtle and recondite meanings in the text but, on the contrary, to save scripture from precisely that kind of misapplied verbal ingenuity. 'I have read and known certain Kabbalistic triflers', he writes, 'whose insanity provokes my unceasing astonishment' (p. 140). Their mistake is just the opposite of that made by the rationalizing exegetes who attempt to square scripture with the dictates of *a priori* knowledge. These 'triflers' have so little regard for truth that they latch onto passages of dubious import and use them as a pretext for indulging in displays of geared-up sophistical invention. This leads them to ignore the first rule of responsible commentary, as Spinoza conceives it: namely, that 'the sacredness of Scripture depends on our understanding of the doctrines therein signified, and not on the words, the language, and the phrases in which these doctrines are conveyed to us' (p. 150). Such truths are accessible to reason alone – like the truths of Euclidean geometry – and in no wise dependent on the fallible tokens of prophecy or the vagaries of written communication.

So the business of scriptural exegesis is to clear away those sources of error and confusion that stand between us and the literal meaning of what the prophets sought to convey. That meaning may itself turn out to be confused, inconsistent or rationally unintelligible, as indeed we ought to expect (on Spinoza's account) given the conditions under which the prophets were writing and the problems of establishing a reliable text. But this need not be thought to impugn the authority of scripture so long as we observe the essential distinction between truths of reason and ideas arrived at through the reading of sacred works. For these latter have their own authority, one that derives from their law-giving power (in modern parlance: their *performative* capacity) to exact obedience and thus preserve the ties of communal and religious obligation. Spinoza makes this point – the difference between 'laws' and 'eternal and necessary truths' – in connection with God's warning to Adam and Eve not to eat the apple from the Tree of the Knowledge of Good and Evil. 'If God had spoken to them without the intervention of any bodily means [i.e. without resort to sense-perception or 'knowledge of imagination'] . . . immediately they would have perceived it, not as a law, but as an eternal truth' (TPT, p. 63). And the same applies to questions of scriptural meaning, in so far as any doubts concerning their validity must be put down to the inherent imperfections of a knowledge arrived at through imaginative signs and tokens, and transmitted through the fallible medium of written words.

II

In the remainder of this book I shall argue that Spinoza anticipates many of the issues that currently preoccupy literary theorists. More than that: he thinks them through with a clarity and persistence often lacking in his present-day descendents. There are problems in Spinoza's work that have to do with his rationalist metaphysics, his extreme mistrust of language (especially written language) as an aberrant or duplicitous medium, and his defence of scriptural truth through arguments that often – knowingly or not – turn out to undermine the very bases of religious belief. These problems are compounded, as we have seen, by the existence of two, radically opposed interpretive traditions, the one (mainly German and English) regarding Spinoza as a visionary thinker in the high Romantic line of descent, the other (mainly French) treating him as a thoroughgoing materialist and a strong precursor of Marxism, semiotics, psychoanalysis, post-structuralism and other such contemporary movements of thought.[16] If one thing is clear it is the fact that Spinoza made the highest possible claims for the pure good of theory, its power to demystify false ideas, bring the mind to an acceptance of truths unavailable through 'bodily' or commonsense perception, and thus achieve a knowledge atop all the strife of competing creeds and ideologies.

It is precisely this aspect of Spinoza's system that has struck many readers as a species of idealist or metaphysical delusion, the result of his assuming a direct correspondence between the order of ideas (or rational thought) and the order of real-world events, processes, causal relations, etc. For it is a truth self-evident to reason, on Spinoza's account, that 'the connection of ideas is the same as the connection of things', since 'the idea of each caused thing depends on the cognition of the cause of which it is the effect' (*E* II, P 7). In which case there could be no question of our having an 'adequate idea' that would not correspond to some real-world state of affairs. Truth would be its own guarantee in the sense that our knowledge (or the structure of logical relations between one idea and another) provided the only possible means by which to conceptualize reality. Thus 'substance thinking and substance extended are one and the same substance, comprehended now through one attribute, now through another' (*E* II, P 7 note). Hence Spinoza's radical monism – the grounds of his quarrel with Descartes – and, following from this, his espousal of a thoroughly deterministic outlook that identifies truth with the inexorable order of causal necessity, and freedom with the willing acceptance of this same condition. To many later thinkers (including Kant) this appeared nothing more than a striking example of the errors to which philosophy was prone when it exceeded the bounds of cognitive grasp and lost itself in the realm of pure speculative reason. Spinoza's mistake – and that of all rationalist metaphysics – was to think that one could gain a direct, unmediated knowledge of reality (or the *Ding-an-sich*) without first establishing the powers and limits of human understanding.

Such was Kant's object in the first *Critique*: to demonstrate the confusions that arise when these limits are ignored, when speculation is given free rein, and when 'ideas of pure reason' are allowed to override the evidence of phenomenal cognition.[17] It was essential to maintain this distinction, he believed, since otherwise there could be no defence against the arguments of sceptics like Hume, those who had rejected the rationalist appeal to a necessary link between the 'order of ideas' and the 'order of things', and who then went on to deny the possibility of our ever giving reasons (or validating grounds) for even the most basic items of commonsense knowledge. Kant's answer was of course that these problems were wholly misconceived, and that Hume's radical scepticism was merely the obverse of Spinoza's metaphysical rationalism. Henceforth philosophy should concern itself *not* with ontological questions ('what is the nature of reality?') but with questions concerning the 'conditions of possibility' for knowledge in general, the *a priori* grounds for different kinds of truth-claim, and the legitimate scope of those various faculties – pure reason, understanding, practical reason, aesthetic judgement – which between them comprised the entirety of human knowledge and experience. This would bring two main benefits, according to Kant. On the one hand it would show that metaphysicians (Spinoza among them) had fallen into error by ignoring the lesson of the first *Critique*, i.e. that if 'intuitions without concepts are blind', then equally 'concepts without intuitions are empty'. And it would also avoid the determinist upshot of Spinoza's arguments by showing that questions of free-will, autonomy or ethical choice are not properly dealt with by the same faculty – that of theoretical understanding – but need to be deduced from quite different principles, as enounced in the second *Critique*. Thus philosophy could be saved from the twin perils represented by Hume and Spinoza: an empiricism forced to entertain extravagant doubts about our knowledge of the external world, and a rationalism that led to the most extreme form of metaphysical determinist creed. The result of Kant's 'Copernican revolution' in philosophy would be to establish once and for all the limits of pure (speculative) reason, and the necessity of referring all truth-claims to the appropriate tribunal, as decided through a process of transcendental-deductive critique.

These arguments of Kant have exerted a deep and lasting influence on the currency of literary-critical debate. They were first taken up by the German and English Romantics (with Coleridge as a principal mediating figure), and are still a main topic – albeit in a highly problematized form – among the present-day exponents of deconstruction in philosophy and literary theory. This chapter of intellectual history has been well covered in a number of recent works, so I shall say no more about it here.[18] What has not been so often remarked is the distinct metaphysical turn – including the revival of Spinozist themes and arguments – across a range of otherwise diverse movements during the past two decades and more.[19] In part this has to do with the various attempts (by thinkers like Foucault, Deleuze and Lyotard) to revoke the Kantian 'Enlightenment' paradigm by arguing that 'man', or the transcendental subject, was really nothing more than a transient episode in the order of shifting discursive regimes, a 'fold' in the fabric of knowledge and representation whose brief hegemony was already coming to an end. On this account, the idea that truth-claims could ever be legitimized – or ultimately ruled out of court – by referring them to the critical tribunal of the faculties was merely a sign of the prestige once enjoyed by that delusive phantom entity. At any rate – so Foucault contends – it is no longer possible to place any credence in the Kantian subject, supposed source of truth and knowledge, that curious 'transcendental-empirical doublet' which somehow took rise within the discourse of the eighteenth-century human sciences.[20] Its claims have been undone by, among other things, the Freudian 'decentring' of self-possessed rational subjectivity; Saussure's structural revolution in linguistics (where thought becomes likewise a purely differential system 'without positive terms'); and the Nietzschean assault on all systems of knowledge and value that mask their will-to-power behind a rhetoric of pure, disinterested truth. There are, to say the least, certain questions that are begged by this wholesale abandonment of critical reason in the name of a new (postmodern) dispensation devoid of transcendental guarantees. But it is part of a wider movement of thought among French intellectuals that has marked a return to metaphysical questions and a striking revival of interest in Spinoza's philosophy.

The earliest and probably the best-known example was Althusser's project of so-called 'structuralist Marxism', a project that explicitly hailed Spinoza as among the great precursors of Marxist dialectic. Althusser made a point of acknowledging this debt in *Reading Capital*, the volume he coauthored with Etienne Balibar in 1965.

> The first man ever to have posed the problem of *reading*, and in consequence, of *writing*, was Spinoza, and he was also the first man in the world to have proposed both a theory of history and a philosophy of the opacity of the immediate. With him, for the first time ever, a man linked together in this way the essence of reading and the essence of history in a theory of the difference between the imaginary and the true.[21]

This passage is remarkable not only for pitching the claims so high but for using a decidedly *metaphysical* language ('the essence of reading', 'the essence of history') by way of asserting Spinoza's credentials as a materialist thinker. The reason may well be Althusser's desire to question the standard (vulgar-Marxist) idea that 'metaphysics' always belongs on the side of idealist mystification, while Marxism reveals such philosophies for what they are, mere illusions in the service of 'bourgeois ideology'. On the contrary, he argues: the only right reading of a work like *Das Kapital* is one that takes a lesson from Spinoza and distinguishes the *real-concrete* from the *concrete-in-thought*, or lived experience (the realm of ideology) from the work of theoretical production which aims at a knowledge – a scientific knowledge – of the 'misrecognition' involved in such appeals to experience as a source of plain, self-evident truth. For Althusser, ideology is best understood as a concept precisely equivalent to Spinoza's 'knowledge of imagination', i.e. the kind of 'natural' or pre-reflective attitude that accepts what is given in a common-sense way, and finds no reason to question or to criticize the grounds of naive sense-certainty. The break with this attitude can only be accomplished through a labour of rigorous conceptual critique, a labour of the kind exemplified in Marx's mature writings, though not (Althusser argues) in those works which predate that discovery and which still bear traces of an earlier – humanist or Hegelian – mode of understanding.

In fact it is no exaggeration to say that the entire project of Althusserian Marxism comes down to this issue of Spinoza *versus* Hegel, or the claims of a Marxist theoretical 'science' as opposed to a subject-centred dialectics of class-consciousness, alienation, 'expressive causality' and other such Hegelian residues. One philosopher at least had anticipated Marx in achieving the 'epistemological break' required to set Hegel back on his feet. Spinoza takes on this privileged role because he, more than anyone, saw the need to maintain a clear-cut distinction between knowledge as arrived at through experience, sensory acquaintance, phenomenal intuition certainty etc., and knowledge as established (or *produced in thought*) through a form of immanent or structural critique. And it was this revolution at the level of theory, quite as much as his heterodox religious views, which resulted in Spinoza's extreme notoriety and his banishment from the company of reputable thinkers. 'The history of philosophy's repressed Spinozism thus unfolded as a subterranean history *at other sites*, in political and religious ideology (deism) and in the sciences, but not on the illuminated stage of visible philosophy.'[22] That is to say, it was not until Marx – and moreover, not until Marx made the break with his own 'pre-Marxist' or Hegelian thinking – that history caught up with the insights attained in Spinoza's work. Indeed. Althusser goes so far as to claim that Spinoza was a veritable structuralist *avant la lettre*, a thinker who managed to formulate the central precepts of the modern 'linguistic turn' without benefit of Saussure's methodological revolution. He was able to achieve this extraordinary feat by rejecting all versions of naive or 'metaphysical' realism and insisting that truth was *entirely and exclusively* a work of theoretical production, i.e. that the only criteria for truth were those arrived at through an immanent critique or a structural analysis of the concepts in question. And it is for this reason – against all the odds, one might think – that Althusser can treat Spinoza not only as a critical thinker of exceptional power but as a radical *materialist* who opened the way to a rigorous (scientific) reading of the Marxist text.

This claim has to do with the concept of 'structural causality', a concept that Althusser thinks indispensable to any such reading. It is aimed squarely against the Hegelian–Marxist notion of 'expressive causality', according to which historical phenomena (class-conflict, forces and relations of production, dominant ideologies and so forth) can best be grasped as the gradual unfolding of a world-historical Idea through stages of a grand dialectical progress whose meaning – or whose inner dynamics of change – they manifest successively from age to age. Althusser detects this idealist notion at work both in early Marx and in those latter-day thinkers (like the Lukács of *History and Class-Consciousness*) who adopt a similar idealist view.[23] At the opposite extreme – and equally mistaken – is the kind of mechanistic determinism that conceives causality as a one-way relation between material (economic) factors on the one hand, and on the other those various ideologies, artforms, belief-systems etc. wherein the 'real conditions' of social life find a partial and distorted image. It is this latter, crudely reductionist habit of thought that has produced the base/superstructure model and the various failed attempts – mostly on the part of Marxist aestheticians and literary theorists – to refine that model and avoid its more awkward implications. The only alternative, as Althusser argues, is to conceive the various modes of production (economic, social, cultural, scientific, etc.) in terms of a 'structural causality', an order of relations where economic factors may indeed play a determining role 'in the last instance', but only as components within a complex ensemble where the other levels maintain their 'relative autonomy' and cannot be reduced to an epiphenomenal or merely derivative status.

It is Spinoza's distinction to have theorized this possibility long before Marx and thus laid the groundwork for a properly scientific understanding of Marxist concepts and categories. On this model, as Althusser and Balibar describe it,

> effects are not outside the structure, are not a preexisting object, element or space in which the structure arrives to imprint its mark; on the contrary, the structure is immanent in its effects, a cause

immanent in its effects in the Spinozist sense of the term, that the *whole existence of the structure consists in its effects*, in short that the structure which is merely a specific combination of its peculiar elements, is nothing outside its effects.[24]

In Spinoza, this argument is conjoined with the strong (metaphysical-determinist) claim that the highest form of knowledge consists in perceiving the entire order of causal relations *sub specie aeternitatis*, or as they might appear to a pure (indeed a God-like) rational intelligence, one that has somehow managed to transcend all merely contingent limitations of time and place. It is remarkable indeed that Althusser should find such thinking amenable to the purposes of Marxist criticism. But in fact he takes this whole metaphysics on board, including the doctrine at the heart of Spinoza's *Ethics*: namely, that our timebound or localized perceptions of cause and effect belong to mere 'knowledge of imagination' and are therefore not to be confused with the order of self-evident, *a priori* truth. Thus Spinoza: 'In the nature of things no contingent thing is given, but all things are determined from the necessity of the divine nature to existing and operating in a certain mode' (*E* I, P 29). From which it follows that history is itself an 'imaginary' construct, that historical time has no reality outside this realm of delusory appearances, and therefore that the end of all rational enquiry is to free the mind from its bondage to inadequate (i.e. historically contingent) ideas. It is by virtue of this power vested in the human intellect – a power to think beyond the false positivity of sensory impressions, empirical self-evidence, history, time-consciousness, etc. – that we can, on rare occasion, bring ourselves to contemplate ideas in their eternal (and eternally necessary) order of logical relations.

Althusser is prepared to follow Spinoza even to the point of accepting these claims for a knowledge – or a mode of 'theoretical production' – that somehow stands outside and above the contingency of historical events. We must recognize, he says,

that the *concept of history* can no longer be empirical, i.e. *historical* in the ordinary sense, that, as Spinoza has already put it, *the concept dog cannot bark*. We must grasp in all its rigour the necessity of liberating the theory of history from any compromise with 'empirical' temporality, with the ideological concept of time which underlies and overlies it, or with the ideological idea that this theory of history, *as history*, could be subject to the 'concrete' determinations of 'historical time' on the pretext that this 'historical time' might constitute its object.[25]

This passage helps to explain one of the most controversial theses advanced by Althusser, namely his argument that ideology 'has no history', that it exhibits a certain invariant structure, a mechanism of 'interpellation' whereby all subjects are assigned a role within the governing order of social relations.[26] The most obvious source of this theory is Lacan's rethinking of Freudian psychoanalysis, in particular his concept of the 'imaginary', that realm of specular misrecognition in which the ego maintains its precarious existence as a figment of narcissistic desire, a subject-position forever unable to achieve self-presence or stability.[27] What is not so often noticed is the close connection between Althusser's theory of ideology and Spinoza's account of how the mind is held thrall to 'knowledge of imagination'. Such knowledge is the source of those empiricist or commonsense delusions (like taking the sun to be *actually* a small red disc suspended in the haze at a middling distance) which result from our not subjecting such ideas to a process of rational critique. More absurdly, it is the kind of category-mistake that Spinoza has in mind when he observes that 'the concept "dog" cannot bark'.

That is to say, imagination misleads in so far as it confuses the two distinct realms of *empirical self-evidence* on the one hand and *necessary truth* on the other. Its structural workings are precisely equivalent to those of 'ideology', in Althusser's understanding of that term. It is false not so much in the sense that it distorts the facts of immediate or real-life experience – since the sun, after all, *does* present itself to our senses in exactly that deceptive shape, just as ideology reveals certain genuine truths about our lived (imaginary) relation to the real conditions of social life. Where the falsehood comes in is at the moment of misrecognition when the subject confuses this limited, partial or historically situated knowledge with a truth that is conceived as holding good for all time, or as transcending mere ideology. For Spinoza, in short, 'Imagination is the idea wherewith the mind contemplates a thing as present; yet this idea indicates rather the present disposition of the human body than the nature of the external thing' (*E* V, P 134). It is the same with ideology, as Althusser conceives it: a pre-reflective or uncritical mode of awareness which cannot be *altogether* devoid of truth – since it gives access to our everyday experience as living, thinking and feeling human agents – but which presents this truth in imaginary form *as if* from the standpoint of a mind in possession of eternal or adequate ideas. Such is indeed the essential ambiguity of the term 'subject', the slippage of meaning that allows it to function as an alibi or means of disguise for the real conditions of social existence. 'In the ordinary sense of the term', Althusser writes, '"subject" in fact means: (1) a free subjectivity, a centre of initiatives, author of and responsible for its actions; (2) a subjected being, who submits to a higher authority, and is therefore stripped of all freedom except that of freely accepting his submission'.[28] It is precisely by means of such equivocal terms that language accomplishes the work of ideology, the process that constructs (or 'interpellates') the subject as a free individual who willingly occupies his or her place within the pre-given order of socialized subject-positions.

One of Althusser's major concerns is to argue against the standard (vulgar-Marxist) account which treats ideology as entirely a matter of 'false consciousness', a realm of delusory appearances that are ultimately determined by conditions prevailing in the socio-economic 'base', but which then serve merely as a distorting mirror that obscures or dissimulates those same ubiquitous conditions. The great problem here – one that has dogged many versions of Marxist *Ideologiekritik* – is to explain how one could possibly theorize such a process, or give any rational account of its workings, from a standpoint that would not have been determined in advance by the very mechanism it seeks to comprehend. For Althusser – again taking his cue from Spinoza – the only way through and beyond this dilemma is to grasp both horns at once, so to speak, and acknowledge that we are always 'in' ideology, but capable of thinking its limits and internal contradictions through an exercise of reason whose truth is in some sense *its own guarantee*. I must quote at some length to convey what is involved in this admittedly abtruse piece of argument. 'It is necessary', he writes,

> to be outside ideology, i.e. in scientific knowledge, to be able to say: I am in ideology (a quite exceptional case) or (the general case): I was in ideology. As is well known, the accusation of being in ideology applies only to others, never to oneself (unless one is really a Spinozist or a Marxist which, in this matter, is to be exactly the same thing). Which amounts to saying that ideology *has no outside* (for itself), but at the same time that it is *nothing but outside* (for science and reality) . . . Spinoza explained this completely two centuries before Marx, who practised it but without explaining it in detail.[29]

To his opponents of a broadly empiricist persuasion – notably E. P. Thompson in 'The Poverty of Theory' – such language must appear nothing more than a case of pseudo-philosophical jargon, a dreadful example of what goes wrong when theory loses touch with the lived actualities of historical experience.[30] Thompson's essay exploits every opportunity for Swiftian satire and downright knock-about polemics. It fastens unerringly on those passages in Althusser which show the full extent of his indebtedness to Spinoza and other such thinkers in the rationalist or high metaphysical tradition. For Thompson, this merely goes to demonstrate the basic absurdity of a self-styled 'Marxist' theory which – as a matter of principle – rejects any appeal to historical fact, to the real conditions of social life and the self-understanding of those men and women whose experience is the only veritable record we possess. In fact he goes further and indicts Althusserian Marxism as a form of theoreticist delusion which translates directly into the politics of neo-Stalinism, that is to say, the belief in a privileged intellectual *cadre* (or 'revolutionary vanguard') whose dictates can then be used to justify all manner of inhuman policy decisions. What begins *in theory* as a perverse misreading of Marx – a notion of 'science' that would somehow transcend lived experience, ideology or history itself – ends up as a covert endorsement of the worst political practices.

Thompson's polemic has considerable force when read in the context of his own work as a chronicler of working-class history from the viewpoint of those who were actively engaged in making that history.[31] It is a statement of faith in the two working principles that are everywhere implicit in his writing. The first is that historical episodes make sense – and not merely in a distorted or 'ideological' way – for those who have lived through them and worked collectively to achieve some political end. And the second – following directly from this – is that historians in turn can best make sense of such episodes when they give due weight to the words, motives and actions of those involved, rather than adopt the kind of high-handed attitude that claims an *a priori* privileged perspective above all mere vicissitudes of time and place. The main point at issue between Thompson and Althusser comes down to their reading of the well-known sentence in Marx's *Eighteenth Brumaire*, that 'men' indeed 'make their own history', but not under circumstances or conditions of their own free choosing.[32] With Thompson, the emphasis falls characteristically on the first part of this sentence, while Althusser stresses the qualifying clause, the extent to which historical agency is always constrained by material factors beyond its power to predict, control or fully comprehend. In short, it must seem from an Althusserian viewpoint that Thompson has fallen prey to a species of naive voluntarism, a subject-centred thinking which ignores the real conditions – the structural limits – placed upon human thought and action. For Thompson, conversely, the upshot of Althusser's theorizing is a form of metaphysical determinism that discounts the very notion of history-in-the-making, rejects any appeal to the living witness of situated human agents, and produces nothing more than a clanking machinery of abstract concepts and categories.

What Thompson fails to recognize – perhaps necessarily, given his own priorities as a working historian – is the fact that these problems cannot be wished away *at the level of philosophy or theory*, even if they pose no obstacle (and indeed appear entirely unreal) at the level of commonsense practical awareness. After all, it is not only in the discourse of Marxist criticism that thought comes up against the issue of freewill *versus* determinism, or the question how far 'men' can 'make their own history' if one concedes the extent to which actions are governed by an order of necessity that scarcely leaves room for the autonomous, self-acting subject. Kant's three *Critiques* set out to adjudicate this question by assigning the faculties each to its own proper realm of competence and judgement. More specifically, he argued that the freewill/determinist antinomy only arose through our habit of confusing *theoretical* knowledge (i.e. knowledge arrived at through an adequate matching-up between concepts and sensuous intuitions) with *practical reason*, or the faculty competent to judge in matters of ethical import. It was this confusion, according to Kant, which led on to the 'paralogisms of pure reason', those chimerical conundra that had so preoccupied thinkers in the old 'metaphysical' tradition. Nowadays philosophers are more apt to make the point in logico-linguistic terms, as for instance by talking of human activities as falling under two different kinds of description, causal-determinist on the one hand and self-willed (or ethically accountable) on the other.[33] But the problem is still there – unavoidably there – no matter what refinements are brought in by way of easing the apparent contradiction. Quite simply, we are unable to abandon the belief that at least *some* actions – our own in particular – result from an exercise of freely-willed choice which does leave room for alternative decisions, themselves the outcome of differing values or priorities. This conviction goes deep, not only as a matter of ethical (and legal) necessity, but as a fact of experience closely bound up with our every conscious thought and action. Yet is is equally the case that any attempt to think this problem through in a consequent way will find itself obliged to accept some version of the determinist argument. For the question remains: what can possibly account for our choosing some particular course of action, if not the fact that we are *already* disposed to behave in that way through cultural conditioning, formative experience, previous value-commitments and so forth? By pushing the argument back a stage – appealing to past choices as the background of present values and behaviour – the champion of freewill merely begs the question or opens the way to an infinite regress. In the end there is no escaping the logic of determinism, but also – paradoxically – no room to deny that we *do* have this experience of choosing, willing, acting on principle, etc. as a matter of inward or intuitive self-evidence.

It is in order to achieve a more adequate grasp of such problems that Althusser proposes his model of 'strucutral causality', as opposed to previous ('expressive' or 'mechanical') versions of deter-minist thinking. This model is intended to explain (1) how ideology 'interpellates' the subject, creating the illusion of autonomous agency, freewill and choice, and (2) how it is nevertheless possible on occasion to achieve a 'scientific' knowledge of this process by means of conceptual clarification or immanent critique. And it is here that Spinoza figures most importantly as the one thinker before Marx who managed to conceive the relation between science and ideology in properly *dialectical* (i.e. non-reductive and historically specific) terms. What produced this break with existing forms of knowledge – a veritable revolution in thought, as Althusser sees it – was Spinoza's attempt to think the limits of ideology (or lived experience) from the standpoint of theoretical reason, but without thereby reducing ideology to mere 'false consciousness' or subjective illusion. For Spinoza, that is to say, there is a knowledge that belongs to our worldly condition, our practical experience as living, situated human agents. This knowledge has its own kind of truth – a truth *sub specie durationis*, or valid in respect of its own time and place – and cannot be dismissed out of hand from the viewpoint of theory or rational critique. But its claims are inevitably partial and (in some degree) distorted, arising as they do from a level of commonsense, empirical or everyday awareness that lacks 'adequate ideas', or concepts framed according to the dictates of critical reason. Such criticism would not be *outside* ideology in the sense of existing only in so far as we suspend all reference to contingent historical circumstances and aspire to an order of timeless, transcendent truth. Rather, it requires that we learn to distinguish these separate (but always co-implicated) orders of knowledge, the one having to do with sense-certainty, empirical self-evidence, lived history etc., while the other is entitled to question such evidence in the name of adequate ideas.

Spinoza makes this point most forcefully in a letter to one of the many perplexed correspondents who requested further instruction. 'It is necessary before all things', he writes, 'to distinguish between understanding and imagination, or between true ideas, and the rest, namely the fictitious, the false, the dubious, and absolutely all those which depend solely on memory' (Letter 37). But elsewhere he makes it clear that 'knowledge of imagination' cannot be regarded as entirely false or misleading, since its origins most often lie in facts of experience which the intellect may indeed be forced to abandon, while the senses continue to perceive them just as before. In the simplest case – that of optical illusion – 'when its [the sun's] true distance is known, the error is removed, but not the imagination' (*E* IV, P 1 note). And this applies equally to 'errors' in the realm of lived (ideological) experience, those brought about by the mind's subjection to a limiting mode of timebound, historical knowledge. Falsehood in such cases 'consists solely in the privation of knowledge which inadequate ideas involve, nor have they any positive quality on account of which they are called false' (*E* IV, P 1). In short, ideology is best understood *not* as a species of mere illusion, bad faith or 'false consciousness', but as a present lack of knowledge that results from the restrictions placed upon thought by its confinement to the here-and-now of immediate, practical concerns. And from this it follows – in Spinoza's view – that thinking can be brought to perceive those limits through an exercise of immanent critique that shows up their logical incoherence, or the points at which commonsense perception conflicts with the order of 'adequate ideas'.

III

There is a passage in the *Ethics* that presents this case in terms strikingly reminiscent of Kant on the sublime. 'Wonder is the conception (*imaginatio*) of anything, wherein the mind comes to a stand, because the particular concept in question has no connection with other concepts' (*E* III, Def. 4). Just as, for Kant, the sublime exceeds all the powers of phenomenal cognition, and thus gives access to a realm of 'suprasensible' ideas, so likewise for Spinoza consciousness is brought 'to a stand' by suddenly encountering the limits of commonsense perception, revealed as such by a knowledge that transcends all contingencies of time and place. It is for this reason that Althusser hails Spinoza as the first to have arrived at a workable theory of the relation between 'science' and 'ideology'. He made it possible, in short, to conceive how subjects might at once be constructed *within* ideology – the precondition of socialized experience in general – and yet achieve a knowledge *of* that ideology from a standpoint that somehow exceeded its structural grasp. That this is not just a version of idealist metaphysics (as opponents like Thompson would argue) is borne out by Spinoza's reiterated point: that lived experience has its own reality – its truth 'for us' in a temporal context – and furthermore, that this reality must also be accounted for in humanly intelligible terms.

Pierre Macherey sees this as the heart of Spinoza's political philosophy, the aspect of his thinking which, more than any other, helps to counteract idealist (i.e. Hegelian) readings of Marx. 'Error is a mechanism regulated by the strictest of conditions which are also those of our everyday subjection [*esclavage*].'[34] Erroneous or confused ideas would then follow from one another with the same necessity that governs adequate (clear and distinct) ideas. That is to say, they would both belong to an all-embracing order of transitive causal connections, but with this essential difference: that adequate ideas give a knowledge *in and of* ideology, a mode of understanding not totally enslaved to commonsense perceptions, while 'knowledge of imagination' thinks itself somehow an exception to the rule, an originating source of actions or ideas, and is thus all the more (since unwittingly) a product of ideological conditioning. This is why Spinoza equates true freedom with the acceptance of a thoroughgoing causal necessity that governs both the 'order of things' and the 'order of ideas'. It is precisely in so far as we lack this knowledge – in the measure that our concepts are defective, 'inadequate' or 'confused' – that we strive after a false (imaginary) notion of the self-caused, autonomous, free-willing agent. Thus, in Macherey's words,

[t]he inadequate idea is an incomplete idea, to the extent that we cannot grasp it without mutilating it: in itself, in God, it is adequate; but, in comprehending it in a partial manner, we are prevented from perceiving its necessity, and it is from this contingency, of which the real causes are in us, that derives the illusion of freewill.[35]

For Althusser and Macherey alike, the significance of Spinoza's conceptual revolution lies in its break with all idealist philosophies of subject and object, mind and nature, the 'for-itself' of thought and the 'in-itself' of sheerly existent material reality. They both read Spinoza as offering an alternative to Hegel, a philosophy that dispenses with the transcendental subject as locus of a truth that would emerge in the fullness of time through the progress of Spirit in its world-historical march toward Absolute Reason, Christianity and the Prussian nation-state. Spinoza's dialectic, conversely, is one that functions

in the absence of all guarantees, in an absolutely causal manner, without the foregone orientation which from the outset equips it with the principle of negativity, without the promise that all the contradictions in which it is engaged will finally be resolved, because they carry within themselves the conditions for their solution.[36]

What Spinoza gives us to think is a principle of sufficient reason that supposes all things to be causally determined (not excepting our own ideas and actions); that equates ideology with the various factors conspiring to prevent or obscure this knowledge; but which also explains how these factors result from a necessity inscribed in the given condition of our existence as historically-situated human knowers and agents. It is a harshly paradoxical teaching which admits of no saving or compromise solutions, such as (for instance) Hegel provides by resolving the subject-object dialectic in a moment of revealed, self-authenticating truth.

For Macherey, this is the crux of Spinoza's philosophy and the point where it comes most closely into contact with the central problematic of Marxist thought. Spinoza gives the lie to Hegelian dialectic by steadfastly refusing the kind of metaphysical comfort that derives from a confidently subject-centred conception of history and ultimate truth. His thinking insistently raises the question: 'What is the limit that separates an idealist from a materialist dialectic?' And it does so by renouncing all premature solutions, by acknowledging on the one hand the force of material circumstance, historical conditions, commonsense knowledge etc., and on the other the claims of a critical reason that inevitably calls such knowledge into question. This thinking must function 'in the absence of all guarantees' to the extent that it renounces the Hegelian faith in a master-narrative of reason and truth, a providentialist 'logic' that knows in advance how the story must eventually turn out. For Spinoza, such notions are strictly unintelligible since they confuse the two realms of *logical necessity* (which has to do with 'eternal' or adequate ideas in the nature of reason itself) and *historical explanation* (where knowledge is always in some degree restricted by its own perspectival character). In which case, Macherey asks: 'might one not just as well say that that which he refutes in Hegelian dialectic is actually not dialectical, that which Marx himself called Hegel's idealism?'[37]

It is by virtue of this resolute anti-idealism – his rejection of all 'final causes', whether in theology or metaphysics – that Spinoza occupies a privileged place in the history of radical thought before Marx. And we should not be misled, Macherey thinks, by the fact that Spinoza couches these arguments in the language of theological debate, as when he identifies 'God' with the ultimate reality (or substance) which exists in and of itself, and in relation to which the two 'attributes' (of mind and body) and the various determinate 'modes' of existence constitute a more or less partial apprehension. For this language is adopted partly as a matter of practical necessity – a means of circumventing censorship – and partly because it enabled Spinoza to address a whole series of urgent *political* questions in terms that would at least make sense to readers brought up in that same tradition. What his thinking demonstrates most clearly is the way that, in Macherey's words, 'an excess of idealism may border on (*toucher à*) a materialism, or at any rate produce certain materialist effects'.[38] That is to say, there is a process of translation involved – a transposition into secular and political terms – if one is to grasp the significance of Spinoza's thought, not only for present-day readers but for those of his enlightened contemporaries who could read between the lines and perceive the real import of his arguments.

What then becomes apparent is that Spinoza shares none of the beliefs that characterize orthodox (whether Jewish or Christian) systems of religious thought. He rejects any notion of God's omnipotence as consisting in the exercise of a sovereign power to will or determine events in a manner contrary to natural necessity. Since

'God' and 'nature' are strictly synonymous – since they function as alternative names for that substance of which all minds and bodies partake under one or the other attribute – it simply *cannot make sense* for God to act against the laws of nature. From which it follows necessarily (1) that human freewill is likewise a species of illusion brought about by our failing to grasp those laws; (2) that all talk of miracles or divine interventions derives from the same incapacity; and (3) that religion – as commonly understood – is itself the *effect* of certain causes to be sought in the mass-psychology of belief, the interests of various state or political systems, and the factors that conspire to prevent individuals from perceiving their subjection to these ideological constraints. This is why theorists like Macherey can claim Spinoza as a radical materialist despite his professed adherence to a form of thoroughgoing metaphysical monism. For the terms of that doctrine, when examined more closely, reveal that it can always be translated point for point into a language of *Ideologiekritik* or socio-political analysis. And this applies even to those concepts and categories (like the 'intellectual love of God') which appear most remote from secular concerns. There is no reason to suppose that Spinoza is deliberately playing a double game, adopting the terms of theological argument – in however heterodox a fashion – in order to deceive the censors, to smuggle in subversive political ideas, or just to avoid trouble.[39] More plausible is the reading that interprets such language *on both levels simultaneously*: that is, as a genuine attempt to resolve theological problems about freewill, determinism, divine omnipotence, scriptural authority, etc., while also conducting a sustained critique of secular institutions and values. Thus the 'intellectual love of God' would signify both a knowledge arrived at through the contemplation of adequate ideas *sub specie aeternitatis*, and also that form of theoretical enquiry that transcends the limits placed upon thought by ignorance, prejudice or commonsense (ideological) habits of belief.

'That thing is called free', Spinoza writes, 'which exists solely by the necessity of its own nature, and of which the action is determined by itself alone' (*E* I, D 6). Construed metaphysically, this means that 'free' is a predicate which applies only to God (or nature), since these terms alone denote a substance that is self-originating (*causa sui*), that depends on no prior conditions of existence or intelligibility, and therefore functions entirely according to its own immanent laws of necessity. But there is also the claim – just as prominent in the *Ethics* and elsewhere – that an increase of knowledge brings an increase of freedom in the secular and political spheres; that the closer we come to comprehending the universal order of causal relations, the less we will be subject to illusory ideas that diminish our capacity for effective thought and action. This follows from the major premise of Spinoza's metaphysics, i.e., that mind and body are the twofold attributes of a single, indivisible substance, so that any acquisition of additional powers in the mental or reflective realm must necessarily entail a commensurate change in the order of bodily well-being. Thus: 'he, who possesses a body capable of the greatest number of activities, possesses a mind whereof the greatest part is eternal' (*E* V, P 39).

It is clear enough, from this and other statements, that when Spinoza speaks of the mind's having access to 'eternity' or 'eternal ideas', these expressions cannot be taken as referring to an afterlife enjoyed by the individual soul in the company of God's elect. Rather, they indicate that reason is 'time-blind' (to adopt a phrase from Jonathan Bennett, one of Spinoza's best modern commentators). Thus 'when reason says that P it announces that *eternally P*, meaning that *necessarily always P*. [And] this leaves no foothold for any concept involving *tempus*, i.e., involving past-present-future or temporal measure'.[40] Bennett reads Spinoza from the standpoint of present-day analytical philosophy, admiring much of what he finds but also offering various attempts at 'rational reconstruction' in the logico-linguistic mode. Thus he argues that Spinoza's case with regard to 'eternal ideas' might be rendered more convincing – or relieved of its surplus metaphysical baggage – if presented in terms of modal logic, or truth 'at all possible worlds'. Nevertheless he treats it as a defensible position and one that requires (on this point at least) only minimal adjustment to meet the demands of analytical clarity and rigour. From a different perspective – more idealist in character – one could cite the following passage by Errol E. Harris which assimilates Spinoza's thinking to a broadly Kantian (epistemological) paradigm. On this account the mind may be said to possess 'eternal ideas' inasmuch as it

transcends time and space in the sense that time and space are *for* it and it is not *in* them . . . The human mind is thus both finite and potentially infinite, both the idea of a finite mode of Extension (and thus itself a finite mode of Thought), and, nevertheless, in being idea, capable of adequate knowledge of the total scheme of things. It is therefore self-transcendent and eternal.[41]

What both these commentators seek to establish is the fact that Spinoza's arguments have an import – a logical consistency or structure of articulated truth-claims – which need not involve any ultimate appeal to God, substance, eternity, or other such 'metaphysical' grounds. More precisely: his system is indeed *metaphysical* through and through, but only in the restrained or descriptivist sense of that term adopted by recent philosophers, notably P. F. Strawson.[42] 'Metaphysics' would then be taken to include all reflection on the powers and limits of human knowledge, all attempts to demarcate the 'bounds of sense', or to comprehend the structures of knowledge and perception through an exercise of critical reason. And the same would apply to any version of materialist critique which claimed – in however subtle or nuanced a fashion – to distinguish 'science' from 'ideology', or the real conditions of social existence from the forces that work to conceal or dissimulate those same conditions, and which thus perform the task of ideological recruitment.

Hence the two central propositions of Althusserian Marxism, propositions which must appear strictly unthinkable (or downright contradictory) from any but a Spinozist standpoint. For it is only on these terms – by conceiving the subject as always and everywhere 'in' ideology, but also as potentially 'in' science to the extent that ideology is fractured, conflictual, producing subject-positions of knowledge outside its self-enclosed sphere – it is only on these terms, Althusser argues, that Marxism makes any kind of conceptual sense. Spinoza's would then be the one philosophy before Marx that managed to articulate this structural problematic in the form of a genuine 'theoretical practice', a discourse that examined truth-effects (i.e. their mode of production for the subject 'in' ideology), but which also kept open the appeal to a critical perspective wherein those effects could be adequately theorized. In other words, he avoided the twin temptations of (on the one hand) an idealist indifference to the realities of lived experience, and (on the other) an empiricist refusal to break with that experience in the name of an alternative, more rigorously theorized knowledge. One can therefore understand why Spinoza became such a focus of interest for left-wing French intellectuals during the period when Althusser's structural Marxism exerted its most widespread influence.

To those who remember it (myself included) that period now seems strikingly remote. In a general way no doubt this has to do with the steady rightward drift in British and US politics, the loss of faith in Marxist ideas (especially those of a high-theoreticist character), and the adoption of policies, even on the left, which increasingly appeal to consensus-values in the name of a so-called 'new realism'. These shifts have been reflected in a large-scale retreat from the kinds of theoretical activity that once (not so long ago) formed the main agenda of Marxist debate. In his recent book *The Detour Of Theory* Gregory Elliott offers a detailed reading of the events – historical, political and intellectual – that contributed to this 'eclipse' of Althusserian Marxism.[43] They include the sense of post-'68 disenchantment on the left, the disarray of many activists (especially CP members) as a result of those wholly unexpected events, and the perceived inability of theorists like Althusser to account for what had happened or explain why the looked-for revolution had failed. One direct consequence was the rise to fame of a group of conservative ideologues (the *Nouveaux Philosophes*) who set out to reoccupy the ground now vacated by left intellectuals. Another was the move towards alternative forms of oppositional discourse, attempts to re-fashion a left cultural politics in terms unbeholden to Marxist (or Enlightenment) notions of truth, reason, history, progress, and critique.

A list of these thinkers would amount to a litany of current 'theoretical' options as debated in the vanguard books and journals. In all of them (Foucault, the later Barthes, Lyotard, Baudrillard, Deleuze) one finds a deep mistrust of explanatory systems, 'meta-narrative' schemas or any attempt to arrive at a position outside or above the register of bodily experience. As Paul Hamilton puts it:

> existentialist and structuralist versions of this access of authenticity are superseded by another vocabulary, simultaneously more mandarin in its negations and yet more physical in its detail than before: 'force'; 'power'; *jouissance*; *figure*; 'desiring machines'; *chora*; the dream-work that works, not thinks; all the post-structuralist resources of exorbitance, and so on. All participate in the self-targeting of reason itself . . . a process which reaches for the extra-philosophical titles of bodily activity, material practice or work the more its reflexivity and relativism advertise its procedures as noetically untenable.[44]

In short, the emphasis has now shifted to what Spinoza calls 'knowledge of imagination', or the kind of knowledge that arises at the level of immediate, pre-reflective experience, rather than subjecting such experience to a process of rational critique. Thus Foucault

Spinoza vs Hegel 51

sees nothing but grandiose delusion in those old meta-narratives (Kantian, Hegelian, Marxist or whatever) which staked their claims on a world-historical progress towards enlightenment and truth. In their place he proposes a detailed 'micrological' analysis of the way that individuals are recruited, disciplined, subjected to various forms of institutional control through the workings of a pervasive 'power/ knowledge' that extends to every aspect of private and public life.[45] It is no longer a question – as the Marxist would have it – of some particular class-interest or machinery of state that maintains itself through the exercise of a sovereign, juridical will-to-power. Rather, it is a case of multiple, decentred 'discourses' which circulate without any clear point of origin, 'technologies of the self' that no longer need to have punitive sanctions attached since they are willingly embraced (or internalized) by subjects in quest of 'authentic' self-knowledge. From the Christian confessional to Freudian psychoanalysis, this process unfolds as a steadily increasing compulsion to make everything a topic for discourse, to expose every aspect of our social, sexual and affective lives to the various forms of knowledge (including the latter-day 'human sciences') that march under the banner of progress and enlightenment.[46]

So we should expect nothing good to come of theory, least of all the kind of mandarin 'theoretical practice' envisaged by Marxist intellectuals like Althusser. Where reason once promised to deliver us from the grip of ignorance, prejudice, injustice and arbitrary rule – exposing them to the lucid, undeceiving gaze of ideological critique – it now appears, on Foucault's account, that reason is a part of the problem, not the solution; that every increase of knowledge brings about an equal increase in the available technologies of power, surveillance and control. The one hopeful aspect of Foucault's diagnosis is the link between *power* and *resistance*, terms which are strictly indissociable – he argues – since power cannot function in the absence of resisting subjects, bodies, or discourses, while resistance takes rise at every point where power is inscribed within social relations. But again, this isn't a matter of developing some *theory* to explain how 'ideology' gives way to 'science', or how the mystified, commonsense view of reality turns out to harbour certain gaps and aporias, thus producing an alternative, more adequate form of knowledge. For Foucault, on the contrary, theory is itself a product of that ubiquitous and implacable 'will-to-truth' which subjugates the body – locus of all genuine, effective resistance – to its various disciplinary regimes. Hence his adoption of a resolutely physicalist language – a language of forces, drives, affects, libidinal investments, bodily impressions, etc. – by way of counteracting this tyranny of concepts.

The same might be said of those other thinkers in the broad poststructuralist camp who have renounced 'theory' as an abstract or totalizing project, and devised a new rhetoric more closely allied to the rhythms and intensities of lived experience. In Barthes this took the form of an erotics of reading, a language of textual *plaisir* or *jouissance*, evoking the relationship between reader and text through an image-repertoire of obsessions, seductions and intimate bodily encounters, such as could scarcely be grasped by any version of high-structuralist poetics or narratology.[47] Thus Barthes's later writings are increasingly devoted to a quest for whatever eludes or frustrates the systematic enterprise of theory. They focus on moments of 'ecstasy', abandonment or loss, moments when the reader is seized by a sense of strange, uncanny, even perverse attachment to the text; when all the scaffolding of method and theory suddenly falls away and one is left with the need to somehow articulate that which uniquely solicits one's interest as a subject of textual desire. In his last book, *Camera Lucida*, Barthes essayed a rhetoric of the photographic image that would not – like so much of his earlier work – reduce in the last analysis to a matter of 'codes' or structural meanings, elements of sense that could then be recomposed at the level of a generalized systemic method.[48] What lent these photographs their special significance, their power to enthral and disconcert, to tease the viewer almost out of thought, was their belonging to a repertoire of bodily affects, of wishes, memories and desires, which in one sense made their analysis a hopeless endeavour (since he alone – Barthes – was the subject in whom those affects uniquely converged), but which also required that he somehow give voice to them, articulate their meaning in terms that would bring at least a measure of shared understanding.

And so we find the last of those binary oppositions (nature/culture, *lisible/scriptible*, *plaisir/jouissance* etc.) that run through the entirety of Barthes's work and which always serve to distinguish a passive, conformist, heavily naturalized, 'commonsense' mode of reading from one that involves an active, self-critical, transformative relation to the text. Here it is the pair of terms *studium* and *punctum*, borrowed from the discourse of scholastic philosophy, the first of which denotes everything in a photograph that belongs to the realm of codified, conventional, publicly-available meaning, while the second signifies just those details that pierce the viewer with strange recollection, that possess some utterly distinctive meaning, yet which cannot be reduced to any order of preexistent codes or structural relations. Like music – which also preoccupies Barthes in some of these haunting and haunted late essays[49] – photography leads criticism to a point where theory no longer has anything useful to say, and where meaning can only be evoked analogically through a language of somatic impulses, bodily desires and sexual connotations. From one point of view – that taken by theorists like Althusser and Macherey – one can hardly imagine a more complete break with the Spinozist principles of rational thought.

2 Of Truth and Error in a Spinozist Sense: Deleuze, Derrida, de Man

I

The work of Gilles Deleuze offers the single most sustained example of this drive 'against theory' in the name of the body as a locus of anarchic, polymorphous-perverse instincts and desires. In his best-known text, the *Anti-Oedipus* (co-authored with Félix Guattari), Deleuze offers not so much a critique of Freudian psychoanalysis as a full-scale polemical assault on its truth-claims and concepts, its social effects, its ulterior motives (of surveillance and control), its normalizing rhetoric and everything else that marks it as just another discourse in the service of latter-day repressive or instrumental reason.[1] The Oedipus Complex is itself nothing more than a tool of social domination, an all-purpose concept that pretends to explain how subjects are recruited into the existing (familial and socio-political) order of power, but which in fact helps to enforce and perpetuate that order by supplying its basic rationale. What is more, the same applies to *any* kind of theory – Marxist, structuralist, post-structuralist or whatever – that seeks to bring conceptual order out of instinctual chaos, or to impose its own tidy schemes of explanation on the rich, chaotic, pre-conscious, non-signifying flux of libidinal energy.

The Deleuzian equivalent of Barthes's binary terms is the distinction between 'molar' and 'molecular' strategies of discourse, the former having to do with tree-structures or hierarchically-ordered relationships of meaning, knowledge and power, while the latter manifest themselves in a 'rhizomatic' pattern of tentacular, criss-crossing networks and nodes which acknowledge no ultimate authority or source, and which thus proliferate far beyond reach of any possible explanatory theory. Karl Kraus's famous remark about

Freudian psychoanalysis – that it offered itself as the cure for cultural disorders of which it was in fact the most striking and visible symptom – is here pursued to the limit of its power to wreak havoc with Freud's (and, more pointedly, with Lacan's) theoretical enterprise. The *Anti-Oedipus* can perhaps best be read as a kind of Rabelaisian satire, an extravagant mixing of genres that combines 'serious' argument with knockabout polemics, that drags theory down to the level of bodily appetites and functions, and which leaves no room for any delusive meta-language that would seek to have the last word, and thus close off the play of polymorphous instincts and drives.

What Deleuze and Guattari set out to demolish by every available means is the will-to-truth within psychoanalysis that sets itself up as a hermeneutic discourse, a language with the power to *interpret and explain* the inchoate symptoms of bodily desire. Hence their strategic recourse to a different language, an idiom of 'desiring-machines', 'schizo-analysis', 'molecular' forces, etc., whereby to contest and subvert the whole idea that symptoms exist, that they have to be interpreted, and that psychoanalysis is the discipline best qualified to decipher their occult meaning and thus speak the truth of the unconscious and its effects. In place of this interpretive-hermeneutic paradigm the *Anti-Oedipus* proposes a whole new range of erotic, libidinal or sensory analogues, terms which function entirely at the level of 'desiring-production', of the body as a locus of forces, affects and conflictual relations that signify nothing beyond themselves. To accept this inversion of received priorities – to abandon the old, Platonist metaphysic that set up a realm of Meaning and Truth as opposed to mere affect, bodily sensation, erotic enslavement, perceptual illusion and the like – is to take the first step (so Deleuze and Guattari argue) toward a break with the various self-regulating structures of capitalist social power. For this is their major claim in the *Anti-Oedipus*: that theories like psychoanalysis, so far from representing a challenge to the capitalist order of social relations, in fact lend support to that order by imposing a system of explanatory concepts – terms such as the 'Oedipus Complex' – whose effect is to *endorse and perpetuate* the social apparatus by confining subjects to their pre-assigned role as bearers of that same repressive structure.

In this sense Freud comes closer to the truth in his late, sombre meditations – works like *Civilization And Its Discontents* – than when he and his disciples lay claim to an essentially liberating power for psychoanalysis, a power to restore the libidinal freedoms now lost through our subjection to an alienating social order. For it is precisely in this effort to interpret or theorize the unconscious – to speak its truth in the name of some higher, more adequate knowledge – that psychoanalysis unwittingly allies itself with the capitalist drive toward an ever-increasing regimentation of bodily drives and desires. Such is the 'territorializing' impulse which permeates every aspect of existence in capitalist society, and which also typifies those various disciplines (like psychoanalysis) which seek to comprehend or interpret that process. The only effective means of resistance is an opposite ('deterritorializing') impulse which rejects all forms of interpretation, hermeneutics, diagnostic commentary etc., which insists on the absolute primacy of the body and its various asemic or non-signifying drives and desires, and which consequently aligns itself with 'molecular' rather than 'molar' structures of desiring-production.

In *A Thousand Plateaus*, their sequel to the *Anti-Oedipus* (and forming Volume 2 of *Capitalism And Schizophrenia*), Deleuze and Guattari pursue this analysis through a form of multi-layered compositional technique that touches on a yet more exorbitant range of topics and themes.[2] This is not the place for a detailed account of a work which in any case defies one's best efforts of summary explication. What interests me here – and resumes the main argument of this book – is the role that Spinoza plays throughout their writing as a kind of elective precursor, one who stands (improbably enough) as source and inspiration for its every strategic move. 'After all', the authors write,

> is not Spinoza's *Ethics* the great book of the Body without Organs? The Attributes are types or genuses of BwO's substances, powers, zero intensities as matrices of production. The modes are everything that comes to pass: wars and vibrations, migrations, thresholds and gradients, intensities produced in a given type of substance starting from a given matrix . . . A continuum of all substances in intensity and of all intensities in substance . . . Drug users, masochists, schizophrenics, lovers – all BwO's pay homage to Spinoza. The BwO is the *field of immanence* of desire, the *place of consistency* specific to desire.[3]

If this passage displays (to say the least) a degree of rhetorical overkill, it nevertheless communicates something of the 'underground' quality, the radical appeal or counter-cultural following that has marked the reception of Spinoza's philosophy almost from the outset. We have seen already how 'Spinozism' figured in the lexicon of eighteenth-century political debate. It became a kind of a code-word more or less synonymous with atheism, materialism and various forms of revolutionary doctrine.[4] To his enemies (conservatives and upholders of orthodox religion) Spinoza was indeed – as Deleuze and Guattari represent him – a thoroughly subversive thinker, one who acknowledged no God except Nature, who rejected any distinction between mind (or soul) and body, and who demanded an absolute freedom of conscience in matters of religious belief. But there were always those who revered Spinoza on exactly the same grounds, as a radical free-thinker whose message required decoding to bring out its real (i.e. materialist and revolutionary) import. In this light one can read the above passage as one more attempt to rescue Spinoza from the clutches of a misconceived pious reading which totally falsifies that message.

It also shows very clearly how the emphasis has shifted in the twenty or so years since Althusser launched his project of structural Marxism explicitly under the aegis of Spinozist ideas. For Althusser, the crucial lesson to be gained from a reading of Spinoza was the need to elaborate a Marxist 'science' of theoretical concepts and categories, one that would respect the relative autonomy of different cultural spheres and so maintain a distinctive role for its own theoretical practice. Where Marxists had tended to confuse the issue was in thinking that a truly *materialist* account of knowledge and cultural production must always involve an *empiricist* philosophy of objects as directly given to perception without intermediary concepts. In fact this amounted to a gross misreading of Marx, one that might not have come about had Spinoza's work been better known:

> Against what should really be called the latent dogmatic empiricism of Cartesian idealism, Spinoza warned us that the *object* of knowledge or essence was in itself absolutely distinct and different from the *real object* . . . the *idea* of the circle, which is the *object* of knowledge must not be confused with the circle, which is the *real object*. In the third chapter of the 1857 *Introduction*, Marx took up this principle as forcefully as possible.[5]

Thus for Althusser, the chief value of Spinoza's thought lies in its rigorous distinction between, on the one hand, 'adequate ideas' (those that can be worked up into a genuine science of Marxist theoretical practice), and, on the other, 'confused' or inadequate ideas that belong to the realm of ideology, commonsense, or every-day lived experience. Only by maintaining this crucial distinction can Marxism achieve any kind of theoretical rigour. For Deleuze and Guattari, on the contrary, what marks Spinoza out as a radical thinker is his total rejection of Cartesian dualism, his insistence that 'mind' and 'body' are attributes of the same indivisible substance, or – in analytical terms – that they function as twin predicates attaching to a single subject. And in this case (so their argument implies) it is the merest of delusions to think of theoretical knowl-edge, or 'adequate ideas', as existing in a cognitive realm apart from the evidence of bodily or sensuous impressions. Quite simply, there is no distinguishing the one from the other, no means of knowing *for sure* what might be the limits of bodily (i.e. causal) explanation, or how far these limits merely reflect our own present ignorance of the body and its workings.

For this is one of Spinoza's main points, in the *Ethics* and elsewhere: that the illusion of freewill, with all its attendant prob-lems and paradoxes, may be nothing more than the result of our simply not grasping the extent of those causal relations – however subtle or far-reaching – which in fact determine our every last act and thought. It is precisely this condition of ignorance, coupled with a certain intellectual disdain for the body and its mechanisms, that gives rise to all manner of confused speculation regarding the supposed freedom or autonomy of human will. In fact, Spinoza writes, the body 'far surpasses in complexity all that has been put together by human art, not to repeat what I have already shown, namely, that from nature, under whatever attribute she be con-sidered, infinite results follow' (*E* III, P 2 note). Thus, according to Spinoza, we are led into error by identifying freedom with the privileged domain of human thought and agency, whereas bodies are envisaged as subject to the laws of a strict causal necessity. But this is to get the matter backward, he argues, since on the one hand ideas (whether true or erroneous) are likewise causally determined, while on the other we are not in a position to know just how complex – and how far beyond present understanding – are the springs and mechanisms of bodily experience. Among his proofs for this claim Spinoza cites the instances of dreaming and somnam-bulism, both of which activities are enough to show 'that the body can by the sole laws of its nature do many things which the mind wonders at' (*E* III, P 2 note).

Of course it might be argued – and Spinoza anticipates this point

– that what's really involved here is just a more occult or subliminal order of mental operation, a sign that the mind possesses powers unguessed-at under normal (waking) conditions. But this line of argument simply won't do since it deepens the confusion yet further. That is to say, it ignores one plain, self-evident fact of experience (that we only have a partial, fragmentary, confused knowledge of the body and its attributes) in order to conjure up a whole new range of insoluble problems and paradoxes. 'Thus, when men say that this or that physical action has its origin in the mind, which latter has dominion over the body, they are using words without meaning, or are confessing in specious phraseology that they are ignorant of the cause of the said action, and do not wonder at it' (ibid). In which case, Spinoza argues, we are obliged to accept the following conclusions: (1) that mind and body are likewise subject to the laws of logical and natural necessity; (2) that this involves a complete rejection of Cartesian dualism and its various offshoots; and (3) that the only genuine freedom – as opposed to imaginary ideas thereof – is that which comes of acknowledging these truths and thus acting in accordance with the dictates of reason and nature alike.

So one can see why Spinoza should recently have figured as a strong precursor for two such utterly disparate movements of thought as Althusserian Marxism and the project of 'schizo-analysis' announced by Deleuze and Guattari. On the one hand his work can be read as endorsing a high theoreticist position, one that insists on a clean conceptual break between the realm of ideology (or lived experience) and the domain of Marxist science (or 'adequate ideas'). On the other – and with at least some degree of interpretive warrant – it lends support to the converse set of claims: that theory is a pointless and delusive endeavour, that concepts must always falsify the nature of lived experience, and that the only reality is that of the body as a complex ensemble of drives, impulses and 'desiring machines' that acknowledge no necessity save that of preserving their own, sheerly physical or sensuous mode of existence. There are many propositions in the *Ethics* which would clearly be open to either reading and whose undecidability cannot be resolved by appealing to context or other such saving ploys. Thus: 'Whatsoever increases or diminishes, helps or hinders the power of activity in our body, the idea thereof increases or diminishes, helps or hinders the power of thought in our mind' (*E* II, P 2 note). And again: 'The mind, as far as it can, endeavours to conceive those things, which increase or help the power of activity in the body' (ibid). One could read both statements in the Althusserian mode, that is to say, as having to do with the essential role of theory, its capacity to clear away sources of 'commonsense' confusion and thus free the mind for an active engagement in the realm of 'theoretical practice'. Such a reading could claim to be perfectly consistent with everything that Spinoza has to say on the topic. But it is also in passages like these that Deleuze and Guattari find warrant for their version of Spinoza as a celebrant of the 'Body without Organs', or that level of polymorphous-perverse instinct and desire that eludes all forms of conceptual understanding, that exists outside the symbolic order (or the Oedipal economy of socialized exchange), and which seeks only to maximize 'intensities' of bodily experience. In short, both parties – theorists and anti-theorists alike – can plausibly lay claim to Spinoza as an advocate on their own side of the argument, one in whose work all their major themes are strikingly rehearsed or prefigured.

In fact Deleuze published two studies of Spinoza before the period of collaborative work with Guattari that marked their decisive turn 'against theory'. One of them (*Spinoza: practical philosophy*) has recently appeared in English translation, and provides a useful point of entry to this whole current debate on the powers and limits of rational understanding. There is, Deleuze writes,

> a double reading of Spinoza: on the one hand, a systematic reading in pursuit of the general idea and the unity of the parts, but on the other hand and at the same time, the affective reading, without an idea of the whole, where one is carried along or set down, put in motion or at rest, shaken or calmed, according to the velocity of this or that part.[6]

What is perhaps most significant about this book – especially in light of Deleuze's subsequent texts – is the fact that it manages to keep both readings in play, despite the strong preference (as manifested here) for an 'affective', as opposed to a purely theoretical or 'systematic' treatment. Thus it offers a cogent exposition of Spinoza's ideas that would seem to be modelled, at least up to a point, on the manner of reasoning *more geometrico* that Spinoza himself adopts in the *Ethics*. In fact a large portion of the book – nearly half its total length – is taken up by a glossary of Spinozist terms and concepts, a series of more or less extended definitions that employ the same technique of elaborate cross-reference by way of analytic commentary. In these passages Deleuze appears mainly concerned to clarify the logical structure of Spinoza's argument, and to do so by means of a 'rational reconstruction' (or mode of conceptual exegesis) which basically respects that structure. For the rest, his book has chapters on the religious and political context of Spinoza's work, on its reception-history (starting out from Spinoza's correspondence with Blyenbergh), and finally – looking forward to *Mille Plateaux* – on the topic 'Spinoza And Us'.

So one could make the same point about Deleuze's text that commentators have often made about the *Ethics*: that it operates on two different levels of address, the one aspiring to an order of logical rigour, consistency and truth, while the other finds room for diverse comments and local *aperçus* whose relation to the overall structure of argument is at times fairly hard to discern. Efraim Shmueli has some useful remarks on this topic in his essay 'The Geometrical Method, Personal Caution, and the Idea of Tolerance'. What is most striking in the *Ethics*, he writes, is 'the difference between the restrained and detached, although controversial assertions dressed in the geometrical form, and the non-geometrical assertions loaded with harsh rebukes, refutations, ridicule, and scorn'.[7] This disparity can best be explained, Shmueli thinks, if we recognize Spinoza's need for a conceptual framework that would give his ideas an objective (or at least a quasi-objective) form, and thus act as a defence against his own more turbulent feelings and the ever-present danger of state or religious persecution. Thus the non-geometrical portions of the *Ethics* 'are agitated by deep apprehensions and intellectual doubt', which in turn suggests 'that the geometrical form served for Spinoza, consciously or semiconsciously, as a device for restraining his strong temper when dealing with views whose treatment by him might have annoyed the public'.[8] But there is also a more principled aspect to Spinoza's choice of presentational form, one that has to do with his liberal-progressive politics, his commitment to the cause of tolerance, democratic government, and freedom in matters of religious belief. What these values entail is the right of each individual to exercise his or her own powers of reason and not be obliged to conform their thinking to the dictates of church or state power. And it is precisely this ideal, so Schmueli suggests, that is embodied in the formal structure of Spinoza's arguments, his laying them out as so many axioms, propositions, definitions, corollaries, scholia and so forth which solicit assent at an intellectual level, and not by means of suasive, rhetorical or other such potentially coercive strategies. Thus 'in Spinoza's mind, the geometrical order, the cautious, impersonal, and universally valid (*ex ipsa ratione*) method of deduction was a call, indeed, for tolerance, but also for self-discipline'.[9] What the method achieved was at once a technique for avoiding trouble with the censors and a means of subjecting his own arguments to the tribunal of enlightened reason.

The alternating pattern that Shmueli notes in Spinoza's work – his oscillation between extremes of passionate involvement and detached, impersonal authority – is a characteristic that can also be observed among the commentators. In Deleuze, this results from his persuasion on the one hand that Spinoza's philosophy makes logical sense, i.e. that it offers a coherent and compellingly-argued system, and on the other his belief that it remains first and foremost a *practical* philosophy, one whose truth-claims cannot be assessed apart from their efficacy in promoting *action* at various levels of bodily and mental existence. It is here – in their similar treatment of passive or 'inadequate' ideas as the source of all human misery and confusion – that Deleuze makes the link between Spinoza and Nietzsche as radically affirmative thinkers. Thus the Nietzschean 'genealogy of morals' finds a parallel in Spinoza's argument against all forms of moralizing doctrine (religious or secular) that conceive virtue in terms of a passive obedience to this or that set of ethical injunctions.[10] For both philosophers, the result of such thinking is to encourage a wholly negative, ascetic or self-denying outlook, a spirit of *ressentiment* (to adopt Nietzsche's term) which, instead of seeking to overcome or transvalue the present limitations of human existence, merely takes them as given and then – by a perverse twist of reasoning – sets them up as its highest ideals. And so it comes about that morality is turned into a system of internalized checks and interdictions, a system whereby reason is deprived of its affirmative, self-acting power, and the body is subjected to a false regime of tyrannizing 'spiritual' disciplines.

Spinoza makes this point most forcefully in connection with the Judaeo-Christian idea of original sin. If Adam and Eve had fully understood the consequences of eating the apple – that is to say, if they had interpreted God's words *not* as an arbitrary command (or mere prohibition) but as offering genuine knowledge and practical guidance – then it is surely inconceivable that they should have fallen into error. (See *TPT*, pp. 63–4.) And the exegetes, for their part, compound this faulty reasoning when they interpret the

Garden of Eden episode as an instance of divine law transcending the limits of human comprehension. Those limits are real enough, Spinoza thinks, but not in the sense that they indicate some ultimate restriction placed upon knowledge in accordance with God's will. Rather, they are the product of a partial or faulty understanding ('knowledge of imagination') which fails to recognize the essential difference between 'laws' and 'eternal and necessary truths'. Thus: 'If God had spoken to them [Adam and Eve] without the intervention of any bodily means, immediately they would have perceived it, not as a law, but as an eternal truth' (*TPT*, p. 63). If the scriptures frequently resort to a performative idiom – a language of divine laws, commands and prohibitions – it is only in order to accommodate their message to the popular imagination. A more adequate reading would treat such passages (as Spinoza treats the Garden of Eden episode) in terms of their underlying rational import, i.e. as 'imaginary' representations of a truth whose significance can only be grasped *sub specie aeternitatis*, or as a matter of 'eternal and necessary ideas'. But we should be wrong to conclude from all this that the body and its modes of sensuous apprehension are mere encumbrances, sources of inevitable error and confusion, obstacles to truth which reason must transcend in the quest for adequate ideas. This might appear to follow from Spinoza's statement that the Fall could never have come about had Adam and Eve construed God's words 'without the intervention of any bodily means'. However, it is clear that Spinoza is here speaking of a *partial and impaired* state of bodily awareness, one that misinterprets the divine ordinance precisely on account of its not enjoying the full, unimpeded, or active exercise of conjoint mental and physical powers. For it is only in so far as it lacks such powers – a deficiency affecting mind and body alike – that the will becomes subject to illusory ideas of divine prohibition, original sin, the corrupting effects of knowledge, etc., ideas that conspire to disable or pervert the very exercise of human reason.

So it appears that Spinoza sees the same confusion at work in Cartesian dualism (or any variant of the mind/body distinction) and the idea of morality as a system of heteronomous laws, commands or prohibitions which thwart the otherwise self-acting, self-preserving tendency of human organisms. Such is at any rate Deleuze's reading of the *Ethics*, a reading that looks to Nietzsche (where Althusser had looked to Marx) for evidence of the continuing force and validity of Spinoza's arguments.

This will be the threefold practical problem of the *Ethics*: *How does one arrive at a maximum of joyful passions?*, proceeding from there to free and active feelings (although our place in nature seems to condemn us to bad encounters and sadnesses). *How does one manage to form adequate ideas?*, which are precisely the source of active feelings (although our natural condition seems to condemn us to have only inadequate ideas of our body, of our mind, and of other things). *How does one become conscious of oneself, of God, and of things?* (although our consciousnesses seem inseparable from illusions).[11]

Deleuze's answer to these questions, as we have seen, is to go all the way with a materialist or thoroughly demystified reading of Spinoza's text. It is a reading that chiefly stresses the mind-body identity thesis, the bad (self-disabling) effect of moral values which deny this thesis in the name of some higher 'spiritual' truth, and the need for a 'transvaluation of values' that would finally lay these false ideas to rest and give full scope to the body's mode of being as a force-field of endlessly multiplied impulses and drives, a nexus of manifold 'desiring machines' whose effects impinge upon our every thought and action, conscious or otherwise, but whose causes – being radically decentred, or immanent to the order of mind-nature as a whole – exceed the powers of self-present conscious grasp. Thus, according to Deleuze:

You will not define a body (or a mind) by its form, nor by its organs or functions, and neither will you define it as a substance or a subject. Every reader of Spinoza knows that for him bodies and minds are not substances or subjects, but modes. It is not enough, however, merely to think this theoretically. For, concretely, a mode is a complex relation of speed and slowness, in the body but also in thought, and it is a capacity for affecting or being affected, pertaining to the body or to thought . . . Affective capacity, with a maximum threshold and a minimal threshold, is a constant notion in Spinoza . . . That is why Spinoza calls out to us the way he does: you do not know beforehand what good or bad you are capable of; you do not know beforehand what a body or a mind can do, in a given encounter, a given arrangement, a given combination.[12]

It is clear enough, from this and many passages in his book, that Deleuze experienced the reading of Spinoza's texts as one such radically transformative 'encounter', a release of energies that went far beyond any purely philosophical conversion. There is no great distance from what he writes here to the arguments, the hyperbolic rhetoric, the strategy of out-and-out warfare on all conceptual systems and truth-claims, that are carried to yet more extraordinary lengths in the *Anti-Oedipus*. And it is remarkable – an irony perhaps without parallel in recent intellectual history – that the self-same work (Spinoza's *Ethics*) should have inspired two such utterly divergent projects as Althusser's structural Marxism and Deleuzian schizo-analysis.

II

But to leave it at that – having registered (and perhaps, to some degree, explained) the existence of these discrepant readings – would, I think, be to miss the most revealing aspects of Spinoza's present-day reception history. For it is not just a question of tracing his influence on thinkers (like Althusser, Macherey and Deleuze) who have overtly acknowledged that influence and made it an integral part of their work. What I want to argue now – having suggested as much all along – is that some of the most crucial issues and debates in modern critical theory are effectively prefigured in Spinoza's writings, even where there is no question of 'influence', direct or oblique. In very general terms this discussion has to do with the powers and limits of theory itself, the relation between different orders of truth-claim (philosophical, historical, literary-critical, etc.), and the question whether language can be thought of as providing a reliable means of access to these and other kinds of knowledge.

Clearly there is a sense in which this last question precedes and subsumes all the others. For Spinoza has a good deal to say about language and what he says must affect our reading of his work at every level of commentary and analysis. In fact there is widespread disagreement among the commentators as to just how far Spinoza went in his principled mistrust of language as a source of 'confused' or 'inadequate' ideas, a medium inherently ill-adapted to the quest for ultimate truth. Certainly there are passages where he seems to suggest that words (or signs) can never be trusted, that they offer mere 'knowledge of imagination' and belong to an order of shifting, unstable and arbitrary sense where adequate ideas can find no place. As we have seen, Spinoza takes this line when he addresses the topic of scriptural exegesis and the problem of maintaining the authority of scripture when faced with such a mass of conflicting truth-claims, variant narratives, chronological enormities, evidence of textual corruption and so forth. His response is to argue on the one hand that the prophets 'perceived by imagination and not by

sure mental laws', and on the other that it is 'one thing to understand
the meaning of Scripture and the prophets and quite another thing
to understand the meaning of God, or the actual truth (*TPT*, pp. 26
& 170–71). But this attitude goes beyond his dealing with questions
of biblical hermeneutics to produce what many commentators have
perceived as a deep and thoroughgoing scepticism with regard to
language in general. For if words are indeed mere arbitrary signs –
if they operate, as Spinoza more than once asserts, on a basis of
transient associative linkage between meanings, images and
(confused) ideas – then it is hard to see how *any* kind of verbal
argument, his own included, could possibly lay claim to *any* kind
of truth. So there is an obvious problem – or a species of self-
reflexive paradox – if one takes this doctrine to apply (as it must)
in the reading of Spinoza's own texts.

David Savan's article 'Spinoza and Language' was the first to
take full account of this paradox and insist on the difficulties it
raised for anyone concerned to understand the *Ethics* at its own
professed level of argument. For Spinoza, he writes,

> an idea is not an image and does not consist of words. A true idea
> can neither arise from experience of words and images nor can it be
> verified through such experience, for experience can give no knowl-
> edge of essences . . . Whereas an idea is certain, words are uncertain.
> Whereas 'that true word of God which is in the mind can never be
> depraved or corrupted', words are corruptible. And whereas it is of
> the nature of reason to consider things as necessary and under a
> certain form of eternity, words are connected with contingency and
> time.[13]

In which case one would have to conclude that Spinoza's arguments,
being couched in language, necessarily partake of the same dubious
character that attaches to all verbal sign-systems. Of course it might
be held (as Spinoza asserts in the case of Old Testament prophecy)
that this is just a matter of accommodating truth to the given
limitations of human understanding; that since (self-evidently) language is essential to the conduct of any philosphical argument –
even one that aspires to an order of reasoning *more geometrico* –
therefore it is pointless to raise such difficulties. But this defence
simply won't do, as Savan remarks, if it involves making a special
case of the *Ethics* while regarding all other texts, religious or philosophical, as purveyors of a knowledge inherently flawed by its
reliance on mere verbal signs. For Spinoza makes the point very
firmly and thus closes off all possible escape-routes for the reader

intent upon squaring or resolving this paradox. If words cannot be 'disengaged from the imagination in order to represent true ideas', then this applies reflexively to every statement in the *Ethics* and Spinoza's other writings. Language is a chief cause of error and delusion *not* on account of some existing defect that might yet be remedied (e.g. by tidying up its logical grammar and semantics), but rather because its very nature aligns it with the sources of inadequate, confused or 'imaginary' ideas. In short, there is no avoiding the awkward conclusion that Spinoza's philosophy self-deconstructs – undermines its own truth-claims – by casting doubt on those very propositions that make up its overt structure of argument.

The existence of this problem will come as no surprise to readers acquainted with the work of Jacques Derrida. For it is his main contention – advanced through the rhetorical close-reading of philosophic texts – that language (especially written language) has always been conceived by thinkers in the Western 'logocentric' tradition as an error-prone, duplicitous, thoroughly unreliable medium, a realm of 'supplementary' or secondary signs where truth all too often becomes lost in the labyrinths of textual undecidability. There is no room here for a detailed account of Derrida's writings on (among others) Plato, Aristotle, Kant, Hegel, Husserl, Saussure, and J. L. Austin.[14] For present purposes (i.e. as regards Spinoza and the problem of construing his remarks about language) the following may serve as some useful points of entry.

Since Plato, philosophy has standardly conceived itself as the discipline uniquely fitted to pronounce on questions of ultimate truth. In its classical form, this entails the claim that reason (*logos*) or knowledge (*episteme*) come about through a power of authentic, inward contemplation (*theoria*) whereby the mind is enabled to transcend mere opinion (*doxa*), or the fallible evidence of the senses, and thus gain access to a realm of eternal, self-validating 'forms' or 'ideas'. It is in virtue of this privileged role that philosophy can criticize other forms of knowledge – poetry, rhetoric, sophistics, all the arts and techniques of mere suasive appeal – as failing to meet its own high standard. These practices ought not to be encouraged since they promote various kinds of illusion, notably that of mistaking mere semblances (whether verbal, sensuous, mimetic or whatever) for the adequate ideas or eternal forms to which those semblances vainly aspire. Thus, for Plato, the only 'good' mimesis is one that aims toward a spiritual wisdom – a truth conceived *sub specie aeternitatis* – and which therefore renounces all forms of outward, material or phenomenal embodiment. And writing is especially an object of suspicion, as Derrida shows in his essay on the *Phaedrus*, since written signs are themselves a species of 'bad' mimesis, doubly harmful in so far as they substitute for spoken words which in turn substitute for the order of authentic, self-present, inward ideas.[15] So philosophy should ideally have no truck with writing and restrict itself – as Socrates taught – to the 'live' dialectic of spoken exchange where words are least apt to obtrude their harmful effects.

But Plato is unable to sustain this argument, not only for the obvious reason that he has *written this dialogue down* (and thus disobeyed the Socratic injunction), but also for other, more intricately textual reasons that emerge from a deconstructive reading of the *Phaedrus*. For it then becomes apparent that the whole Platonic doctrine of truth, self-presence and adequate ideas is dependent on a certain *metaphorics* of writing – a 'good' mimesis or 'writing in the soul' – which the dialogue is at paints to distinguish from its 'bad' counterpart, but which cannot in fact be thus distinguished except by adopting a mainstream (Platonist) view and ignoring the evidence of the text. One such piece of evidence is the word *pharmakon*, a term that Plato associates with writing at various points in the dialogue, and whose range of meaning encompasses the starkly antithetical senses of 'poison' and 'cure'. Writing is a poison, as Socrates (on Plato's account) expressly argues, since it threatens to destroy the very sources of authentic, inward truth by supplying a mere mechanical apparatus, a mnemotechnic device that substitutes not only for speech but also for the effort of thinking, reasoning, actively getting things 'by heart'. But there is another logic that runs athwart this reading of Plato's text and constitutes a challenge to all its associated precepts and values. For writing is also a 'cure' in the sense that it supplements (makes up for) the inherent limitations of an oral, pre-literate culture. Quite simply, writing is the *precondition* for those various disciplines or knowledges – science, history, philosophy itself – which could never have advanced beyond a primitive stage in the absence of a written archive. Thus what Derrida remarks in the *Phaedrus* is not just a series of striking 'ambiguities' in the key-term *pharmakon*, but a structural fault-line that runs through the text, a double logic (or aporia) which marks the very limit of Platonist thought.

This pattern repeats itself in Derrida's essays on Rousseau, Husserl, Saussure, Austin and others. In each case there emerges a 'logic of the supplement', a curious (even 'perverse') undoing of normative concepts and priorities, whereby what *ought* to be the secondary or derivative term in a given pair – e.g. 'writing' as opposed to 'speech' – in fact turns out to be always already at work in any definition of its positive counterpart.[16] The case of Husserl (and especially Derrida's reading of his essay *The Origin of Geometry*) is perhaps most relevant to the problem of construing what Spinoza has to say about language and its inherently unreliable, duplicitous character. For Husserl, like Spinoza, geometry figures as the paradigm case of *a priori* knowledge, of truths that are (or ought to be) self-evident to reason through a process of pure 'eidetic inspection', aside from all merely contingent factors of historical time and place.[17] Of course Husserl can scarcely deny that such truths have a 'history' in the sense that they were once unknown (or confusedly perceived), and therefore required the conceptual labours of a thinker like Euclid before they gained acceptance as a matter of universal knowledge. But this doesn't alter the basic point, according to Husserl: that conclusions arrived at by reasoning *more geometrico* have a character of ideal necessity (or apodictic truth) which was always, so to speak, *there waiting to be discovered*, and cannot be conceived as merely the outcome of episodes in this or that contingent history of thought.

Thus Husserl follows Spinoza (and Plato) in regarding geometry as grounded in a knowledge of 'eternal ideas' to which reason has access by virtue of its own, immanent laws. And this leads him to argue, like them, that language – especially written language – is a hindrance to the mind in its quest for such ultimate truths, language being at best an unstable, deceptive medium where signs stand in for adequate ideas and thought becomes subject to all the vagaries of time and chance. For Husserl, the communality of knowledge – or the conveyance of ideas from mind to mind – should ideally take place in a realm of 'primordial intuitions' that would stand quite apart from the documents, the history or the written archive wherein these discoveries are recorded. But again, as with Plato, there is a marked discrepancy between Husserl's *express thesis* – that writing is at best a mere technical necessity, a means for communicating adequate ideas – and what his argument effectively *constrains him to say*: that in the absence of writing (or of language in general) we could have no access to the truth-claims of geometry or any kind of knowledge. Thus, in Derrida's words, 'the possibility of writing will assure the absolute traditionalization of the object, its absolute ideal Objectivity . . . Writing will do this by emancipating sense from its actually present evidence for a real subject and from its present circulation within a determined community'.[18] And this despite Husserl's repeated statements of the contrary position, i.e. that the only source of indubitable truths is a reasoning grounded in primordial intuitions (or eidetic self-evidence), and having nothing to do with mere linguistic signs.

Here as elsewhere in Derrida's texts, it would be wrong to understand the term 'writing' in its commonplace, restricted or literal sense, i.e. as applying to systems of graphic notation (or phonetic-alphabetical script) which in turn represent the elements of spoken language. Certainly this has been the dominant assumption among philosophers, for whom – as Derrida shows in many instances – speech has at least possessed the relative virtue of a close proximity to live, self-present ideas, while writing has figured as 'the sign of a sign', and hence as a doubly deceptive medium.[19] But this idea should not go unquestioned, Derrida argues, if analysis reveals that a certain insistent problematics of writing inhabits the texts of philosophy at precisely those points where reason asserts its essential non-dependence on the written word. Such is the case with Plato, Husserl and those other thinkers in the mainstream (logocentric) tradition whose texts manifest this curious ambivalence with regard to their own status. For the question of writing is always within reach of the further question whether *any* kind of language – written or spoken – can provide a reliable access to truth. If writing is indeed the 'sign of a sign', then this condition must apply to spoken language also, since speech-acts make sense only in so far as they belong to some pre-existent set of codes, conventions or signifying structures, and not by virtue of their power to articulate ideas self-present to the mind of this or that individual speaker. Thus 'writing' is the name (a synecdoche or metonym) for everything in language that frustrates the desire for conceptual mastery, self-presence or truth. And where philosophers cast doubt upon the capacity of writing to convey 'adequate ideas', what is really at stake is philosophy's claim – an inherently aporetic claim – that reason can somehow escape or transcend all these bad liabilities of language while arguing its case, of necessity, through the medium of verbal signs.

As I have said, Spinoza exhibits this problem raised to a high point of self-reflexive principle. Savan states the case most succinctly:

So sharply does Spinoza separate words from adequate ideas that it is difficult to make out for language any useful philosophical function at all. It is no more possible for us to discover and express true knowledge through language than it is for a somnambulist to communicate intelligently with the waking world . . . If he was aware of this situation, then he cannot have intended that the *Ethics* should be a simple and straightforward exposition of his philosophy.[20]

What Savan describes here is something very like the structure of opposed and unresolvable truth-claims that Derrida locates in Husserl's *Origin of Geometry*. That is to say, Spinoza occupies a likewise anomalous position as author of the *Ethics*, on the one hand declaring his mistrust of language as a source of inevitable error and confusion, but on the other presenting his reasons for this attitude through a series of verbal propositions. Of course it might be argued – in keeping with Spinoza's views on the topic – that those same propositions are set out in a form which aspires to the order of demonstrative reasoning achieved in Euclid's *Elements*, and which thereby avoids the charge levelled against language in its everyday, un-self-critical mode. But this defence also fails since it is far from clear that Spinoza's use of the analogy really holds up, or that arguments like those pursued in the *Ethics* could possibly be justified *more geometrico*. In fact it is generally agreed among the commentators that this 'method' serves more as an organizing principle, a quasi-objective formalist device, or perhaps (as Shmueli persuasively argues) a means of avoiding sectarian dispute through its seeming reliance on truths arrived at by the exercise of pure, disinterested reason.[21] At any rate there are few who would take seriously Spinoza's claim – if indeed it was his claim – to have wrought such a change in the groundwork of ethics, metaphysics or philosophy of mind that they could henceforth be treated on Euclidean terms as purely *a priori* disciplines.

This still leaves room for other attempts to save the situation by arguing that Spinoza is *not* in fact committed to a form of self-disabling epistemological scepticism. Thus G. H. R. Parkinson comes up with a series of possible rejoinders to Savan's article, one of which involves the early-Wittgensteinian distinction between 'showing' and 'stating' as alternative forms of philosophical argument. 'The inadequacy of language', he suggests,

is not so much stated by Spinoza as shown – shown by the contradictions in the *Ethics* itself, which, it might be suggested, is regarded by Spinoza as the most coherent system that can be constructed with

words. This seems to be a valid answer, though it will be noted that
it implies that the *Ethics* does contain serious contradictions, and
that this was recognized by Spinoza.[22]

On this account, Spinoza would have placed himself quite knowingly in the same position that Wittgenstein occupies at the close
of his *Tractatus*. That is, he would have stated all that it was possible
to state (i.e. to articulate in the form of verbal propositions) about
language, logic and the limits of conceptual representation. As for
what lay beyond those limits – a 'beyond' that encompasses, in
Wittgenstein's view, the whole domain of ethics, metaphysics and
other questions of ultimate concern – on these matters, famously,
one is in no position to 'state' anything at all, and had therefore
best remain silent.[23] On this reading it would be possible to argue
that Spinoza was likewise consciously engaged in a form of therapeutic exercise, one that sought to *show* (not to state) those same
essential limits by pressing language to its highest point of 'geometrical' purity and rigour, and only then – through a self-deconstruc-
tive move – pointing to the insufficiency of any such approach. In
which case, as Parkinson says, the *Ethics* would possess some claim
to coherence at the level of performative strategy, but would still
create problems for anyone concerned to make sense of its logical
structure.

In fact Parkinson doesn't rest content with this Wittgensteinian
analogy but goes on to propose what he takes to be a more convincing line of defence. This has to do with Spinoza's concept of
'intuitive knowledge', that which (as defined in the *Ethics*) 'proceeds
from an adequate idea of the formal essence of certain of the
attributes of God to an adequate knowledge of the essence of
things.'[24] Of all Spinoza's categories this is the one that has caused
most trouble for the commentators, even those (like Jonathan
Bennett) who are otherwise predominantly well-disposed and anxi-
ous to make the best logical sense of his arguments. Intuitive
knowledge is classified by Spinoza as the third (and highest) form
of cognition, one that combines the positive elements of the two
lower orders ('knowledge of imagination' and 'knowledge of
intellect'), but combines them in such a way as to cancel or transcend
their inbuilt restrictions. So the three kinds of knowledge exhibit a
progressive – even, one could say, a dialectical – relationship.
Imagination is a 'lower' faculty than reason in so far as it depends
upon bodily mechanisms (sense-data, images, memories, random

associations, 'confused ideas', etc.) whose nature is inherently passive, or incapable of rising to an adequate knowledge of their own causal provenance. Reason is that which enables the mind to break with this commonsense or pre-reflective attitude by framing adequate ideas which then give access to a knowledge beyond mere sensuous perception. But reason still lacks the capacity to link up this knowledge with the concrete particulars of everyday, self-evident experience, a mode of cognition that cannot be dismissed as purely a product of fantasy or false consciousness. And it is here – in the gap (so to speak) between commonsense and pure reason – that Spinoza inserts the superior truth-claim of 'intuitive knowledge', or that which transcends this bad antinomy by reconciling concepts with sensuous intuitions.

As Bennett remarks, this claim looks very like the Kantian argument that 'intuitions without concepts are blind', whereas 'concepts without intuitions are empty'.[25] In which case Spinoza would at this point be quitting the realm of metaphysics, in Kant's pejorative sense of that term. He would be entering on the path of a true 'critical philosophy' concerned to delimit the bounds of theoretical knowledge (where concepts match up with phenomenal intuitions), and thus to ensure that ethics – or the realm of 'supersensible ideas' – fulfil its proper role in the Kantian scheme of things and not be made subject to the order of causal or natural necessity. But there are problems with this reading, despite its attractiveness from a modern (post-Kantian or epistemological) viewpoint. For on Spinoza's account of it 'intuitive knowledge' extends far beyond the domain of theoretical understanding to encompass not only 'eternal ideas' but also the 'intellectual love of God' wherein those ideas discover their ultimate ground or justification. It fails to remark that crucial Kantian distinction between *concepts of understanding* and *ideas of pure reason*, and thus remains subject – as Bennett ruefully concedes – to all the old, 'metaphysical' puzzles and perplexities.

Indeed, the last chapter of Bennett's book reads like a series of exasperated school-report entries: 'showed great promise, worked hard all along, but let himself down rather badly in the final examinations'. At times there is a sense of real hurt or betrayal, as if Bennett himself is the one who has worked hard to make logical sense of Spinoza's ideas, only to find himself at last confronted with these utterly nonsensical doctrines. Thus:

> those of us who love and admire Spinoza's philosophical work should in sad silence avert our eyes from the second half of Part 5 [i.e., that portion of the *Ethics* that treats of the mind's eternity, intuitive knowledge, and the 'intellectual love of God']. I wanted to do so in this book; but I would have had to say why, and could hardly offer my judgment . . . without defending it. I have hated writing this chapter, and have scruples and fears about publishing it. But it defends a negative judgment which is important if true and will be liberating if it is believed. (Bennett, p. 375).

This passage is all the more remarkable for coming at the close – as the very last sentence – of a book whose style and intellectual temper are otherwise very much attuned to the ethos of current analytical philosophy. Like the *Ethics* itself, Bennett's reading of Spinoza is firmly committed to the intellectual virtues of clarity, logic and straightforward orderly exposition. But this commitment is strained to the limit and beyond, as Bennett suggests, by those three utterly unredeemable doctrines that Spinoza presents as the terminus or high-point of all his philosophical labours. Worse still, those doctrines (or variants of them) had previously stood up rather well under the rigours of a logical-reconstructive approach, since Spinoza had there confined his argument to the first two orders of cognition, and had not – or not yet explicitly – invoked the bad magic of 'intuitive knowledge'. Thus, as we have seen already, Bennett was able to reformulate Spinoza's talk of 'eternal ideas' in the language of present-day modal logic, that is to say, as applying to truth-claims that necessarily held good in this and all possible worlds. But this approach doesn't work with Part 5 of the *Ethics*, where the argument takes a decidedly mystical turn. For here it is all too evident (in Bennett's submission) that Spinoza is indeed equating *eternity* with *immortality*, or the highest, most active properties of mind with the wisdom that comes of a union with God (or Nature) through 'knowledge of intuition', thereby transcending all mere contingencies of time and place. It is at this point that Bennett throws up his hands in sad disbelief and declares the relevant passages beyond all hope of rational reconstruction.

He is equally disenchanted with the commentators, or those among them (like Stuart Hampshire and Frederick Pollock) who over-extend the principle of charity by stretching it to encompass these deplorable passages. Against Hampshire: 'I contend that instead of implying that Spinoza has brought us "beyond the limits of literal understanding" and that this is acceptable because it is inherent in his chosen topic, we should say openly that Spinoza is talking nonsense and that there is no reason for us to put up with it' (Bennett, p. 373). As for Pollock, who describes the doctrine of the mind's eternity as among 'the most brilliant endeavours of speculative philosophy', one that 'throws a sort of poetical glow over the formality of his [Spinoza's] exposition', Bennett is yet more scathing in his response. Thus he writes: 'when a commentator as shrewd as Pollock is reduced to such babbling by his desire to praise the final stretch of the *Ethics*, that is further evidence that this material is worthless. Worse, it is dangerous: it is rubbish which causes others to write rubbish' (p. 374). This is, by any standard, a remarkable outburst of sheer bad temper and all the more startling for the fact that elsewhere he professes high regard for Hampshire and Pollock as sources of clear-headed commentary on the text.

To some extent the tone of these remarks can be explained by Bennett's commitment to the analytic mode, his rejection of mystical truth-claims in whatever form, or his extreme frustration at this point, having come so far in the logical exposition of Spinoza's thought only to encounter such a mass of intractable material. But the difficulty clearly goes deeper and extends well beyond the offending Part 5, as one can see by reading his book over again with an eye to those numerous passages where Bennett states it as his aim to improve, clarify, reformulate, express more cogently or make better sense of Spinoza's cloudier pronouncements. Thus, to take a few examples more or less at random: 'fortunately, we can find something better to say on his behalf . . . '; 'there are two sorts of demonstrations that can be regarded as valid, but not perfectly realized on the page'; 'his demonstration that there is only one substance . . . is a creaky, leaky affair which cannot be fully salvaged'; 'while we have him making that plea, we had better cram into his mouth an explanation of what looks like an inconsistency in his text' (Bennett, pp. 357–75 passim). In each of these sentences Bennett seems committed to a double and contradictory line of argument. Thus Spinoza manifestly *cannot be right* when he lays claim to a knowledge transcending all the powers of linguistic or logical grasp. In which case the commentator is clearly entitled to set such unfortunate passages aside and concentrate his efforts on making better sense of those doctrines that lend themselves to reconstruction in the logical or analytic mode. But this leaves Bennett in the awkward position – awkward by his own exegetical lights – of claiming to know better than Spinoza (or better than the *Ethics* can put into words) what the text really means, or should be taken to mean on the best, most adequate reading. Thus 'the courtly deference which pretends that Spinoza is always or usually right, under some rescuing interpretation, is one thing; it is quite another to look to him, as I have throughout this book, as a teacher, one who can help us to see things which we might not have seen for ourselves' (p. 372). But again, this raises the obvious problem as to how – given Bennett's resolute mistrust of readings that go beyond the 'literal' sense of the text – he could possibly claim to explicate its arguments on a level of rigour or consistency higher than that achieved by the text itself.

One could multiply such instances from almost every page of Bennett's book. What they suggest is not merely a series of localized interpretive problems but a deep-laid discrepancy between, on the one hand, Bennett's tough-minded analytical approach – his desire to reconstruct or to 'salvage' Spinoza's doctrines – and, on the other, that whole dimension of the *Ethics* that claims access to a truth surpassing the reach of verbal or propositional knowledge. Hence his quarrel with Hampshire's willingness to regard those problematical passages as taking us 'beyond the limits of literal understanding', and doing so for reasons somehow 'inherent in his chosen topic'. For this is *not*, as Bennett would have it, a problem that arises only when philosophy goes off the rails and begins to entertain irrationalist or mystical ideas. In fact it is much akin to those antinomies that Derrida discovers in his reading of Husserl, brought about by the desire for a grounding or foundational discourse of philosophic reason, one that would achieve intuitive self-evidence and thus not be subject to the vagaries of verbal or written transmission. I have already examined this kinship between the two thinkers as it bears upon Spinoza's second order of cognition, i.e. the realm of 'adequate ideas' where intellect surpasses naive sense-certainty or 'knowledge of imagination'. But the relationship is closer (if more problematic) when one moves on to Spinoza's claims for the third and highest order, that of 'intuitive knowledge', where ideas of pure reason are supposedly united with the realm of concrete, sensuous particularity.

Of course it may well be objected at this point that there is really no comparing the two projects since Husserl's is a thoroughly secular critique of truth, knowledge and representation, while Spinoza ultimately rests his claims on the existence of 'eternal ideas' seemingly vouchsafed to the mind through the 'intellectual love of God'. But this objection clearly carries less weight once it is recognized – as most commentators would agree – that Spinoza very often adopts such language by way of avoiding doctrinal dispute, or simply to communicate with readers trained up in theological ways of thought. The parallel with Husserl will then appear less far-fetched. Both thinkers offer arguments for the following theses: (1) that *a priori* knowledge is indeed possible, (2) that it belongs to a realm of absolute ideal objectivity that transcends all merely local or contingent observations, and (3) that philosophy should therefore be concerned with enquiring back into the grounds, sources or constitutive principles that justify such claims. Thus Husserl draws a sharp distinction between his own project – that of 'transcendental phenomenology' – and those other, less demanding variants which fail to attain this degree of self-critical rigour.[26] And it should be noted that Derrida follows Husserl in remarking the necessity of just this distinction, i.e. the loss of rigour that results when questions of a factual, empirical, or existential import are allowed to deflect enquiry from its proper (Husserlian) aim. Thus, in the words of Rudolf Bernet:

> Derrida's almost unqualified defence of Husserl's understanding of history repeatedly forces him into a polemical confrontation with the relevant literature, especially that of the 1940s and 1950s. Husserl's phenomenology of history is emphatically distanced from the kind of hermeneutic philosophy which invokes the name of Dilthey, as well as from the ontology of facticity inspired by Heidegger . . . Transcendental phenomenology investigates the essential conditions of the possibility of the constitutive origin of objective spirit and not its origin as a peculiar fact.[27]

It is precisely at the point where he claims to establish this 'constitutive origin' of thought that Husserl has to recognize the essential role of language – more specifically, of writing – as the sole means by which such truths can attain the condition of 'absolute ideal objectivity'. On the one hand, as we have seen, this creates real problems for the attempt to ground knowledge in a self-present access to primordial intuitions or truths arrived at strictly *more geometrico*. For it is just because writing continues to function in the absence of all present guarantees – in the absence, that is, of utterer's intentions, realized meanings, 'inward' accompaniments of whatever kind – it is just for this reason that writing figures as the ground or precondition of knowledge in general. So Derrida is undoubtedly pointing to a difficulty at the heart of Husserl's entire project. But he also insists very firmly that there is no adequate response to such problems except through the kind of rigorous 'transcendental' critique that Husserl, more than anyone, sought to provide.

This aspect of Derrida's essay needs stressing since so many readers (or non-readers) take deconstruction for just another variant of the 'end-of-philosophy' thesis, the idea that all concepts come down to metaphors – or all truth-claims to a species of rhetorical imposition – in which case there is simply no point in pursuing those old 'metaphysical' themes. But this reading is radically mistaken, as one can see not only from his various essays on Husserl but also from those later texts where Derrida engages with Kant and the tradition of Enlightenment critical reason.[28] What deconstruction seeks to reveal is *not* the obsolescence of that whole tradition but, on the contrary, the need to think its truth-claims through *to the limit* and thereby determine their relation to problems that remain, of necessity, unthought (or unthinkable) on its own terms of analysis. With Kant – as Rodolphe Gasché has shown in a fine recent book – these problems arise in connection with certain basic but unquestioned (and in this sense pre-critical) elements of the system, like Kant's requirement that concepts of understanding *must* match up with sensuous intuitions in order to claim any kind of theoretical adequacy.[29] One result of a deconstructive reading is to highlight those passages in the Kantian text where the argument comes up against a certain inbuilt resistance to its own more dogmatic or stipulative claims. For Gasché, this resistance can best be located by uncovering the signs of a different, ulterior logic at work, a logic whose textual operations are suggested by the various Derridean key-terms: 'arche-writing', 'trace', '*différance*', 'supplement', etc. Their effect is to bring about a subtle displacement of Kantian concepts and categories, a shift of attention from the overt to the covert structure of argument, such as to challenge certain presuppositions that would otherwise (and not without reason) be hidden from view.

These terms are neither 'concepts', strictly speaking, nor 'themes' peculiar to this or that Derridean text. Rather, they are names for a process that functions at a level anterior to all philosophical reflection, all attempts to ground the discourse of philosophy in truths self-evident to reason. So these effects are not confined to Derrida's writing, where the terms in question play a prominent role. They can also be detected in the work of other thinkers – for Gasché, most importantly, Kant and Hegel – where problems arise as to the status of conceptual truth-claims *vis-à-vis* writing or philosophy's reliance on a textual mode of transmission. But this is not to say – far from it – that the Kantian project is thereby discredited or shown up as a kind of intellectual dead-end. On the contrary, as Gasché insists: the only way to think the limits of this or any other philosophical system is to follow out its furthest, most rigorous implications and apply them reflexively to statements in the system that appear problematic on its own conceptual terms. Thus the question of writing takes on this capacity to subvert or unsettle the truth-claims of Kantian reason only after those claims have been subjected to a process of analysis, appraisal and critique *in the Kantian mode*. And the same applies to Derrida's reading of Husserl, a reading carried out with scrupulous respect for the aims and imperatives of transcendental phenomenology. Certainly Derrida questions that project by showing it to rest on a series of axioms or grounding suppositions which are neither self-evident nor indeed sustainable if one applies the full rigours of a deconstructive critique. But such a reading will simply not be possible unless it follows in the path laid down by Husserl's phenomenological enquiries, a path which – as Derrida repeatedly insists – cannot be abandoned by deconstruction or by any philosophy that sets out to criticize the heritage of 'Western metaphysics'.

So there is clearly no question of philosophy's being somehow discredited or put out of business by the demonstrable fact of its reliance on writing as the sole means of establishing its claims to truth. On the one hand this argument does raise fundamental doubts as to whether the Husserlian project could ever achieve its wished-for condition of a pure, indubitable, self-present access to the realm of primordial intuitions. But it is equally the case, as Derrida shows, that Husserl's own texts conduct a powerful (if covert) critique of such ideas, to the point where writing comes implicitly to figure as the structural *a priori* or condition of possibility for thought in general. As Bernet puts it:

> Language and, in particular, writing are always simultaneously and undecidably the 'movement of the essential and constitutive possibility of embodiment' as well as 'the place of factual and contingent sensible embodiment'. If we ascribe a moment of essential and thus irreducible facticity and materiality to writing in this way, then the danger of the 'annihilation of the world' or even merely a burning

of books affects writing not simply as sensible body but as spiritual corporeality as well. The spiritual essence of a universally valid sense which is deposited in writing is always endangered by factual events and defencelessly exposed to acts of individual caprice or the brutal violence of natural catastrophe.[30]

Bernet's main point (following Derrida) is that this realization only comes about through an interrogative reading of Husserl's essay which fully respects the Husserlian injunction to suspend all taken-for-granted beliefs and subject them to the undeceiving rigours of a transcendental critique. It is precisely in so far as it upholds this requirement that deconstruction can arrive at the point where writing and its various co-implicated terms – 'supplement', 'trace', *différance* etc. – turn out to be constitutive for Husserl's entire project. And by the same token that project must be seen to harbour the suspicion – despite and against its own express claims – that the 'absolute ideal objectivity' of truth may after all be subject to accidents of an historical, empirical or 'merely' factual nature. Thus the upshot of Derrida's reading is to question *both* the assurance (characteristic of philosophy) that truth exists in a realm apart from such crassly contingent factors, *and* the idea (common to all forms of pragmatist or historicist thinking) that these factors account for everything that philosophy has hitherto – mistakenly – regarded as proper or essential to its own calling. For such questions only arise as the result of a thinking-back into the genesis and structure of philosophic truth-claims which cannot be dismissed *tout court* without abandoning the very ground of historical reflection.

III

We are now perhaps in a better position to grasp why Spinoza's writings have been subject to such radically divergent interpretations. On the one hand they carry to its furthest extreme that view of philosophy as a transcendental project – a quest for knowledge *sub specie aeternitatis* – which remains (indispensably, as Derrida would argue) a constitutive part of its enterprise. On the other, in his more overtly 'political' works, they seem to support just the opposite reading, one that would emphasize the determinant role of historical and material factors in producing every kind of knowledge, not least the 'truths' of philosophy and religion. Thus, as Leszek Kolakowski remarks, the 'German reception', or, more generally, the pantheistic reception, takes from the philosopher the motif of the whole and the part, hope for ultimate reconciliation with the absolute through the mystical renunciation of individual affirmation. The 'French reception' fortifies the threads of republican free thought, generalizes the slogans of liberty, repeats with satisfaction the sallies against the clergy and the church. The optics of a political radical and the optics of a metaphysician trying to tame infinite being: two points of view so different that it would indeed be highhanded to reproach his inconsistency on this point . . . as if anyone in history had actually succeeded in bringing that double observational standpoint – directed toward being and toward the object – into union with one another.[31]

But in fact, as we have seen, the situation is more complicated than this might suggest, since there are differences of view within each camp that run just as deep as the differences between them. Thus Althusser and Deleuze both offer a 'political' reading of Spinoza, though their versions have just about nothing in common beyond this vague similarity. In fact one could argue that Althusser's project – his attempt to reconstitute Marxist 'theoretical practice' through a rigorous application of Spinozist concepts and categories – relates more closely to a certain branch of the current analytical reception, an approach (like Bennett's) concerned with matters of intra-philosophical consistency and truth. For it is, to say the least, a curious feature of Althusser's reading that it rests very largely on precepts derived from the *Ethics* – or from Spinoza's theory of knowledge at its most abstract – and pays little regard to those other texts that engage directly with political and historical issues. In Deleuze, conversely, the attack on all forms of theoretical reason goes along with a 'materialist' celebration of the body, the senses and the polymorphous energies of pre-Oedipal desire which often leans over into a mystical rhetoric with distinctly pantheist overtones. So Kolakowski's account of the two reception-histories – which he offers, to be fair, only as a 'simplified schema' – does begin to lose credibility when applied to the modern commentators.

All the same it is difficult (maybe impossible) to avoid this dualistic habit of thought, one that treats philosophers *either* as engaged in a quest for ultimate truths, *a priori* concepts, self-validating grounds etc., *or* as historically-situated thinkers whose work reveals the pressure of contingent circumstances and events. Such is the pattern that Derrida detects in his essay on Husserl: an alternating movement of thought wherein reason claims the right to exclude or suspend all short-term, historical or culture-specific interests, while in fact bearing witness to the opposite case – the sheer *impossibility* of attaining this ideal – through the knowledge that its truths can only be preserved in the material, destructible, accident-prone form of writing. This conflict between *de jure* and *de facto* orders of truth-claim is one that figures constantly in Derrida's work. Most often it involves (as with Plato and Rousseau) the discovery of a double or 'supplementary' logic at work within the text, such that its overt, principled statements of meaning or intent are thrown into doubt – or rendered undecidable – by the presence of conflicting motifs. But it is above all in the writings of Husserl (and especially his essay on the origin of geometry) that this aporetic structure reveals itself as always and everywhere bound up with the project of philosophic thought. For, according to Husserl, it should rightfully be the case (*de jure*) that geometrical self-evidence has nothing to do with the contingent facts of discovery, transmission or archival storage. Such truths (like those of transcendental phenomenology) should exist in a realm of 'absolute ideal objectivity' where writing is at most an adjunct or an instrument in the service of clear and distinct ideas.[32] But this argument encounters resistance – comes up against *de facto* problems in the nature of its own undertaking – when it emerges that no such distinction can be drawn. For geometry, like every other discipline of thought, has a history (a written history) whose survival is prerequisite to thinking in general. And it is on these grounds precisely that Derrida names writing as the one essential object of thought that Husserl can neither exclude altogether from his field of enquiry nor account for explicitly within that field, since its effects would disrupt his project at source.

It might appear from all this that the 'history' in question is a highly generalized affair that has no point of contact with *real* historical conjunctures or turns of event. Thus it seems to be defined, in Derrida's usage, by the threefold condition of (1) being associated with writing, in an equally generalized sense of that term; (2) being opposed, in some ultimate way, to the transcendental truth-claims of philosophic reason; and (3) having the power to subvert such claims by reminding philosophy of the problems that arise whenever it attempts to repress or to sublimate the knowledge of its own historically-contingent character. But in fact there is a much more specific kind of history involved with these interpretive issues. It can best be understood by asking the question: what exactly is left out of account when one treats the writings of Husserl (or Spinoza) as those writings expressly demand to be treated, i.e. as giving access to truths of reason (or 'eternal ideas') independent of time and change? In Husserl's case the relevant history would include certain facts about his essay *The Origin of Geometry* – facts having to do with its date and circumstances of publication – which nowhere figure explicitly in the text but which cannot, all the same, be regarded as mere 'background' data since their very absence must itself give rise to questions of a jointly philosophic and historical import. At this point we can turn to Paul de Man's essay 'Crisis and Criticism' for another reading of Husserl that confronts precisely these questions.[33]

De Man, like Derrida, sets out at one level to 'deconstruct' the claims of transcendental phenomenology, or to show that there exists *de facto* evidence (in Husserl's own text) of those claims failing to meet the self-imposed standards of ideal purity and rigour required *de jure* of any such project. Husserl's *Origin of Geometry* itself had its origin as part of a much larger enterprise, one whose first programmatic statement was a 1935 lecture ('Philosophy and the Crisis of European Humanity'), and which later appeared as a book under the title *The Crisis of the European Sciences and Transcendental Phenomenology*.[34] The 'crisis' in question was identified by Husserl with the emergence of various irrationalist or relativist doctrines, ideas that went back to the anti-Enlightenment thinking of philosophers like Nietzsche, and which now threatened to undermine reason itself by reducing all truth-claims to mere contingent products of this or that socio-cultural context. It is against this levelling consensus-view of reason, knowledge and truth that Husserl asserts the case for his own approach to the ultimate questions of philosophy. Thus thinking must henceforth suspend all appeals to commonsense, the 'natural' attitude, the immediate self-evidence of the senses, or other such seemingly secure grounds of knowledge which the sceptic can always call into doubt. The most urgent task in reason's defence is to question everything that can possibly be questioned and thus give no hostages to the relativist argument. Only then – at the end of this critical procedure – can philosophy claim to have arrived at a point where any further doubts would simply *not make sense*, since by now it is a question of concepts, categories, primordial intuitions, structures of perceptual experience and so forth which are presupposed by our very existence as thinking, perceiving subjects. And this would be enough, Husserl argues, to turn back the tide of irrationalist ideas which otherwise looks set to dissolve philosophical enquiry into those various pseudo-disciplines (like the 'sociology of knowledge') that display no regard for reason or truth.

De Man begins by noting that Husserl's language is everywhere marked by a 'rhetoric of crisis', an insistence that philosophy is currently confronted with problems of a quite unprecedented nature. There is, he remarks, 'a very modern note in Husserl's description of philosophy as a process by means of which naive assumptions are made accessible to consciousness by an act of critical self-understanding' (*BI*, p. 15). In fact this description could equally apply to de Man's project in *Blindness And Insight*, a sequence of essays on various critics and philosophers whose work exhibits both a strong demystifying impulse and a marked tendency to ignore or occlude the moments of self-induced mystification in their own work. 'We must ask ourselves', he writes, 'if there is not a recurrent epistemological pattern that characterizes all statements made in the mood and the rhetoric of crisis' (p. 14). This pattern is a kind of oscillating rhythm, one that gives rise to de Man's central thesis: that the moments of significant 'blindness' in a text are also, for us as critical readers, moments of the greatest potential 'insight'. And this applies all the more in the case of a thinker like Husserl, one who identified the character and destiny of European thought with its power to elucidate the blindspots of prejudice that had so far resisted such treatment. For there is – de Man argues – a notable instance of prejudice *in Husserl's own text* which entirely (and necessarily) eludes his grasp as a thinker in that same Enlightenment tradition. And this blindness emerges in precisely those passages where Husserl puts forward his loftiest claims for the saving power of a 'universal' reason equated – as if by natural right – with *European* culture and thought. Speaking himself as a member of that privileged community, 'it seems that Husserl escapes from the necessary self-criticism that is prior to all philosophical truth about the self' (p. 16). That is to say, his whole project grows out of the conviction that there exists a present 'crisis of the European sciences', that this crisis has drastic implications (intellectual, moral and political), and that only by subjecting their own truth-claims to an equally drastic critique can those sciences regain their rightful position as arbiters of universal truth. Hence the striking fact that, in Husserl's writings of this period, 'two words remain constant: the word "crisis" and the word "European"; [and] it is in the interaction of these two concepts that the epistemological structure of the crisis-statement is fully revealed' (p. 14).

De Man makes this point *not* by way of impugning Husserl's good faith or intelligence, but to draw attention to the alternating pattern – the dialectic of 'blindness' and 'insight' – that tends to develop when the calling of philosophy comes up against the pressures of historical circumstance. 'Since we are speaking', he insists, 'of a man of superior good will, it suffices to point to the pathos of such a claim at a moment when Europe was about to destroy itself as centre in the name of its unwarranted claim to be the centre' (p. 16). In short, all the vigilance that Husserl musters on the side of enlightenment, reason and critique cannot save him from harbouring this ethnocentric prejudice at the very heart of his philosophy. For it is not just an accidental blindspot, or momentary lapse into a naive, pre-critical attitude, one that Husserl might have remedied had he but noticed the fact before committing his thoughts to print. Rather, as de Man argues, this prejudice turns out to be a *structural prerequisite* for the entire project of transcendental phenomenology, a project that can only exercise its claim to superior cognitive grasp by discovering some other (naive or mystified) state of awareness upon which to focus its critical vision. Thus:

> Husserl speaks repeatedly of non-European cultures as primitive, prescientific and pre-philosophical, myth-dominated and congenitally incapable of the disinterested distance without which there can be no philosophical meditation. This, although by his own definition philosophy, as unrestricted reflection upon the self, necessarily tends toward a universality that finds its concrete, geographical correlative in the formation of supratribal, supranational communities such as, for instance, Europe. Why this geographical expansion should have chosen to stop, once and forever, at the Atlantic Ocean and at the Caucasus, Husserl does not say. (p. 15)

It may be seen from this how wide of the mark are those attacks on deconstruction that treat it as a species of mandarin 'textualist' activity culpably indifferent to larger (historical or political) concerns. What de Man is presenting here – like Derrida in his essay on *The Origin of Geometry* – is an argument that goes by way of meticulous close-reading, but which also (and inseparably) raises questions about the background history and implied politics of Husserl's enterprise.

So it is wrong to suppose that such concerns are excluded by an interest in the rhetorical workings of language, even where that interest consistently leads to the point of doubting whether texts can ever mean exactly what they say, or be taken as referring unproblematically to a world of extra-textual events or realities. For it is de Man's main contention – in this passage on Husserl and elsewhere – that 'the rhetoric of crisis states its own truth in the mode of error' (p. 16). That is to say, there comes a point in the deconstructive reading when textual analysis can presently do no more, having shown up the various conflicts that develop between 'constative' and 'performative' levels of meaning, or – in de Man's later terminology – between the logical, grammatical and rhetorical orders of signification. At this stage the focus of attention shifts to those interests of a socio-political nature that determine what the text is able to say (and, equally, what it has to conceal) about its own ideological commitments. In Husserl's case, specifically, 'the privileged viewpoint of the post-Hellenic, European consciousness is never for a moment put into question; the crucial, determining examination on which depends Husserl's right to call himself, by his own terms, a philosopher, is in fact never undertaken' (p. 16). And the omission is all the more striking when one considers that Husserl was announcing this radical new departure for philosophy against the background of – and in response to – those very events that were threatening to negate the heritage of enlightened thought.

At one level these events had to do with the brute self-evidence of a German nationalist revival which had already (in 1935) gone far along the path toward revoking every last precept and value represented by that same tradition. But they also bore witness – so Husserl argued – to a 'crisis' whose origins went much further back, and whose ominous character could only be grasped through a diagnostic reading of the symptoms apparent in late nineteenth-century German thought and culture. There is a parallel here with what Lukács was to argue, some two decades later, in his book *The Destruction of Reason*: namely, that the intellectual roots of National Socialism are to be found in that deep-laid irrationalist trend whose early avatars (Nietzsche chief among them) had turned against the Kantian Enlightenment paradigm in search of more 'authentic', spontaneous or primordial values.[35] For Lukács, of course, such episodes only made sense in light of a Marxist historical overview, one that interpreted the fateful swerve as evidence of a path not taken at this crucial juncture in the history of thought. Thus Nietzsche reacted to the inbuilt problems and antinomies of Kantian critical reason by renouncing that entire tradition, attacking reason itself in the name of the 'will-to-power', 'eternal recurrence', the 'transvaluation of values' and other such dangerous ideas. But it was Marx who first recognized the twofold necessity of thinking both *within* and *against* the Enlightenment public sphere, preserving what remained of its critical thrust (the power to challenge received ideologies) while working to expose the interests concealed behind its own universalist rhetoric, its elevation of bourgeois-liberal reason into the last word on issues of knowledge and truth. Thus Lukács, like Husserl, sees a direct link between the rise of a militant irrationalist strain in nineteenth-century German philosophy and the collapse of social-democratic institutions that marked the end of the Weimar Republic. And he likewise argues that the only hope for reason in face of this historical catastrophe is to think its way back to the decisive turning-point – for Lukács, the 'choice' between Marx and Nietzsche – where philosophy first confronted these questions in the nature of its own undertaking.

Of course this comparison cannot be pushed too hard. Husserl is very far from agreeing with Lukács that Marxism – or any form of socio-political analysis – can set philosophy back on the high road of history and reason forsaken by thinkers in the bad (post-Nietzschean) line of descent. In fact, he treats such arguments as nothing more than symptoms of the same deep malaise – the slide into relativist habits of thought – for which his own project (that of transcendental phenomenology) is the one truly effective antidote or cure. All the same the parallel is worth pursuing for the light it throws not only on Husserl's philosophy but also on de Man's reading of Husserl as a figure set about by all the conflicts and antinomies of reason at a time of extreme historical duress. In de Man's words:

> Speaking in what was in fact a state of urgent personal and political crisis about a more general form of crisis, Husserl's text reveals with striking clarity the structure of all crisis-determined statements. It establishes an important truth: the fact that philosophical knowledge can only come into being when it is turned back upon itself. But it immediately proceeds, in the very same text, to do the opposite. The rhetoric of crisis states its own truth in the mode of error (*BI*, p. 16).

There are several points to be made about this passage in connection with the Lukács/Husserl comparison. One is that Husserl can indeed be criticized (or his text 'deconstructed', i.e. read against the grain of its express philosophical convictions) at the points where he displays this peculiar 'blindness' to questions of an urgent political import. To this extent de Man might be said to take Lukács's side in making *history* the last court of appeal, and diagnosing the sources of this latter-day 'crisis' in the failure of reason to reflect adequately on its material conditions, its historical provenance and social responsibilities. But it is also very clear to any reader of de Man that the 'history' in question cannot, for him, be conceived in terms of a totalizing model, a dialectics of 'base' and 'superstructure', or the access to some ultimate truth behind transient (ideological) appearances. In fact his work contains numerous statements to the effect that such ideas are delusory, that they involve a premature recourse to historical absolutes, as if the truth-claims of history somehow existed in a realm apart from the various forms of rhetorical, textual or narrative representation.[36] And this goes along with his high regard for Nietzsche – utterly contrary to Lukács assessment – as a powerful demystifying thinker, one who subjected all such claims to a process of rigorous sceptical critique, and who did so (like Derrida and de Man after him) by means of an intensive rhetorical close-reading. For it is precisely in so far as he avoids this negative labour – in so far, that is to say, as he takes his own concepts as possessing an ultimate validity or truth – that Husserl falls prey to residual forms of ethnocentric prejudice or blindness.

So in the end one cannot separate the 'question of the text', as raised by conceptual rhetoricians like Nietzsche and de Man, from questions of a wider political and socio-historical bearing. But this doesn't mean – far from it – that one should henceforth regard those 'Enlightenment' values of truth, reason and critique as so many fictions or rhetorical ploys that merely serve to disguise such ideological interests. For if indeed it is the case, as de Man argues, that 'the rhetoric of crisis states its own truth in the mode of error', then there is simply no substitute for the kind of meticulous, closely-reasoned and socially responsive critique that Husserl himself (as 'a man of superior good will') set out to provide in his complex meditations on the destiny of European thought. Anyone who determines to criticize the blindspots in Husserl's undertaking will do so from a standpoint that necessarily shares those same essential values and assumptions. And this will apply even to those readers (like de Man) who evince a deep mistrust of all 'demythologizing' projects, all attempts to occupy a privileged position of ideal, self-validating knowledge *outside and above* the errors they denounce. Certainly de Man sees this as one major source of that blindness to its own presuppositions that marks the discourse of 'enlightened' thought. Thus:

> the need to safeguard reason from what might become a dangerous *vertige*, a dizziness of the mind caught in an infinite regression, prompts a return to a more rational methodology. The fallacy of a finite and single interpretation derives from the postulate of a privileged observer; this leads, in turn, to the endless oscillation of an intersubjective demystification. (*BI*, p. 10)

De Man's specific instance here is the structural anthropology of Claude Lévi-Strauss, caught up (as he reads it) in a similar 'oscillating' rhythm between insight and blindness, the detection of ethnocentric prejudice in others and the failure to perceive such elements in one's own thinking.[37] But de Man is just as firm in making the point (here as with Husserl) that 'a fundamental discrepancy always prevents the observer from coinciding fully with the consciousness he is observing' (p. 10). Thus it is not so much a weakness or a corrigible fault in Lévi-Strauss's methodology as a kind of reiterated structural *a priori* that affects all versions of the quest for a knowledge beyond what is given at the level of 'naive' self-evidence or commonsense awareness.

De Man makes this point to maximum effect by juxtaposing the passages on Lévi-Strauss and Husserl. He thus casts doubt on what might otherwise appear – at least in Husserlian terms – the absolute, categorical *difference* between, on the one hand, a project of applied anthropology and, on the other, a set of 'transcendental' truth-claims purporting to establish the grounds and conditions of human knowledge in general. This certainly indicates a large degree of scepticism concerning such immoderate (and, as de Man would have it, such inherently 'blind' or self-deluding) claims. Thus 'there are no longer any standpoints that can *a priori* be considered privileged, no structure that functions validly as a model for other structures, no postulate of ontological hierarchy that can serve as an organizing principle' (p. 10). But it is equally the case that thinking cannot proceed – least of all the kind of critical, interrogative thinking that Husserl and Lévi-Strauss both exemplify to a high degree – without presupposing some such privileged standpoint for its own operations. In short, the dialectic of enlightenment consists in precisely this constant 'oscillation' between a principle of reason that lays claim to a knowledge beyond mere appearances, commonsense wisdom, etc., and a sceptical impulse which extends that suspicion to all discourses, its own included. Husserl keeps faith with this critical imperative in so far as he defines philosophy as 'a prolegomenon to a new kind of praxis, a "universal critique of all life and all the goals of life, of all man-created cultural systems and achievements" and, consequently, "a criticism of man himself . . . and of the values by which he is consciously or pre-consciously being governed"' (p. 15). He fails to live up to it only at those points where critique hardens into dogma, where 'the superior theoretical man observes the inferior natural man' (ibid).

It is in these moments that Husserl reproduces the archetypal scene of encounter which, according to de Man, continues to haunt the discourse of structural anthropology, even in the writings of a thinker like Lévi-Strauss, one who sets out to purge his work of all such ethnocentric residues. And yet there is no dispensing with enlightened critique – with the effort to demystify received concepts and categories – since it is only by way of such a vigilant procedure that thought can detect the hidden workings of prejudice. It is impossible for theory ever to achieve that full measure of lucid, enlightened or self-critical grasp that would place it once and for all beyond reach of further demystification. But it is equally out of the question for philosophy (or the human sciences in general) to renounce all such principles and values on account of their inherent partiality, or the blindness that goes along with their claim to a privileged order of insight. Thus Husserl, in de Man's words, 'conceived of philosophy primarily as a self-interpretation by means of which we eliminate what he calls *Selbstverhülltheit*, the tendency of the self to hide from the light it can cast on itself' (*BI*, p. 15). Yet this project turns out to be 'radically blind to the light it emits', caught up in a structure of self-imposed mystification which eludes even Husserl's most vigilant efforts to overcome all such sources of prejudice. So we are left, at the end of de Man's essay, with a double (and seemingly paradoxical) injunction: that thought must continue to respect the highest standards of enlightened reason and critique while maintaining this awareness of its own inevitably partial, flawed or error-prone character.

IV

I have argued that these questions are absolutely central to Spinoza's philosophy and the various debates that have grown up around his work. To summarize very briefly, there are three main areas where that work impinges on the interests of present-day critical theory. One has to do with the relationship between language, reason and truth, or more specifically the question whether language gives access to anything other than confused, inadequate or 'imaginary' ideas. The second – following directly from this – concerns the powers and limits of historical criticism, or the question of just how far (and on what precise terms) theory can articulate a mode of knowledge that surpasses the lived experience of situated human agents. Hence, as I have suggested, the very different readings of Spinoza advanced by commentators (like Althusser, Macherey and Deleuze) who come out strongly either 'for' or 'against' the claims of theoretical *Ideologiekritik*. And the third area – again closely related to the previous two – is that of deconstruction, as exemplifed here by de Man's and Derrida's readings of Husserl.

What is perhaps most striking in this regard is Spinoza's insistence (in his treatise *On the Improvement of the Understanding*) that erroneous judgements, as well as true ideas, must ultimately yield to a causal explanation that assigns them a place within the overall determinist scheme of things. In fact, it is by way of this theory of error – a theory which resembles some of de Man's statements in *Blindness and Insight* – that Spinoza comes closest to forging a link between the two (otherwise disparate) aspects of his work, i.e. the high metaphysical concerns of the *Ethics* and the interests that led to his engagement with issues of a social, religious and political nature. The connection appears most clearly when Spinoza identifies 'inadequate ideas' with the determirate *privations* of knowledge or reason brought about by material circumstance. That is to say, if every error has its proximate cause – a factor that prevents reason from perceiving the truth as revealed *sub specie aeternitatis* – then indeed it is the case, in de Man's terminology, that fallacious or inadequate judgements 'state their own truth in the mode of error'. Such is Spinoza's attitude when dealing with the truth-claims of revealed religion, with prophecies, miracles, divine interventions and the like. These delusive beliefs can be accounted for largely in terms of their social efficacy, i.e. their power to impose obedience, self-discipline and respect for law on an otherwise fractious and well-nigh ungovernable populace. And the same must apply (so Spinoza argues) to every form of religious superstition, including the orthodox idea of God as an executive deity whose will and whose desires, commands or prohibitions we are required to obey on pain of eternal punishment. Such vulgar errors may still be of use in extracting at least the semblance of virtue from an ignorant and credulous people. But they have no place in any rational religion based on an adequate knowledge of God, a knowledge that conceives 'his' attributes and powers as wholly coextensive with – or immanent in – the order of natural necessity.

As we have seen, this doctrine gave rise to accusations that Spinoza, whether wittingly or not, had undermined every last tenet of genuine religious belief. But what I want to stress here – recalling de Man's commentary on Husserl – is the relation that obtains between a form of *Ideologiekritik* (a discourse, that is, on the social and political causes of commonsense mystification) and a structure of argument that identifies error with the failure to conceive adequate ideas in accordance with the laws of reason. For there is a similar argument everywhere implicit in de Man's writings, a conviction that error is essentially privative, that it only arises from a present incapacity – determined, most often, by pressures of historical circumstance – to reason out the full implications of one's own argumentative standpoint. Hence the extraordinary case of Husserl, 'demonstrating the urgent philosophical necessity of putting the privileged European standpoint into question', but at crucial points remaining 'entirely blind to this necessity, behaving in the most unphilosophical way possible at the very moment when he rightly understood the primacy of philosophical over empirical knowledge' (*BI*, p. 15). What relates such passages to Spinozist doctrine is the assumption on de Man's part that the truth of Husserlian phenomenology can only be read 'in the mode of error', or to the degree that understanding is able to substitute 'adequate' for 'inadequate' ideas. And it can do so – as he argues – only on condition that those errors are themselves treated as *significant* lapses, swerves from the truth that reveal some intelligible motive, purpose or causal factor which has brought them about.

De Man makes this point very firmly when he distinguishes mere 'mistakes' (which can always be put down to careless reading or thinking) from determinate 'errors' (which cannot be so easily dismissed since they always involve a conflict of aims or a deeper disparity of meaning and intent). This distinction is the basis of de Man's argument in his essay 'Heidegger's Exegeses of Hölderlin', where he claims that the philosopher has misread the poet at crucial points, but misread him in such a way as to bring out important truths in respect of both his own and Hölderlin's work. 'At this level of thought', de Man writes, it is difficult to distinguish between a proposition and that which constitutes its opposite. In fact, to state the opposite is still to talk of the same thing though in an opposite sense, and it is already a major achievement to have, in a dialogue of this sort, the two interlocutors manage to speak of the same thing . . . Whatever one may otherwise reproach in Heidegger's commentaries, their great merit remains to have brought out the central 'concern' of Hölderlin's work; and in this, they surpass other studies. Nevertheless, they reverse his thought.[38]

So Heidegger's readings are not just *mistaken* in the sense that he might have cleared away the sources of confusion by attending more closely to the text or learning to discipline his own unruly responses. Rather, they are errors that result directly from Heidegger's basic, overriding philosophical concern, namely his desire to discover in Hölderlin a poet who speaks the very language of Being, and who thus points a way beyond the bankrupt legacy of Western 'metaphysical' thought. For Heidegger, quite simply, 'Hölderlin is the greatest of poets . . . because he states the essence (*Wesen*) of poetry. The essence of poetry consists in stating the parousia, the absolute presence of Being' (*BI*, p. 250).

De Man finds this reading erroneous on two main counts. Firstly, it is impossible that poetry should achieve such immediate or self-present access to truth, since language *by its very nature* – its existence as a realm of mediating signs – prevents this dream from ever being carried into effect. Thus 'as soon as the word is uttered, it destroys the immediate and discovers that instead of stating Being, it can only state mediation' (p. 259). And this objection at the level of generalized argument is borne out (de Man claims) in the reading of Hölderlin's poems, since in fact these turn out to say just the opposite of what Heidegger would have them say. Far from achieving the wished-for moment of *parousia*, or of Being self-presently manifest in language, their burden is to state the realization that this moment can only be endlessly deferred, since language itself becomes the obstacle to any such power of transformative vision. It is only by ignoring certain crucial details of the text – details that would throw his whole project into question – that Heidegger can make out this case for Hölderlin as the poet of unmediated presence. And the upshot of his reading – as de Man argues – is to enlist Hölderlin as prophet and witness to his own philosophical vocation, his attempt to think back beyond the history of Western metaphysics to a language of revealed, self-authenticating truth.

So Heidegger's exegeses of Hölderlin have a value, for de Man, that exists quite apart from any claim to speak the truth of the text as encountered in the 'words on the page'. Certainly he holds Heidegger to account for sometimes straightforwardly *misreading* those words, as for instance by ignoring the subjunctive (optative or conditional) force of certain verbs and treating them as declarative statements, an error that fits in all too readily with Heidegger's preconceived purpose. But to point out such swerves from the poet's 'proper' meaning is not to suggest that they might have been rectified had Heidegger only been more attentive to subtleties of phrasing and style. For his misreadings have about them something of that compulsive, inescapable character that marks the essential difference between 'errors' and 'mistakes'. One is reminded of the passage in *Ulysses* where Stephen Dedalus delivers himself of the oracular claim that the artist 'makes no mistakes', that his 'errors are volitional', and must therefore be seen – if we read them aright – as the very 'portals of discovery'. De Man's reading of Heidegger is of course not pitched at this level of high romantic argument. But it does make the point, more cautiously, that the difference between what Hölderlin says and what Heidegger wishes him to say is a difference that reveals significant truths about the poetry and the criticism alike. Thus 'any exegetical project', as de Man sees it,

> will ultimately have to come to grips with the same problem: how to elaborate a language capable of dealing with the tension between the ineffable and the mediate. The ineffable demands the direct adherence and the blind and violent passion with which Heidegger treats his texts. Mediation, on the other hand, implies a reflection that tends toward a critical language as systematic and rigorous as possible, but not overly eager to make claims that it can substantiate only in the long run. (*BI*, p. 263)

In short, Heidegger's errors cannot be understood unless one takes account of the motivating interest – even, as de Man says, the 'blind and violent passion' – that emerges in his readings of Hölderlin. To regard his exegeses as merely inaccurate (or mistaken) is to trivialize the issue by failing to acknowledge the depth of engagement that Heidegger brings to his encounter with the poetry.

This is not to say that those readings must therefore be exempt from criticism since they operate at a level of profoundly 'philosophical' thinking where the workaday standards of interpretative truth simply don't apply. On the contrary: de Man is quite unyielding in his requirement that Heidegger's claims be assessed *at every point* against the detailed evidence of Hölderlin's text. Furthermore, those claims will need to be demystified – subjected to a close rhetorical scrutiny – if thinking is to become 'as systematic and rigorous as possible', and thus remain true to its critical vocation. But at the end of this process one arrives at a point where there is simply no resolving the tension that exists between a hermeneutic reading aimed toward Being and truth and a 'reflective' or 'mediated' reading that respects the imperatives of clarity and rigour. Thus 'when it [i.e. the discipline of textual analysis] is negated by an equally excessive mysticism or scientism, it gains in increased self-awareness and provokes the development of methodological movements within the discipline itself, which ultimately reinforce it' (*BI*, p. 264). Such is the process of reflective critique – the dialectic of 'blindness' and 'insight' – that de Man will pursue through all the essays collected in his volume of that title. It involves (as we have seen with his reading of Husserl) a continuing commitment to the 'Enlightenment' values of reason, truth and critique, but also a sense of the factors that conspire to prevent those values from being properly or consistently carried into practice. And this is where de Man puts forward what amounts to a Spinozist theory of truth and error. That is to say, he treats the symptoms of localized 'blindness' in thinkers like Husserl and Heidegger as indicative of a project that *necessarily* miscarries, that is somehow predestined to be wide of its intended mark, but which none the less (or for that very reason) requires that we attend to the truths implicit in its own distinctive mode of error. And most often those truths have to do with historical or socio-political pressures that cannot be acknowledged explicitly in the text without calling its methods and motives into question.

I have written elsewhere about the complex interplay of history, politics and interpretive theory that marks both Heidegger's reading of Hölderlin and de Man's reading of Heidegger.[39] Sufficient to say that a certain pattern repeats itself here, a pattern of determinate blindspots or lapses into mystified thinking which can be seen to affect de Man's as well as Heidegger's arguments. And again, the most important lesson to be drawn – especially in view of de Man's much-publicized wartime writings[40] – is that errors like this have a truth-telling character, a tendency to reveal ulterior meanings, motives and interests that inevitably point to circumstantial factors beyond the author's power to control or comprehend. In short, there comes a moment when questions of critical theory or method inescapably lead on to questions in the realm of social or political thought. And it is here that Spinoza figures most directly as a philosopher whose work (and whose own life-history) obliged him to confront both kinds of question as a matter of urgent necessity. It is perhaps worth recalling that Spinoza interrupted his work on the *Ethics* at a time (1665) when factions supporting the House of Orange, in league with Reformed Church clergy, were threatening to revoke all the hard-won freedoms of conscience and belief that Spinoza so valued in the Dutch republic. Perhaps, as one commentator puts it, 'only the most intense feeling could have drawn Spinoza from the speculative heights . . . and embroiled him in the turmoil of contemporary events'.[41] But then again one could argue – on the evidence of Spinoza's texts – that there was never, for him, such a radical disjunction between metaphysics and politics, reason and history, or the need to comprehend experience 'under the aspect of eternity' and the need to account for that same experience in temporal (or historically relevant) terms. On the one hand it is impossible to read a work like the *Ethics* without noticing the numerous passages where Spinoza turns aside from the business of argument *more geometrico* and strikes a more combative, polemical tone. On the other, it is clear that his 'worldly' writings – the two treatises on politics and religion – are themselves informed at every point by Spinoza's philosophical doctrines.

Among the commentators also one finds this uneasy tension – uneasy because they feel it somehow shouldn't exist – between a reading that respects Spinoza's highest truth-claims and a reading attentive to matters of historical circumstance. Thus Paul Wienpahl, in his book *The Radical Spinoza*, puts forward a whole series of arguments that purport to establish the compatibility of these two approaches, but often betray a distinct anxiety as to which should take precedence in any given case. Of the *Tractatus Theologico-Politicus* he remarks:

> while it is true that the traditional terms in which it is written and the notoriety it achieved are further evidence for the notion that the book was composed for the occasion [i.e. as a defence against religious and political intolerance], I think that it is *also* written *sub specie aeternitatis*, that is, that it is a basic and basically a philosophical book.[42]

Wienpahl's intention, as his title suggests, is to offer a reading responsive to present-day social and political concerns. Thus he sets out explicitly to reclaim Spinoza for the purposes of a 'radical' philosophy that would find inspiration in his view of nature ('a tree is an arboreal mode of being'), his democratic politics and his argument against all forms of coercive or state-sanctioned religious doctrine. Nor is Wienpahl alone in this, as can be seen from the various viewpoints adopted by Marxist or left-wing commentators, as well as from Spinoza's importance to the work of a 'deep ecologist' like Arne Naess.[43] But it is clear from the above-quoted sentence that Wienpahl has a problem in reconciling his two claims, firstly that Spinoza was a philosophical genius of the highest calibre, and secondly that his thinking on political questions had an urgency and relevance that still come across in the context of current debate. Thus his comment suggests that we *must* draw a distinction, at some level, between those aspects of Spinoza's work that qualify as 'basic philosophy', and those aspects that belong to the order of temporal events, and which thus gave rise to the book's stormy reception-history. But this argument comes up against the obvious objection that it was just as much Spinoza's 'metaphysical' doctrines – advanced in a work of 'pure' philosophy like the *Ethics* – that earned him the titles of 'atheist', 'apostate Jew' and so forth. And conversely, one could argue that there is something rather odd about Wienpahl's claim for the *Tractatus* as a work of 'basic' philosophy – a text composed *sub specie aeternitatis* – since here, if anywhere, Spinoza is directly and explicitly concerned with issues of a socio-political import. What is so difficult to decide, it seems, is the question as to whether Spinoza is first and foremost a thinker of 'eternal ideas', or whether those ideas should always be read in the context of his embattled life-history.

I have put the case that in fact these two dimensions of his thinking are inseparable, and that modern critical theory has much to learn from the way that Spinoza brings them together. The point can best be made by returning to his treatise *On the Improvement of the Understanding*, since it is here that we find Spinoza's most explicit and detailed arguments concerning the relation between truth, error and historical understanding. These passages leave no doubt that he is firmly committed, like Althusser, to a high theoreticist standpoint from which the falsity of inadequate ideas (or 'commonsense' representations) can be brought to light through a sustained effort of conceptual analysis and critique. Thus:

when the mind devotes itself to any thought, so as to examine it and deduce therefrom in due order all the legitimate conclusions possible, any falsehood which may lurk in the thought will be detected; but if the thought be true, the mind will readily proceed without interruption to deduce truths from it . . . Further, since method is reflective knowledge, the foundation which must direct our thoughts can be nothing else than the knowledge of that which constitutes the reality of truth, and the knowledge of the understanding, its properties and powers. (*OIU*, p. 23)

This follows directly from Spinoza's doctrine of the *privative* character of false ideas, their failure to achieve adequate knowledge through some erroneous perception, some lapse or defect of reasoning, brought about by causes that presently exceed one's powers of intellectual grasp. Thus 'false and fictitious ideas have nothing positive about them . . . which causes them to be called false and fictitious; they are only considered as such through the defectiveness of knowledge' (p. 18). And such falsehoods come about only on account of our not fully perceiving all the causes, relationships and interconnections that operate *both* in the realm of natural phenomena *and* within the order of adequate (i.e. clear and distinct) ideas. In fact, Spinoza argues, this distinction is itself radically misconceived, since there is no possible way of getting outside our normative truth-claims, theoretical commitments, standards of valid reasoning etc., in order to check that they somehow 'correspond' with objects, processes or events in the outside world.

This is why Spinoza says in the *Ethics* that 'substance thinking and substance extended are one and the same substance, comprehended now through one attribute, now through the other' (*E* II, P 7 note). His point is to remedy the bad effects of Cartesian dualism by showing that nobody could possibly perform the requisite thought-experiment, or succeed so far in doubting or suspending every item of received knowledge that nothing would remain save the solitary *cogito* of Descartes's curious fable. According to Spinoza, we can see the false reasoning that leads to this quandary as soon as we reflect on the sheer *impossibility* of achieving such an abstract, remote or disembodied standpoint with regard to the truths of experience. Thus 'the idea which forms the essence of the mind involves the existence of the body so long as the body exists' (ibid). The dualist illusion only takes hold to the extent that we lack adequate knowledge, a knowledge that would bring us to the point of comprehending all the causes (physical and mental) that had previously worked to reinforce that illusion. We should then be fully proof against the cardinal error (as Spinoza sees it) of equating true wisdom with the power to transcend mere bodily or worldly experience. But he also insists that such knowledge cannot be gained except through a rigorous sorting of adequate from inadequate ideas, these latter most often treated as a product of bodily illusion, or of the mind's being subject to limits placed upon the order of sensuous (or phenomenal) cognition. So there is a certain lack of symmetry in Spinoza's doctrine, despite what appears (in comparison with Descartes) a thoroughgoing form of metaphysical monism.

I have pursued this point at some length because it helps us to grasp what is at stake not only in Spinoza's theory of truth but also in his more overtly political writings. For the one great purpose of his work is to vindicate the claims of enlightened reason in all matters touching on ethical, social and religious practice. And he thinks it essential to any such endeavour that reason should fulfil its implied universalist promise, and not be conceived as subject to the limiting perspectives of this or that socio-political order. Hence the main precepts of Spinoza's philosophy: that truth is 'its own sign', that it can only be arrived at through an immanent critique of 'false' or 'fictitious' ideas, and – following from this – that there is nothing in the order of nature or reality *so far as we can possibly know it* that doesn't bear witness to the same structure of inbuilt rational necessity. Anyone who denied this last thesis would be placed in the untenable position of claiming to know – or to have good grounds for asserting – truths that went against all existing ideas of what must count as veridical knowledge. All of which leads to Spinoza's conclusion that

> the more things the mind knows, the better does it understand its own strength and the order of nature; by increased self-knowledge it can direct itself more easily, and lay down rules for its own guidance; and, by increased knowledge of nature, it can more easily avoid what is useless. (*OIU*, p. 15)

This is why Spinoza takes it as axiomatic that there must exist some ultimate correspondence between the 'order of things' (or natural phenomena) and the 'order of ideas' as revealed to a mind in full possession of the requisite intellectual powers. In this respect his argument finds a parallel in the work of certain recent analytical philosphers, especially those (like Donald Davidson) who have challenged any form of relativist doctrine as regards questions of language, truth and interpretation.[44] It may be useful to pursue this connection in some detail since it shows just how live are the issues raised by Spinoza's seemingly arcane – not to say archaic – metaphysical idiom.

3 Language, Truth and Historical Understanding

I

We can best start out from Frege's cardinal distinction between 'sense' and 'reference', developed in an essay of 1922 which set the agenda for much subsequent debate.[1] His argument can be summarized very briefly as follows. Sense (*Sinn*) is a matter of those meanings, semantic attributes or predicates which allow some particular expression to play its role in a sentence of the language concerned. Terms possess significance not in and of themselves but only in so far as they make a specific contribution to establishing the truth-conditions of a sentence, i.e. its proper meaning, since meaning is here defined as what makes the sentence demonstrably true in some given context of utterance. And it is their sense thus construed in logico-semantic terms which enables sentences to pick out those real-world objects or states of affairs which establish their referential bearing. Thus the use of a word like 'gold' is predicated on our knowledge of certain attributes – its colour, value, chemical composition and so forth – which decide what shall count as a proper use of the term. Sense determines reference, in Frege's view, since the ability of language to designate objects is dependent on the various semantic criteria that are brought to bear in establishing the referential scope (or extension) of any given term. On the other hand propositions can only be fully or properly meaningful in so far as their sense carries through, so to speak, and refers to some real or factually warranted state of affairs. Sentences about fictive or non-existent entities – like Spinoza's 'ideas of imagination' – would then be construed as possessing sense but not reference, and therefore as belonging to a deviant sub-class with no truth-conditional status.

Allowing for the obvious differences of idiom one can see how Spinoza makes a similar point in his treatise *On the Improvement of Understanding*. Thus 'the less men know of nature, the more easily can they coin fictitious ideas, such as trees speaking, men instantly changed into stones, or into fountains, ghosts appearing in mirrors, something issuing from nothing, even gods changed into beasts and men, and infinite other absurdities of the same kind' (*OIU*, pp. 21–2). And the object of his argument, like Frege's, is not so much to prevent us from imagining such things – since this would be a hopeless endeavour, given our propensity for myths, fictions, metaphors and so forth – but to point out the confusions that arise when we mistake them for genuine or veridical sources of knowledge. 'Many things we affirm and deny, because the nature of words allows us to do so, though the nature of things does not. While we remain unaware of this fact, we may easily mistake falsehood for truth' (p. 33). And the surest way to avoid such errors is to follow Spinoza's cardinal precept and determine whether or not the idea thus formed has its place in the order of rational necessity established *a priori* through the exercise of critical thought. Thus it follows, according to Spinoza, that 'fiction cannot be simple, but is made up of several confused ideas of diverse objects or actions existent in nature, or rather is composed of attention directed to all such ideas at once, and unaccompanied by any mental assent' (p. 24). The process of distinguishing truth from falsehood (or falsehood from 'fictions' knowingly and safely entertained) will thus take the form of a rigorous immanent critique, one that examines the truth-conditions for possessing adequate ideas. For it is, as we have seen, Spinoza's central premise – and Althusser's after him – that truth is necessarily 'its own sign', so that 'that which constitutes the reality of a true thought must be sought in the thought itself and deduced from the nature of the understanding' (p. 22).

This argument can be re-stated in Fregean or logico-linguistic terms without too much in the way of revisionist licence. Thus 'sense determines reference' to the extent that reality (as we know and name it) is always a construction out of ideas, predicates, semantic categories, etc. which constitute the entire class of meaningful propositions in a language. But in order properly to assess the status of those same propositions – in order, that is, to distinguish veridical from false statements, or falsehoods pure and simple from fictive or imaginary ideas – we also need to grasp how the truth-conditions operate for language in its paradigmatic (referential or truth-telling) aspect. And so it comes about, in Spinoza's words, that

> when the mind devotes itself to any thought, so as to examine it and deduce therefrom in due order all the legitimate conclusions possible, any falsehood which may lurk in the thought will be detected; but if the thought be true, the mind will readily proceed without interruption to deduce truths from it. (*OIU*, p. 23)

Of course it might be argued that any such comparison ignores the crucial difference between these thinkers. Thus Spinoza raises ontological questions and subscribes to a form of thoroughgoing metaphysical monism, while Frege is concerned with issues in the province of language, logic and conceptual analysis which – as he would certainly wish to claim – must be treated quite apart from those old (and misconceived) notions of ultimate truth. But in fact this objection soon breaks down if one asks what reasons Frege could provide for his insistence, firstly, that the meaning of a sentence is a matter of the relevant truth-conditions, and secondly, that although 'sense determines reference' in the final analysis, nevertheless we must take veridical sentences (those that refer to some real-world state of affairs) as somehow the operative standard or type-case for all uses of language. For otherwise, as he argues, we will be in no position to distinguish true from false statements, or downright untruths from that special class of utterance (i.e. fictions) which cannot be judged in terms of this bivalent system. 'I can feign', Spinoza writes, 'so long as I do not perceive any impossibility or necessity; if I truly understand either one or the other I should not be able to feign, and I should be reduced to saying I had made the attempt' (p. 19). Frege is advancing much the same case – albeit in a fairly remote technical idiom – when he offers the distinction between true, false and fictitious orders of utterance. In short, Frege's argument does entail certain ontological commitments, despite his desire to cut logic free from all such (to his mind) fruitless and misguided interests.

One thing this theory sought to explain was how sentences asserting the equivalence of two distinct names for the same referent – like 'The morning star is the evening star' – were not merely tautological. That is, one can use such sentences to impart information, to clear away muddles in the everyday usage of names, despite the fact that both terms have a common referent (the planet Venus) which would otherwise, on a non-Fregean account, reduce them to the level of circular definition or purely analytic truth. Another example would be that of two explorers approaching the same mountain from different directions, each having a name for it – the name supplied by their respective languages or cultural communities – and then coming to realize, when their paths eventually cross, that both names designate the same physical object. Or again, there is the instance of scientific statements asserting an identity between chemical formulae and various substances belonging to the discourse of everyday, familiar knowledge. In each case something quite specific is being said: namely, that terms with different senses (i.e. distinct ranges of use and application) turn out to have identical referents, which may indeed constitute a new item of knowledge for those who had previously thought them to signify discrete physical realia. So one use of the sense/reference distinction is to show how such seeming tautologies have a role in communicating truths about the meaning of identity-statements which would otherwise be wholly redundant. Thus language can be seen as providing the conceptual grid, the network of logico-semantic implications that structure our basic understanding of the world. But in Fregean terms this idea goes along with the insistence that truth-conditions are paramount, that the sense of any genuine, valid proposition will always be a function of its possessing the appropriate referential aspect.

In post-structuralism – as in some post-Fregean philosophy of language – this latter requirement is problematized to the point where truth is often seen as wholly relative to the conventions or 'conceptual schemes' that operate within different cultures. And it is not hard to see how this shift came about. If it is accepted that 'sense determines reference' – that our knowledge of the world is to this extent a product of the concepts, categories, semantic fields or grammatical relations that make up some particular language-scheme – then the way is clearly open to a species of cultural and linguistic relativism that goes clean against Frege's logical or truth-conditional approach. There is no room here to elaborate at length on the various forms taken by this current relativist drift. They would include the kind of epistemological scepticism endorsed by philosophers like Quine, i.e. his argument that distinctions between 'analytic' and 'synthetic' orders of truth-claim are always bound up with a given network of beliefs, assumptions and tacit ontological commitments, such that some new piece of evidence – whether on the 'periphery' of empirical observation or right in at the core of *a priori* beliefs – may effect the most far-reaching change in what is regarded as manifest, self-evident truth.[2] Then again, there is the line of neo-pragmatist argument of which Richard Rorty is currently the most prominent and resourceful advocate.[3] This holds that philosophy took a wrong turn when it assumed, with Descartes and Kant, that knowledge stood in need of ultimate foundations – a bedrock of epistemological certitude and truth – if it was ever to defeat the twin perils of scepticism and relativist doctrine. On the contrary, says Rorty: truth is indeed, as William James thought, 'what's good in the way of belief', and philosophy must therefore give up its delusions of epistemological grandeur and accept its role as just one more voice in the ongoing cultural conversation. Modern philosophers who continue in the old ways of thought are merely displaying their own inability to catch up with the new pragmatist rules of the game. For on Rorty's view there is no escaping the conclusion that truth is a product of our cultural needs, our consensus-values or communal ideas of what should count as true for all practical purposes.

Thus Rorty's pragmatism can take heart from what he sees as the collapse of analytical philosophy, or at least that version of it to be found in the present-day systematizing heirs of thinkers like Frege and Russell. The signs of this collapse are there to be read – Rorty argues – in a whole range of present-day discourses, from Quine's dissolution of the Kantian paradigm to the writings of post-structuralist literary critics, 'strong misreaders' like Barthes or Harold Bloom who deny the very notion of interpretive truth. Or again, it finds expression in Foucault's Nietzschean 'genealogies' of power/knowledge, his treatment of truth as an essentially-contested concept, a domain of plural interpretive strategies where what ultimately counts is the power to impose some particular, self-interested reading of events against other competing accounts.[4] The virtue of such ideas, according to Rorty, is their courage in rejecting the old idea of truth as a matter of grounds, foundations, *a priori* concepts or whatever, and their acceptance of the straightforward fact that interpretation *goes all the way down*; that philosophy, like every other kind of discourse, can rest on nothing more than the language-games or cultural forms of life that keep the whole enterprise in business. Quite simply, there is no alternative standpoint, no position from which to criticize those practices according to some standard of validity or truth that would not always need to make good its own claims within a given community of interests, values and beliefs.

So there are clear points of contact between this current 'post-analytical' trend in philosophy and those ideas about language, discourse and power/knowledge that characterize recent post-structuralist theory. They also find support in the kind of ethno-linguistic relativism espoused by thinkers like Whorf and Sapir; namely, the argument that 'reality' is structured through and through by concepts, categories and 'grammars' of perception that vary considerably from language to language, and which therefore may provide no reliable means of translating from one universe of discourse to another.[5] Quine takes this as grounds for asserting the impossibility of 'radical translation', the fact that we can never know for sure that any word or expression in the target-language has been adequately rendered or carried across into words or expressions of our own. Such is Quine's doctrine of 'ontological relativity', the idea that speakers of different languages may inhabit incommensurable worlds where there is no guarantee of shared understanding on basic assumptions about truth, reference, logical entailment, speech-act implicatures and so forth.[6] Here again, the upshot is to relativize these concepts and view them as essentially language- or culture-specific, valid for our own current practical purposes but possessing no absolute validity. Of course I am not suggesting that Quine, Rorty, Whorf and Foucault are all engaged in the selfsame enterprise, or that they wouldn't disagree on some basic matters of argumentative validity and method. But their projects do have this much in common: a belief that such questions can no longer be addressed from the standpoint of a rational commitment to truth-claims taken as transcending all mere relativities of language and cultural context.

This is where Davidson enters the picture as a thinker squarely opposed to such relativist ideas. He attacks them most forcefully in his 1974 essay 'On the Very Idea of a Conceptual Scheme', where the argument may be summarized very briefly as follows.[7] There is a mistaken line of reasoning common to many philosophers, linguists and workers in the field of comparative anthropology, as well as those theorists of science, like Kuhn and Feyerabend, who stress the degree to which different 'paradigms' or frameworks of knowledge may set up wholly incommensurable orders of truth-claim. Their mistake is to be over-impressed by the sheer variety of languages or world-views on offer, which leads them to treat cases of misunderstanding as the norm, rather than those other, more frequent cases where we do make a fair shot at grasping the beliefs, ideas and knowledge-constitutive interests that characterize discourses other than our own. This error takes hold through the widespread habit of thinking in terms of 'conceptual schemes', or of truth-claims as making sense only relative to some given language or set of deep-laid ontological assumptions. Thus Whorf points out the differences that exist bewteen Hopi Indian and the structure of our own and related languages, arguing that the speaker of Hopi must inhabit a conceptual universe so remote from ours that translation should be well-nigh impossible. And yet, as Davidson points out, Whorf does manage to convey a lively impression of the differences involved, thus achieving in practice a 'translation' of Hopi grammar, concepts and categories into those of his English-speaking readers.

The same applies to those philosophers of science who adopt a radically conventionalist view. Thus 'Kuhn is brilliant at saying what things were like before the revolution [i.e. the advent of modern scientific ideas] using – what else? – our post-revolutionary idiom' (Davidson, p. 184). And likewise with the problem of 'radical translation' as Quine conceives it: namely, the question whether we could ever make a start in understanding the language of some alien culture or speech-community, given that their whole metaphysics of language and experience might fail to correspond with ours at every point. For Davidson, such arguments are strictly incoherent, since we cannot be in any position to judge where understanding might have gone awry unless we assume that the language in question resembles our own in certain crucial respects. And these would have to include (among other things) the referential capacity to pick out objects by an act of designative naming, and the existence of constraints upon the class of sentences held true within the language as a whole.

This is why Davidson rejects all talk of 'conceptual schemes' and proposes instead that we adopt the criterion of truth (or holding-true) as a kind of logical primitive. Where the sceptics go wrong is in supposing that language – or the conceptual grid imposed by some particular language – must always organize our thoughts and perceptions in accordance with its own immanent structure. But this is to get the matter upside-down, Davidson suggests, since the basic condition for *any* understanding of language is that we grasp which sentences are held to be true and then, on this basis, go on to construct a more general 'theory' for the language in question. Hence what Davidson calls the 'principle of charity', the threefold assumption that languages make sense, that their ways of making sense cannot differ radically from one culture to another, and therefore that the generalized principles of inference that work for our own language will also work – at least up to a point – for the language we are given to translate. And this leads on to his central claim:

> Since charity is not an option, but a condition of having a workable theory, it is meaningless to suggest that we might fall into massive error by endorsing it. Until we have successfully established a systematic correlation of sentences held true with sentences held true, there are no mistakes to make. Charity is forced on us; whether we like it or not, if we want to understand others, we must count them right in most matters. If we can produce a theory that reconciles charity with the formal conditions for a theory, we have done all that could be done to ensure communication. Nothing more is possible, and nothing more is needed. (p. 197)

Of course it is not the case – as Davidson concedes – that all languages have a common ontological structure, or that predicates in one will necessarily be identical (i.e., possess the same extension or range of reference) with predicates in another. To this extent he acknowledges the force of those arguments for linguistic relativism put forward (from very different theoretical standpoints) by thinkers like Whorf, Quine and Foucault. But he sees this as no reason for abandoning his principle that truth-conditions are basic to all known or conceivable languages; that the pattern of beliefs held true is a perfectly good starting-point for the process of radical translation; and that any differences between one 'conceptual scheme' and another will at most produce effects of localized misunderstanding which the interpreter can always correct by referring them back to an overall 'theory' that works for the language as a whole.

In fact Davidson is quite happy to dispense with the notion of reference so long as the theory can still find room for those basic regularities that must play a role in any act of linguistic understanding. He can therefore go along with Quine's arguments on the topic of 'ontological relativity', but still claim to offer a better, more adequate theory, one that avoids the idea of incommensurable 'schemes' or of translation as in some sense a radically impossible enterprise.

> What I have added to Quine's basic insight is the suggestion that the theory should take the form of a theory of absolute truth. If it does take this form, we can recover a structure of sentences as made

up of singular terms, predicates, connectives and qualifiers, with ontological implications of the usual sort. Reference, however, drops out. It plays no essential role in explaining the relation between language and reality. (p. 225)

Commentators on Davidson are divided as to just how strong a theory of 'absolute truth' might be in question here. Some (like Richard Rorty) treat it as a largely redundant technicality, since what counts as true in any given language must always be a matter of the ideas, beliefs and convictions that happen to prevail at the time. Thus Rorty sees no obstacle to claiming Davidson as a kind of half-way or honorary pragmatist, one who hasn't yet quite managed to free himself from the old metaphysical quest for truth, but whose work nevertheless points in that direction if one reads it aright. Thus, according to Rorty,

the purpose of constructing a 'truth theory of English' is not to enable philosophical problems to be put in a formal mode of speech, nor to explain the relationship between words and the world, but simply to lay out perspicuously the relation between parts of a social practice (the use of certain sentences) and other parts (the use of other sentences).[8]

On this account truth, as well as reference, can simply drop out of the picture, since it offers no more than a kind of psychological back-up for arguments which would otherwise be just as well served by appealing to the current consensus of ideas and beliefs. For it is impossible, Rorty argues, to provide any stronger theory of truth, any meta-linguistic or 'absolute' theory that could adjudicate the issue from a standpoint outside this context of consensual values. In short, Davidson is a pragmatist *malgré lui*, one whose best insights are enough to controvert his own more questionable claims.

In support of this reading Rorty could point out that Davidson does make some sizable concessions to the pragmatist case, as by saying that truth must always be contextualized, i.e. that particular utterances can only be interpreted through the role they play within some language as a whole, or the entire class of sentences held true in any given speech-community. It is this holistic aspect of Davidson's theory – his apparent willingness to weaken the idea of truth to the point where it might just as well be a matter of consensus belief – that Rorty understandably finds most congenial. Furthermore, Davidson has to acknowledge the fact that any assignment of truth-conditions to a sentence will need to take account of its enunciative modality, that is, those aspects of the speaker's situation that may render a statement truthful in one context and false in another. 'Where indexical or demonstrative elements are present, it cannot be sentences that are true or false, but only sentences relative to a speaker and a time' (Davidson, p. 74). Taken along with his assertion elsewhere that any formal of theory of truth will have to 'go relative' when applied to a natural language – as distinct, that is, from the formalized languages constructed by logicians – this might seem to bear out Rorty's claim that what Davidson is proposing is a broadly pragmatist line of approach where 'truth' functions only as a honorific term.

It is also possible to argue – like S. Pradhan in a recent essay[9] – that Davidson's thinking has much in common with Derridean deconstruction, in the sense that it adheres to a 'minimalist semantics' which rejects the idea of meaning as conveyed by conceptual schemes, structures of semantic implication or whatever, since no such account could conceivably encompass the sheer range of situations and contexts in which speech-acts do possess significance. Thus Davidson's approach, like Derrida's, lays stress on the way that such utterances can be 'grafted', carried across from one situation to another, beyond all hope of devising a semantic theory that would sort out proper from improper uses, as for instance by appealing to speaker's intentions or the context in which they acquire 'genuine' performative force. Such attempts go wrong (Davidson argues) because they remain captive to the illusion of meaning as a matter of semantic identity, of that which enables signs (or sentences) to preserve something of their original sense across a range of more or less remote or deviant contexts. Hence also his argument against all those theories of metaphor, from Aristotle down, that try to explain the workings of figural language in terms of some intra-semantic relationship between the literal meaning of an expression and its use in contexts that seem to require an alternative, metaphorical sense.

> Metaphor runs on the same familiar linguistic tracks that the plainest sentences do. What distinguishes metaphor is not meaning but use . . . And the special use to which we put language in metaphor is not – cannot be – to 'say something' special, no matter how indirectly. For a metaphor *says* only what shows on its face – usually a patent falsehood or an absurd truth. And this plain truth or falsehood needs no paraphrase – its meaning is given in the literal meaning of the words. (Davidson, p. 259)

This is not to say that metaphors are 'meaningless' in the sense of conveying no insights, perceptions or new ways of looking at the world. Rather it is to claim that such effects come about, not through some complex process of semantic adjustment or translation from one level of meaning to another, but more simply by our grasping the literal sense and then working out what relevance it might have in the present context of utterance. There is no special 'meaning' or structure of semantic implication that would account for this relevance and thus enable the analyst of metaphor to come up with a plain-prose, literal paraphrase. In short, we make sense of figural language by perceiving that normal truth-conditions don't apply, and then going on to devise some way of matching up words with context. What we *don't* do in such cases – according to Davidson – is construct an elaborate translation-scheme which would explain how metaphor creates new meanings.

This might seem to lend support to Pradhan's deconstructionist reading of Davidson. 'Minimalist semantics' would then be another name for what Derrida terms the 'iterability' of meaning, the capacity of speech-acts to function across a vast (potentially infinite) range of contexts, such as to defeat any possible explanation in terms of their semantic properties.[10] This reading goes in much the same direction as Rorty's pragmatist account. That is to say, it ignores the many passages where Davidson insists that truth-conditions, not meanings, are the basis of linguistic understanding, and instead chooses to emphasize his talk of such truths being relative to language as a whole, or the entire class of sentences held true at some given time. But in so doing it effectively discounts what is most distinctive and important in Davidson's argument. For his point is that we couldn't make sense of any language unless we possessed this more basic grasp of what it takes to make a sentence true. And this applies not only to remote foreign languages but to instances of metaphor, deviant usage or – another related Davidsonian topic – malapropism. For even where speakers constantly misuse words and expressions, to the point where no scheme of semantic substitution could unravel their sense, still it is often possible to assign truth-conditions by examining the context of their utterance and then forming a reasonable inference as to what they must have meant by the speech-act in question. Thus for Davidson, malapropism is much like metaphor in requiring that we take the literal sense – and not some alternative, conjectural meaning – as the basis for valid interpretation. 'As philosophers', he remarks, 'we are peculiarly tolerant of systematic malapropism, and practised at interpreting the result. The process is that of constructing a viable theory of belief and meaning from sentences held true' (p. 196). And what enables us to do so is the fact that language makes sense against a background of normative assumptions about truth, meaning and valid inference which in practice offers a good enough starting-point for the process of 'radical translation'.

It is clear that these arguments, if accepted, would cast considerable doubt upon post-structuralist ideas about the inscrutable nature of reference, the ultimate relativity of meaning, and the absence of any standard by which to adjudicate issues of right interpretation. According to Davidson, we could never be in a position to make such claims, since they presuppose the availability of an independent standpoint, a neutral high ground of theory from which we could compare different languages, cultures or 'conceptual schemes', and judge them wholly incommensurable one with another. But of course this argument reduces to nonsense, since the relativist case would then have to be stated in a meta-language conveniently exempt from its own implications. Davidson is far from suggesting that this commonplace riposte to relativist arguments could in any way provide a substantive set of claims as to the universality of human understanding. Even if, as he asserts, there is 'no intelligible basis on which it can be said that schemes are different', all the same it would be equally wrong 'to announce the glorious news that all mankind – all speakers of language, at least – share a common scheme and ontology. For if we cannot intelligibly say that schemes are different, neither can we intelligibly say that they are one' (p. 198). Davidson's point is that these problems would seem less pressing – and perhaps disappear altogether – if we gave up thinking of truth as relative to this or that conceptual scheme, and recognized instead that belief (or the attitude of holding-true) is a precondition for our possessing language at all. And this is enough, he thinks, to justify dispensing with all those problematic theories of language and representation which make it more difficult to envisage any means of overcoming the relativist impasse.

II

It seems to me that Spinoza anticipates these arguments point for point in numerous passages of the *Ethics* and his treatise *On the Improvement of Understanding*. Thus he takes it as axiomatic, like Davidson, (1) that truth is in some sense 'its own sign', (2) that all languages necessarily incorporate some truth-conditional logic or structure of assumptions – since otherwise they would simply not work as languages – and (3) following from this, that where errors exist (whether of 'understanding', in Spinoza's terminology, or of 'translation' in Davidson's idiom) they can be brought to light through a process of reasoning that invokes those same standards of consistency and truth. But we have also seen how Davidson's claims lend themselves to a quite different reading, namely, a version of the widespread neo-pragmatist doctrine that rejects all talk of truth, theory, principles of reason or suchlike (supposedly obsolete) ideas. And one can readily understand why this flipside interpretation should have come about. For if indeed it is the case – as Davidson asserts – that we *can't get outside* those basic assumptions about truth, meaning, validity etc. which characterize our own worldview, then the pragmatist can turn this argument right around and say that it is impossible (or just pointless) to raise any question concerning their adequacy when measured against the standards of right reason, theoretical understanding, logical consistency or whatever. Quite simply, there are no such 'grounds' or 'principles' that won't turn out, on subsequent reflection, to be always already a part of our taken-for-granted beliefs as to what must count as an adequate argument. Thus we may want to think (and genuinely believe) that theory has important consequences, that it can bring about changes not only in the 'order of ideas' but also in the order of practical, real-world events. And this conviction would seem to be important for anyone who engages in theoretical activity, whether with a view to clearing up sources of conceptual confusion (as in much analytical philosophy), or with the aim of getting people to think their way out of some prejudice, some mistaken set of values or ideological beliefs. But we are deluded – so the pragmatist argument runs – if we imagine that theorizing *really* has this power to undermine existing habits of thought or produce some radical change in the currency of ideas.

Thus according to Stanley Fish, the most vigorous proponent of this viewpoint, theory is a strictly useless or redundant activity, one that cannot possibly make any difference to the ongoing debate about values, beliefs, principles and so forth.[11] Fish has three main arguments in support of his anti-theoretical case. One is the point – developed at length in a number of recent books and articles – that theory can never do more than offer a post-hoc rationalization of beliefs that must already be in place if the argument is to carry conviction with us or other members of our own 'interpretive community'.[12] On its broadest definition this latter may extend to the whole socio-cultural context or framework of values within which we live, work and think as late-twentieth-century citizens of one or another Western bourgeois democracy. More narrowly, it signifies our membership of various more specialized interest-groups – political parties, academic disciplines, professional bodies and so forth – which also set the terms for what shall count as an effective, worthwhile or acceptable contribution to debate. On the one hand, any truly radical theory – any argument that broke altogether with existing interpretive constraints – would *ipso facto* be wholly unintelligible to people within the relevant community, and would thus be either ignored, misconstrued or consigned to the limbo of 'incompetent' or 'eccentric' thought. On the other, any theory that *claimed* to be 'radical' but in fact enjoyed widespread acceptance – or even a modest degree of comprehension among like-minded colleagues – would for this very reason have to be seen as part of an existing consensus, no matter how small or how marginal its membership. In short, critical theorists cannot have it both ways, assuming an imaginary standpoint of knowledge outside and above their interpretive community, while expecting their ideas to be received, taken up or merely understood by members of that same community. They are caught (so Fish would argue) in a classic double-bind predicament, since their claims to speak genuinely on behalf of an alternative, dispossessed or minority culture must become less plausible with each new step toward gaining a wider currency for their views.

This leads on to Fish's second point: that theory cannot have 'consequences' in the strong sense of effecting some change in the social, political or intellectual sphere that could not have been effected by other (i.e. non-theoretical) means.[13] Of course, as he concedes, it may have *results* in persuading us or others that the beliefs we hold are more than just beliefs; that they possess some ultimate validity or truth that can only be arrived at through theory. But if so then this remains an empirical fact about the psychology of assent or the workings of persuasive argument. That is to say, it offers no grounds whatsoever for the strong thesis that theory makes a difference *in and of itself*, that by learning to criticize received ideas from a higher, theoretical standpoint we can change those ideas and thus bring about a more adequate, enlightened or progressive state of knowledge. Fish puts this argument most succinctly in the opening paragraph of a recent essay. 'In what follows', he writes,

> I will contend (1) that in whatever form it appears the argument for theory fails, (2) that theory is not and could not be used . . . to generate and/or guide practice, (3) that when 'theory' is in fact used it is . . . in order to justify a decision reached on other grounds, (4) that theory is essentially a rhetorical and political phenomenon whose effects are purely contingent, and (5) that these truths are the occasion neither of cynicism nor of despair.[14]

His last item here is intended as a simple recognition of the fact that, just as 'doing theory' has absolutely no consequences, for better or worse, so giving up theory will have no real effect on the quality, range or intellectual level of debate. As for his own arguments – and the obvious question as to what would be the 'consequence' if people found them wholly convincing – Fish can afford to take a relaxed line. The ideal outcome, he implies, would be a couple of letters saying 'You're right!' and then a complete silence on the topic of theory (for or against) and a switch of attention to other, more important matters. But really nothing much will have changed since the theorists were always debating those matters – starting out from various kinds of value-judgement, political conviction, disciplinary interest or whatever – and producing theoretical arguments or truth-claims only to achieve an extra degree of persuasive force. So the real benefit of ceasing to talk about theory is that it would remove these obstacles in the way of straightforward discussion and thus leave us free to continue the argument exactly where we last left off.

Fish's third point has to do with the distinction between 'positive' and 'negative' versions of theory. The positive theorists are those who think we need reasons, principles, or justifying grounds for the conduct of debate on interpretive questions. They would include, for instance, a thinker like E. D. Hirsch whose early book *Validity in Interpretation* came up with a range of theoretical arguments for the case that an author's intentions are constitutive for the meaning of his or her text, and that critics should therefore make every effort to recover the 'original' meaning before going on to raise questions of present-day 'significance' or meaning-for-us.[15] But to Fish this whole enterprise seems nothing more than a massive example of misapplied scholarly ingenuity. For it is simply a fact about the way we understand language – whether everyday speech-acts or literary texts – that we *do* try to figure out the utterer's intentions and thus make sense of their meaning to the best of our ability. And when this effort doesn't pay off for some reason (maybe on account of confused expression, changes of linguistic usage or wilful obscurity) then no kind of theory can possibly help us to determine what the speaker or the author might have had in mind. And the same goes for theorists in other disciplines – notably exponents of liberal jurisprudence – who argue for the existence of 'grounds' or 'principles' by way of backing up their interpretive claims. Here again Fish finds their thinking inconsequent in the sense that it simply can't make any difference whether or not one's beliefs come equipped with some notional apparatus of theory. Of course there are reasons – strategic or rhetorical reasons – for taking an avowedly principled stand on this or that question, and thus claiming to occupy the moral high ground. But in the end such talk comes down to a species of self-induced mystification. What it has to ignore is the straightforward fact that we believe what we believe on various issues of politics, justice, social values etc., and that nothing follows – in theory or in principle – from adopting these suasive techniques.[16]

The 'negative theorists' (i.e. the deconstructors) are in even worse trouble, according to Fish. For it is their main argument – at the opposite extreme from a hardline intentionalist like Hirsch – that texts very often *don't and cannot* mean what they say; that there is simply no access to authorial intentions (or original meaning) since language complicates the process of reading to the point of an ultimate 'undecidability'; and therefore that we had best discount all these various surrogates for the author's self-present voice and instead pay attention to the conflicts that develop between logic, grammar and rhetoric, or language in its literal and figural modes.[17] Then again, there is the Marxist version of 'negative theory' which holds that texts may be seen to conceal their true (class-specific or historically determinate) meaning in the interests of some dominant ideology whose workings can best be exposed to view through an immanent critique of their blindspots, contradictions or moments of unwitting self-revelation. Much the same applies to the Freudian distinction between 'manifest' and 'latent' sense, or indeed to any form of diagnostic reading that claims this prerogative of somehow knowing more than the author can plausibly be held to have known about his or her meanings, motives or intent. In each case the critic effectively disowns any belief in the maxim that language, for the most part, means what it says and says what it means.

Fish's response to all this – as might be expected – is a downright denial that it could ever apply to our experience as members of an interpretive community engaged in making sense of literary or other kinds of text. For it is a precondition of belonging to any such community that one's readings will only be acceptable in so far as they are addressed to the common understanding of like-minded scholars, critics, informed laypersons, competent judges and so forth. And beyond these relatively specialized sub-groups there is also the larger – maybe universal – set of assumptions about meaning, intention, or speech-act implicature which simply define what it is to 'make sense' in any given context of utterance. So the negative theorists cannot be taken seriously, Fish argues, when they put forward their case for a modern 'hermeneutics of suspicion' that would somehow revoke one or all of these basic conventions, and thus produce readings that go clean against every notion of common-sense interpretive grasp. Once again it is a version of the Cretan Liar dilemma: *either* these readings are intelligible to the wider community (in which case they can't be as radical as they claim), *or* they really do subvert all established ideas of readerly competence (in which case nobody could begin to understand them). And since the theorists concerned are mostly prominent figures on the academic scene it is the first option that clearly provides the best means of resolving this pseudo-paradox.

There is no denying the elegance and persuasiveness of Fish's arguments when applied to some of the more wayward examples of modish all-purpose scepticism. But his real target – among 'positive' and 'negative' thinkers alike – is the claim that theory can indeed make a difference, and not the idea (which in fact he would very willingly endorse) that it amounts to just one more species of persuasive rhetoric. One can best view Fish as the latest in a line of debunking anti-philosophers which goes back at least to Protagoras and his quarrel with the truth-claims of Socratic reason. This is why he is able to beat the modern sceptics (or some of them at least) at their own game. It also gives a handle for other players, following Fish, who go along with the whole neo-pragmatist case 'against theory' but then proceed to catch him out in some covert theoretical move or failure to stick with his own principles.[18] To which Fish responds – quite predictably – by showing that these critics have misconstrued his argument, and done so moreover since they themselves are in the grip of some residual theoreticist illusion. Clearly there can be no end to this game so long as one carries on playing by the same rules. The real question is not so much whether Fish wins out on ground of his own choosing. For the current neo-pragmatists have this much in common with the sophists, the sceptics and other such purveyors of a knock-down case against theory. That is to say, they can always have the last word if once it is conceded – as Davidson apparently concedes – that truth can be defined for all practical purposes as what is 'good in the way of belief'. The way is then open for the pragmatist to urge, like Rorty on Davidson, that we drop all this otiose talk of truth-conditions, logical primitives etc., and simply get on with playing our role in the 'cultural conversation of mankind'.

From a Rortyan standpoint the same would apply to all those philosophers, past and present, who have thought they were doing something more than just conversing on this or that subject of topical interest. One would only have to show – as Rorty argues in connection with Plato, Descartes, Kant, Hegel, Heidegger and others – that in fact their various orders of truth-claim came down to so many 'final vocabularies', different ways of talking that prom-ised some ultimate or privileged access to truth, but whose real purpose was to win credence and keep the conversation going.[19] And it is not hard to see how this argument might work – or at least gain a certain *prima facie* plausibility – in Spinoza's case. Thus Rorty could point to those passages in Spinoza where truth is defined in what appears to be a purely redundant or circular fashion, i.e. as consisting in 'adequate ideas' whose validity 'needs no sign' since it must be self-evident to reason, or known *a priori* by any mind in possession of the requisite logical powers. And it is on this point precisely that Rorty takes issue with Davidson, or at least with any reading of Davidson that takes his talk of 'truth' to entail something more than an attitude of mind, a psychology of belief or a simple acceptance of the pragmatist position.

In fact Spinoza anticipates this argument – that his reasoning is circular and begs all the relevant questions – in a passage which could be seen as merely restating the problem without any hint of an adequate response. 'It may provoke astonishment', he writes,

> that, after having said that the good method is that which teaches us to direct our mind according to the standard of the given true idea, we should prove our point by reasoning, which would appear to

indicate that it is not self-evident . . . To this I make answer that, if by some happy chance anyone had adopted this method in his investigations of nature – that is, if he had acquired new ideas in the proper order, according to the standard of the original true idea, he would never have doubted the truth of his knowledge, in as much as truth, as we have shown, makes itself evident, and all things would flow, as it were, spontaneously toward him. (*OIU*, p. 16)

Rorty or Fish could accept all this and still draw their lesson that the only kind of truth-claim in question here is one that reduces to an empty tautology or a product of circular definition. That is to say, Spinoza 'proves' quite convincingly that the truth of our beliefs is presupposed by the fact of our having those beliefs in the first place; that there is no real difference between believing this or that to be the case and taking it as true (or self-evident to reason) that the case is indeed what we think it. But his proof is quite compatible with the pragmatist claim that truth is *nothing but* what we are given to believe by the currency of ideas, opinions or values that happens to prevail within some existing consensus. For if the attitude of holding-true is in the nature of a necessary presupposition – if it is, as Spinoza claims, the point from which we always start out when offering further reasons, arguments, deductive chains of inference etc. in support of that 'original true idea' – then it might seem to follow that nothing could count as evidence either for or against our settled habits of thought. In which case clearly Fish would be justified in arguing that theory has no 'consequences', since it cannot affect those foregone assumptions one way or the other. All it can do is provide a kind of reassuring technical back-up for beliefs that are always already in place before we get around to the pointless activity of examining those beliefs 'in theory'. And Spinoza's *Ethics* could then be seen – ironically enough – as a text that allows no escape from this process of endless circular reasoning, and which thus provides a massive (albeit unintentional) endorsement of Fish's neo-pragmatist position.

It should be clear from everything I have written so far that mine is a very different reading of Spinoza's achievement in the *Ethics* and elsewhere. It differs chiefly on the question – crucial to present-day philosophy and critical theory – as to whether thinking can ever attain to a standpoint that wouldn't be determined in advance by prevailing beliefs or consensus values. Fish takes the view that this is simply impossible and that anyone who fails to see the point of his arguments can best be coaxed down from the heights of theoreticist delusion by a series of well-rehearsed therapeutic moves. What he won't allow – since it would render these moves ineffectual – is the idea that theory *can* make a difference by bringing us up against limits, contradictions or blindspots in the discourse of commonsense knowledge which resist all attempts to wish them away in the name of some notional 'interpretive community'. This is why I have offered a sequence of extended comparisons between Spinoza's thinking and the various positions occupied by theorists like Althusser, Macherey, Deleuze, Derrida, and de Man. These positions encompass the widest extremes of what Fish would call 'positive' and 'negative' theory. Thus Althusser (like Macherey) argues for a version of Marxist *Ideologiekritik* which follows Spinoza (or one reading of Spinoza) in placing the maximum possible distance between 'science' and lived experience, or theoretical knowledge and the various forms of commonsense practical grasp. Deleuze comes out in fierce opposition to any such 'totalizing' claims, since they are always advanced (so his argument runs) under the flag of some putative master-discourse of science, history, mind, Spirit, or universal reason. What he finds in Spinoza is therefore – to repeat – a celebrant of the 'Body without Organs', a thinker of 'molecular' desires, energies and sheer anarchic instinct, as opposed to the 'molar' or self-maintaining structures of repressive (Oedipal) power. His Spinoza is one for whom 'the modes are everything that comes to pass: wars and vibrations, thresholds and gradients, intensities produced in a given type of substance starting from a given matrix'.[20]

With Derrida and de Man there is no such evidence of Spinozist ideas as an overt or decisive 'influence' on their work. But there are – as I have suggested – aspects of Spinoza's work that do relate closely to issues raised in the deconstructive reading of philosophical and other kinds of text. Most significant here is the relation between philosophy as a discourse aimed toward ultimate truth – 'positive theory', in Fish's terms – and that other strain of 'negative' or demystifying thought which plays a large role in Spinoza's political texts. To some extent these two projects can be seen as leading in opposite directions. For clearly there is a sense in which a mind that surveyed the entirety of nature from a standpoint of 'eternal' or 'adequate' ideas could have no use for the kinds of short-term, practical knowledge that arise from our everyday interests and involvements. 'It would be impossible', Spinoza writes, for human infirmity to follow up the series of particular mutable things, both on account of their multitude, surpassing all calculation, and on account of the infinitely diverse circumstances surrounding one and the same thing, any one of which may be the cause for its existence or non-existence. (*OIU*, p. 37)

In which case philosophy at its highest level would consist in the pursuit of eternal truths self-evident to reason and ideally unconcerned with matters of a secular, this-worldly, or 'mutable' character. Its characterizing mark would be the will to transcend such limiting perspectives and attain – or at any rate aspire – to a knowledge beyond all mere particularities of time and place. But we have seen already what problems the commentators face when they attempt to do justice to this aspect of Spinoza's thought by taking him at his word, as far as possible, and offering various interpretive guidelines – or modes of 'rational reconstruction' – which would somehow make sense of these high metaphysical claims. Their responses range from good-willed bafflement to a style of brisk, no-nonsense commentary and, beyond that, to the tone of sheer exasperation that marks the closing pages of Bennett's book when he at last loses patience with Spinoza's talk of 'intuitive knowledge', 'eternal ideas' and other such (as he would have it) plainly nonsensical doctrines. And there is a similar problem for commentators like Wienpahl, determined to represent Spinoza *both* as a genuine 'radical' whose ideas are still relevant to issues in present-day political debate, *and* as a thinker whose ultimate concern – if we read him aright – is with matters of a timeless or transcendental import.

It is not that Wienpahl is wrong to adopt this dual perspective. In fact, as I have argued, one can scarcely begin to make sense of Spinoza's philosophy unless one takes account of the tension that develops between these aspects of his thinking. But the problem with Wienpahl's even-handed approach is that it underrates the sheer resistance encountered by any attempt to reconcile the claims of absolute reason with those of a worldly or secular outlook concerned to adjudicate principles of justice, political interests, questions of state authority, censorship, freedom of thought and speech etc. Wienpahl's position is that of a modern left-liberal – albeit quite markedly to left of centre in present-day American terms – who wants to preserve the existing consensus of broadly agreed-upon values while allowing that there must be room for 'radical' voices that challenge this consensus from a standpoint inimical to mainstream interests and values. This means that his arguments are always at risk of falling into Fish's ingenious and well-laid trap. What is lacking in Wienpahl's account is a sense of this basic – perhaps irreducible – conflict between opposed discourses, orders of truth-claim, or standards of argumentative validity. On the one hand philosophy asserts its privileged position as the sole discipline capable of arriving at 'adequate ideas' by renouncing all concern with the order of short-term, contingent episodes and events. For 'in proportion as the mind's understanding is smaller, and its experience multiplex, so will its power of coining fictions be larger, whereas, as its understanding increases, its capacity for entertaining fictitious ideas becomes less' (*OIU*, p. 210). In which case the true path of philosophic wisdom would lead on and up through stages of increasing detachment from the pressures of real-world circumstance, to a point where the mind could contemplate ideas *sub specie aeternitatis*, or as viewed from a quasi-divine perspective of pure, disinterested knowledge. But on the other hand Spinoza is acutely aware of the factors that conspire to prevent such knowledge from appearing as even a remote possibility under present socio-political conditions. It is this awareness that impels him to publish his tracts in defence of the Dutch republican party, in support of a proper separation of powers between church and state, and against any form of coercive legislation applied to matters of religious, political or moral conscience.

In the end these two endeavours go hand in hand since it is – Spinoza argues – only with the advent of a just political system that thinking can attain the freedom to pursue its quest for adequate ideas. But he also acknowledged that this wished-for state of things was so far from being realized in any past or present society that the philosopher had no choice but to engage those manifold errors of prejudice, contorted reasoning, narrow self-interest etc. which had so far stood in the way of achieving a rational polity. And it is here that Spinoza most strikingly anticipates many of the central issues and concerns in present-day critical theory. I have suggested already – through the comparison with de Man's reading of Husserl – that the Spinozist treatment of 'confused' or 'imaginary' ideas can be seen as a form of deconstructive analysis *avant la lettre*, one that goes by way of a detailed critique of language and representation, and which sets out to locate those blindspots of prejudice in the discourse of enlightened reason where thought falls prey to unacknowledged motives and interests in its own undertaking. This comparison may serve to dispel any notion that Spinoza's 'metaphysical' doctrines prevent him from perceiving the extent to which language complicates the quest for philosophical truth. But it is important to remember also that Spinoza is a thoroughgoing rationalist who believes (unlike Derrida or de Man) that truth is 'its own sign', that thinking must be regulated according to the standard of clear and distinct ideas, and that words are most often sources of confusion which get in the way of an adequate intellectual grasp. Thus (to cite just one of many such passages):

> Since words are a part of the imagination – that is, since we form many conceptions in accordance with confused arrangements of words in the memory, dependent on particular bodily conditions – there is no doubt that words may, equally with the imagination, be the cause of many and great errors, unless we keep strictly on our guard. (*OIU*, p. 33)

One could scarcely envisage an argument more completely at odds with the current understanding – at least among literary theorists and philosophers who have taken the 'linguistic turn' – that the order of concepts just *is* the order of language, discourse or representation, since there is no possibility of framing ideas outside the presently-existing range of linguistic forms and resources. In this regard, certainly, Spinoza's rationalist convictions place him at the furthest remove not only from thinkers like Derrida and de Man, but also from just about everything that has happened in philosophy and theory over the past few decades. Nothing I have said should be taken to suggest that this distance is illusory or merely the result of our not having 'deconstructed' Spinoza to the point where such distinctions lose all pertinence or force.

Nevertheless it seems to me that there do exist grounds for comparison, especially if one examines the implicit truth-claims, structures of argument, tacit presuppositions and so forth which continue to operate in the discourse of criticism even where it thinks to have broken with all such 'metaphysical' ideas. Derrida makes this point about Foucault in his reading of the latter's *Madness and Civilization*.[21] Foucault may profess to be writing a book that eschews all the ground-rules and protocols of reason, that refuses to occupy the standpoint of 'enlightened' modernity, and which will thus give voice to that repressed or marginalized language of madness which has always been condemned to silence by the doctors, philosophers, psychoanalysts, historians and other such rational seekers-after-truth. But the problem with this stance, as Derrida remarks, is that it cannot be sustained by any discourse that effectively *argues its case* through a series of sentences, statements or consecutive propositions. Foucault thus provides yet another instance – perhaps the most extreme – of a relativist position that self-deconstructs as soon as one asks how its claims stand up under the test of reflexive application. And this applies all the more to a text like *Madness and Civilization*, one that marshals an impressive range of historical evidence, and which sets out moreover to analyse that evidence from a critical or diagnostic standpoint. It is impossible for such writing ever to achieve the kind of radically aberrant or anomalous status that Foucault seems to envisage. For if it did so – as Fish would be quick to point out – then not only would its arguments lack all force but each sentence would be meaningless by any standard one could possibly bring to bear.

Thus, despite his protestations to the contrary, Foucault is engaged in a sense-making enterprise which cannot but respect certain rational or 'enlightened' criteria, and this with regard both to his own judgements and those to be found in his various case-histories and source-texts. In Derrida's words:

> By its essence, the sentence is normal . . . It carries normality and sense within it, and does so whatever the state, whatever the health or madness of him who propounds it, or through whom it passes . . . In its most impoverished syntax logos is reason and, indeed, a historical reason . . . So that any philosopher or speaking subject (and the philosopher is but the speaking subject par excellence) who must evoke madness from the *interior* of thought (and not only from within the body or some other extrinsic agency) can do so only in the realm of the *possible* and in the language of fiction or the fiction of language. (*CHM*, p. 54)

The immediate reference here is to Descartes's sceptical thought-experiment and Foucault's use of it as a prime instance of how reason establishes its sovereign claims over against the imaginary threat of a madness equated with the failure, the delirium, or the total absence of reason. But this argument misfires, according to Derrida, since Foucault himself fails to recognize the extent to which rational constraints still govern both the Cartesian experiment with 'hyperbolic doubt' and his own treatment of it as a text-book example of reason's domineering claims. 'Thereby, he [Foucault] reassures himself against any actual madness – which may sometimes appear quite talkative, another problem – and can keep his distance, the distance indispensable for continuing to speak and to live' (p. 54). So there can be no question of taking Foucault on trust when he claims to have exceeded or transgressed the bounds of reason and thus (in his own words) to have written 'a history not of psychiatry but of madness itself, in its most vibrant state, before being captured by knowledge' (cited by Derrida, p. 34).

But Derrida is equally emphatic on the point that this difficulty cannot be put down to any mere confusion on Foucault's part or any oversight that might have been corrected with a bit more attention to detail. It is – to borrow de Man's terminology – a clear case of significant 'error', rather than just a local, accidental or inconsequential 'mistake'. For the necessity of applying rational criteria even when criticising reason and all its works is one that affects not only the arguments of Descartes and Foucault but every discourse on the powers and limits of reason. So this is not, Derrida writes,

> a weakness or a search for security proper to a given historical language (for example, the search for certainty in the Cartesian style), but is rather inherent in the essence and the very project of all language in general; and even in the language of those who are apparently the maddest; and above all in the language of those who, by their praise of madness, by their complicity with it, measure their own strength against the greatest possible proximity to madness . . . In this sense I would be tempted to consider Foucault's book a powerful gesture of protection and internment. A Cartesian gesture for the twentieth century. (CHM, p. 55)

As I have said, Spinoza is not 'important' for Derrida in the way that (say) Plato, Kant, Hegel, Husserl or Heidegger figure as constant points of reference in his writing. But it strikes me that his entire line of argument in the debate with Foucault bears witness to at least an elective affinity with Spinozist ideas. Thus Derrida repeats against Foucault what Spinoza argued against Descartes: namely, that the venture into radical doubt *cannot make sense* or be understood at all unless from a standpoint which has to accept the truth of certain reasonable presuppositions. And again, he makes the point that any such venture will necessarily have recourse to imaginary ideas (in Derrida's words, 'the realm of the possible . . . the language of fiction or the fiction of language' [p. 54]). For it is impossible for thinking to entertain the notion that it might be systematically deceived – that all (or nearly all) its basic ideas are the result of some malign cosmic joke or whatever – without thereby laying claim to a knowledge somehow exempt from the general curse.

In Spinoza, this leads to the familiar conclusion: that truth is and must be 'its own sign', since otherwise we should have no certain means of distinguishing truth from falsehood, or of seeing (as with Descartes) where fictive hypotheses take over, so that the true/false distinction no longer applies. Obviously Derrida is far from subscribing to any such set of high metaphysical truth-claims. But he does insist that deconstruction is *not* – as some opponents would have it – an activity indifferent to standards of right reason, or one that would blithely dispense with all notions of truth and falsehood. These declarations have become more frequent of late – and taken on a certain polemical edge – when Derrida finds himself attacked by critics (like Habermas and Searle) who evince small knowledge or understanding of his work.[22] Hence the following passage from his 'Afterword', written in 1988, to the well-known exchange with Searle on the topic of Austinian speech-act theory. How is it possible, Derrida asks, that his texts should be so grossly and perversely misconstrued by opponents who charge him with those self-same faults from a confidently orthodox or mainstream standpoint? 'The answer is simple', Derrida asserts:

> this definition of the deconstructionist is *false* (that's right: false not true) and feeble; it supposes a *bad* (that's right: bad not good) and feeble reading of numerous texts, first of all mine, which therefore must finally be read or re-read. Then perhaps it will be understood that the value of truth (and all those values associated with it) is never contested or destroyed in my writings, but only reinscribed in more powerful, larger, more stratified contexts. And that within interpretive contexts (that is, within relations of force that are always differential – for example, socio-political-institutional, but even beyond these determinations) that are relatively stable, sometimes apparently almost unshakeable, it should be possible to invoke rules of competence, criteria of discussion and of consensus, good faith, lucidity, rigour, criticism, and pedagogy.[23]

I have quoted this passage at length because it states very clearly the terms on which Derrida expects to be read by anyone presuming to discuss or criticize his texts. Despite the markedly polemical tone it comes toward the close of a detailed argument in the course of which Derrida shows – among other things – that Searle has himself confused the main issues, abandoned the distinction between truth and falsehood (which Derrida asserts as a *sine qua non* of 'competent' philosophical thought), and succeeded in committing each and every one of those faults that he attributes to Derrida's reading of Austin. But the chief point to be remarked in this context is the fact that he endorses the pertinence and the would-be force of those criticisms even while turning them back upon Searle through a series of classic *tu quoque* moves.

The same applies to his comments on Habermas, offered in response to the latter's reading of deconstruction as merely one more deplorable sign of the current ('postmodern') retreat from reason into forms of relativism, nihilism or mere 'literary' posturing.[24] Derrida counters – and I think with some justice – that Habermas not only misconstrues his arguments but appears to have read only a fraction of his work, and that with minimal attentiveness to detail. What are we to make of this curious attitude in a thinker whose writings constantly proclaim the need for reciprocal understanding, for free and open exchange on topics of shared interest, with a view to achieving that 'ideal speech-situation' which is Habermas's regulative model for the conduct of all such debate? 'With a stupefying tranquillity', Derrida writes,

> here is the philosopher of consensus, of dialogue and discussion, the philosopher who claims to distinguish between science and literary fiction, between philosophy and literary criticism, daring not only to criticize without citing or giving a reference for twenty-five pages but, even more, justifying his non-reading . . . by this incredible alibi: 'Since Derrida does not belong to *those philosophers who like to argue* . . . it is expedient to take a closer look at his disciples in literary criticism . . . in order to see whether this thesis really can be held'.[25]

My purpose in citing these passages is not so much to establish the truth or justice of Derrida's claims – which I have attempted at greater length elsewhere[26] – but to underline the point that such considerations (i.e. of truth and justice) are integral to his work yet entirely ignored by critics like Habermas and Searle. And I think that by pursuing the comparison with Spinoza we can see more clearly why this should be the case.

III

Deconstruction can invoke standards of truth and falsehood because, as I have argued in connection with de Man, it locates those moments of resistance in a text where the sense holds out against simplified or premature forms of interpretive grasp. This is why critics like Habermas are wrong – demonstrably wrong – when they treat it as just another version of the modish neo-pragmatist outlook which reduces all texts to a dead level of consensus thinking or meanings that happen to enjoy a certain currency in this or that 'interpretive community'. It is also de Man's main reason for insisting that criticism continue to respect the distinction between logic, grammar and rhetoric, even while showing that rhetoric (or language in its figural or tropological aspect) creates all manner of problems for any such clear-cut separation of realms.[27] For if rhetoric is taken to command the whole field of linguistic possibility – if everything reduces to a species of suasive utterance – then clearly there is no counter-argument to Fish and his claim that truth and falsehood are redundant values which can henceforth be replaced by a straightforward appeal to what's good in the way of belief. And the upshot of any such argument, according to de Man, is to 'empty rhetoric of its epistemological impact' by treating it as simply a matter of suasive or performative efficacy, and thus ignoring the conflicts that emerge between the different orders of signification.

The pragmatist can therefore dismiss all appeals to reason, truth, adequate ideas and so forth on the grounds that they offer nothing more than a species of 'rhetorical' back-up for beliefs that are always already in place. 'It is as if . . . rhetoric could be isolated from the generality that grammar and logic have in common and considered as a mere correlative of an illocutionary power' (RT, p. 19). There could then be no question of language putting up that resistance to mainstream, conventional or orthodox readings which de Man brings out in his deconstructive treatment of Rousseau, Husserl, Heidegger and others. For such claims would always be subject in the end to Fish's standard line of response: that since texts can never 'mean' anything other than what we take them to mean in some existing context of usage, conventions, or interpretive ground-rules, therefore there is simply no point in coming up with ingenious proofs that they mean something different. De Man takes issue with

Fish on precisely this crucial point. 'What awakens one's suspicion', he writes,

> is that it [i.e. the pragmatist argument] relegates persuasion, which is indeed inseparable from rhetoric, to a purely affective and intentional realm and makes no allowance for modes of persuasion which are no less rhetorical . . . but which are of the order of persuasion by *proof* rather than persuasion by seduction. (*RT*, p. 18)

For a fuller understanding of de Man's phrase 'persuasion by proof' one would need to consult other texts, notably his late essay on Pascal, where this distinction is pursued at much greater length.[28] But it is enough for present purposes to note the following main points at issue. First: the term 'rhetoric' is commonly used with two different (and indeed contradictory) senses. It can signify *either* the deployment of language to suasive or performative ends – in which case rhetoric 'works' in so far as it secures the desired effect – *or* that discipline whose function it is to analyse the various tropes, figures and devices that operate everywhere in language. Second: this ambivalence must inevitably give rise to a conflict of aims, since the efficacy of language in its suasive aspect decreases in proportion as we become more aware of those same rhetorical devices. And third: it is the business of critical theory to maintain this awareness at the highest level and not give way to a generalized notion of performative utterance which leaves no room for such conflicts to appear.

This is why, in de Man's words, 'the equation of rhetoric with psychology rather than with epistemology opens up dreary prospects of pragmatic banality' (*RT*, p. 19). For once this move has been made there is simply no avoiding Fish's conclusion, in which case 'theory' is either played off the field (as the pragmatist would wish), or condemned to an endless rehearsal of arguments which always beg the same question at some crucial point. It is only by respecting that critical dimension – what de Man calls the 'epistemology of tropes' – that theory has the means to escape this closed circle and to demonstrate how reading can indeed go against the consensus of mainstream or orthodox ideas. From this standpoint rhetoric is conceived as the disruptive element, the name for those unruly tropes or aberrant figures which have always created certain problems for philosophy, at least in so far as the latter has sought to establish a straightforward, one-to-one relation between language, logic and the forms of phenomenal cognition. De Man makes this point in terms of the classical *trivium* (logic, grammar and rhetoric) where 'grammar stands in the service of logic which, in turn, allows for the passage to the knowledge of the world', while rhetoric on the contrary obeys no rules derived either from logic or the structure of real-world appearances. And this for the reason that 'tropes, unlike grammar, pertain primordially to language . . . they are text-producing functions that are not necessarily patterned on a non-verbal entity, whereas grammar is by definition capable of extra-linguistic generalization' (*RT*, pp. 14–15).

So it is here that problems can be seen to arise with the classical paradigm, i.e. when rhetoric gets out of hand, exceeds the compass of an orderly 'system' of tropes, and thus threatens to disrupt the continuity that should otherwise run from logic, via grammar to a knowledge of the world. At this point 'it is no longer possible to ignore the epistemological thrust of the rhetorical dimension of discourse . . . no longer possible to keep it in its place as a mere adjunct, a mere ornament within the semantic function' (p. 14). But it is equally the case that such a theory would lack all critical force – be devoid of 'consequences', in Fish's terms – if rhetoric were reduced to its purely illocutionary, performative or suasive dimension. For it would then be self-evident that language just *does* have the meaning we are persuaded to place upon it according to this or that dominant consensus, speech-act convention or set of prevailing interpretive norms. And this would count decisively against the strong claim – advanced by both Derrida and de Man – that deconstructive readings not only make sense but involve values of truth and falsehood that respect (even while they do much to complicate) the exigencies of classical logic. This is why it turns out (in de Man's words) that 'the relation between trope and perfor-mance' is 'actually closer but more disruptive' than anything envis-aged by neo-pragmatists like Fish or by proponents of speech-act philosophy in its commonplace, received or un-self-critical form. Such approaches are designed – quite explicitly in Fish's case – to cut out theoretical activity at source by making its arguments appear either trivially true (if they carry enough weight with people in the relevant 'interpretive community') or manifestly false (if they fail to persuade and are therefore rejected as muddled or meaningless).[29] But this case only holds up if one accepts Fish's major premise: namely, that rhetoric can never do more than confirm one's foregone assumptions and beliefs by falling in with some accepted language-game, cultural consensus or whatever. For otherwise it can always be asserted, as by de Man, that 'speech-act oriented theories of reading read only to the extent that they prepare the way for the rhetorical reading they avoid' (p. 19).

As I have said, Pascal is the thinker whom de Man singles out for his most detailed treatment of the problems that arise when a rationalist metaphysic – the seventeenth-century 'way of ideas' – comes up against the need to justify its claims by way of persuasive reasoning.[30] It is an essay of extraordinary subtlety and power, starting out from Pascal's work in the field of geometry and pure mathematics, going on to discuss how that work relates to his philosophy of mind and language, and then showing how the truth-claims of reason necessarily have recourse to fictive, rhetorical or 'literary' modes of expression in order to gain the reader's assent. Of course it might be said that this reading tells us nothing radically new, since it was – after all – quite explicitly a part of Pascal's own project to establish the limits of analytic thought and thus to make room for religious faith, or for 'reasons of the heart' which could never be grasped by the unaided rational intellect. But what distinguishes de Man's essay is its refusal to take the Pascalian wager (or 'leap of faith') as a pretext for abandoning the strictest protocols of logical argument and analysis. In the end he seems to assert – like Pascal – that such thinking cannot be self-sufficient, that it always stands in need of some further justifying ground, and that ultimately there is no avoiding the resort to language in its suasive or performative aspect. But he also makes it clear that any such conclusion has to be earned (so to speak) through a rigorous critique of the values and assumptions that gave rise to this distinction in the first place. For otherwise it is impossible for commentary to avoid what de Man calls 'the tendentious and simplistic opposition between knowledge and faith which is often forced upon Pascal' (*PAP*, p. 7). And the trouble with this latter line of approach is that it manages to bypass all the most crucial interpretive issues in the reading of Pascal's texts. That is to say, it gives no sense of the close but problematical relationship between, on the one hand, Pascal's rationalist metaphysics (including his attempt to reformulate epistemological questions in the mode of geometrical reason) and, on the other, his desire to save the truth-claims of religion and the grounds of ethical good faith by precisely delimiting the scope and competence of reason itself.

De Man's point is that these issues cannot be grasped unless one reads *both* with the maximum degree of analytical care and precision, *and* with an eye to those rhetorical devices which make it impossible, finally, to maintain any such clear-cut distinction of realms. 'Why is it', he asks, 'that texts that attempt the articulation of epistemology with persuasion turn out to be inconclusive about their own intelligibility in the same manner and for the same reasons that produce allegory?' (*PAP*, p. 2). And again, more succinctly: 'What is it, in a rigorous epistemology, that makes it impossible to decide whether its exposition is a proof or an allegory?' (p. 5). These questions may seem to be 'merely' rhetorical in the sense that they invite a sceptical response, i.e. that all forms of demonstrative 'proof', all truth-claims or orders of logical reasoning (even those practised *more geometrico*) will at last come down to so many instances of suasive or performative rhetoric. But it is important to be clear that this is not at all the lesson that de Man draws from his reading of Pascal. On the contrary: he treats it as a matter of necessity – a prime obligation on the reader's part – that thinking should *as far as possible* respect the different orders of validity or truth-claim laid down by the classical distinction between logic, grammar and rhetoric. For this model provides the only adequate terms of analysis for a deconstructive reading that sets out to reveal the limits of any such rationalist paradigm when applied to texts as complex and rhetorically self-aware as those of Pascal.

One can therefore see why de Man's later writings (notably 'The Resistance to Theory') show a marked preoccupation with topics that arise in the discourse of rationalist metaphysics. The following passage is perhaps the clearest statement of this interest, as well as suggesting how Spinoza stands out as a figure central to this entire history of thought, though curiously absent from de Man's account of it.

> Seventeenth-century epistemology, at the moment when the relationship between philosophy and mathematics is particularly close, holds up the language of what it calls geometry (*mos geometricus*), and which in fact includes the homogeneous concatenation between space, time and number, as the sole model of coherence and economy . . . This is a clear instance of the interconnection between a science of the phenomenal world and a science of language conceived as definitional logic, the precondition for a correct axiomatic-deductive, synthetic reasoning . . . [But] this leaves open the question, within the confines of the *trivium* itself, of the relationship between grammar, rhetoric and logic. And this is the point at which [rhetoric] intervenes as a decisive but unsettling element which, in a variety of modes and aspects, disrupts the inner balance of the model and, consequently,

its extension to the outside world as well. (*RT*, p. 13)

These remarks have an obvious pertinence and force when applied to Spinoza's philosophy. They help to explain how his work can find room for those two distinct theories of mind and language – a thoroughgoing rationalist monism and a version of *Ideologiekritik* based on the analysis of errors, falsehoods and fictions – which have so often divided the commentators. And they also point toward the close relationship that exists between Spinoza's political thinking and his treatment of language as a prime source of intellectual confusion or 'inadequate ideas'.

For it is clear from what Spinoza has to say on this topic that any resistance to the obfuscating powers of language, ideology, commonsense belief and so forth will involve on the one hand a rational critique of the interests that conspire to produce such confusion, and on the other an analysis of language itself carried out by means of a critical (demystifying) rhetoric. Thus 'words are formed according to popular fancy and intelligence, and are, therefore, signs of things as existing in the imagination, not as existing in the understanding' (*OIU*, p. 33). But the only hope of locating such errors – and thus of providing a remedy – is a method that would somehow formulate *in language* those truths (supposedly self-evident to reason) which language does its utmost to obscure or distort. And this predicament is one that repeats itself in every aspect of Spinoza's thought. Thus his theory of truth has struck some critics – Jonathan Bennett intermittently among them – as trivial (or simply invalid) since it leaves no room for matters of contingent fact, i.e. truths that apply to the way things are in the world, and which cannot be either confirmed or falsified by appealing to essences, necessary attributes, eternal ideas or whatever. For Bennett, in short,

> many of Spinoza's philosophical moves are invalid if there is no contingency: for example, his uses of the concept of a thing's *essence*, meaning those of its properties which it could not possibly lack, are flattened into either falsehood or vacuous truth if there are no contingent truths; because then every property of every thing is essential to it.[31]

But then the question must arise as to just what is left of Spinoza's philosophy if one substracts the high metaphysical truth-claims and attempts to salvage a credible version in accordance with modern (post-Kantian or analytical) precepts. And the same applies to Spinoza's doctrine of 'adequate ideas' as somehow consisting in a perfect correspondence (more exactly: an absolute identity) of bodily and mental states, but also as resulting from the mind's innate power to transcend the limits of phenomenal experience. In each case one's reading will at some point encounter a moment of choice between radically opposed interpretations which cannot be decided by appealing to the evidence of this or that crucial passage.

As we have seen, this produces some marked divergences among the present-day commentators, with some (like Althusser) electing to pursue the high road of theory while others (like Deleuze) interpret Spinoza as a thoroughgoing radical materialist. Then again, there is the question of how we should read those notoriously difficult statements in Book V of the *Ethics* having to do with 'eternal ideas', the 'third kind of knowledge', and 'the intellectual love of God'. Opinions range from Bennett's attitude of downright contemptuous dismissal, through various attempts to 'save' these doctrines by recasting them in a less metaphysical form, to the case argued by Alan Donagan in his recent study, where they are presented – albeit with certain reservations – as the crowning statement of principles intrinsic to Spinoza's entire system of thought.[32] What these debates have in common is a deep disagreement as to how far theory – or pure reason – can detach itself from the errors, uncertainties and pressures of day-to-day contingent or historical circumstance. And the response to this question hinges very largely on the role that language is conceived to play in the production or communication of adequate ideas. For if language is indeed – as Spinoza argues – a deceptive and unreliable medium ('since we form many conceptions in accordance with confused arrangements of words in the memory, dependent on particular bodily conditions' (*OIU*, p. 33), it is none the less the only means available for tracking those confusions to their source and arriving at a better, more adequate knowledge.

It would, to say the least, be a somewhat parochial line of approach that treated these questions solely with regard to their relevance in the context of present-day literary theory. On the contrary, as I have argued: they are posed inescapably by every form of philosophical enquiry that aims to do more than just reflect or reinforce some existing doctrinal consensus. In short, they have defined the very project and self-image of philosophy, starting out from Plato's seminal distinction between *doxa* and *episteme*, or received opinion as opposed to those truths attained through the exercise of reason. But it is only in recent years – with the advent of 'postmodern', neo-pragmatist, or other such anti-philosophical movements of thought – that this claim has been expressly disowned in favour of a straightforward conformist appeal to consensus values and beliefs. So I should not wish to argue – or be taken as having argued – that these issues are of special and unique concern to the warring schools of current literary-critical debate. But I have thought it worth pointing out at some length (and mainly for the benefit of literary theorists) that much of this debate is prefigured in controversies on and around Spinoza's work. It therefore remains for me to follow this argument through and suggest more precisely what the deconstructors, post-structuralists, New Historicists and others might have to learn from a reading of Spinoza.

One major point on which these critics divide is the issue of historical understanding in relation to theory, especially those high-powered versions of theory – Marxist or otherwise – that claim what amounts to a privileged epistemological status, a position somehow outside and above the contingencies of lived experience. Such is the stance adopted by philosophers like Althusser and Macherey, and resisted with equal tenacity and force by the recent school of radical anti-theorists, among them Deleuze, Foucault and (more ambivalently) the New Historicists. What these latter have in common – despite their seeming disparities of style and approach – is a deep suspicion of all such claims to comprehend history from a cognitive standpoint possessed of some superior knowledge, theory or mode of 'meta-narrative' grasp. That is to say, they all reject the overweening truth-claims of an 'Enlightenment' discourse which supposedly embodies the worst – the most repressive, monological or doctrinaire – aspects of instrumental reason. Hence Foucault's well-known aversion to Marxism in whatever refined or sophisticated form, as well as Deleuze's crusade against theory in the name of the 'Body-without-Organs' and its long repressed repertoire of polymorphous-perverse pleasures. That Deleuze can cite Spinoza as his single greatest ally in this same crusade – and thus turn the tables completely on theorists like Althusser and Macherey – is perhaps the most ironic chapter to date in a reception-history full of such strange reversals. But one could equally point to the New Historicists – a school, to my knowledge, quite untouched by any direct Spinozist influence – and argue that here also there has been a move 'against theory' and 'back to history' which raises all the questions that Spinoza first raised about the kinds and modalities of critical understanding.[33] In fact – as I suggested in my opening chapter – it makes little sense to ask whether or not Spinoza 'influenced' the various schools of modern hermeneutics, critical theory or interpretive method. For these disciplines are so fundamentally indebted to a work like the *Tractatus Theologico-Politicus* that their later development is scarcely thinkable without taking account of the issues first posed in Spinoza's work.

With regard to the New Historicism, those issues can be stated very briefly as follows. If there is one principle that serves to identify this otherwise quite disparate movement, it is the maxim 'Always contextualize!', or 'Always read in such a way as to open up so-called "literary" works to the widest possible range of intertextual comparisons and cultural cross-references'. The effect of such readings – as seen in Stephen Greenblatt's various essays on Renaissance poetry and drama – is to challenge the idea that literature should enjoy a privileged status *vis-à-vis* those other kinds of text (historical, documentary, sociological etc.) which have standardly been treated as so much ancillary or 'background' material for the critic's selective use.[34] And along with this levelling of the genre-distinction between literature and non-literature goes a similar move to treat literary theory as just another kind of writing, one whose high truth-claims must invite suspicion in so far as they affect a superior vantage-point of cognitive mastery and power. Thus the New Historicists follow Foucault (and ultimately Nietzsche) in their principled mistrust of 'totalizing' narratives, their treatment of history as a force-field of contending rhetorical and interpretive strategies, and their consequent rejection of theory – especially Marxist theory – as an enterprise premised on false ideas of what criticism ought to be about. It is worth noting here that in these respects they differ somewhat from their British 'cultural materialist' counterparts, most of whom acknowledge a strong Marxist influence and continue to practise a form of *Ideologiekritik*, albeit one that has also taken lessons from Foucault and French post-structuralist thinking.[35]

So the New Historicists are clearly a part of that widespread movement 'against theory' which has played such a prominent and well-publicized role in recent critical debate. More specifically, their work repudiates the notion – so vital to Althusser and the adepts of Marxist 'theoretical practice' – that thinking can break with ideology (or 'lived experience') to the point of establishing its own autonomy as a discourse of immanent critique. The following passage by Terry Eagleton – written very much under Althusser's influence in the mid-1970s – may help to recall just what this claim amounted to, as well as bringing out the markedly Spinozist structure of ideas that characterized that whole episode. 'Literature', Eagleton argues,

> is the most revealing mode of experiential access to ideology that we possess . . . It is a mode more immediate than that of science, and more coherent than that normally available in daily living itself. Literature presents itself in this sense as 'midway' between the distancing rigour of scientific knowledge and the vivid but loose contingencies of the 'lived' itself. Unlike science, literature appropriates the real as it is given in ideological forms, but does so in a way which produces an illusion of the spontaneously, unmediatedly real . . . Like science, literature appropriates its object by the deployment of certain categories and protocols – in its case, *genre*, symbol, convention and so forth. As with science, those categories are themselves the elaborated product of perception and representation; but in the case of literature that elaboration is not carried to the point of producing *concepts* – rather to the point of certain forms which, while performing an *analogous* function to that of concepts in science, tend simultaneously to conceal and naturalize themselves, standing in apparently intimate, spontaneous relation to the 'materials' they produce.[36]

This passage – like so many in Althusser and Macherey – could be taken as a point-for-point transposition of Spinozist arguments into the idiom of latter-day Marxist debate. And it also shows very clearly just what is involved when literary critics come out against 'theory' in favour of a more open-ended, pragmatic or contextualist approach to questions of historical understanding. Their argument takes rise from the root conviction that no such method – indeed, no *method* as such – can possibly do justice to the sheer variety of possible 'fits' between language, ideology and the realm of lived experience. To this extent they are fully in agreement with a thinker like Rorty, one for whom any attempt to 'cut nature at the joints' – any quest for some ultimate conceptual scheme that would perfectly match or mirror the structure of reality – is inherently a hopeless and misguided endeavour. And of course their work is much indebted to Foucault, especially those late texts (like the *History of Sexuality*) which make a programmatic point of eschewing all truth-claims, the better to reveal the various discourses of power/knowledge that contend for mastery at any given time. Here again it is Nietzsche – the 'new Nietzsche' of current post-structuralist fashion – whose sceptical genealogies of truth and method are the starting-point for a wholesale critique of such values carried out under the sign of history, rhetoric and counter-Enlightenment thinking.[37]

Yet one could argue that Spinoza belongs just as much within this tradition as he does within the high theoreticist line espoused by thinkers like Althusser and Eagleton. For it soon becomes evident to any reader of the *Tractatus Theologico-Politicus* that this text raises questions about history, politics and the 'worldly' or situated character of human understanding which in many ways prefigure the New Historicist approach. Certainly there is a tension – perhaps, at the limit, an ultimate conflict of aims – between Spinoza's quest for 'adequate' or 'eternal' ideas and his view of philosophy as a discipline that answers to immediate socio-political concerns, and is thus obliged to make constant allowance for the various *ineliminable* sources of error and confusion in human affairs. But if this problem remains unresolved in Spinoza one can see how its negative counterpart persists in the work of those critics who reject all versions of the appeal to theory but continue to write *as if* from a standpoint where the failures of theory would be shown up at last through demonstrative reasoning. Thus when Rorty and Fish deny that it is possible to criticize existing consensus-values from a position outside or above those values, they fail to perceive how this very line of argument commits them to holding a distinctive *theory* about the non-availability of any such thing.

This is the point that Derrida makes so tellingly in his essay on Foucault's *Madness and Civilization*. It is also, I think, what Althusser means by his cryptic statement that 'ideology has no outside (for itself), but at the same time is nothing but outside (for science and reality)'.[38] One could paraphrase this statement roughly as follows: (1) that we are always 'in' ideology to the extent that human knowledge is inevitably timebound, partial, and a product of specific historical conditions; (2) that any theory addressed to those conditions will need to take account of its own constitutive (ideological) interests; but also (3) that this form of 'theoretical practice' can at times give rise to a different mode of knowledge, one that involves an immanent critique of the errors, illusions and 'commonsense' ideas that compose the realm of ideology (or 'lived experience'). Taken together, these three propositions form the basis of Althusser's critical epistemology. But they also – he would argue – provide the only means of justifying theory *both* in terms of its relevance to real-world political events *and* in respect of its further claim to give a knowledge of those events which cannot be attained by situated historical agents (or subjects 'in' ideology). For otherwise there is no resisting the pragmatist argument that theory must always reduce to what is presently thinkable within this or that interpretive community, or – more simply – what is 'good in the way of belief'. To avoid this conclusion one has to explain how criticism can preserve its worldly or situated character while not thereby giving grounds for the charge that it can *do no more* than reflect or reproduce existing forms of knowledge. And here it is worth recalling Althusser's claim that 'Spinoza explained all this [i.e. the relationship between "science" and "ideology"] two centuries before Marx, who practised it but without explaining it in detail'.[39]

The New Historicists would no doubt reject such ideas as belonging to that old 'meta-narrative' paradigm which elevated reason to a sovereign status above all the various competing discourses of ideological representation. But in so doing they ignore the simple point – as Derrida remarks of Foucault – that 'since the revolution against reason, from the moment it is articulated, can operate only *within* reason, it always has the limited scope of what is called, precisely in the language of a department of *internal* affairs, a disturbance' (Derrida, *CHM*, p. 36). That is to say, one cannot offer a single assertion in support of the case 'against theory' which would not bear witness to the contrary by virtue of its own propositional structure, as well as its role in a sequence of articulated argument. And from this it follows – according to Derrida – that 'a history, that is, an archaeology against reason doubtless cannot be written, for, despite all appearances to the contrary, the concept of history has always been a rational one' (p. 36). Of course this should not be understood in terms of some grand Hegelian synthesis, some ultimate convergence of history and reason with the advent of Absolute Knowledge. Nor can it be grasped solely by reference to that aspect of Spinoza's thinking which equates the possession of adequate ideas with the mind's innate power to transcend mere contingencies of time and place. On the contrary: what Derrida is arguing here is that reason (or theory) provides the only means of resisting such premature absolutes in so far as it enables thought to perceive the blindspots of prejudice, the self-imposed errors and aporias, that result from the drive to conceptualize history in accordance with a sovereign narrative schema or rational masterplan.

Hence what he sees as the complex double irony of Foucault's reading of Descartes, a reading that denounces the Cartesian gesture of rational containment or mastery, but which itself has no choice but to repeat that gesture in its every last detail of argument. For this is not, Derrida writes, 'a specifically Cartesian weakness . . . not a defect or mystification linked to a determined historical structure, but rather is an essential and universal necessity from which no discourse can escape, for it belongs to the meaning of meaning' (p. 54). In which case not only is Foucault deluded in thinking to escape this necessity but his writing achieves its greatest critical force in precisely those passages where the truth-claims of reason are pressed to their limits and beyond.

4 The Claim of Reason: Spinoza as a Left-Cartesian

It is here that Spinoza's work holds lessons for present-day literary theory. He brings out more clearly than any other thinker the way in which questions of a high metaphysical nature – 'ultimate' questions about knowledge, truth, the structure and modalities of human understanding – may none the less connect with issues in the realm of real-world history and politics. But at the same time he shows that one cannot just sidestep those ultimate questions by adopting a postmodern-pragmatist line or assuming (like the New Historicists) that they will simply drop out of the picture when we recognize how various are the contexts, discourses or systems of value that operate within any given cultural community. This is why the best commentators on Spinoza – with one or two exceptions, notably Jonathan Bennett – have always felt obliged to give some account of his life-history and political involvements, even when their first concern is to elucidate matters of a 'purely' philosophical import. And conversely, it has meant that writers more committed to the 'life and times' approach have found themselves inevitably drawn to raise questions in the province of speculative reason.

Alan Donagan speaks for the former tendency when he begins his recent book with a short section – less than three pages – under the title 'What Students of Spinoza's Thought Need to Know about his Life, and What They Need Not'.[1] According to Donagan, it is enough to have the following facts in mind: that Spinoza's family was of Sephardic Jewish origin; that his father (a noted free-thinker in religious and political matters) had left Portugal as a result of Catholic persecution; that the family had then settled in Amsterdam, where the Jewish community was well established and enjoyed a large measure of freedom guaranteed by the Estates General; that the young Spinoza acquired a reputation for heterodox thinking, with the result that he was finally expelled from the Synagogue, cursed and denied all contact with other members; that his ideas occasioned lively controversy among a small though highly influential group of philosophers, scientists and political thinkers; and really nothing much beyond these basic points of information. In short, Donagan takes it that anyone *seriously* interested in Spinoza's philosophy will have little use for the kind of historical-contextualist approach that insists on tracing back ideas to their source in this or that socio-political milieu. 'Generally, his life was of a piece with what he wrote: discoveries about its details – apart from facts about his intellectual exchanges – bear dubiously on disputed questions about what he thought' (Donagan, pp. 10–11). Furthermore, 'it does not appear that any question about his political theories will be resolved by discovering what he did or said on issues of practical politics' (p.11). And indeed, Donagan's book respects this principle by concentrating on issues in the Spinozist philosophy of mind and knowledge, and by treating the politics mainly with a view to its role within the larger (metaphysical) scheme of things.

For it is Donagan's belief – one shared by Stuart Hampshire and other recent commentators – that metaphysics, despite all the criticisms levelled against it by philosophers from Kant to the logical positivists, still has a claim to articulate questions (and even provide answers) which cannot be expressed in any other form. Thus, although he remarks certain lapses in Spinoza's reasoning – at least when treated from a modern analytic standpoint – Donagan is a good deal readier than Bennett to regard them as local and corrigible errors, standing in need of only minor adjustments to render them thoroughly acceptable. And this goes along with Donagan's view that Book V of the *Ethics* cannot be dismissed as (in Bennett's words) 'an unmitigated and seemingly unmotivated disaster', or a sad decline from logical rigour into specious pseudo-profundity. In fact he is able to present these doctrines – leading up to Spinoza's most problematic statements on the 'intellectual love of God' -- as both a fitting conclusion to the *Ethics* as a whole and a worthy example for the better conduct of our social and individual lives. Thus: 'if God is what Spinoza believed he is, there is nothing greater to which human beings can aspire than to love him without desiring that he should love them in return' (p. 206). And this follows, in Donagan's view, from the principle which stands at the heart of all

Spinoza's reasoning: namely, that the highest good of intellectual
enquiry is 'the very Love with which God loves himself, not insofar
as he is infinite, but insofar as he can be explicated by the human
Mind's essence, considered *sub specie aeternitatis*' (p. 206). At this
point – in his book's closing sentence – one must suppose that
Donagan's detailed reservations have at last been overcome, and
that the viewpoint thus achieved is offered as a genuine and ultimate
good, rather than a mere re-statement or paraphrase of Spinoza's
thinking.

So it is not hard to see why Donagan should reject any version
of the (old or new) historicist claim that such doctrines can only be
interpreted through a knowledge of the cultural contexts, material
conditions, pressures of circumstance etc., that first gave rise to
them. This approach would go clean against his conviction that
Spinoza's metaphysical system – or a large part of it – lays claim to
an order of essentially *timeless* validity and truth which cannot be
accounted for on any such reductive terms. Yet there are several
passages in his book where Donagan does make concessions to the
case for reading Spinoza 'in context', or for treating his ideas as to
some extent the product of their own specific time and place. Thus:
'except with respect to its principles, Spinoza's political theory
cannot be appraised simply as philosophy; for, as he acknowledged,
all political theory must be tested by what he calls "experience" –
that is, by history, recent or remote' (Donagan, p. 174). Now it
might well be argued that this passage in fact concedes rather little;
that it applies only to Spinoza's political writings, and to these in
so far as they cannot be connected with the 'principles' that characterize his deeper (i.e. philosophical) thought. In such matters it may
be useful – Donagan thinks – to turn aside briefly from conceptual
exegesis and offer some account of Spinoza's relationship to other
political theorists (notably Hobbes and Machiavelli), along with a
handful of relevant facts about his own life-history. But this doesn't
mean that one has thereby achieved a more adequate understanding
of Spinoza's ideas, or 'explained' them to the point where metaphysics gives way to politics, history or the sociology of knowledge. For
it is important not to lose sight of the difference between these two
activities: on the one hand that of giving *reasons* (or offering conceptual justification) for this or that item of Spinozist thought, and on
the other that of *explaining* such ideas through various modes of
causal, determinist, or socio-historical argument. On Donagan's
view only the former should count as a properly philosophical

reading. For the rest is merely background, anecdotal evidence, 'history of ideas' or whatever; relevant to those whose interests lie in that direction, but of no possible use when it comes to assessing the validity (or otherwise) of Spinoza's claims. And of course this distinction finds warrant in the *Ethics*, where Spinoza teaches that 'the more an affect is known to us, the more it is in our power, and the less the mind is acted on by it'; or again, that 'an affect which is a passion [i.e. both passive and confused] ceases to be one as soon as we conceive a clear and distinct idea of it' (*E* V, P 3c & *E* V, P 3; cited by Donagan, p. 186). In which case Donagan would seem to be justified in maintaining this order of priorities, respecting Spinoza's metaphysical truth-claims, and not yielding ground to historicist arguments for the time-bound or socially-conditioned character of all human understanding.

Nevertheless, there are passages where his commentary runs into problems for exactly this reason; where the analytic way of 'clear and distinct ideas' comes up against a knowledge of history, contingency, time and change which tends to subvert (or at least somewhat to complicate) its own *a priori* claims. Thus Spinoza writes:

> the true cognition we have of good and evil is only abstract or universal, and the judgement which we make about the order of things and the connection of causes, in order that we may be able to determine what in the present is good and evil for us, is imaginary rather than real. (*E* IV, P 62s)

Donagan cites this sentence in support of his case that there is in fact a reasonable working model of human self-knowledge, motivation and desire to be found in the *Ethics*, and furthermore that this model – though amounting to a kind of philosophical anthropology – also joins up in a convincing way with Spinoza's metaphysical doctrines. Thus he glosses the above passage by remarking that 'in most human beings, imaginative ideas of real things present to them and causing sadness will exclude abstract reasoned ideas of the harmfulness of the excessive pleasure that sadness will restrict' (Donagan, p. 187). But one could just as well read it as entailing the opposite conclusion, i.e. that 'true cognition' (or knowledge arrived at by way of adequate ideas) is indeed 'only abstract and universal', and therefore cannot have any application in matters of practical ethics, politics, psychology etc. For as the passage makes clear, these latter must be treated as belonging to the order of 'imaginary' ideas, concepts that we form *sub specie durationis*, or in accordance with the limits necessarily imposed by our existence as creatures of history and circumstance. That is to say, what we grasp of 'the order of things' or 'the connection of causes' is always the product of a partial and short-term purview, a finite mode of understanding which cannot attain to the status of 'true cognition'. And this would make it hard to avoid the conclusion that Spinoza's metaphysical doctrines – those ideas which, according to Donagan, constitute the heart of his philosophy – can have little bearing on matters of real-life ethical or social concern.

This is not to say that Donagan would endorse such a reading of his own arguments. In fact, as I have mentioned, he does make a case for regarding the Spinozist theory of knowledge as capable of at least some generalized extension to the realm of practical choices and commitments. Thus 'what he [Spinoza] calls "dictates of reason" are descriptions, in conditional form, of how a model human being who is the adequate cause of his own conduct, and whose ideas of his own conduct are adequate, conducts himself' (p. 167). But this amounts to nothing more than a circular re-statement of those same metaphysical doctrines in a language of the utmost abstract generality. What Donagan evidently cannot concede – in keeping with his own doctrinal stance – is that factors of a merely contingent or historical nature should bear *in any crucial or decisive way* on the interpretation of Spinoza's thought. In other words, his book is at the opposite extreme from a reading in the New Historicist mode, one that would attach no importance to questions of validity, truth or right reason, since these would be seen as values produced within a given context of cultural debate, and hence as lacking all claim to determine what should count as an adequate 'philosophical' treatment. It is for this reason that Spinoza makes such an interesting test-case for the various interpretive schools, methods and theories that have grown up over the past few decades. Pursued in one direction – as has often happened – his thinking leads to a high plateau of metaphysical truth from which all questions of historical 'background' become either totally invisible or shrouded in the mists of error, contingency and 'knowledge of imagination'. Yet there is also, as we have seen, that 'other' dimension of Spinoza's work that insists on the primacy of historical understanding (especially as regards questions of scriptural exegesis); which constantly adverts to the social, political and material conditions of knowledge-production; and which thus anticipates much of what the current New Historicists have to say. Without wanting to push this parallel too far I would at least argue that it helps us to see how much is left out of the picture *on principle* by any reading, like Donagan's, firmly committed to the high metaphysical view.

But it is equally the case that Spinoza's philosophy demands much more in the way of rigorous intellectual engagement than could ever be provided by a New Historicist reading. And this applies not only to what Donagan would consider his core metaphysical doctrines, but also to those passages that do clearly call for some form of socio-historical commentary. On the one hand it is useful to be reminded that metaphysical systems don't take wing in some heaven of pure thought; that (for instance) the rationalist theory of mind and the ideal of reasoning *more geometrico* were seen throughout Europe – and especially in Holland at the time – as embodiments of a liberal-humanist outlook opposed to all forms of religious dogmatism.[2] But again, these reminders will serve no purpose if they halt at the point of merely drawing comparisons, multiplying relevant 'contexts', or reducing Spinoza's arguments to one more episode in the history of shifting discursive regimes envisaged by a postmodern sceptic like Foucault. What is wrong with so much recent thinking in this area is precisely the idea that one can only get 'back' to history by renouncing all forms of theoretical enquiry, all versions of *Ideologiekritik*, or all attempts to distinguish the kinds and levels of knowledge involved in philosophical, historical, and literary texts. For the ultimate result of this levelling process – if it were really carried as far as these thinkers suggest – would be to cast criticism adrift on the seas of a limitless 'intertextuality' with no anchor-points for argued debate on the merits of this or that reading.

To some extent no doubt this reaction took rise from the widespread disenchantment with Marxist thinking in the wake of 1968, and more specifically the sense that theorists like Althusser had failed to meet the challenge or live up to their role as a self-professed intellectual vanguard. As a result there emerged a whole range of alternative discourses, all of them avowedly 'post'-theoretical and united in a deep mistrust of Marxism and other such supposedly 'totalizing' creeds. This retreat from grand theory went along with the claim – as enounced most dramatically in a work like Foucault's *Madness and Civilization* – to be somehow speaking up for those various oppressed or minority discourses that had so far been either consigned to oblivion or treated as mere aberrations from the path of enlightened secular critique. But once again this raises the awkward question (as Derrida puts it in his reading of Foucault) as to how one could possibly advance such claims in a language that renounced all rational constraints, all the standards of discursive coherence or logico-semantic entailment. For a discourse that truly achieved this condition would be lacking in precisely that critical force – that capacity to question received values and normative ideas – which Foucault believes to be the sole justification for any such activity. It is also worth recalling what Derrida argues in his latest (and most forceful) response to John Searle: that although any given speech-act may function across a vast (and potentially infinite) range of conceivable contexts, this doesn't at all mean that philosophy can relax its standards of analytic rigour and henceforth take refuge in a vague appeal to the open-ended character of speech-act conventions.[3] On the contrary, it is only by treating problematic cases with the utmost *conceptual* precision that theory can arrive at the point of enouncing certain general propositions about the limits of its own enterprise.

It seems to me that this argument has a wider application to the New Historicism and kindred schools where the current terminology of 'context' and 'discourse' takes on a kind of talismanic virtue. For the result of such thinking – a consequence quite knowingly embraced by its proponents – is to cut language off from any means of assessing its various distinctive orders of validity-claim, and thus to reduce it (as happens with Fish and Rorty) to a dead level of suasive or rhetorical effect. This is how it has come about that, in de Man's words, 'the resistance to theory . . . which is also a resistance to reading, appears in its most rigorous and theoretically elaborated form among the theoreticians of reading who dominate the contemporary theoretical scene' (*RT*, p. 13). One way of grasping de Man's point here is to unpack the various meanings contained in this string of seemingly redundant or pleonastic terms. These critics are still theorists (or 'theoreticians') to the extent that they offer, like Fish, a generalized account of the reading process which in turn links up with speech-act philosophy, hermeneutics and rhetoric in its widest, most inclusive sense. More than that: their work can indeed be called 'rigorous' and 'theoretically elaborated' in so far as it provides a persuasive and – on its own terms at least – a simply *irrefutable* case for believing that theory can never do more than reproduce existing consensus-ideas of what counts as a competent, qualified reading. That is to say, the whole drift of such theories is to show that conventions go all the way down; that meaning is a product of interpretive codes (or moves in the game of reader-response) that define the very nature of literary competence; and therefore that it simply cannot make sense for theory to reject these conventions in favour of some other, more 'radical' line of approach.

But it is precisely de Man's point that this argument involves a 'resistance to theory' which is also and inseparably a 'resistance to reading', or a means of avoiding those obstacles that rhetoric puts in the way of a straightforward consensus-theory of meaning and truth. For Fish's case will only seem convincing – only carry the kind of knock-down force it is clearly intended to possess – if one accepts his implicit confinement of rhetoric to language in its suasive, performative or strictly non-cognitive aspects. It is by means of this concealed premise, this avoidance of what de Man calls the 'epistemology of tropes' (i.e. rhetoric as a form of immanent critique) that Fish can always show, or persuasively 'prove', how pointless and redundant are the truth-claims of theory. And so it turns out, in de Man's words, that 'the resistance to theory is in fact a resistance to reading, a resistance that is perhaps at its most effective . . . in the methodologies that call themselves theories of reading but nonethless avoid the function they claim as their object' (*RT*, p. 15). For what emerges from a properly rhetorical close-reading is the fact that these two dimensions of rhetoric (the suasive and the cognitive, or the performative and the epistemological) are bound up with each other at every point and cannot be neatly separated out in the manner that Fish requires. In short – as de Man argues most forcefully in his essay on Pascal – one has to take account of those structures of sense 'which are no less rhetorical and no less at work in literary texts, but which are of the order of persuasion by *proof* rather than persuasion by seduction' (*RT*, p. 18). For otherwise there is simply no accounting for the way that texts can and do have a power to resist our most stubborn preconceptions, or to change our minds by not falling in with this or that prevailing consensus, ideology or settled habit of response.

Curiously enough, one can find what looks like a strong statement of exactly this position in the works that Fish wrote before arriving at his current neo-pragmatist standpoint. These books (*Surprised By Sin*, his study of Milton, and its sequel *Self-Consuming Artefacts*) were aimed squarely against the formalist presumption that literary meaning was somehow objectively 'there' in the text, embodied in certain distinctive attributes of form, structure or style.[4] The American New Critics had raised this belief into a matter of doctrinal orthodoxy. For them, the poem was a 'verbal icon', a structure of inwrought 'irony', 'paradox' or other such privileged tropes, and hence sealed off in a realm of timeless aesthetic values indifferent to the mere vicissitudes of reader-response.[5] Fish set out to counter this high formalist position by proposing what he called an 'affective stylistics', an account of what happened from moment to moment in the process of interpreting texts, negotiating various problems or obstacles, and often coming up with ingenious solutions in face of some particular interpretive crux. In the Milton book this approach went along with a claim that the reader was thereby placed in the same situation as characters in the poem like Satan, Adam and Eve, confronted with a series of complex and wholly unpredictable choices which they – characters and readers alike – had to make on the instant and without any guidance from rules or conventions already in place. And with *Self-Consuming Artefacts* – as the title suggests – this approach was extended to various poems and prose-texts which (as Fish read them) could be seen to subvert any notion of autonomous, self-possessed 'form' by bringing the interpreter up against a series of blocks or resistances to easy comprehension, and thus giving rise to a constant quest for new and more adaptable strategies of reading. So on the face of it nothing could be further removed from Fish's later line of argument, his insistence that texts can only be construed in accordance with some preexisting set of interpretive values and protocols. In fact he would appear to have swung right over from a position that maximizes reader-involvement, unpredictability and *resistance* in the text, to one that completely rejects these notions in favour of a blanket consensus-theory where nothing could ever come as a surprise since everything is always known in advance.

But this shift of allegiances will look less drastic if one recalls what de Man has to say about the effect of any theory that equates rhetoric with language in its purely suasive dimension, and which thus avoids taking cognizance of rhetoric in the other, more unsettling or troublesome sense of that word. For it can then be seen that Fish has not so much renounced his earlier convictions as devised a different model of reader-response, one that is still conceived in *psychological* rather than epistemological terms. That is to say, he has simply switched from a theory that focuses on what goes on 'in' the individual reader to one that takes the whole community of readers (or those properly qualified to judge) as its final court of appeal.[6] In neither case does he leave any room for those tensions that arise – as de Man argues – between rhetoric considered as a mode of persuasion and rhetoric as a form of immanent critique (or an 'epistemology of tropes') that inherently tends to question or problematize those same persuasive effects. Thus, although the early Fish thinks always in terms of resistances, obstacles or blocks – textual features that get in the way of some habitual mode of reading – still those effects are treated psychologically, as conflicts that arise from some local interference of attitudes, mind-sets or readerly expectations. In short, there is no question for Fish – early or late – that language might harbour a potential for the kind of disruptive, self-critical undoing of its own rhetorical devices that de Man finds everywhere at work in the texts of literature, criticism and philosophy. His theories (both of them) are able to achieve such a high degree of persuasiveness and force precisely because they take no account of this complicating factor in the analysis of language. Hence – to repeat – de Man's observation that 'to empty rhetoric of its epistemological impact is possible only because its tropological, figural functions are being bypassed. It is as if . . . rhetoric could be isolated from the generality that grammar and logic have in common and considered as a mere correlative of an illocutionary power' (*RT*, pp. 18–19). For the upshot of all such arguments – whether advanced under the banner of reader-response theory or that of 'interpretive communities' – is to render it strictly unthinkable that language should muster an effective resistance to the workings of suasive ideology.

I have suggested that this issue has a relevance far beyond the current controversy sparked off by neo-pragmatists like Fish and Rorty. It is also the single most important question raised by Foucauldian genealogies of power/knowledge, by the various forms of 'postmodern' revolt against theory, reason or Enlightenment values, and finally by critics of a New Historicist persuasion who likewise reject such notions in favour of a thoroughgoing contextualist approach. This is where Spinoza comes in, so to speak, as a thinker who anticipated much of this recent debate, and who did so, moreover, in historical circumstances which gave his arguments an added urgency and force. To this extent there would be some warrant for a New Historicist reading that showed small interest in his 'purely' philosophical doctrines, focusing instead on those various material factors – economic, social, political etc. – which in turn took shape in the multiple 'discourses' surrounding his life and work. Such an approach would have the merit of illuminating aspects of Spinoza's thought that are either ignored or treated as so much anecdotal 'background' by philosophers in the mainstream tradition. But there would still come a point where it had to engage with issues in Spinoza's theory of mind, his account of the various kinds or modalities of knowledge, and his treatment of problems in the realm of historical understanding. For these issues are posed inescapably by *any* reading of Spinoza's work, no matter how sceptical that reading might be with regard to questions of ultimate validity or truth.

That is to say, one cannot grasp the relevance of this or that historical 'context' without also raising a series of *theoretical* (and eminently Spinozist) questions concerning – for instance – the conditions of possibility for historical knowledge in general, the relation between 'science' and 'ideology' as modes of discursive production, and the problematic status of theory itself as a discourse that claims access to 'adequate ideas', but which does so always from a partial or situated viewpoint, one that must therefore partake to some degree of the limits placed upon all human understanding. Of course the New Historicist could argue that this last point is enough to discredit the entire theoretical enterprise, or at least to show it up as naive and self-deluding in so far as it ignores the plain fact of its own historically-contingent character. But to take this line is also to evade the central question of all Spinoza's work: namely, whether criticism could have any purpose – any sense of its own distinctive aims and powers – without presupposing the basic distinction between truth and falsehood, knowledge and ideology, or adequate and inadequate ideas. For these are not just so many optional notions in the service of an outworn 'Enlightenment' creed, one that has now succumbed to the advent of a postmodern-pragmatist cultural consensus, and should therefore be abandoned without further ado. Rather – as Derrida shows in his reading of Foucault – they are truth-claims built into the very structure of all argumentative discourse, and never more so than when criticism seeks to interrogate its own grounding suppositions in the hope of revealing the power-interests that mask behind a rhetoric of pure, disinterested reason.

Spinoza was the first to articulate this self-understanding of critical philosophy as a discourse that was obligated *both* to take account of its own historical conditions of emergence *and* to subject those same conditions to a form of rigorous immanent critique. It is therefore understandable that his work has given rise to such widely differing interpretations. In fact, as I have argued, one can trace Spinoza's influence in just about every school and tendency of present-day critical thinking. Sometimes that influence is overtly acknowledged, as by Althusser, Macherey, and Deleuze. More often – as with the New Historicists – it is implicit in various dominant ideas about language, ideology, the power of cultural representations, and the way that forms of religious belief work to legitimize structures of socio-political power. It would hardly be too much to say that Spinoza invented – or at any rate strikingly prefigured – the very terms of debate by which these present-day thinkers measure their reciprocal agreements and differences. On the one hand his philosophy provided a model for all subsequent forms of negative hermeneutics, demystifying discourse, or Marxist *Ideologiekritik*. The following passage from Macherey – one of many that might be cited in this context – will serve to demonstrate how close are the links between the Spinozist theory of truth and error and the interests of Marxist criticism.

> Spinoza's theory of liberation involves a new attitude to language; the hollow speech of the imagination must be halted, anchored; the unfinished must be endowed with form, determined (even though the indeterminate depends on a certain kind of necessity, since it can be known) . . . There is a profound difference between the vague language of the imagination and that of the text . . . [and] in this space where language confronts itself, is constructed that true distance which is the condition of any real progress – the discourse of the book. This does not mean that the book is able to become its own criticism: it gives an implicit critique of its ideological content, if only because it resists being incorporated into the flow of ideology in order to give a *determinate representation* of it. Fiction, not to be confused with illusion, is the substitute for, if not the equivalent of, knowledge. A theory of literary production must show us what the text 'knows', how it 'knows'.[7]

This leaves no doubt of Macherey's position with regard to the various issues raised in current literary-critical debate. It amounts to the strongest possible endorsement, not only of the Marxist case for treating 'science' as a mode of theoretical production quite distinct from ideology, fiction, or 'lived experience', but also of Spinoza's preeminent role in having set this enterprise on course by providing its most basic concepts and categories. But on the other hand his influence is equally strong – if seldom acknowledged as such – in the work of those critics who come out against theory in the name of a New Historicist or Cultural Materialist approach. Here also Spinoza stands out as the single most impressive early instance of a method (more exactly: a strategy of reading) the effects of which are still powerfully at work in the discourse of present-day criticism. For he was – by widespread scholarly assent – the first thinker to practise a form of textual exegesis based on a reading of canonical works (in this case the Old and New Testament scriptures) which treated them *not* as sources of revealed truth but as documents in the history of changing civil and political institutions. To this extent at least he belongs in the company of Nietzsche, Foucault and the New Historicists: those who have set out to document the workings of a 'political economy of truth', or to offer an applied 'genealogy of morals' that would analyse the social production of knowledge-effects.

II

It now remains to bring these various lines of argument together and ask more directly what critical theorists have to gain from a reading of Spinoza. I have suggested three main areas of interest where his thinking has valuable lessons to impart. Firstly there is Spinoza's theory of knowledge, one that anticipates much of what Derrida and de Man have to say about the rhetorical structures of language, the relationship between truth and error as equally determinate modes of understanding, and the way that deconstruction can lead on to questions in the realm of ideology and historical criticism. In this aspect of his thinking Spinoza provides a needful corrective to the widespread idea that deconstruction reduces philosophy to just another 'kind of writing', a licence for critics to interpret texts pretty much as they like, with no regard for the protocols of reason or logical accountability.

Secondly, Spinoza makes it clear that such practices of negative critique cannot be sustained to any purpose or effect unless they are combined with a positive commitment to principles of right understanding, social justice, or truth at the end of enquiry. This point could be made in summary style by saying that Spinoza left a double legacy: on the one hand pointing forward to Nietzsche, Foucault and the current New Historicist school, while on the other offering the first elaboration of precepts that were later developed – especially by Kant – as the basis of Enlightenment or liberal-democratic thought. But in Spinoza these two kinds of argument are so closely intertwined that one cannot make sense of his negative theses (i.e. those having to do with falsehood, error and the sources of ideological illusion) without relating them back at every point to his substantive principles in the realm of ethics, politics and social philosophy. That these are currently seen as conflicting standpoints – postmodern genealogy *versus* the claims of Enlightenment reason – is one more sign of the distance we have travelled from Spinoza's way of treating such questions.

This results in the kind of drastic antinomy to be found not only in Foucault's studies of madness in the epoch of reason, but also in the New Historicist idea that theory and history just don't mix, so that the only way to 'liberate' the hitherto repressed or marginalized voices of history is to topple theory from its privileged vantage-point and treat it as merely one discourse among others, a discourse whose only characterizing mark is its eminent capacity for self-delusion. For Spinoza, on the contrary, historical understanding can only come about through a reasoned appraisal of the causes and conditions that have worked to produce various forms of state and civil society. As Robert Duff points out:

> the political history of the Hebrews becomes in his hands a fascinating text from which principles of wide application are derived . . . Roman history, the constitution and government of Turkey, of Arragon, of Venice and Genoa, of Spain and Holland, of Portugal and China are all pressed into service to give point to some general truth.[8]

That is to say, there is always an appeal open from the detailed analysis of particular societies, political systems, or structures of state power to the principles of justice and liberal democracy against which those systems can be measured or assessed. Like Kant, Spinoza sees that these principles are far from being realized in any past or presently-existing society. But they are still indispensable if one wants to go beyond a mere descriptive or comparative account to one that raises more fundamental questions of ethics and politics alike. Although his philosophy finds no explicit role for Kantian 'ideas of pure reason' as the source of such as-yet unfulfilled political ideals, this is I think the role that these principles play: a set of regulative concepts and values which provide the only possible working basis for a critique of political institutions.

Certainly Spinoza is very far from believing, like Foucault, that 'progress' and 'enlightenment' are delusive notions, or that they operate merely as legitimizing terms for an ever more powerful and refined apparatus of social surveillance and control. As Michael Walzer has remarked, this leads Foucault to ignore the very real differences that exist between various forms of modern (post-feudal) state and civil society.[9] What Foucault offers through his all-purpose rhetoric of power/knowledge is essentially an updated version of the Hobbesian thesis that naked self-interest is the sole motivating force in human affairs, and that state authority is merely the outcome of a contract entered into for the sake of limiting its more destructive effects. Up to a point Spinoza goes along with this analysis, at least in so far as he treats social structures as marked through and through by relations of force, differentials between 'active' and 'passive' modes of being which in turn give rise to differing capacities for effective, self-promoting agency. This kinship with Hobbes comes out in his treatment of the affects or passions as issuing from an omnipresent will-to-power by which social beings – as 'finite modes' within the overall economy of causal relations – strive to maintain their highest level of intensity or (as Deleuze would have it) their maximum potential for peak experiences. But Spinoza differs very markedly from Hobbes in his conviction that it is only through the exercise of reason that individuals and collectivities alike can set about transforming 'passive' into 'active' ideas, and thus achieve a more adequate grasp of the forces that must otherwise hold them in thrall to an alien and oppressive social order.

It is on these grounds that Spinoza argues the case for democracy as the highest, most evolved or enlightened form of social existence, one that gives the greatest scope for this exercise of rational self-determination. In comparison with the other main forms – aristocratic and monarchical – it involves the least sacrifice of freely-willed assent on the part of thinking individuals, citizens who agree to relinquish some of their freedoms in the cause of maintaining civil peace and a communal *modus vivendi*. Ideally, 'if human nature were such that men desired nothing but what true reason prescribes, a society would need no laws whatsoever; for men to do of their own free will what is really for their benefit it would be enough to teach them true moral precepts' (*TPT*, p. 73). For there would then be no problem in translating ethics directly into politics, or dispensing altogether with laws, governments and other such forms of self-imposed collective restraint. But this can never be realized in practical terms since, as Spinoza says, 'no society can exist without government and force, and hence without laws to control and restrain the unruly appetites of men' (ibid). In which case there might seem to be no great difference between Spinoza's and Hobbes's views on the function of state power and the evils of anarchic individualism. But this is to ignore the crucial point about Spinoza's political thought: namely, his argument (anticipating Kant) that it is an abuse of power for the state to interfere in matters of judgement, opinion or conscience, and therefore that democracy – in so far as it respects these freedoms – proves itself the form of government best suited to the interests of reason and justice. Thus according to Spinoza:

> in a democracy . . . all make a covenant to act, *but not to judge and think*, in accordance with the common decision; that is, because all men cannot think alike, they agree that the proposal which gets the most votes shall have the force of a decree, but meanwhile retain the authority to revoke such decrees when they discover better. Thus, the less freedom of judgement men are allowed, the greater is the departure from the most natural condition, and, in consequence, the more oppressive is the government. (*TPT*, p. 259)

Spinoza's distance from Hobbes on this point can be seen from the very different sense he attaches to the phrase 'natural condition'. For Hobbes the state of nature is a chaos of conflicting wills, interests and desires, a perpetual warfare of all against all which can only be restrained by the sovereign imposition of state authority and power. For Spinoza, on the contrary, the 'natural condition' is a life conducted in free-willed accordance with the dictates of reason, or in pursuit of common goods – like justice, liberty and truth – which reason perceives as the highest objects of civilized social existence.

So it is here that I would locate the third main point of contact between Spinoza's thinking and the interests of present-day critical theory. He offers a singularly impressive example of the way that philosophy can fix its sights, so to speak, on the highest ideals of reason and truth, while continuing to work with the given realities of socio-political life. This example is all the more worthy of attention in view of the current deep rift between thinkers like Habermas, committed to preserving what they see as the emancipatory promise of enlightenment (or the 'philosophic discourse of modernity'), and those who would reject such beliefs outright as mere symptoms of a deep-laid continuing malaise. To Spinoza, such quarrels would appear misconceived in so far as they ignore the essential and enabling relationship between *reason* as a source of affirmative ideals and *critique* as a means of exposing the obstacles – the barriers of prejudice, religious dogma, erroneous belief and so forth – that have up to now stood in the way of achieving a just and rational polity. Hence the main object of his writings: to demonstrate (as against cynical philosophers like Hobbes) that realism in matters of political judgement is perfectly compatible with a high regard for the powers and prerogatives of reason. And this double aspect extends, as we have seen, across the whole range of Spinoza's intellectual activities, from his interpretation of scriptural texts to his theory of knowledge and his reading of political history.

Nor can it be said that his works divide into two main categories: on the one hand a text like the *Ethics*, arguing its case at the highest level of abstract 'metaphysical' enquiry, and on the other his socio-political writings where reason is brought up against the *de facto* limits of its applicability to practical affairs. For, as Deleuze remarks,

> The *Ethics* is a book written twice simultaneously: once in the continuous stream of definitions, propositions, demonstrations, and corollaries, which develop the great speculative themes with all the rigours of the mind; another time in the broken chain of scholia, a discontinuous volcanic line . . . setting forth the practical theses of denunciation and liberation. The entire *Ethics* is a voyage in immanence; but immanence is the unconscious itself, and the conquest of the unconscious. Ethical *joy* is the correlate of speculative affirmation.[10]

And this points to a further complicating fact about Spinoza's philosophy: that one cannot always or easily distinguish the 'positive' ideals of reason and truth from the 'negative' conditions of a creaturely existence lived out *sub specie durationis*, or the endless conflicts of knowledge and desire that we experience as finite modes of apprehension, incapable of attaining ultimate wisdom. For Deleuze, understandably, it is this latter aspect of Spinoza's thought that possesses the greater appeal, since it fits in with his own project for unleashing the forces of affect (or libidinal energy) against the repressive 'Oedipal' structures of theory, reason or critique. From this point of view 'the categories of possible and contingent are illusions, but illusions based on the organization of the existing finite mode'.[11] That is to say, there is no denying the primacy or force of those instinctual drives and desires, even if – from Spinoza's more elevated standpoint – they belong to an order of causal relations which the mind fails to grasp through its reliance on passive or inadequate ideas. But Deleuze is a good enough reader of Spinoza to see that his entire system rests on the need to subject such 'illusory' modes to the knowledge attained through critical reflection on the sources of ignorance, prejudice and error. In short, 'it is characteristic of inadequate ideas to be signs that call for interpretation by the imagination, and not *expressions* amenable to *explication* by the lively intellect'.[12] For it is precisely through this work of converting passive into active ideas – or achieving more adequate self-knowledge through the 'lively intellect' – that reason is able to confront and overcome the 'sad passions' which always result from the mind's subjection to an alien causality.

It is worth noting that Deleuze makes this point *both* in relation to Spinoza's theory of signs, language and scriptural exegesis, *and* in connection with his thinking on topics of an ethico-political import. For in each case there is the same double movement of thought: a diagnostic reading of the errors that result from false, prejudicial or otherwise 'inadequate' modes of knowledge, and a compensating stress on the benefits to be had by transforming those errors into a source of critical strength or improved understanding. I have already suggested that there is a parallel to be drawn with de Man's essays on the 'rhetoric of crisis' – or the curious pattern of co-implicated 'blindness' and 'insight' – in thinkers like Nietzsche, Husserl and Heidegger. What I want to stress here is the close connection in Spinoza's thought between *epistemological* values such as truth, falsehood, error and fiction, and arguments concerning the relative goodness – the degree of rational accountability – attained by various orders of political existence. Democracy is the best such order, he argues, since it is able to combine the two main virtues of preserving the peace through a common assent to laws laid down for the general good, while at the same time allowing freedom of thought and conscience for those who (quite rightly) grant that assent only on condition that these freedoms be respected. 'Could thought be controlled as easily as speech', Spinoza writes,

> all governments would rule in safety, and none would be oppressive;
> for everyone would live as his rulers wanted, and his judgements of
> true and false, good and bad, fair and unfair, would be determined
> entirely by their will. (*TPT*, p. 262)

But this is not the case, at least in any condition of civil society that has passed beyond the stage of passive acquiescence in laws, customs or decrees whose force is a matter of absolute sovereign will. For reason is unable to accept such decrees once it has recognized the need for the state to *legimitize* its own authority and power by claiming to achieve the best working balance between the interests of communal security and peace and the interests of rational self-determination on the part of enlightened citizens. Thus: 'it is impossible for thought to be completely subject to another's control, because no-one can give up to another his natural right to reason freely and form his own judgement about everything, nor can he be compelled to do so' (ibid). In this respect Spinoza's political philosophy looks forward directly to Kant's emphasis on the free exercise of religious, moral and political conscience as an absolute prerequisite of all enlightened social orders.

It is the same set of principles that Spinoza brings to bear in his reading of the Hebrew scriptures and other such documents whose chief characteristic – from his point of view – is their drive to suppress liberty of thought in the name of revealed religious truth. Such theocratic doctrines were justified, he argues, at a time when the Jewish people had just recently thrown off the Egyptian yoke, and as yet possessed no sense of collective identity – no settled constitution or power of determining their own best interests – by which to avoid an unending succession of internecine civil feuds. But it is nothing less than a betrayal of reason (and, besides that, a dangerous concession to the powers of arbitrary church-and-state authority) to read those documents *now* in the way that they were originally intended to be read. Thus questions of interpretive or hermeneutic method are never far removed from questions of history, politics and state power. For Spinoza, this connection was clearly borne out by the social and religious antagonisms which threatened to undermine all the hard-won achievements of liberal democracy in Holland. This threat came partly from conservative supporters of the monarchist House of Orange, and partly from their allies, the Dutch Calvinists, who were bent upon restoring the absolute authority of scripture and the principles of a theocratic state. One can therefore see why Spinoza, as spokesman for the liberal-democratic interest, felt obliged to conduct his arguments at so many levels simultaneously. For it was necessary (1) to make the case for democracy as the only tolerable form of government for citizens who had once experienced such freedoms; (2) to discredit those fideist or literal-minded readings of scripture which claimed divine warrant for returning to the monarchist *status quo ante*; and (3) to argue against thinkers like Hobbes, those who identified the 'natural condition' with a state of unending civil discord, and who thus lent support to the conservative cause by counselling a passive acquiescence in decrees handed down – supposedly for the public good – by some ultimate law-giving power. Otherwise there could be small hope of preserving the values of tolerance, freedom and justice represented by the federal Dutch republic.

So Spinoza's defence of democratic values went along with his defence of a rational hermeneutics, one that would allow each interpreter of scripture to apply his or her best efforts to the task of extracting some rational sense, cr (failing that) some message that *once* made sense against a certain background of religious or socio-political needs. Here again, it is the question of signs and their interpretation that leads Spinoza to formulate his theory of the difference between theocratic orders (where obedience to divinely-sanctioned law is the only true measure of social virtue) and enlightened democracies (where virtue is achieved through the freely-willed exercise of rational choice). Deleuze lays particular stress on this point, so it is worth quoting his comments at some length:

> God reveals to Adam that the fruit will poison him because it will act on his body by decomposing its relations; but because Adam has a weak understanding he interprets the effect as a punishment and the cause as a moral law, that is, as a final cause operating through commandment and prohibition. Adam thinks that God has shown him a sign. In this way, morality compromises our whole conception of law, or rather moral law distorts the right conception of causes and eternal truths (the order of composition and decomposition of relations) . . . And the most serious error of theology consists precisely in its having disregarded and hidden the difference between obeying and knowing, in having caused us to take principles of obedience for models of knowledge.[13]

Spinoza's hermeneutics and his ethico-political theory both take rise from this basic distinction between, on the one hand, law as a matter of revealed truth, divine injunction or sovereign command and, on the other, law conceived as an order of rational necessity, one that corresponds to our own best interests, could we but grasp them from the standpoint of an adequate knowledge. Hence his firm rejection of belief in miracles, divine interventions, prophetic modes of utterance or other such affronts to rational intelligence. And from this it follows, according to Spinoza, that we are obliged to take nothing on trust from the scriptures, or nothing that requires us to suspend the powers of reason and adopt an attitude of unquestioning faith. Thus the prophets 'perceived by imagination, and not by sure mental laws' (*TPT*, p. 26). And again: since 'the highest power of Scriptural interpretation belongs to every man', therefore 'the rule for such interpretation should be nothing but the natural light of reason which is common to all – not any supernatural light nor any external authority' (p. 119).

This distinction could be put in speech-act terms by saying that the ancient Hebrew texts very often had resort to downright performative commands – or coercive prohibitions resting on divine fiat – where a later, more enlightened polity would appeal to rational (constative) norms by way of legitimizing argument. Thus the prophets should be seen as charismatic figures whose authority – despite its resting on mere 'knowledge of imagination' – was *at that time* the only possible means of imposing discipline on a fractious and otherwise ungovernable nation. But there was no place for such stratagems, so Spinoza believed, in a social order like that of the Dutch republic, one whose existence could only be maintained by respecting the essential freedoms and prerogatives of a people who had progressed far beyond that primitive stage. Robert McShea provides perhaps the best short statement of Spinoza's thinking on the question of just why religion should persist at all once deprived of its illusory transcendent guarantees:

> Although religion is, from the standpoint of the rational man, false, it should not be discarded. It plays a major political role in forming the national character at the original founding of the state. The need for religion diminishes, but is not wholly lost, as the state gains support from other sources – rational self-interest, patriotic fervour, and the inertia of habitual compliance, for instance. The social, and only, function of religion at all times is to teach obedience to the rational demands of society by those persons who cannot be rationally compelled or persuaded.[14]

So there are two main aspects to Spinoza's critique of religious beliefs and institutions. One takes the form of a functionalist or social-utility argument, treating religion as a stabilizing force in the service of political interests, but seeing no role for it beyond the more primitive stages of social evolution. From this point of view, as McShea comments, 'in the ideal state . . . religion might cease to exist at all'. But there is also the more radical suggestion – taken up in different ways by Feuerbach and Marx on the one hand, and Nietzsche and Foucault on the other – that religion is the site of a struggle for power between various ideologies (or 'discourses'), the

effects of which go far beyond the grasp of any simplified functionalist model.

Thus, according to Feuerbach, the 'truths' of religion are best
understood as expressions of an alienated human essence, of desires
that cannot be fulfilled under existing conditions of social life, and
which are therefore projected – in imaginary form – onto the
attributes of a divine personage.[15] For Marx, famously, this critique
stopped short at the point of an essentialist metaphysics, one that
fell back into the same old trap of identifying 'human nature' with
some timeless, transcendent set of values and ideals. Hence his
argument in the 'Theses on Feuerbach': that one could only break
out of this charmed circle, this realm of specular misrecognition,
by acknowledging the historically-contingent character of 'human
nature' in its various forms, and the fact that all such notions took
rise from the 'real foundations' of socio-economic life.[16] The other
line of thought, running from Nietzsche to Foucault, has no use
for what it sees as the residual rationalist premises that underpin
the Marxian critique of ideology as false consciousness or imaginary
projection. It denounces such arguments as a mere continuation of
the 'Enlightenment' drive to make all history conform to its own
narrow set of universalist precepts and values. This quarrel has
resulted in the current stand-off between Foucauldians, New Historicists and their like, who regard 'power/knowledge' as the bottom
line, the point beyond which critical theory becomes just another
form of self-deluding enterprise, and on the other hand those –
Marxists among them – who wish to defend at least some version
of the claim that theory gives a knowledge unattainable from within
ideology, lived experience, or the discourses of socially legitimized
truth.

I have argued that this is the single most contentious issue in
present-day literary-critical debate. But it is also a question that is
raised inescapably whenever any discipline – philosophy, hermeneutics, political theory, sociology of knowledge, historiography –
lays claim to an order of conceptual or explanatory power beyond
what is given at the level of first-hand, self-evident, or commonsense
truth. And this question has always presented itself in political as
well as philosophical terms, giving rise to arguments – some of
which I have examined in the course of this book – about the
powers and limits of *Ideologiekritik*, the relation between 'positive'
and 'negative' theories, and the extent to which all thinking is
subject (as the current neo-pragmatists would have it) to beliefs and

values already current within some existing interpretive community. This latter argument has close affinities, not only with Foucault's *tout court* equation of power and knowledge, but also with a long tradition of thought – going back well beyond Hobbes – that assimilates what is rational in any given social context to what best serves the interests of established authority. And ranged on the opposite side of this debate are those thinkers (albeit a fairly mixed company) who argue that theory is indeed capable of mounting a resistance to accepted beliefs, and that knowledge is not – or not always and everywhere – an effect of power-interests that determine in advance what shall count as veridical belief.

Of course one reason why the company is mixed has to do with the fact that there is no direct or necessary link between philosophic doctrines on the one hand and political commitments on the other. Thus, for instance, Hume and Russell were both radical empiricists, thinkers who shared a whole range of common assumptions about language, logic, and the nature of philosophical enquiry. But where Hume took these assumptions to warrant a basically conservative or social-conformist outlook, Russell could argue with equal plausibility that they supported his adoption of a left-liberal stance and an attitude opposed to just about every orthodox social value. Derrida has commented to similar effect that 'there can always be a Hegelianism of the left and a Hegelianism of the right, a Heideggerianism of the left and a Heideggerianism of the right . . . and even, let us not overlook it, a Marxism of the left and a Marxism of the right. The one can always be the other, the double of the other'.[17] To which it might be added that deconstruction – at least in its US-domesticated forms – has proved itself just as adaptable to readings of a mixed political character. So clearly there is no question of a generalized 'politics of theory' that would line thinkers up to 'left' or 'right' on a series of well-defined philosophical questions. But this argument does make sense with regard to the basic distinction between those who espouse a consensus-model of interpretive truth, or who regard knowledge as entirely a product of vested power-interests, and those who envisage a critical role for theory beyond the mere passive reproduction of received ideas. For the latter, what then becomes the crucial question is just how theory can achieve this aim, given the fact – so amply documented by thinkers like Foucault – that knowledge can never be entirely disengaged from the social contexts or power-interests that affect its production. It is not a matter of arguing, as against Foucault, that theory can somehow rise clear of these irksome constraints and achieve an order of serene, self-validating truth. On the contrary: it is only where thinking comes up against a certain 'resistance to theory' – a resistance encountered in the reading of texts or through reflecting on its own historical conditions of emergence – that criticism escapes the closed circle of interpretive foreknowledge.

What makes Spinoza's thought so instructive in this regard is the fact that he gives full weight to both arguments, acknowledging the force of the social-determinist case while holding nevertheless that reason can attain to an order of insight or critical grasp which liberates the mind from its condition of passive enslavement to external causes. Such is indeed the end-point and justification of all philosophical enquiry, as Spinoza conceives it. 'If we separate emotions or affects from the thought of an external cause, and join them to other thoughts, then the love or hate toward the external cause is destroyed, as are the vacillations of mind arising from these affects' (*E* V, P 2). On the face of it this passage recommends nothing more than an attitude of studious contemplative detachment from an otherwise all-embracing order of causal necessity. But it can also be read as a statement of the conditions that apply to *any* theoretical activity, any thinking that seeks a more adequate knowledge of events, meanings or mental processes than can be had at the level of first-hand, self-evident belief. Edwin Curley puts the argument as follows in his recent study of the *Ethics*:

> Ridding ourselves of a belief may involve a difficult process of looking again at our evidence for the belief, testing alternative theories which might explain that evidence equally well, criticizing the logic by which we have arrived at the belief, and so on.[18]

Curley's main interest here is in the way that such thinking can benefit the individual subject in his or her progress toward rational self-knowledge. Thus 'if a certain belief is an essential component in a particular affect, and if we can destroy that belief, or weaken it, then we will have destroyed or weakened the affect of which it is a component'.[19] Philosophical reflection would then be closely allied to the kind of therapeutic technique that Freud, at least toward the end of his career, held out as the one last source of hope for civilization and its discontents.

However, this comparison cannot be pushed too far since it accounts for only one aspect of Spinoza's thinking. There is a crucial difference between Freud's pessimistic and conservative assessment of the prospects for social change, and Spinoza's conviction that the exercise of reason can achieve real benefits, not only in terms of psychological adjustment but also at the level of history, politics and collective human well-being. And this difference arises from Spinoza's understanding of the constant *interaction* between 'passive' and 'active' ideas, or the extent to which errors brought about by force of circumstance – by the pressure of contingent historical events or material conditions – may yet become the starting-point for a process of critical reflection that points a way beyond those errors. Only thus can one avoid the twin temptations of a rationalist metaphysics devoid of worldly consequence and a doctrine of cynical *Realpolitik* which renounces all hope of enlightened progress.

III

It is on this account that Spinoza deserves to be recognized as a signal precursor of current debates about the politics of theory. On the one hand he perceives (like Nietzsche and Foucault) that thinking is never carried on in some abstract heaven of pure ideas; that it is always demonstrably an *effect* of certain knowledge-constitutive interests, rather than a self-caused activity of the rational mind; and that only by concealing this awkward fact about its own contingent or motivated character can theory hang on to its high claims as an arbiter of ultimate truth. To this extent – as I have argued – he belongs in the company of those thinkers for whom knowledge is an epiphenomenal occurrence, a product of the epistemic will-to-power that masquerades as disinterested reason. But to single this out as the most important lesson of Spinoza's work is to ignore everything that counts against the pragmatist reduction of truth to what is 'good in the way of belief', or – in Foucault's idiom – of 'knowledge' to a matter of undifferentiated 'power/knowledge'. David Bidney provides perhaps the best brief statement of Spinoza's attitude with regard to these two main traditions of Western political thought.

> Plato had said: All virtue is knowledge. Francis Bacon added: All knowledge is power. Spinoza concluded: Therefore all virtue is power. Spinoza accepts the Platonic doctrine that virtue is knowledge but interprets knowledge in the Baconian sense of efficient power.[20]

In short, there is no criticizing past or present forms of political injustice, tyranny or oppression without this appeal to countervailing positive principles, 'ideas of reason' – as Kant would describe them – which hold out the promise of a better, more just and equitable social order. And to Spinoza's way of thinking these ideas found their highest expression to date in the articles of a liberal-democratic charter such as existed (albeit under constant threat) in the Dutch republic of his day.

This is why his writings constitute a test-case of the complex relation between *theory* as a mode of speculative reason aimed toward the highest philosophical ideals, and *history* as the province of contingent actions and events where those principles must at last be tried and tested. It is significant that some of Spinoza's best modern commentators have themselves written under pressures of historical circumstance that bore a marked resemblance to conditions obtaining in his own place and time. Thus Lewis Samuel Feuer (*Spinoza and the Rise of Liberalism*, 1958) addresses his study to a series of questions which have as much to do with post-war American politics as with the fortunes of liberal democracy in seventeenth-century Holland.[21] The fact that he describes Spinoza's trial before the elders of the Amsterdam Synagogue as 'an investigation into un-Dutch activities and modes of thought' (Feuer, p. 110) is enough to suggest that Feuer has present-day comparisons in view. Lest any doubt remain he remarks at one point that Spinoza had reason to be 'acutely aware that an inquisition, a police state, a society of informers and hysterics can stamp out men [sic] of independent mind' (ibid). And clearly Feuer is thinking not only of events in the Soviet Union but also of developments nearer home for which those events served as a handy pretext.

In short, his book is offered – at least in part – as a latter day defence of liberal-democratic values against the same kinds of threat that Spinoza perceived as coming from the Calvinists, the watchdogs of religious orthodoxy (Christian or Jewish), and the supporters of a resurgent monarchist interest centred on the House of Orange. As Feuer reads it, Spinoza's entire life's work was devoted to this purpose of providing philosophical support – even, one could say, doing high-class propaganda – for the republican party whose chief representative was his patron, the Dutch Grand Pensioner, Johan de Witt. And this argument gains credence from the fact that de Witt was himself not only a leading light among progressive European intellectuals of his day, but also the author of a treatise, *Deduction of the States of Holland*, which claimed to derive these liberal precepts through the same mode of reasoning *more geometrico* that Spinoza adopted in the *Ethics*.[22] For both, this amounted to a kind of formal declaration that the most important truths – in philosophy, ethics and politics alike – were accessible to reason by virtue of its own innate rational capacities, and in no wise dependent upon faith, revelation, doctrinal adherence or other such causes of social strife.[23] Hence their allegiance to what Feuer calls the 'left-Cartesian' strain of seventeenth-century rationalist thought. That is to say, they inherited Descartes's quest for 'clear and distinct ideas' as the source of all genuine, indubitable knowledge, but at the same time sought to make such truths more widely available by bringing them out into the public domain, presenting them *not* (or not only) as arrived at through a species of inward eidetic inspection, but as following one from another in the chain of rational-deductive argument. It is worth recalling that Spinoza's first published work was a critical exposition of Descartes's philosophy laid out in precisely this manner.[24] And the object of the exercise – very much in keeping with Spinoza's liberal-Enlightenment views – was firstly to clarify the more obscure aspects of Cartesian thought, and secondly to show that this could be achieved without resorting to the notion of a privileged epistemic standpoint.

Here again, there is a useful comparison to be drawn with Habermas's theory of communicative action, a theory that claims to carry on the project of enlightened critical reason, but which also acknowledges the force of current anti-foundationalist thinking.[25] For Habermas – as for Spinoza and the left-Cartesians – this indicates the need to offer something more than a first-hand appeal to eidetic self-evidence or *a priori* truth-claims grounded in the nature of human understanding. The trouble with such claims is that they are always open to the kind of counter-argument standardly adduced by a whole range of modern (post-Kantian) thinkers, from out-and-out sceptics like Nietzsche and Foucault to Kuhnian philosophers of science, neo-pragmatists like Rorty and Fish, radical empiricists like Quine, and historicists of various persuasion from Hegel on down. But it is a mistake, Habermas argues, to draw the conclusion that enlightenment is a thing of the past, that the 'philosophic discourse of modernity' has now at last run its course, so that henceforth any appeal to values of reason, truth or critique will merely be evidence of a lingering attachment to the old foundationalist paradigm.[26] For this is to ignore what Habermas sees as the single most promising alternative: a 'transcendental pragmatics' (or theory of communicative action) which can happily give up all ideas of privileged epistemic access so long as it preserves the regulative concept of an 'ideal speech situation', or a public sphere of free and equal discourse aimed toward removing the various obstacles of prejudice, self-interest and coercive ideology that presently stand in its way. Spinoza is claiming a similar advantage for his method of reasoning *more geometrico* in the treatise on Descartes and the formal portions of the *Ethics*. That is to say, he regards this method not only as the surest, most reliable means of attaining 'adequate ideas', but also as the form of philosophical argument inherently best suited to the interests of liberal-democratic thought.

From one point of view (call it New Historicist) this would simply go to show that *all* philosophical systems – even, or especially, those that purport to deliver timeless truths – are in fact bound up with discourses of power/knowledge specific to the interests of this or that social group. Feuer is himself quite willing to entertain such ideas, as when he remarks that 'the modern theory of liberal republicanism was born as a theory of Dutch exceptionalism', or when he poses the question: 'why did the radical democratic thought of the seventeenth century find pantheistic metaphysics its natural expression?' (Feuer, p. 55). Indeed, his whole approach has this much in common with the New Historicist programme: that it shows small patience with the various forms of *a priori* discursive categorization that have standardly served as disciplinary markers in philosophy, literary criticism, and the history of ideas. In this respect Feuer stands at the opposite extreme from commentators like Bennett or Donagan, those for whom Spinoza's *philosophical* arguments are the only real topic of interest, and who therefore pay minimal attention to matters of so-called historical 'background'. To Feuer, on the contrary, such distinctions would appear at best a matter of specialized scholarly convenience, and at worst a technique for evading or disguising the political implications of Spinoza's thought.

Indeed, one could press the New Historicist analogy a good deal further by reading Feuer's book alongside the essays of a critic like Stephen Greenblatt, especially where these engage with issues in the sociology of religious belief, the emergence of oppositional (or 'atheist') discourses, and the role of literature as one such discourse where these interests are often in play.[27] For here also – as I remarked in chapter 1 – there is a primary focus on the various contexts (political and socio-economic) which tend to be ignored by more orthodox forms of literary scholarship. One of Greenblatt's major themes is the way that Renaissance colonial expansion brought about an encounter between Christian and other varieties of religious belief, with the result that those other beliefs were first denounced as mere priestly impostures, and then gave rise to a sceptical questioning of all religions, Christianity included. As he reads it, this offers a striking example of Foucault's thesis: that resistance is always an effect of power in so far as it can only mobilize its forces or define its interests *over and against* some hegemonic discourse of self-authorized truth. What is wrong with the standard (liberal-Enlightenment or Marxist) view is that it sets up a simplified dualist scheme of values, such that 'power' is automatically equated with repression, passivity, false consciousness, mass-manipulation and so forth, while 'resistance' comes about through the mind's capacity to criticize such false ('ideological') perspectives, thus achieving an active, transformative stance *vis-à-vis* its social conditions of existence. The New Historicists follow Foucault in rejecting both terms of this implicit equation between, on the one hand, *history* as a teleological process aimed toward the final overcoming of untruth, error and prejudice, and on the other *reason* as an ultimate ground, a transcendental guarantee that this process leads up to truth (or enlightenment) at the end of enquiry. For them, this whole argument needs to be turned around, allowing us to see that its central terms (truth, reason, enlightenment, progress, the transcendental subject) were products of a certain period-specific discourse of power/knowledge whose effect was precisely to place such values beyond reach of critical scrutiny. And in Greenblatt's work this perception is pushed back to that originating moment in the European 'sciences of man' – the moment of encounter between colonist and colonized, Christian and pagan, imperial power and localized resistance – when these opposites were visibly inscribed in a complex play of differential forces and relationships which cannot be subsumed under any of the standard (dialectical or 'Enlightenment') modes of explanation.

Now there is no doubt that Spinoza can be enlisted on the side of a radically contextualist approach that would bear out many of these New Historicist claims. Thus Feuer offers a whole series of arguments for reading him *not* as a 'pure' metaphysician, one whose philosophy rose serenely above the material conditions of its own time and place, but on the contrary as a thinker whose best efforts were devoted to the defence of liberal-republican values in a context of recurrent legitimation crises. The parallel is yet more striking if one considers Feuer's claim that their overseas trading interests brought the Dutch into contact with alien cultures and alternative modes of religious belief, an experience which in turn did much to strengthen their attitude of tolerance and freedom of thought in matters of individual conscience. Thus 'the fact and problem of coloured races was imposing itself on the Dutch in the seventeenth century, in Java, Japan and in Brazil' (Feuer, p. 238). And moreover, these contacts may well have produced the kind of reflex response – the intensified self-questioning and scepticism with regard to *all* forms of religious orthodoxy or doctrinal adherence – which Greenblatt locates in the underground discourse of so-called Renaissance 'atheism'. Spinoza himself had cause to reflect on this nexus of religious and socio-economic interests since, as Feuer notes, his expulsion from the Amsterdam synagogue most likely came about for several such reasons. That is to say, it was a drastic remedy, a sanction of last resort, prompted not only by Spinoza's heterodox religious views but also by the fear that such thinking might precipitate yet further crises in the complex balance of powers and allegiances that made up the Dutch body politic.

This threat was twofold: on the one hand to the immigrant Jewish community (whose civic position and mercantile interests depended on maintaining a sense of common purpose), and on the other to their host culture, the Dutch Estates General, which had faced a whole series of challenges – the struggle for independence from Spain, trade wars with France and Britain, the continuing challenge from Calvinist fanatics and monarchist interests centred on the House of Orange – and whose survival was often in doubt from one such crisis to the next. As Feuer remarks,

> Spinoza is the early prototype of the European Jewish radical . . . The Jewish elders were monarchist in their sympathies, loyal to the House of Orange, friendly to the Calvinist party, stockholders in the Dutch East India and West India Companies. Spinoza was an ardent republican, a follower of de Witt, a critic of the Calvinist party, its ethics, and its theocratic pretension . . . The Amsterdam Jewish leaders could tolerate theological disagreement; they could not tolerate a political and economic radical. (Feuer, p. 5)

The result of all this, one might conjecture, was to give Spinoza a particular insight into the workings of socialized power/knowledge, or a grasp of how political interests could operate across the whole range of human cultural activities, especially – in his own case –

that of theological dispute. To this extent at least it is fair to say that Spinoza lived out the truth of one main item on the New Historicist agenda: the idea that all discourses are bound up with the drive to secure themselves a position of power in respect of rival claimants to the same privileged position. And one could further suggest that it brought home to him the intimate relation between power as achieved through such effects of discursive mastery, and resistance to power as likewise engendered by the complex dynamics of cultural exchange between different orders of knowledge-production. This is why, in all his writings, Spinoza gives such weight to the role of the affects (or the constant struggle between 'active' and 'passive' modes of creaturely existence), even where his philosophic sights are fixed on a knowledge that would somehow transcend such conflicts by attaining to a vantage-point of ultimate truth *sub specie aeternitatis*.

But again there are limits to this New Historicist analogy, limits that emerge most clearly if one looks into the *reasons* for Spinoza's resignation to the non-perfectibility of social arrangements, the regressive nature of human desires, and the failure of the Dutch experiment to secure universal assent by virtue of its appeal to the common interests of toleration, justice and peaceful coexistence. For this was Spinoza's main problem, as Feuer perceives it: 'how to found a democracy if a people is prone to unreason and hatred and capable of destroying its benefactors?' (Feuer, p. 75). In this case the benefactor was de Witt himself, set upon and murdered by a panic-stricken mob during the French invasion crisis of 1672. And of course Spinoza had personal grounds enough for holding public opinion (or its orthodox representatives) in no high esteem. But the essential point here is that Spinoza reached this position through a process of unwilling disenchantment which registered the setbacks to liberal democracy – or what he saw as the nearest thing to it in contemporary Europe – while yet holding on to a principled argument (and *not* just a belief or preferential attitude) that democracy was the best, most enlightened or rationally-accountable form of political justice. And in this, once again, he anticipated Kant, especially those passages in the later writings (recently the subject of some interesting commentary by Lyotard) where Kant distinguishes between judgements arrived at in conformity with the evidence of past or present real-world events, and judgements of reason in its speculative mode having to do with ideas like freedom, progress, and the notion of perpetual peace.[28] These latter may indeed be 'unwarranted' in the sense that they cannot appeal to historical examples, or rest their case on any other form of demonstrative proof through experience. For as Lyotard remarks – not without a touch of post-'68 cynical *Schadenfreude* – all the evidence to date would have to count against the idea that such values could ever be successfully carried into practice or, once achieved, retain their force as a guiding set of regulative concepts and ideals.[29]

Kant himself bore witness to one of many such historical disappointments with the collapse of those hopes which he and like-minded liberal thinkers had invested in the French Revolution. And Lyotard obligingly goes on to enumerate the subsequent events that would tend to confirm this gloomy diagnosis, at least at the level of a straightforward appeal to 'the facts' as they strike a reasonable mind in possession of the relevant historical data. Such judgements fall under the rule that applies to all determinate (theoretical or cognitive) truth-claims, i.e. that 'intuitions without concepts are blind', while 'concepts without intuitions are empty'. In which case – if this were the only ground of appeal – there could be little reason to suppose that future developments might bring about a change in the well-attested pattern of ideals betrayed, hopes brought to naught, or revolutions foundering on the rocks of prejudice, self-interest, or counter-revolutionary violence. Hence Lyotard's melancholy catalogue, offered by way of a standing reproof to those nineteenth-century 'philosophies of history' which assumed – unlike Kant – that the signs of progress were there to be read as a matter of self-evident or manifest truth.

> The names which are those of 'our history' oppose counter-examples to their claim. – Everything real is rational, everything rational is real: 'Auschwitz' refutes speculative doctrine. This crime at least, which is real . . . is not rational. – Everthing proletarian is communist, everything communist is proletarian: Berlin 1953, Budapest 1956, Czechoslovakia 1968, Poland 1980 (I could mention others) refute the doctrine of historical materialism: the workers rose up against the party. – Everything democratic is by and for the people, and vice versa: 'May 1968' refutes the doctrine of parliamentary liberalism. The social in its everydayness puts representative institutions in check . . . The passages promised by the great doctrinal syntheses end in bloody impasses. Whence the sorrow of the spectators in this end of the twentieth century.[30]

For Spinoza likewise, all the evidence suggested that the great Dutch experiment in liberal democracy had very nearly run its course; that the trade-wars, the death of de Witt, the French invasion, Calvinist intrigues and other such crises had already signalled its imminent demise; and therefore that philosophy had lost its wager on the continuing progress of social institutions and could only make terms with the obdurate facts of human perversity, self-interest and party prejudice. In short, one could take the above-quoted passage of Lyotard and substitute episodes from Spinoza's life-history that would lead point-for-point to the same disenchanted conclusion.

Nor were these reflections confined to events on the Dutch political scene. There was also the example of the English Civil War, starting out (with Spinoza's spirited approval) as a revolt against monarchist pretensions and an overweening High-Church interest, and ending up with what he saw as the bad resort to regicide, the irruption of sectarian strife, and then the melancholy return full-circle to something very like the *status quo ante*. Commentators – Feuer among them – have remarked on the parallels between Spinoza's thinking and ideas that were circulating on the 'radical left' of the English revolutionary movement. In fact it seems that Spinoza was a close observer of political events during and after the interregnum. His admiration for Cromwell – whom he saw, to begin with, as a figure in the same heroic mould as de Witt – was abandoned when the former set himself up as Lord Protector and then fell victim to civil discords which opened the way to the restored monarchy. Spinoza seems at first to have sympathized with those visionary thinkers, like the Digger, Winstanley and the Leveller, John Lilburne, who shared his own commitment to liberal (ultimately communist) principles, and also his materialist reading of scripture as a text that prefigured current events and pointed the way to an earthly fulfilment of the Old and New Testament prophecies. But these hopes were misplaced, or rather – since this distinction is the main point at issue here – they were not borne out as it happened by the record of subsequent socio-political events. For Spinoza, as indeed for his contemporary John Milton, the post-revolutionary period was a chapter of successive bitter defeats, all the more bitter in Spinoza's case since the Restoration of Charles II led on to British trade wars with Holland which in turn hastened the decline and near-collapse of the Dutch republican interest.[31] Hence – as Feuer argues – the marked change of attitude that appears in his later writings, where radical hopes have at last given way to a mood of disenchantment and a reinforced conviction of the fallible, error-prone nature of human understanding.

But I think that Feuer somewhat exaggerates the extent of this shift in Spinoza's political beliefs. For as we have seen, his high claims for the *potential* liberating power of reason go along with a keen, often painful sense of the obstacles that rise against it on account of our limited perspectives, our confused states of knowledge, or our failure to grasp the causal relations that determine such erroneous beliefs. This is why, as Spinoza says,

> the mind has no adequate knowledge of itself, nor of its body, nor of external bodies, but only a confused knowledge, as often as it perceives things in the common order of nature, that is to say, as often as it is determined to the contemplation of this or that *externally* – namely, by a chance coincidence, and not as often as it is determined *internally* – for the reason that it contemplates several things at once, and is determined to understand in what they differ, agree, or oppose one another; for whenever it is internally disposed in this or in any other way, it then contemplates things clearly and distinctly. (*E* II, P 29 schol.)

The point of this passage and others like it is *not* to place reason in a realm quite apart from the messy contingencies of everyday life (or 'the common order of nature'). Still less is it to argue, in Cartesian fashion, that the mind has access to genuine truths only in so far as it withdraws from the world of fallible commonsense perception and attains to an order of contemplative knowledge where ideas are effectively their own formal guarantee. To be sure, Spinoza holds out this ideal as a limit-point of rational enquiry, a point that might be reached could the mind but achieve such a God-like ultimate perspective. But he is also convinced that knowledge comes about through an arduous churning of facts and theories – or truths of experience and truths of reason – which will always partake *in some measure* of the limits imposed upon human understanding by the given conditions of history, circumstance, or received opinion. And this is why his thinking cannot be encompassed within the current New Historicist or Foucauldian paradigm. For Spinoza, it is no argument against the ideas of reason, truth, political justice, enlightenment, progress etc. that these ideas have as yet found no lasting embodiment in the record of human social institutions. What keeps them alive is precisely the perceived mismatch between the way things are and the way they might become had reason attained a more adequate knowledge of its own best interests and those of humanity at large.

5 From Scriptural Hermeneutics to Secular Critique

I

I have argued that present-day critical theory is still working out the implications of Spinoza's thinking, even where there is no question of 'influence' or of tracing any direct line of intellectual descent. Take the following passage from Barbara Johnson's fine book *The Critical Difference*, a passage that has to do with the ubiquity of error as a force to be reckoned with in human affairs, not only as it bears upon the activity of reading (her immediate concern) but also in the realms of history, politics and day-to-day practical choice. 'Far from being a negative or non–existent factor', she writes,

> what is not known is often the unseen motivating force behind the very deployment of meaning. The power of ignorance, blindness, uncertainty, or misreading is often all the more redoubtable for not being perceived as such . . . The 'unknown' is not what lies beyond the limits of knowledge, some unreachable, sacred, ineffable point toward which we vainly yearn. It lies, rather, in the oversights and slip-ups that structure our lives in the same way that an *X* makes it possible to articulate an algebraic equation . . . It is not, in the final analysis, what you don't know that can or cannot hurt you. It is what you don't *know* you don't know that spins out and entangles 'that perpetual error we call life'[1]

This might seem to go clean against Spinoza's argument that falsehood and error can only be characterized in negative terms; that they come about solely through the mind's privation, its *not* having access to adequate ideas, and hence its failure to take full account of the causes and conditions that must otherwise produce erroneous thinking. But again, one can point to numerous passages where Spinoza qualifies this doctrine by insisting that errors have very real consequences, not only for the lives of particular individuals (in so far as they think or act on mistaken assumptions), but also at the level of history and political events, where a false understanding – in Johnson's terms, a misreading of the signs – can be carried into practice and thus bring about determinate material effects. Such was indeed Spinoza's analysis of the misfortunes (more precisely: the multiplied errors of collective reasoning and judgement) which overtook the Dutch experiment in liberal democracy. Its failure was evidence *not* that such ideals were unattainable in practice, but that here, in this particular instance, they had come up against a range of adverse factors (political and socioeconomic) which in turn gave a hold for prejudice, narrow self-interest, and other such regressive habits of mind.

So Feuer is right to see Spinoza as sadly disenchanted by the course of events up to and after 1672. He is also quite justified in viewing those events as a strong counter-instance to Spinoza's early faith that reason would prevail over prejudice and error in the managment of Dutch political affairs. Where Feuer goes wrong is in supposing that the weight of *de facto* evidence (i.e. the testimony of events in Holland and England) must have led Spinoza – like so many embittered ex-liberals, then and since – to the point of abandoning *not only* his immediate hopes but also his belief in enlightened critique as the agent of progressive political change. As he puts it:

> defeat and melancholy replaced the buoyancy of youth. In a later age, young Europeans, after the failure of the Revolution of 1848, turned from philosophies of social reconstruction to the pessimism of Schopenhauer. Spinoza lived through the crisis-experience and wondered which of his youthful principles had survived the test of history, how much of his youthful vision would withstand the revision of experience. (Feuer, p. 229).

But this reading tends to assume – like the New Historicists – that theory (or political philosophy) can never be anything other or more than a 'discourse' whose limits are inexorably fixed by the social conditions that obtain in this or that context of utterance. That is to say, it ignores the possibility that reason may propose an alternative to the way things are (or the way they have turned out so far) which cannot be validated by any appeal to factual self-evidence, but which none the less answers to a rational (enlightened) self-interest on the part of good-willed subjects whose judgement is not clouded by currently prevailing forms of prejudice. To discount this possibility – or treat it as just another form of self-deluded utopian reverie – is tantamount to claiming that we cannot conceive of any social order that would represent a definite stage of advance beyond past or present modes of collective life. And this attitude goes along with a certain kind of philosophical confusion, namely that which would seek to delimit the interests of speculative reason according to the terms and conditions laid down for cognitive judgements (i.e. knowledge of real-world objects and events).

Of course these distinctions don't figure expressly in Spinoza's metaphysics, belonging as they do to a later (epistemological) framework of enquiry. But they are none the less implicit in what he has to say about the various modalities of knowledge, the prevalance of 'confused ideas', and the way that error comes about as a determinate effect of material causes whose nature may yet be accessible to reasoned analysis. Only thus can philosophy hope to comprehend why the promise of enlightenment (or social progress) has so often given way to the dreary chronicle of revolutions defeated or high hopes collapsing into cynical *Realpolitik*. For there remains, when all the evidence is in, a margin for hope in the very fact that such discrepancies exist between the documentary record and the interests of reason as a mode of enlightened speculative thought. Such is the standpoint that Kant adopts in those late writings where he addresses the question of how philosophy can maintain its principled commitment to values of freedom, democracy, and progress, while at the same time acknowledging the various well-documented failures (like that of the French Revolution) which would seem to throw all such values into doubt.[2] What is required is a clear sense of the distinction between judgements that issue in cognitive truth-claims (and which therefore involve an appeal to intuition or phenomenal self-evidence), and judgements that derive from the *sensus communis* of a shared commitment to as-yet unrealised values and ideals. On this basis one can not so much ignore as re-evaluate those instances of failed opportunity that would otherwise present an overwhelming case against the prospects for genuine and lasting social change.

In the first *Critique* it is Kant's main concern to prevent pure reason (or speculative thought) from straying over onto the terrain of genuine knowledge, and thus creating all manner of 'metaphysical' puzzles and perplexities. But after that – with the second and third *Critiques* – the emphasis shifts to those other modes of judgement (ethical and aesthetic) whose validity cannot be established by appealing to any form of factual, phenomenal, or cognitive self-evidence. And it is here – as recent commentators have noted – that the two aesthetic categories of the beautiful and the sublime (especially the latter) come to play a significant role in the entire Kantian structure of argument.[3] For what the sublime figures forth most strikingly is the existence of feelings that answer to something in the nature of our experience as sentient, thinking individuals, but which cannot be verified (or checked against 'the facts') in so far as they exceed any form of phenomenal cognition. Thus, as Lyotard writes:

> Enthusiasm is a modality of the feeling of the sublime. The imagination tries to supply a direct, sensible presentation for an Idea of reason (for the whole is an object of an Idea, as for example, in the whole of practical, reasonable beings). It does not succeed and it thereby feels its impotence, but at the same time it discovers its destination, which is to bring itself into harmony with the Ideas of reason through an appropriate presentation. The result of this obstructed relation is that instead of experiencing a feeling for the object, we experience, on the occasion of that object, a feeling 'for the Idea of humanity in our subject'.[4]

Lyotard's point in all this is to argue – like Kant – that the 'signs' of history cannot be read as so many items of documentary evidence presented to the mind through a straightforward review of the facts as they offer themselves for stocktaking judgement. For this is to confuse the two distinct orders of *theoretical understanding* (where the rule is that every concept must have reference to some given intuition), and *speculative reason* (where Ideas themselves give the rule by appealing to the interests of a *sensus communis* which points the way beyond any past or present state of historical affairs).[5]

Failure to observe this distinction may in turn give rise to two different sorts of confused understanding. One is the tendency of 'enthusiasts' (revolutionary partisans) to suppose that history has *already* attained to the point where those Ideas can be translated directly into practice. This attitude produces the characteristic form of transcendental illusion: 'seeing something beyond all bounds of sensibility, that is, believing that there is a direct presentation when there isn't any . . . cognizing something beyond the limits of all cognition'.[6] The other – as we have seen – comes about most often in the aftermath of failed revolutions, and typically gives rise to a conservative backlash or a mood of generalized cynical disenchantment. Once again, it involves a basic confusion between truths arrived at on the basis of experience (or through a knowledge of past events), and Ideas of reason whose validating rules are not to be sought in any form of *de facto* or evidential grounding. But here the effect is to render such Ideas strictly unthinkable – or place them beyond all hope of fulfilment – by equating reason in political affairs with a straightforward appeal to the past record of abortive revolutions, corrupted ideals, liberal reforms that came to nothing or ran up against the obstacles of prejudice, self-interest, and so forth. It would then be nothing more than a species of wishful thinking – a perverse disregard for all the evidence so far – to imagine that history might yet offer grounds for the enlightened critique of existing social institutions.

For Spinoza, as for Kant, such evidence may give rise to a sobering reflection on the weaknesses and errors to which subjects are prone when denied the full exercise of those rational powers that belong to them properly as social beings in a genuine community (or 'commonwealth') of free and equal discourse. But this doesn't mean that one is driven to renounce such ideals since, whenever they have been put into practice – in however partial or tentative a form – they have encountered obstacles that eventually led to their more or less complete abandonment. For the very term 'commonwealth' signifies, in Spinoza, a commitment to principles of freedom and justice which cannot be falsified or countermanded by the inauspicious record so far. Thus:

> human right or freedom is a nonentity as long as it is an individual possession determined by an individual power; it exists in imagination rather than in fact, since there is no certainty of making it good . . . Besides, it is hardly possible for men to maintain life and cultivate the mind without mutual help. I therefore conclude that the right of nature peculiar to human beings can scarcely be conceived save where men hold rights as a body. (*PT*, p. 296)

Here again, Spinoza parts company with those theorists – from Hobbes to Foucault – who regard power-interests as the sole determinant of social or cultural values, and who therefore tend to level the difference between various political systems or orders of civil society. For him, the word 'commonwealth' carries certain strongly-marked evaluative overtones, including the idea (an 'Idea of reason', in Kantian parlance) that any social order meriting that name will display at least a notional or principled commitment to the values of liberal democracy. From which it follows that the term cannot be applied – or if so, then only with explicit reservations amounting to a form of immanent critique – in the case of any government that attempts to curtail the basic liberties of thought, speech, and religious conscience.

Thus 'commonwealth' figures in Spinoza's discourse as a regulative idea, a term whose full meaning cannot be grasped by reference to this or that existing state of society, but whose usage involves an implicit appeal to values and principles attained through the exercise of reason. In this respect it anticipates much of what Kant has to say about the politics of enlightenment, the prospects for social change, and the need to interpret the 'signs' of history under an aspect that will often exclude any direct appeal to historical or documentary evidence. It also finds a parallel in Habermas's theory of communicative action, one that takes its bearings from an 'ideal speech-situation' conceived very much in Kantian terms, though also designed (as we have seen) to head off anti-foundationalist objections by abandoning the epistemological frame of reference and adopting the idioms of speech-act theory, 'transcendental pragmatics', and related modes of enquiry.[7] Thus Spinoza, like Habermas, equates the highest good of a commonwealth with its capacity for promoting the free and equal discourse of various interest-groups, political viewpoints, or specialized communities of knowledge. This can only be achieved in so far as governments respect the proper limits of their own executive power, and refrain from any attempt to legislate in matters of ethical, religious or political conscience. For at this point there would develop a genuinely autonomous 'public sphere' of enlightened debate where such issues could be argued out by all parties with the object of attaining a rational consensus uncoerced by any form of orthodox opinion or power-seeking interest.

Like Spinoza, Habermas regards this ideal as a kind of best-case scenario, a limit-point of speculative reason which as yet has no model – no exemplary warrant – in the history of social institutions. But he also claims that this ideal (i.e. the notion of uncoerced rational agreement) is implicit in our every act of communicative exchange, each attempt to understand what others are saying or have them understand what we ourselves mean. Furthermore, it is presupposed by the knowledge we have, in particular cases, that somehow this ideal has *not* been attained, that understanding has been blocked – in whatever degree – by the workings of prejudice, self-interest or erroneous belief. For we could have no idea that such failures had occurred were it not for our sense of the existing disparity – the mismatch or non-alignment between meaning and intent – that had opened up in the course of some ongoing dialogue. Habermas's great contribution is to have extended this argument from the level of speech-act pragmatics (or conversational implicature) to that of a generalized *social* theory of knowledge-constitutive interests whose aim is to provide normative standards for the conduct of rational debate.

But it is precisely this commitment to universal values – to a regulative discourse of validating truth-claims applicable across the whole range of human activities and interests – which has led some of Habermas's critics to question both the usefulness and the political implications of his work. For liberals (among them Michael Walzer) its weaknesses are those that are also to be found in the entire tradition of ethical and political theory descending from Kant.[8] That is to say, Habermas pitches his claims at the highest level of abstract generality, and offers little help toward a better understanding of the nuances, the detailed practicalities, or the essentially *contingent* character of real-life ethical choice. This criticism is joined to a Popperian mistrust of *any* theory – Kantian, Marxist or whatever – that thinks to adjudicate present-day issues on the basis of some privileged standpoint identified with truth, reason, or the forward march of historical events. And the charge is taken up even more vigorously by opponents – often of a post-structuralist or postmodernist persuasion – who attack Habermas for adopting what they see as a belated variant of the old Enlightenment paradigm, the belief in reason (or truth at the end of enquiry) as a means of imposing yet another 'grand narrative' in support of its own, self-authorized claims.[9]

Typical of this tendency, they argue, is Habermas's reading of Freud in *Knowledge and Human Interests*, a reading that interprets psychoanalysis as the bringing-to-light of unconscious motives, meanings and desires which would otherwise block or frustrate the drive toward rational self-knowledge.[10] For his critics, on the contrary, the chief lesson that Freud has to offer is the sheer *impossibility* that reason should achieve such a measure of consummate lucidity and grasp, such mastery over – or transparent access to – the workings of unconscious desire. Their starting-point is Lacan's well-known series of pronouncements to the effect that the unconscious is 'structured like a language'; that language is itself marked through and through by the symptoms of that which it can never fully articulate; that reason is always and everywhere in thrall to forces (or structures of signification) that escape its self-conscious grasp; that the ego-ideal is an 'imaginary' construct, the product of a delusive narcissistic craving for origins and presence; and therefore, in short, that reason is quite literally *in no position* to explain, elucidate or rationalize the unconscious and its effects. This argument receives its most striking formulation in Lacan's re-writing of the Cartesian dictum: 'I am not wherever I am the plaything of my thought; I think of what I am where I do not think to think'.[11]

So one can see why Habermas's work has encountered such hostility from Lacanians and other post-structuralist thinkers. For them, the main effect of Freud's 'Copernican revolution' was to bring about a radical *decentring* of the subject, a challenge to those theories of mind and knowledge – from Descartes down – that had rested their claims on the presumed self-evidence of a transcendental ego in sovereign possession of 'clear and distinct ideas'. Habermas's account of Freud – and the entire philosophical project of which it forms a part – must strike them not only as a retrograde move (in so far as it aims to reinstate the values of an obsolete Enlightenment discourse), but also as a gesture of containment and mastery, one whose political implications can be read in the history of 'enlightened' reason as applied to various deviant, oppressed or minority cultures. In short, what they criticize in Habermas is exactly what Foucault speaks out against in *Madness and Civilization*: the way that a certain, historically situated discourse of power/knowledge has managed to impose its own normative categories to the point where other, more subversive forms of discourse are silenced or treated as merely pathological.[12]

I have suggested already that Foucault's approach runs up against insuperable problems if it is asked just how one could accept these sceptical claims – amounting as they do to a wholesale rejection of the criteria for rational argument – and still take his proposals seriously, or seriously enough to engage them at the level of sustained critical debate. The same applies to those critics of Habermas who denounce his appeal to enlightened rationality as a species of oppressive, monological discourse, but who clearly expect that their own arguments will be judged as constructive interventions in a dialogue whose outcome they are scarcely disposed to entrust to the free-floating vagaries of the Lacanian signifier. As Derrida remarks in his critique of Foucault, there is simply no escaping this necessity of reasoned argument, even where the main point at issue is precisely the juridical question – so crucial to philosophy from Descartes and Kant to the present – of just what authorizes reason to pronounce in matters of truth and falsehood or right and wrong. To this extent Habermas is surely justified in claiming that there do exist normative constraints on the activity of giving reasons, engaging in dialogue, arguing one's case etc. But these constraints are not coercive or in any sense a product of the will to exclude or marginalize deviant forms of discourse. Still less are they complicit – as the Lacanians would have it – with that 'Enlightenment' drive for mastery and power which others (Adorno among them) have diagnosed as the chief symptom of modernity and its discontents. On the contrary: they serve as a regulative ideal that holds out the prospect of uncoerced rational agreement against all the numerous contending forces of prejudice, self-interest, and unargued doctrinal adherence.

Spinoza is very clear on this point in his defence of democratic institutions (more specifically: the Dutch States General) as the form of government best suited to maintaining the interests of justice, security and peace. Thus he argues that a 'commonwealth' in the genuine, evaluative sense of that word must be judged according to the scope it provides for the free expression of dissenting views, religious and political, and the extent to which those views can then be assessed – weighed up on their merits – in the 'public sphere' of open rational debate. In this respect his thinking has close affinities with Habermas's 'transcendental pragmatics', a theory that identifies social well-being with the achievement of broad-based consensus values, but which also requires that these be arrived at through a *critical* reflection on the arguments advanced in support of various specific group interests, and not just allowed to emerge in accordance with the dominant ('commonsense') view of those interests. It is on this point that Spinoza differs most markedly with contract theorists like Hobbes. For them, the only source of legitimate state power is the fact that, without it, society would revert to a condition of anarchic civil discord – the *bellum omnium contra omnes* – which Hobbes regards as the 'natural' state of unrestrained appetitive desire. Hence the need for citizens to set up some ultimate law-giving source of authority, since otherwise the social order would be torn apart by the warring forces of sectarian dispute or the naked expression of a will-to-power on the part of various class-factions. There is clearly no room on this Hobbesian view for the idea that there might exist rational restraints – or forms of *a priori* collective enlightened self-interest – which could act as a check upon those same disintegrating forces.

This is why I have suggested that the issue between Spinoza and Hobbes to some extent prefigures the current debate between a rationalist philosopher like Habermas and those 'postmodern' thinkers in the Nietzsche-Foucault line of descent whose project entails a radical rejection of all such Enlightenment ideas. Spinoza's 'commonwealth' would then signify something very like the Habermasian ideal of a 'speech-situation' that held out the promise of a genuine working consensus, a forum (or Kantian 'tribunal' of the faculties) set up in the interests of maintaining civil peace on the basis of uncoerced rational debate. It would thus stand in sharp contrast to those versions of the contract-model, from Hobbes to Foucault, that regard power-interests as the chief (indeed only) reality of social life, and which therefore discount any appeal to enlightened or progressive values as just another form of mystifying rhetoric in the service of liberal ideology.

But having said all this, one must also recognize that Spinoza *does* take a Hobbesian view to the extent of denying that political science can serve any useful purpose if it disregards the facts of 'human nature' as manifest in the history of social institutions to date. And this follows from his doctrine – enounced very clearly in the *Ethics* and elsewhere – that although reason is alone capable of giving access to ultimate truths, i.e. the kind of knowledge that permits us to pursue our best interests as citizen-members of a democratic state, nevertheless there is nothing unreal or delusory about the various material causes and factors that very often conspire to prevent us from achieving that happy condition. In the *Political Treatise* he makes this point by remarking on the sheer irrelevance of political theories that fix their sights on some as-yet unattained – and most likely unattainable – state of social existence. His own approach will sensibly avoid such utopian reveries by respecting the limits of accountable knowledge and not giving free rein to the speculative impulse. Thus:

> as we are treating here of the universal power or right of nature, we cannot here recognize any distinction between desires, which are engendered in us by reason, and those which are engendered by other causes; since the latter, as much as the former, are effects of nature, and display the natural impulse, by which man strives to

continue in existence . . . For man, whether guided by reason or
mere desire, does nothing save in accordance with the laws and rules
of nature, that is, by natural right. (*PT*, p. 292)

And in the opening paragraph of the *Treatise* Spinoza has yet more
caustic remarks about those thinkers who address themselves to
real-life issues from such a height of theoretical abstraction that the
whole course of history appears nothing more than a woeful chaos
of conflicting interests and desires. Such thinkers 'conceive of men,
not as they are, but as they themselves would like them to be'. And
from this it has come to pass, Spinoza writes, that 'instead of ethics,
they have generally written satire, and they have never conceived a
theory of politics which could be turned to use, but such as might
be taken for a chimera, or might have been formed in utopia, or in
that golden age of the poets when, to be sure, there was least need
of it' (*PT*, p. 287).

So there is clearly a strain in Spinoza's political thought that goes
against the aspects I have emphasized so far: those aspects, that is
to say, which anticipate Kant (and Habermas) on the 'idea of
history' – or the 'ideal speech-situation' – as regulative concepts
which hold out the promise of an end to civil discord or the ills
brought about by mutual misunderstanding. And it is here that
Spinoza comes closest to acknowledging the force of those objections
that are nowadays levelled – by Foucauldians, Lacanians, post-
structuralists and others – against any version of the Kantian desire
for an enlightened collectivity of rational subjects with a perfect
understanding of their own best interests achieved through a process
of transparent self-reflection. For there is always, in Spinoza, a
countervailing stress on the degree to which 'error' – most often
identified with the 'passive affections', or ideas and feelings brought
about by causes beyond our intellectual grasp – may none the less
play an *essential and constitutive role* in the shaping not only of
individual lives but of social institutions, political systems, and the
very course of historical events as determined by precisely such
contingent factors.

To this extent one could say that he agrees with the Lacanians,
at least as regards the limited capacity of consciousness (or the self-
present Cartesian ego) to account for those effects that necessarily
exceed its power of reflective grasp. Deleuze makes this point most
succinctly when he asks:

What does Spinoza mean when he invites us to take the body as a model? It is a matter of showing that the body surpasses the knowledge that we have of it, *and that thought surpasses the consciousness that we have of it*. There are no fewer things in the mind that exceed our consciousness than there are things in the body that exceed our knowledge. So it is by one and the same movement that we shall manage, if possible, to capture the power of the body beyond the given conditions of our knowledge, and to capture the power of the mind beyond the given conditions of our consciousness. One seeks to acquire a knowledge of the powers of the body in order to discover, *in a parallel fashion*, the powers of the mind that elude consciousness, and thus to be able to *compare* their powers.[13]

In effect, this passage re-states the distinction between metaphysics (as an enquiry into the nature and conditions of experience in general), and epistemology (as a later, more specialized branch of philosophical thought which raises questions about consciousness, knowledge, and the status of various kinds of truth-claim).

It might appear – from all his talk of 'adequate ideas' and the like – that Spinoza is as much an epistemologist as a metaphysician. And one could likewise argue that his whole philosophical project amounts to a kind of rationalist ego-psychology, an attempt to explain how self-knowledge comes about through the conscious, disciplined reflection on hitherto repressed or recalcitrant desires. Such is indeed the reading of his work that Feuer offers by way of locating it in the mainstream of liberal-Enlightenment thought. Thus 'when we know the causes of our irrational behaviour, the irrational motives themselves lose their force, and we can then act rationally in accordance with our desires as we now clearly apprehend them' (Feuer, p. 221). In which case Spinoza could fairly be regarded as a strong precursor of Freud, or at least as having anticipated that version of ego-psychology – so fiercely denounced by the Lacanians – which views the unconscious as a 'dark continent', an unknown region whose innermost depths must be explored and opened up to the daylight clarity of rational self-knowledge. But this is to ignore two main points about the structure and implications of his thinking. One is the aspect to which Deleuze draws attention: the fact that Spinoza refuses to privilege *consciousness* as a source of ultimate truth, or as a locus of 'clear and distinct ideas' that would somehow transcend the conditions of bodily experience. His argument is rather that mind and body are the two distinct 'attributes' of an otherwise unitary phenomenon whose variable capacity for 'active' or 'passive' existence is determined by its possession of more or less 'adequate' ideas. So it is an error to suppose – in Cartesian or epistemological terms – that the mind gains access to veridical truths only in so far as it transcends or discounts the evidence of bodily knowledge. From which it follows – the second main point – that his system finds room for affects or impulses which may never become *conscious* (that is: never attain to the status of 'clear and distinct ideas'), but which can none the less be *known* through the manner in which they influence our thoughts, actions, or states of conjointly mental and bodily experience.

This distinction between consciousness and knowledge is crucial to Spinoza's entire philosophy. It is the basis of his argument – as against Descartes – that the only measure of 'adequate' ideas is their capacity for transforming *passive* into *active* knowledge, or the extent to which they enable beings to grasp the determinate conditions of their own existence, and thus to lessen the degree of their enslavement to causes beyond their powers of active comprehension. In which case one could argue that Spinoza belongs squarely to that tradition of thought – taken up by Habermas in his reading of Freud – which identifies progress (individual and collective) with the overcoming of obstacles in the way of lucid self-knowledge or open dialogical exchange. But again, this fails to take account of the way in which knowledge-effects (as Spinoza describes them) can always surpass the limits imposed upon reflective or self-conscious thought. Thus, according to Deleuze, 'the conditions under which we know things and are conscious of ourselves condemn us *to have only inadequate ideas*, ideas that are confused and mutilated, effects separated from their real causes'.[14] These conditions may be such as to bring about all manner of illusory ideas, erroneous perceptions, or 'knowledge of imagination'. But this doesn't mean – far from it – that consciousness can somehow transcend those conditions through an effort of disciplined Cartesian self-knowledge that releases the mind from such merely contingent or material constraints. Here again we might recall Barbara Johnson's insistence on the stubborn *facticity* of error, the way that, as she puts it, 'the power of ignorance, blindness, uncertainty, or misreading is often all the more redoubtable for not being perceived as such', so that 'far from being a negative or non-existent factor, what is not known is often the unseen motivating force behind the very deployment of meaning'.[15]

In Spinoza's philosophy this awareness takes various forms, all

having to do with what Johnson describes as the 'redoubtable' force
of illusory effects, their power to produce determinate errors of
judgement which then become the very terms of cognition for
situated human knowers. His address to this topic ranges from
scriptural exegesis (where 'error' and 'blindness' are treated diagnos-
tically as the outcome of contingent socio-historical events), to the
writings on politics and affairs of state where Spinoza reflects – not
without a measure of disillusioned hindsight – on the factors that
conspire to prevent democracy from achieving its highest aims. In
each case the emphasis falls squarely on those limits to the power
of enlightened self-knowledge or rational self-determination which
affect both the individual's quest for 'adequate ideas' and the pursuit
of collective well-being through projects of enlightened liberal
reform. In short, there is no escaping the *real and material* effects
of cognitive error, even where error is conceived – as Spinoza
conceives it – in purely negative terms, as a 'privative' condition
determined by the absence of adequate ideas.

II

So we cannot, after all, read Spinoza as subscribing *absolutely* to a
version of socialized ego-psychology, one that equates the highest
interests of a rational polity with those of an 'ideal speech-situation'
whose participants enjoy transparent access to their own and other
people's motives, meanings, and intentions. Nor, for that matter,
should Habermas be read in this way, since he nowhere suggests that
such transparency is actually *attainable* under the given conditions of
social existence; only that it serves as a regulative standard for
assessing the various kinds and degrees of communicative failure
brought about by the present unequal distribution of power, knowledge, and information-access. All the same, his critics are right to
infer that the optimized conditions of communicative reason envisaged by Habermas are such as would tend – so to speak 'in the last
analysis' – to efface all signs of that 'other' language whose effects
are manifest in the symptoms of unconscious, repressed or subliminal desire. It is here that Spinoza offers the alternative of an outlook
that shares the Habermasian commitment to ideals of communicative reason, participant democracy, and enlightened consensus, but
which also finds room for a clear recognition of those factors –
psychic resistances and structures of regressive socialized desire –
that prevent such ideals from ever being carried fully into practice.

To this extent at least he agrees with the Lacanians: that any theory of language or society that ignores these countervailing forces will always be subject to unlooked-for disruptive effects – a veritable 'return of the repressed' – whose workings will create all manner of difficulty for its own self-assured project. But at the same time he insists, in contrast to these present-day apostles of unreason, that knowledge (though not always *conscious* knowledge) is indeed an ultimate good; that its benefits extend beyond the individual psyche to the government of the well-ordered commonwealth; and further-more, that the exercise of rational thought conduces to an 'active' use of those faculties that would otherwise be held unwittingly in thrall to the forces of natural causality. And so, as Spinoza writes,

> I am altogether for calling a man so far free, as he is led by reason; because so far he is determined to action by such causes, as can be adequately understood by his unassisted nature, although by these causes he be necessarily determined to action. For liberty . . . does not take away the necessity of acting, but supposes it. (*PT*, pp. 295–6)

Feuer is therefore right to associate Spinoza with Freud as a thinker whose efforts were devoted to the task of 'reclaiming' instinctual energies and drives, raising them to the level of 'adequate ideas', and thus putting them to work in the interests of a better, more enlightened social order. But he ignores the extent to which Spinoza makes allowance for those irrational motives which can never gain access to the realm of conscious, articulate reason, or – in Haber-mas's terms – the 'public sphere' of socially accountable meanings and actions. In fact it was Spinoza's recognition of this point – his unflinching acceptance of the error-prone, eccentric, or fallible nature of all understanding – that saved him from the kind of post-revolutionary defeatist or cynical outlook which Feuer attributes to the later works.

We should recall once again that Feuer was writing at a time (1958) when Western liberals were suffering a widespread failure of nerve brought about on the one hand by events in the Soviet Union, and on the other by Western anti-communist hysteria whipped up in support of Cold-War militarist policies. It is not hard to see why his reading of Spinoza falls into the basically tragic pattern of a narrative that leads from high liberal hopes, *via* numerous setbacks, to a mood of disenchanted stoical acceptance. I have suggested two main reasons for rejecting this interpretation. One is the fact that

Spinoza, like Kant, finds grounds for believing in justice, freedom, progress and 'perpetual peace' as *ideas of reason* that cannot be disproved – or written off as utopian fantasies – by simply pointing to the record of historical events, past and present. This might be called the 'positive' aspect of his thinking, though without any suggestion that it amounts to just looking on the bright side, making the best of a bad job, or whistling in the dark. In fact, as I have argued, it is an attitude that derives from Spinoza's most rigorous and consequent reflections on the capacities of human reason, the conditions of historical knowledge, and the replacement of 'passive' by 'active' ideas as a form of enlightening social critique. And on the 'negative' side, what Feuer fails to recognize is the role played by error (or the various effects of imaginary misrecognition) as a constant theme of Spinoza's philosophy, and not just a fact that was suddenly brought home to him by events in Holland after 1672. It is this double perspective – this idealism tempered by a wry knowledge of human fallibility – that enabled Spinoza to confront such disappointments without falling prey to the familiar syndrome of post-revolutionary doubt and despair.

This is not to deny that his confidence was shaken – tested to the limits and (sometimes) beyond – by the series of episodes that began with William II's *coup d'état* in 1650 and continued with the restoration of monarchy in England, the subsequent trade-wars, Calvinist intrigues, the French invasion, the murder of de Witt by a frenzied mob, and other such disheartening events. Nor is it to pass over those passages – more frequent in his later writing – where Spinoza apparently renounces his commitment to a politics of full-scale participant democracy and instead reflects harshly on the fickleness of popular opinion, the ever-present dangers of mob-rule, and the predominance of prejudice over reason as a motivating force in human affairs. Feuer sees all this as plain evidence that Spinoza had indeed learned the lesson of history and retreated, like so many after him, into regions of abstact speculative thought where such realities could no longer obtrude. 'The courageous political pamphleteer was gone; not the courage, but the impulse to persuade people to a rational polity, was gone. The liberal philosopher adjusted himself to resigned existence in a time of reaction' (Feuer, p. 115). And along with this loss of faith in 'the people' went a corresponding change in Spinoza's ideas about the powers and limits of legitimate state rule. In short, he moved over from a 'radical' position – one that identified democracy with the attainment of full civil rights and the unrestrained exercise of reason in all matters of opinion, conscience or belief – to a standpoint more closely resembling that of Hobbes where such freedoms were seen as always open to sectarian or populist abuse, and where the true public interest was conceived to lie in the maintenance of a strong executive power. Thus 'he appealed to governments to be rational, but if governments were irrational, Spinoza resignedly advised only submission' (p. 117). And in Feuer's view this drastic change of heart was not just a matter of emotional response to specific historical events, but a profound intellectual upheaval which shook the very foundations of Spinoza's system.

> The *Tractatus Theologico-Politicus* is a manifesto of freedom, but it ends with freedom's voice muffled and subdued: 'I have written nothing which I do not most willingly submit to the examination and approval of my country's rulers; and I am willing to retract anything which they shall decide to be repugnant to the laws, or prejudicial to the public good'. (p. 115)

In this passage Feuer reads nothing less (or nothing more) than a last-ditch abandonment of all those principles that Spinoza had so strenuously sought to maintain against the forces of reaction and bigotry. It thus provides a fitting if melancholy epilogue, not only to the narrative of Spinoza's life-history but also to the running subtext of Feuer's book, where he figures as a prototype for all liberal thinkers caught up in some retrograde turn of political events.

As I have said, this reading has a certain *prima facie* plausibility if one assumes – like Feuer and the New Historicists – that philosophical ideas are intelligible only as the products of this or that historical conjuncture or nexus of knowledge-constitutive interests. One would then have to agree that the failure of republican hopes and ideals must indeed have struck Spinoza as sufficient grounds for abandoning – or at any rate drastically re-thinking – his erstwhile political convictions. But Feuer's case will seem less persuasive if one takes the following points into account. First, there is the argument – presented most forcefully by Leo Strauss in his book *Persecution and the Art of Writing* – that in approaching such works one must always remember that they were written under threat of religious or political persecution, and may therefore contain covert meanings at odds with their surface declarations of pious or orthodox intent.[16] It would take no very ingenious application of the principle to detect this dissimulating strategy at work – one message for the literal-minded censors, another for the knowing reader – in the passage that Feuer cites as evidence of Spinoza's defeatist attitude. Second, that passage gives no warrant for the claim that Spinoza had significantly changed his views as to the prevalence of error (or 'inadequate ideas') in the normal course of human experience. It is on account of this fact – which he had always acknowledged, and which found confirmation in the untoward turn of Dutch political events – that Spinoza conceded the necessity for strong government, at least in matters concerning state security and the maintenance of civil peace. But it is precisely his aim, throughout the *Tractatus*, to explain how such measures may be justified in various specific historical or socio-political contexts, while none the less asserting that the interests of reason can transcend such short-term practical imperatives. This was one reason why Spinoza elected to present his political ideas partly in the form of a scriptual hermeneutics, or a theory of truth and error as applied to the ancient Jewish and Christian texts. For it was then possible to argue his case in an oblique or suggestive form, and thereby provide himself with at least some defence against charges of subversive intent. But also – more importantly – this approach enabled him to distinguish between *meanings* placed upon the text as a matter of orthodox or canonical requirement, and *truths of reason* arrived at by the exercise of uncoerced critical thought. And on this basis Spinoza could suggest – at least to those readers capable of decoding the signs – that interests of state as defined (or imposed) by their currently authorized upholders were not identical with the interests of reason as perceived through the power of active intellect.

Frank Kermode has drawn attention to this aspect of Spinoza's work in his book *The Genesis of Secrecy*, a study of the various hermeneutic methods brought to bear upon religious and secular texts.[17] What chiefly interests Kermode – writing from the standpoint of a professed 'outsider', one for whom the sense of scripture cannot be a matter of revealed or self-evident truth – is the constant dialogue between orthodox readings and those that admit some degree of interpretive licence, some novel understanding more keenly responsive to the pressures of social or doctrinal change. At such moments there occurs a kind of paradigm-shift, a swerve from the 'literal' (i.e. the received or canonical) reading of a text to one that more knowingly accommodates scripture to the needs of present understanding. And the result of this process is to generate narrative 'secrets', or meanings of an occult, arcane or specialized nature that reveal themselves only to readers in possession of the requisite hermeneutic skills. It is precisely through this interplay of literal and figurative readings that the texts of tradition (whether sacred or secular) continue to provoke debate among adherents to various creeds and ideologies. Such is indeed the character of the 'classic', as Kermode defines it: a work whose meaning is perpetually open to acts of interpretive revision, so that no single reading – orthodox or otherwise – can possibly exhaust its manifold signifying potential.[18] If the orthodox version lays claim to *truth* through divine inspiration or self-authorizing warrant, the rival account can always challenge that authority by affording the pleasure of a privileged access to *meanings* (or subtleties of hermeneutic insight) that necessarily elude the self-appointed guardians of mainstream tradition.

And so it has come about, according to Kermode, that techniques originally developed by biblical scholars – often with the purpose of reconciling variant truth-claims – have now migrated into the field of secular literary studies, giving rise to the numerous competing schools of present-day critical theory. These parallels are perhaps most striking in the discourse of French post-structuralism, a poetics that attaches maximum value to the notions of plural meaning, creative misprision, 'intertextuality', or reading as a process of transformative engagement with codes and conventions beyond the grasp of any orthodox interpretive method.[19] For Kermode, such ideas are best understood as a secularized version of the approach adopted by biblical scholars when they read some passage from the Gospels as 'fulfilling' an obscure Old Testament prophecy, or when they treat the latter as in some sense prefiguring the advent of revealed Christian truth.[20] What occurs in these transactions is a complex process of typological adjustment where reading is at once constrained by the codes of some existing 'interpretive community', and allowed sufficient scope to negotiate the gap between past and present modes of understanding. In periods of relative stability there will emerge a prevailing doctrinal consensus which sets the basic terms for debate and effectively excludes any marginal or deviant reading. At other times – epochs of religious or political upheaval – this consensus will often break down to the point where all manner of novel interpretations arise and the ground-rules are changed to accommodate the readings, rather than the other way around.

Kermode's main point is that we cannot understand the dynamics of tradition (or canon-formation) without taking stock of these constant shifts in the balance of power between orthodox and unorthodox modes of understanding. Thus there is always – even in turbulent periods – a certain degree of institutional control, a set of tacitly acknowledged values or criteria which determine what shall count as a competent, valid or worthwhile contribution to debate. To this extent Kermode is in agreement with Fish, arguing as he does that it is strictly inconceivable that any theory (or reading) should break altogether with existing hermeneutic constraints, since if it did so (*per impossibile*) then it wouldn't make sense to anyone qualified to judge. But there is a crucial difference of emphasis between these critics, since Kermode shows more willingness to allow for real changes in the currency of received opinion, changes brought about by a conflict of interests or principles which cannot be resolved through any straightforward appeal to consensus values. For Fish – as we have seen – such conflicts can amount to nothing more than a localized divergence of interpretive aims, a divergence that only makes sense on condition that all parties subscribe to certain other, more basic norms of consensual understanding. Kermode is himself at least half-way convinced by this line of argument. Yet his book offers plentiful evidence – from religious and secular sources alike – that in fact these disagreements have often run so deep as to necessitate a large-scale revisionist approach to the very ground-rules of interpretive method. And it is here that Spinoza figures most importantly as a thinker whose approach to questions of scriptural exegesis did much to break the hold of that orthodox model which had so far subjugated critical reason to the dictates of religious or doctrinal truth.

The following passages from *The Genesis of Secrecy* explain very clearly why Spinoza played such a crucial role in this liberating movement of thought. 'The story of modern biblical exegesis', Kermode writes, 'tends to confirm the view that it takes a powerful mind to attend to what is written at the expense of what it is written about.'[21] And Spinoza's contribution was to make this possible by severing the hitherto sacrosanct tie between textual meaning and revealed truth, and thus leaving criticism free to pursue its enquiries without interference from the authorized custodians of scriptural tradition.

> The Bible, he held . . . is of divine origin, but it is accommodated to human understanding, which may ascertain its meanings, but must not confound them with truths. 'It is one thing to understand

the meaning of Scripture, and quite another to understand the actual truth.' Five centuries of Jewish interpretative rationalism stood behind Spinoza; but he was addressing the problems of his own day, and saw that the confusion of meaning and truth might result in the suppression of religious liberty. His pious book seemed blasphemous in 1670, so powerful is the atavistic preference for truth over meaning.[22]

This is certainly one reason for Spinoza's notoriety among Christian and Jewish believers alike. But when Kermode equates 'truth' with revealed *religious* truth – God's word vouchsafed to the elect through a species of privileged hermeneutic insight – he overlooks that other kind of truth that Spinoza regards as the highest object of all philosophical enquiry, and which offers the only reliable means to criticize erroneous habits of belief. Thus in the sentence that he cites from Spinoza in the passage above Kermode seems not to recognize the crucial ambivalence that inhabits this term. On the one hand 'truth' is the presumptive warrant that authorizes mainstream exegetes (clerics and commentators) to impose their own interpretation of scripture as possessing absolute validity. On the other, it signifies the capacity of reason to examine such claims, whatever their source, and determine whether or not they meet the required standard of truthful (adequate) ideas. For otherwise there could be no grounds of appeal against those various forms of prejudice, dogmatism, or unthinking doctrinal adherence that all too often result – in Spinoza's view – from the confusion between meaning and truth.

This helps to explain what several commentators have noted about Kermode's work since *The Genesis of Secrecy*: namely, his tendency to vacillate on the question of just how far readings are determined by the pressures of institutional control, or the resistance to change exerted by prevalent modes of consensus thinking. Very often this criticism is couched in ideological terms, as a doubt concerning Kermode's even-handedness – his studied ambivalence, as some would have it – between an interest in the more advanced or radical forms of post-structuralist theory and a lingering attachment to tradition, continuity, and the status of the 'classic' as a means of transcending these otherwise awkward antinomies.[23] One could equally argue – from a sympathetic standpoint – that Kermode is engaged in a project of revisionist theory that values texts for their plurality of meaning, or their openness to new interpretations, while also giving a more radical edge to Fish's talk of reading as a communal activity. My concern is not to adjudicate this issue but to ask what bearing it might have on his account of Spinoza, as summarized above. And it is significant here that Kermode's restatement of the truth/meaning distinction is one that puts 'truth' very firmly on the side of authority, tradition and vested institutional power, while 'meaning' is aligned with the interpreter's freedom to challenge or transform those values, to read texts always in light of changing historical or cultural concerns, and thus to save the 'classic' – or the idea of 'tradition' – from becoming a mere slogan in the service of a closed or reactionary system of beliefs. Thus 'truth' figures mainly as a kind of sacred preserve, a repository of values inherently resistent to time and change. 'Meaning', on the other hand, is that which denies all forms of canonical closure, all attempts to identify the interpreter's role with the faithful transmission of original, self-authorizing truths.

To this extent Kermode might be thought to approximate the stance of a strong revisionist critic such as Harold Bloom, one for whom the best, most productive readings are those that engage – like the poets before them – in an agonistic struggle with their source-texts (or Oedipal precursors), and which thus lay claim to an order of imaginative insight unglimpsed by more orthodox interpreters.[24] But Kermode clearly differs with Bloom in believing that there do exist powerful constraints upon any such revisionist programme, among them those forms of 'institutional control' that provide at least a background of consensual understanding against which to judge any radical departures. On this point he agrees with Fish: that criticism is a communal sense-making enterprise, one that requires some measure of continuity (or deference to established norms), even in periods like the present when it appears that just about every such convention is subject to doubt and disagreement. What emerges in the end from Kermode's treatment of this question is a refusal – a deliberate and principled refusal – to decide between these seeming alternatives, since both play a necessary role in every act of commentary or criticism. And indeed, there is no escaping this conclusion if one accepts, like Kermode, that meaning is entirely a product of interpretive codes and conventions, a matter of perpetual adjustment (as hermeneutic theorists would have it) between the 'pre-understanding' that constitutes tradition and the needs of some present community of readers engaged in making sense of that same tradition. For it then becomes clear that any new interpretation – any challenge to the current institutional *status quo*

– will have to make terms with the existing consensus of qualified opinion, at least if it wants to gain a hearing among readers deemed competent to judge on such questions.

Of course this predicament is by no means unique to Kermode's way of stating the issue. In fact it is a version of the 'hermeneutic circle', as described by philosophers like Heidegger and Gadamer: the argument that all interpretation takes place within a given cultural context of beliefs, values and knowledge-constitutive interests which can never be fully articulated – let alone subjected to radical critique – since they operate at a level of tacit presupposition which alone makes it possible to exchange ideas on a basis of shared understanding. (Other variants include the Wittgensteinian appeal to 'language-games' or 'forms of life' and of course the theory of 'interpretive communities' developed in the work of Stanley Fish.) On this view it is strictly inconceivable that a text could put up the kind of stubborn resistance to consensus values – or provoke the kind of stubbornly resistant reading – that would constitute a genuine challenge to prevailing institutional norms. There could thus be no question of criticizing consensus-values from an alternative (more rational or enlightened) standpoint, since this would entail the impossible claim that thinking can achieve an order of knowledge ideally independent of the beliefs, meanings, or presuppositions that make up a given cultural 'form of life'. And from this line of argument it can readily be deduced – as happens with the more conservative applications of Wittgensteinian or neopragmatist doctrine – that there is simply *no point* in offering criticisms which will either be altogether lacking in persuasive force (in so far as they flout all the relevant conventions), or otherwise be obliged to make tolerable sense on terms that have always been decided in advance by some given interpretive community. For if thinkers like Gadamer are right – if understanding is always and inevitably confined to the 'hermeneutic circle' of tacit foreknowledge – then it is hard to conceive how reading could break with the currency of accepted ideas or commonsense belief.

Habermas makes the point very forcefully when he criticizes Gadamer and other theorists in the hermeneutic camp for their failure to envisage any way beyond this self-enclosed realm of traditional values. For Gadamer, in short, 'any attempt to suggest that this (certainly contingent) consensus is false consciousness is meaningless since we cannot transcend the discussion in which we are engaged . . . From this he deduces the ontological priority of linguistic tradition before all possible critique'.[25] What Habermas objects to in this way of thinking is the fact that it forecloses any grounds of appeal to a better, more enlightened or liberal consensus where participants would not be disadvantaged through unequal access to the public sphere of informed debate. On the contrary, he argues:

> every consensus, in which the understanding of meaning terminates, stands fundamentally under suspicion of being pseudo-communicatively induced . . . the prejudgemental structure of the understanding of meaning does not guarantee identification of an achieved consensus with a true one.[26]

It is on this point – his insistence that values of truth and falsehood cannot be assimilated wholly to the sphere of *de facto* consensual belief – that Habermas differs with Gadamer and other proponents of the hermeneutic circle. As we have seen, he has two main arguments against this view, both designed to show that understanding is not exhausted – or brought up against the limits of rational explanation – as soon as one appeals to some background context of legitimizing values and truth-claims. On the one hand there are knowledge-constitutive interests ('ideas of reason', in the Kantian sense) which hold out the prospect of a *genuine* working consensus that would not be subject to the errors, distortions and partial understandings that characterize current debate. This possibility may never be realized in practice, since it exists as an ideal limit-point, a regulative notion that can always encounter new obstacles thrown up by the imperfect conditions of real-life social exchange. But it still has a vital role to play, not only in locating the nature and the source of those same imperfections, but also in suggesting how they might be overcome in pursuit of a better, more highly evolved sphere of communicative reason. And this leads on to Habermas's second objection: that the 'hermeneutic circle' as theorized by thinkers like Gadamer would effectively rule out the perception of *error* as a determinate fact of human cognitive experience, a fact that makes itself felt wherever knowledge encounters some resistance to its quest for adequate ideas. For if theory and interpretation are really such ultimately circular activities – if nothing can ever count as meaningful or true unless allowed for in advance by some existing consensus, language-game, or communal 'form of life' – then of course it is out of the question that our thinking should be changed by the experience of error as something that occasionally gets in the way of our knowledge-constitutive interests.

In short, this version of the hermeneutic paradigm ends up in a prison-house of its own elaborate devising where there is no longer any role for the values of truth and falsehood, since everything is decided by preemptive appeal to beliefs that hold good for us (or our own 'interpretive community'), and which therefore operate to screen out any evidence that doesn't fit in with the prevalent consensus-view. We can now go back to that passage from Kermode and see just what is wrong with the idea of Spinoza as having more or less invented modern hermeneutics by severing the link between meaning and truth. In fact Kermode himself gives reason to doubt this claim when he recalls (midway through the same passage) that Spinoza 'expressed a particular dislike for the practice of distorting meaning "in order to make it conform with some meaning already entertained"', and furthermore that 'he neatly convicts his illustrious predecessor Maimonides of this offence, which he thinks intellectually disreputable and liable to favour political authoritarianism'.[27] For one then has to ask *by what standard* precisely readings may be judged as 'distorting' the text in accordance with 'some meaning already entertained'. What Spinoza has in mind when he criticizes Maimonides is the habit, among biblical commentators, of starting out from a position of assumed authority – an orthodox stance with regard to questions of doctrinal truth – and then finding ever more elaborate and ingenious ways of bringing the text into line with that initial prejudice. Hence his objection to those 'Kabbalistic triflers' whose stock-in-trade it is – so Spinoza argues – to produce all manner of hermeneutic subtleties or swerves from the literal meaning of scripture while failing to respect the most elementary rules of historical and textual scholarship. By such means they are enabled to pass clean over any signs of resistance in the text, any obstacles, inconsistencies, or disruptions of narrative coherence (as between the various Old and New Testament books) that would call their whole approach into doubt.

For Spinoza, on the contrary, the proper business of scriptural exegesis is to apply its best efforts to the task of rational reconstruction, that is, to explaining just *how it came about* – under what precise historical conditions, what pressures of circumstance, doctrinal adherence, and so forth – that the texts in question should so often have resorted to inadequate (i.e. 'imaginary') techniques for enforcing their message. And this requires in turn that reason be allowed full scope for the exercise of a critical hermeneutics that distances itself equally from both major schools of interpretive thought. On the one hand it is a matter (as Kermode well sees) of liberating commentary from those preemptive truth-claims that mistake their own *de facto* authority – their orthodox standing or purely institutional warrant – for some privileged mode of access to God's truth as revealed through scripture to the minds of a pious priestly elect. To this extent, certainly, Spinoza's great achievement lay in his having dissociated questions of 'truth' from questions of interpretive method. But he is equally insistent – as against Kermode – that criticism cannot make a start in challenging these false claims to truth unless it acknowledges the existence of other, more enlightened or rational forms of interpretive procedure. For otherwise thinking will indeed be trapped in an endless process of specular self-confirmation, a 'hermeneutic circle' which allows texts to mean only what they *must* be construed as meaning in accordance with the dictates of this or that readerly prejudice. Such prejudice may take the form of an adherence to orthodox canons of interpretive response which derive their authority from law, tradition, or respect for 'truth' as identified (mistakenly) with the sacred word of scripture. But it can also be seen in those counter-canonical or 'strong revisionist' readings which reject all appeals to authority and truth in the name of a new-found hermeneutic freedom. For here also there is nothing to prevent mere prejudice from making what it will of the text, this time in the guise of a liberation-movement which merely reproduces an alternative set of prejudicial truth-claims, meanings and values.

III

This is why Spinoza has such harsh things to say about commentators who 'distort' or disfigure the text in pursuit of novel interpretive ideas. It is also one reason why he cannot be assimilated (*pace* Kermode) to that line of thought which begins by questioning the privileged status of scriptural truth-claims, and which ends – in our own day – with post-structuralist, neo-pragmatist, hermeneutical, Foucauldian and other such arguments against *all* forms of truth as mere impositions of a will-to-power that masquerades in the guise of knowledge, science, critique etc. For Spinoza is very firm in maintaining the contrary position: that truth is what *resists* such encroachments of unreason by offering good argumentative grounds for not taking scripture (or anything else) on trust, but subjecting its claims to the tribunal of critical reason.

This conviction is manifest at every level and in every aspect of his work. It informs his writings on scriptural exegesis through Spinoza's insistence, firstly, that the texts be read with an eye to their internal contradictions and downright absurdities – claims that are simply unacceptable to reason – and secondly, that these problems should not be set aside by appealing to divine inspiration (or the paradoxical nature of revealed religious truth), but should rather be traced back to their source in the socio-political conditions prevailing at the time when they were first set down. In short, Spinoza sees absolutely no virtue in the kind of hermeneutic subtlety that developed in the reading of biblical texts, and whose influence has undoubtedly carried across into the practice of present-day secular literary criticism. For there is no denying Kermode's central claim: that this influence may be traced in many of the privileged key-terms (ambiguity, paradox, intertextuality, 'revisionary ratios' and so forth) which have characterized the discourse of advanced critical thinking over the past fifty years and more. But to see Spinoza as a signal precursor of these and related developments (e.g. modern hermeneutic philosophy) is to read him with a mind more closely attuned to such modern ideas than to anything in his own work. For it is precisely his aim to *prevent* interpretation from working its sophistical mischief, that is to say, its capacity for inventing new pretexts, new varieties of ingenious reader-response, in order to avoid the problems involved in making rational sense of the scriptures.

Hence Spinoza's sceptical attitude with regard to miracles, prophecies, divine interventions and other such dubious items of faith, adopted – as he argues – solely with the purpose of persuading ignorant and credulous minds, and lacking any semblance of rational truth. Thus 'all the arguments deployed by Moses . . . are to be understood in the same manner: they are not drawn from the armoury of reason, but are merely modes of expression calculated to instil with efficacy, and present vividly to the imagination the commands of God' (*TPT*, p. 159). Where the subtle-minded exegetes go wrong is in attempting to *reconcile* these passages with the requirements of a latter-day 'interpretive community', one whose members cannot (or at any rate should not) be so easily imposed upon by suchlike persuasive techniques. In short, 'we may explain the words of Scripture according to our preconceived opinions, twisting them about, reversing or completely changing their literal sense, however plain it may be' (*TPT*, p. 117). But this approach is misguided – a source of manifold errors and delusions – in so far as it substitutes mere ingenuity (or interpretive flair) for the much more difficult business of analysing texts in relation to their socio-historical conditions of production. What makes it especially danger-ous (and seductive) is the scope this method offers for new ways of reading which appear to contest the orthodox account, but which in fact just involve some accommodating 'twist' – some convenient swerve from the literal sense – by which to head off any real question as to the nature of scriptural 'truth' and the interests of those who purport to expound it.

So Spinoza is quite definitely *not* saying – as Kermode would have him say – that new readings must always 'accommodate' the old through a harmonizing process of interpretive revision which aims to reconcile discrepant details by shedding all illusions of ultimate validity or truth. Certainly he seeks to liberate commentary from the kinds of preemptive doctrinal truth-claim that would treat scripture as a timeless repository of divinely sanctioned commands. Interpreters who take this line are merely demonstrating their own inability to resist those habits of partial and self-interested reading that have propped up various forms of priestly or institutional control down through the ages. To be sure, Spinoza seeks to challenge this authoritarian regime of truth by removing scripture from the custody of those who would claim some unique, self-validating access to the Word of God as revealed through various arcane techniques of divinatory reading or hermeneutic exegesis. But it is precisely on account of his desire to resist such unwarranted impositions – such manipulative strategies designed to place power in the hands of a privileged interpretive elite – that Spinoza argues the case for a different order of truth-claim, one that goes by way of philological scholarship, historical criticism, the detailed comparison of biblical source-texts, along with an analysis of social institutions, the politics of religious belief, and what amounts to a genealogical critique of all such value-systems. For he sees very clearly that scriptural hermeneutics, if pursued in isolation from these other kinds of study, must always lead back to a self-enclosed realm of preemptive institutional constraints.

Any resistance to received ways of reading and thinking will therefore involve something more than a 'strong revisionist' approach to questions of scriptural meaning. It will have to take account of *material* factors – history, circumstance, prejudice, error, contradictions in the scriptural record, and so forth – which find no place in the hermeneutic model of textual understanding as a circular exchange between tradition (the realm of pre-established meanings and values) and modernity (the point where those values are harmonized with present-day interpretive interests). What drops out of sight in this treatment of the question is any possibility that texts – some texts at least – might *not* be amenable to readings that adopt such a smoothly accommodating line. This is why, in Leo Strauss's words,

> Spinoza demands of Bible science that it should be a means of unprejudiced understanding of Scripture. Unprejudiced understanding is equivalent to historical understanding. Scripture is not being understood if the interpreter is introducing his own insights or convictions into the text, if he is not taking Scripture as it presents itself . . . In accord with this, he defines the purpose of interpretation to be the bringing about of knowledge of Scripture in so far as the message of Scripture is other than the interpreter thinks, believes or feels.[28]

It is hard to conceive how such resistance could arise – how any text could communicate a meaning *against or despite* what the reader expects – if it were really the case (as Gadamer argues) that all understanding necessarily occurs within the 'hermeneutic circle' of interpretive foreknowledge. For Gadamer, the very word 'prejudice' needs to be revalued – given a more positive sense – in view of the fact that we cannot even begin to comprehend the texts of our own (or any other) cultural tradition without acknowledging the tacit values, the structure of shared meanings, beliefs and 'pre-understandings', that make up the enabling background of each and every interpretive act.[29] As I remarked in connection with Fish, there is a basic truth to this position – a kind of flat good sense – so long as it is not then raised into an argument for upholding current consensus-values and rejecting all forms of oppositional critique. For it then becomes necessary to argue – like Spinoza – that understanding is *not* confined to the hermeneutic circle of endless interpretive visions and revisions, since there do exist grounds (historical, philosophical and textual grounds) for reading consistently against the grain of received ideological belief.

So Spinoza's example is immensely significant in the context of present-day critical theory, though not in quite the way that Kermode suggests. His influence has been greatest on those thinkers (like Althusser, Macherey and Deleuze) whose work is aimed squarely 'against interpretation', or at any rate against the view – widely-held among literary critics – that the object of reading is somehow to release the largest possible range of meanings from a given text or passage. This idea can of course be traced back to Coleridge and his set-piece examples of 'practical criticism' as applied to Shakespeare, Wordsworth and others. But its real apotheosis came at the point when T. S. Eliot – in a series of canonical essays – effectively identified the proper interests of criticism with those of close-reading or rhetorical exegesis. The subsequent story is familiar enough, from William Empson's *Seven Types of Ambiguity* – where multiple meaning is taken as the hallmark or touchstone of poetic language – to the American New Criticism, French post-structuralism, and at least one variety of deconstruction as practised by literary critics (among them Geoffrey Hartman and J. Hillis Miller) for whom it offers a degree of hermeneutic freedom denied by other, more orthodox schools. It might be argued, in support of Kermode's central claim, that this whole complex chapter of developments grows out of – and at various points returns to – its origin in the practice of scriptural interpretation. Thus Eliot wrote an essay on Lancelot Andrewes, the seventeenth-century Anglican bishop, drawing attention not only to his historical importance as a defender of orthodox (High Church) interests, but also to the highly distinctive prose-style of Andrewes' sermons, in particular his technique of 'dividing the word of God', or practising a form of minute textual exegesis which closely resembled certain aspects of Eliot's own practice.[30] And at the opposite extreme – 'opposite' at least in terms of doctrinal persuasion – one finds Geoffrey Hartman, in his recent essays, offering the example of Jewish Midrash as a model for the kind of commentary that breaks with orthodox interpretive constraints and ranges freely over a multitude of source-texts, analogues, and rival commentaries.[31] So to this extent Kermode has good warrant for his view that modern criticism derives in large part from techniques invented for the purpose of scriptural exegesis.

But he errs – as I have argued – in counting Spinoza among the adepts of that same tradition. Spinoza belongs much more in the company of those critics and theorists who have held out against the dominant idea of *interpretation* as the normal mode of literary-critical activity, and of multiple meaning (or the 'plural text') as its most rewarding object of study. This alternative tradition goes right back to Aristotle, with his stress on the virtues of an orderly, disciplined method of approach that starts out from observed regularities of structure in various types of text, and then proceeds inductively to specify the rules or conventions governing that genre. The most obvious heirs of Aristotelian thinking are those modern formalist or structuralist movements which likewise see no virtue in producing ever more sophisticated interpretations of individual texts, but concentrate rather on the various poetic devices (or modes of narrative emplotment) that characterize literary discourse in general. However, there are other reasons – more germane to my argument here – why critics have come to view interpretation with a certain principled mistrust, a sense that it falls in all too readily with conformist or institutionalized habits of thought. And I think that Kermode indicates one source of these misgivings when he locates the point of departure for modern hermeneutics in the severance of that link between truth and meaning which had previously governed the practice of scriptural commentary. For it now became possible for interpreters to claim that theirs was a wholly autonomous activity, a practice of reading ideally unconstrained by any obligation to respect the imperatives of reason, logic, historical scholarship, or other such 'non-literary' standards of cognitive accountability. That is to say, there developed a specialized discourse of literary-critical debate where those standards were perceived as strictly extraneous to the structures of inwrought meaning – ambiguity, paradox, irony and so forth – which set poetry apart from all forms of everyday communicative language.

For the New Critics especially this became a high point of principle, a dogma connected with the orthodox ban on readings that failed to pay close enough attention to 'the words on the page', and which thus fell back into the bad habit of invoking historical, biographical, or suchlike strictly irrelevant kinds of knowledge. Where these readings offend most gravely is in failing to respect the difference between the mode of *sui generis* imaginative 'truth' that poetry is uniquely able to provide, and those other sorts of truth that involve the application of factual or logical criteria. Hence the various 'heresies' anathematized by W. K. Wimsatt, the high priest and guardian of 'old' New Critical orthodoxy.[32] Worst of all was the heresy of paraphrase, since this involved the notion – an affront to their every last precept and principle – that poetic meaning could be somehow re-stated in the simplified form of a rational prose discourse that would have no need of devices like irony and paradox. And behind this there loomed the yet more threatening prospect of a criticism that would take poems seriously *in the wrong way*; that would treat them as offering arguments, advancing truth-claims, or engaging with issues beyond their proper realm of self-enclosed meaning and value. Indeed, one could view this whole modern enterprise – in the wake of Eliot's pioneering essays – as a kind of elaborate *cordon sanitaire*, a system of self-authorizing checks and interdictions designed to insulate poetry (or the criticism of poetry) from any contact with history, politics, or questions of a wider socio-cultural import.

This project discovers its best, most satisfying form in a work like Cleanth Brooks's *The Well-Wrought Urn*, a sequence of neatly turned interpretive essays on poets from Donne and Marvell to Wordsworth and Keats, each chapter leading up to the same (wholly circular) conclusion: that all good poetry is paradoxical through and through, since paradox or its kindred rhetorical tropes (ambiguity, irony etc.) are of the essence of poetry, and can therefore provide an indubitable index of aesthetic worth.[33] Very often such judgements emerge from a reading that is by no means innocent of its own historical bias or ideological *parti pris*. The most obvious example is his chapter on Marvell's 'Horatian Ode: upon Cromwell's Return from Ireland', a set-piece essay in rhetorical close reading which takes its cue from Eliot's well-known remarks about the poem's eminently 'graceful' and 'civilized' demeanour. Thus when Brooks praises the 'Horatian Ode' for its qualities of ironic equipoise – its managing to sustain a finely-held balance between Royalist and Cromwellian sympathies – one can see that he has not only contrived to smuggle in a sizable amount of 'extraneous' historical baggage, but has also signalled his own strong preference for Marvell's tactful way of handling (or evading) the issue, as compared, say, with Milton's unambiguous commitment to a politics of radical change.[34] It is no coincidence that Brooks's aesthetic criteria have this effect of valuing poetry in proportion as its rhetoric negates, resists, or disowns any statement of political belief. In fact one could argue that this entire New Critical lexicon – 'parodox', 'irony', 'wit', 'balance', 'impersonality' and so forth – was invented for the purpose of elevating poets (like Donne or Marvell) whose work displayed a fine indifference to politics, and devaluing other (like Milton or Shelley) who espoused any kind of republican or left-wing stance. At least this would go some way toward explaining why Eliot, for one, mounts his case against Milton and Shelley on technical grounds that scarcely account for the sheer vehemence of his attack.[35] So when Leavis wrote that Milton's 'dislodgement' from the canon had been accomplished with 'remarkably little fuss', he was speaking in the name of a critical movement – a confidently orthodox movement – whose aversion to left-wing politics could now be passed off as involving nothing more than a respect for poetry itself, or the imperatives of textual close-reading.[36]

More recently, critics have become very aware of this alignment between the idea of poetry as an autonomous, self-enclosed realm of meaning, and the covert presence of a certain 'aesthetic ideology' that discovers its elective homeground in precisely such a mystified rhetoric of form and value. One of the earliest to make this connection was William Empson in his book *The Structure of Complex Words* (1951).[37] By this time Empson had developed deep misgivings, not only with regard to the American New Criticism – which he saw as promoting an irrationalist doctrine in league with a widespread 'Neo-Christian' revival – but also in respect of his own early work, since *Seven Types* could be taken as a virtual manifesto for just the kind of reading that Empson now deplored. For it seemed to many readers of the earlier book – especially its passages on Donne, Herbert, Hopkins and other religious poets – that Empson was drawing a straightforward equation between literary value and the sheer multiplicity of meaning to be found in this or that instance. And furthermore, his method appeared to work best with poems where 'ambiguity' shaded into 'paradox', or where the mere possibility of 'alternative reactions to the same piece of language' – a description roughly covering Types One to Three – gave way to 'full-blown states of psychological conflict', states which very often resulted (in Empson's view) from a neurotic struggle with the more sinister implications of Christian theology. Thus if the book has any ordering principle, Empson writes, it is the progress through stages of 'increasing logical and psychological complication', to the point where 'ambiguity' is a term hardly adequate to convey the clash of contradictory beliefs or value-systems.

The most striking example is his treatment of Herbert's 'The Sacrifice', a passage that has also given maximum offence to critics of an orthodox (Christian or scholarly) mind. But what Empson found so disturbing in retrospect was the way that *Seven Types* had been taken up as a primer or source-text for the kind of rhetorical close-reading that identified 'paradox' as the chief value and distinguishing mark of poetic language in general. For interpreters could then go on to claim – as did the New Critics, some of them explicitly, others through various forms of analogical transfer – that poetry and religion were deeply akin, since both gave access to imaginative truths beyond reach of mere analysis or plain-prose reason. Thus for Cleanth Brooks it is a matter of principle – inevitably borne out in the reading – that 'what Wordsworth wanted to say demanded his use of paradox . . . [and] could only be said powerfully through paradox'.[38] Hence the great danger, as Empson saw it, that this powerful new mode of rhetorical exegesis would indeed take the path that Eliot had signalled in his essay on Lancelot Andrewes. That is to say, it showed all the signs of developing into a form of surrogate religious orthodoxy, one that came equipped with the full apparatus of doctrinal rules and prohibitions. And then there would be nothing to prevent it from reverting – as Eliot and some of his disciples clearly wished – to that stage of pre-critical consensus belief when religious doctrine was the only measure of interpretive truth, and when meaning (as revealed through scriptural exegesis) placed absolute limits on the exercise of rational thought.

In fact the New Critics had problems with Empson, not least on account of his anti-Christian crusade, his attitude of sturdy commonsense rationalism, and – very much in keeping with this – his flat refusal, in *Seven Types*, to treat poetic language as a privileged mode of utterance, requiring that one not apply the usual standards of sense-making logic and consistency. One sign of his recalcitrance in this regard was Empson's habit of paraphrasing poems, most often by recording multiple attempts to tease out the sense of some particular passage, and then leaving the reader to sort them all into some kind of working synthesis. What this method implied – in stark opposition to New Critical doctrine – was that poetry *could and should* be made accountable to reason; that its interests were continuous with those of our practical, everyday understanding; and therefore that interpreters were merely practising a form of high-priestly mystification when they erected it into a point of principle that poetry should not be paraphrased. All the same Empson had to recognize that there were passages in *Seven Types* – notably the treatment of Herbert – which lent themselves to a reading totally at odds with his tough-minded rationalist stance. This was why he set out, with *The Structure of Complex Words*, to develop a theory of multiple meaning that couldn't be annexed to any form of religious or quasi-religious exegetical technique.

There is no room here for a detailed account of this brilliant, quirky, at times problematic, but often superbly convincing and original book. Sufficient to say that it develops the following theses: (1) that 'complex words' can best be understood as containing verbal 'equations' (or structures of logico-semantic entailment) which condense whole arguments into a single key-word, or a sequence of such words in context; (2) that the best, most rewarding instances – like 'wit' and 'sense' in Pope's *Essay on Criticism*, or 'sense' in a whole range of literary works, from *Measure for Measure* to *The Prelude* and *Sense and Sensibility* – will display an especially rich, complex, or problematical use of these semantic resources; and (3) that where the method comes up against resistance – where the key-word in question proves wholly unamenable to any kind of logico-semantic analysis – then here we have a case of some irrational doctrine, some attempt to short-circuit the structures of intelligible sense and impose what amounts to a species of irrationalist (or merely 'rhetorical') truth-claim. The approach tends to work best with a poem like the *Essay on Criticism*, where Pope is clearly running through a whole gamut of witty variations on the possible senses of 'wit' and 'sense', a virtuoso performance that responds ideally to Empson's analytical technique. Elsewhere, as in the chapters on Wordsworth and Milton, he is obliged to admit that the method hasn't worked, at least to the extent that something in the poetry – some structure of deviant equations, alogical entailment or downright 'paradox' – has proved resistant to any kind of truth-functional analysis. But even here, Empson argues, it is important to see just *why* the analysis fails; to understand how the poets (Wordsworth in particular) are exploiting rhetorical devices which do, undeniably, have great persuasive force, but whose effect is none the less dependent on our not enquiring too closely into their mode of structural-semantic operation.

In the background of this argument one detects not only Empson's rationalist antipathy to all forms of religious mystery-mongering, but also his distinctly Orwellian sense of the dangers implicit in any use of language that gives rhetoric the upper hand over reason, or which treats paradox as a purveyor of ultimate truths beyond or above rational scrutiny. Thus he sees little difference, in rhetorical terms, between the Christian statement 'God is Love' and the various slogans – like 'War is Peace' – through which Orwell conveys the complicity of language with forms of totalitarian thought-control. In fact Empson doesn't go along with Orwell's gloomy prognosis, since he believes that language (at least in its 'normal', undistorted condition) carries structures of logical entailment that most often act as a check upon the power to impose such irrationalist or paradoxical injunctions. In this respect he takes something like a Habermasian line, conceding the existence of forces – social and linguistic – that operate to block or frustrate the desire for rational communication, but also holding out the redemptive prospect of an 'ideal speech-situation' where these obstacles would no longer work their mischief and language would achieve at least the possibility of a working rational consensus. However, Empson differs with Habermas in maintaining that this principle extends to poetry – or literary language in general – rather than applying only to those discourses where questions of truth and falsehood are more obviously raised. For it is Empson's belief, as we have seen, that any too-willing acquiescence in poetry's power to insinuate paradoxes, straightforward falsehoods, or 'profound' pseudo-truths may itself give rise to serious distortions in our dealing with language in its everyday uses. And criticism can only make things worse by raising 'paradox' into a veritable touchstone of poetic value, and thus encouraging a form of wholesale irrationalist abandon. This is how Empson began to feel about some of his own earlier criticism. Thus it seemed, in re-reading the passage on Herbert from *Seven Types*, 'that my attitude was what I have come to call Neo-Christian: happy to find such an extravagant specimen, I slapped the author on the back and egged him on to be even nastier'.[39]

The difference between Empson and Habermas is best brought out in the following passage from the latter's *Philosophical Discourse of Modernity*. In it, Habermas argues the case for treating fiction and poetry as categorically distinct from those other kinds of discourse (criticism included) where validity-claims are always in question, whatever their pretensions to 'literary' form or style. Thus, as Habermas argues,

> the rhetorical element occurs *in its pure form* only in the self-referen-
> tiality of the poetic expression, that is, in the language of fiction
> specialized for world-disclosure. Even the normal language of every-
> day life is ineradicably rhetorical; but within the matrix of different
> linguistic functions, the rhetorical elements recede here . . . The
> same holds true of the specialized language of science and technology,
> law and morality, economics, political science, etc. They, too, live
> off the illuminating power of metaphorical tropes; but the rhetorical
> elements, which are by no means expunged, are tamed, as it were,
> and enlisted for special purposes of problem-solving.[40]

Derrida is the main target here, in particular his habit (as Habermas sees it) of collapsing the vital 'genre-distinction' between literature and philosophy, and thus producing a promiscuous confusion of realms where philosophy is deprived of its critical force and becomes just another 'kind of writing', a collection of texts (or rhetorical strategies) on a level with poetry or fiction. In fact this is a gross misreading of Derrida, as I have argued at length elsewhere.[41] But my immediate purpose in citing this passage is to point up the significant contrast that emerges when one compares it with Empson's resolute stand in defence of *poetic* validity-claims. For Empson – unlike Habermas – there is no question of fencing poetry off in some privileged domain of 'aesthetic' truth where the standard requirements simply don't apply. On the contrary, he argues: any adequate reading of a poem will make every effort to explicate its sense in rationally-accountable terms. Only then – at the point of ultimate resistance – will the critic have to recognize that there may indeed be structures of meaning that elude his or her logical grasp, though *not* because they somehow embody a wisdom (or an order of 'paradoxical' truth) that shows up the inherent limitations of rational thinking as applied to poetic language. For if this were the case then one would have no choice but to regard poetry – and the best poetry at that – as belonging to a realm of 'aesthetic' value where questions of truth and falsehood were simply irrelevant. And it is no exaggeration to say that Empson's criticism after *Seven Types* was devoted almost entirely to the task of rebutting what he saw as the pernicious effects of this aestheticizing creed.

Other commentators – Gerald Graff among them – have likewise perceived how the move to cut poetry off from any appeal to the rational prose virtues may lead toward a wholesale mystification of social and political thought. In his earliest book (*Poetic Statement and Critical Dogma*, 1970) Graff took issue with the New Critics on precisely this ground: that their approach came down to an expert technique for disregarding truth-values in literature, or for treating any 'statements' that a poem might make as hedged about with so many qualifying attitudes – ambiguity, irony, paradox and so forth – that it became simply impertinent to ask whether such statements possessed any kind of validity or truth.[42] And in the sequel (*Literature Against Itself*, 1979) he extended this critique to post-structuralist, postmodernist and other such forms of fashionable anti-mimetic doctrine which, according to Graff, continued the 'old' New Critical drive to dissociate literature from cognitive interests of any kind, or from what was now thought of as the 'repressive' regime of Enlightenment rationality and truth.

> In a world in which nobody can look outside the walls of the prison house of language, literature, with its built-in confession of its self-imprisonment, becomes once again the great oracle of truth, but now the truth is that there is no truth. In a curious inverted restatement of the religion of literature, the literary work is made the sole source of truth only in the sense that it alone refuses to succumb to the delusion that truth can be spoken. Where reality has become unreal, literature qualifies as our guide to reality by de-realizing itself.[43]

I would want to pick some detailed quarrels with Graff's blanket diagnosis, in particular his view of deconstruction as just another symptom of this widespread postmodernist malaise, one that exhibits the same indifference to issues of truth and falsehood. What I have written here about Derrida and de Man will I hope give the reader some idea of what is wrong with this undifferentiating line of attack. But his two books are none the less valuable in pointing up the link between those various forms of irrationalist doctrine – from New Criticism to the current postmodernist turn – which have taken it more or less for granted that any 'statements' to be found in literary texts are pseudo-statements only, or propositions whose truth-value cannot be judged according to normative (factual or logical) criteria. To Graff's way of thinking, on the contrary, '[w]hat compels the theory that literary works make no statements is not the nature of literary works themselves but the cultural constraints upon our theorizing about literary works'.[44] Thus it has more to do with the prevailing conditions of late twentieth-century cultural politics than with anything so radical as a wholesale assault on the codes and conventions of classic 'bourgeois' realism.

The effect of such ideas is all the more disabling, as Graff sees it, on account of that pervasive sense of unreality that has come to characterize our conditions of existence in a world given over to mass-media techniques, fictive appearances masquerading as truth, and the widespread distortion of consensus interests in the name of political 'realism'. For at this point the difference between fact and fiction becomes so impossibly blurred that a curious reversal begins to take place, with theorists proclaiming that the real is unknowable except by analogy with the literary text, and moreover with the kind of postmodern text that constantly adverts to its own fictive character, thus working to undo the old mimetic illusion that held us in thrall to false ideas of objectivity and truth. Thus 'one of the defining aspects of the current situation is the penetration of literary ideologies and paradigms into areas heretofore impervious to them – with a consequent loss of oppositional tension between literary culture and general society'.[45] In support of this argument one could point to various disciplines (notably philosophy and historiography) where the claim is now made, by 'advanced' thinkers in the field, that any notion of truth must henceforth be abandoned since the only knowledge worth having is one that accepts the self-interested nature of all such values and the fact that 'truth' is what presently counts according to this or that language-game, narrative schema, or consensus of informed opinion. As we have seen, Richard Rorty puts this case in respect of philosophy as just another 'kind of writing' on a level with poetry, literary criticism, and the human sciences at large. And Hayden White has argued to similar effect: that historians had better catch up with developments in the area of narrative poetics – or study of the various tropes and figures involved in the production of historical texts – if they want to avoid the kind of old-fashioned positivist thinking bound up with the claim to tell it like it really was ('wie es eigentlich gewesen').[46]

What these proposals have in common is a turn toward literary models – and models of a distinctly postmodern or post-structuralist provenance – with a view to subverting received ideas of rational or veridical discourse. This is why Graff (like Habermas) diagnoses the advent of postmodernist thinking as a loss of that productive 'oppositional tension' that previously marked the relationship between literature and the other humanistic disciplines. It has led to what he sees as a widespread failure of intellectual nerve, not only among literary critics but also – and perhaps more disturbingly – among those have invoked literary theory as a source of new procedures or interpretive paradigms for the human sciences at large. In chapter 6 I shall turn to Spinoza once again for some alternative (and I think more satisfactory) ways of construing this relationship.

6 Fiction, Philosophy and the Way of Ideas

I

I have argued that Spinoza occupies a crucial position in the history of thought that stands behind these developments in present-day critical debate. For Kermode, as we have seen, that significance lies in his having been the first to dissociate questions of meaning from questions of truth, and hence to set modern hermeneutics on its path as a discipline freed from the constraints of doctrinal adherence or orthodox belief. But this is to ignore Spinoza's equal and contrary emphasis on the need to make sense of scriptural texts *as far as possible* with reference to the standards of rational understanding, and only then – where they finally resist such treatment – fall back upon the various saving devices of hermeneutical commentary. Thus the scriptures are 'in many places inexplicable, or at best mere subject for guesswork' (*TPT*, p. 112). But such problems only arise, according to Spinoza, when 'we endeavour to follow the meaning of a prophet in matters which cannot be perceived, but only imagined, not in things whereof the understanding can give a clear and distinct idea' (p. 112). And prophecy is itself an inferior kind of knowledge – most often defective or erroneous – in so far as it relies upon mere 'imagination', or the witness of events (like miracles or divine interventions) whose nature places them beyond reach of analysis or rational critique. Hence Spinoza's view that the prophets 'made more legitimate use of argument in proportion as their knowledge approached more nearly to ordinary knowledge' (p. 159). In short, Kermode's claim should be modified to this extent at least: that Spinoza saw not only the undesirability – the potentially authoritarian upshot – of subjecting interpretation to revealed or dogmatic truth, but also the dangers of 'accommodating' scripture to

the variable currencies of meaning and belief that succeeded one
another with the passage of time. For then there would be nothing
– no evaluative standard of reason, truth, or enlightened critique –
against which to assess the various forms of ideological illusion.

Graff makes a closely related point when he discusses Kermode's
argument (in *The Sense of an Ending*) that 'fictions' are the only
means we possess of interpreting experience, explaining events, or
imposing some provisional order of sense upon the otherwise chaotic
and disparate mass of historical data.[1] The trouble with this argument, he suggests, is that it collapses the difference between story-
telling interests – which may indeed articulate our deep desire for
narrative consistency and shape – and those other kinds of interest
(cognitive or critical) which allow us to hold out against delusory
or mystified forms of understanding. The question then arises

> whether this theory of making sense itself makes sense . . . for the
> very formulation seems self-contradictory: is the statement that we
> make sense of the world by means of fictions itself a fiction? Kermode
> distinguishes between good fictions (open) and bad (closed,
> dogmatic), and he says that the good kind are not simply 'escapist',
> sentimental, easily consoling. 'Fictions too easy we call "escapist"',
> he says. 'We want them not only to console but to make discoveries
> of the hard truth here and now, in the middest.' But it is not clear
> how fictions can help us to make 'discoveries' unless they refer to
> something that is not a fiction, and how anybody can refer to some-
> thing that is not a fiction within Kermode's epistemological universe
> is not clear. Nor is it clear how we can choose intelligently between
> one fiction and another. (Graff, p. 169)

In other words, it is hard to see what could count as an *objection*
to some existing narrative paradigm – maybe some potent myth of
origins adopted in the interest of a dominant power-group – if there
is no ground of appeal outside the conditions of intelligibility created
by this or that fictive economy of truth.

Such is indeed the situation envisaged by those advocates of a
postmodern outlook (like Lyotard in his earlier work) who propose
that since we have now lost faith in the old Enlightenment 'grand
narrative' of critique, reason, progress and truth, therefore we had
best make terms with this condition and instead seek to maximize
the sheer multiplicity of stories (or sense-making strategies) on offer.
What this amounts to is yet another version of the much-touted
'hermeneutic circle', the idea that interpretation goes all the way
down, so that any attempt to theorize the nature and conditions of

narrative understanding will end up by producing just one more narrative, on a level with the first-order fictions and stories it aims to comprehend. In which case – as Graff remarks – there is a problem in grasping Kermode's distinction between those 'easy' forms of narrative fulfilment that merely go along with our present wishes and desires, and those other, more demanding kinds that somehow acquaint us with 'the hard truth here and now'. For this to happen there would have to be some element of *resistance* in the text – some determinate structure or constraint upon the freedom of interpretive choice – which imposed its necessity *despite and against* our readerly expectations. But it is precisely this possibility that Kermode excludes when he treats the difference between 'truth' and 'meaning' as equivalent to that between 'closed' and 'open' readings, or dogmatic institutional control on the one hand and interpretive licence on the other. In short, '[his] overstatement of the truth that the reader is an active participant in the creation of meaning seems to derive from his assumption that any degree of control exercised over the reader is a kind of totalitarianism' (Graff, p. 188). The result of such thinking is to set up the interpreter – or the 'strong' creative reader – as a champion of hard-won hermeneutic freedoms, as against the typecast orthodox position that would claim privileged access to the truth of the text. For we are easily persuaded, as Graff remarks, 'to view the relativizing of belief as a liberalizing strategy because it dissolves the authority of dogmatic and totalitarian systems of thought'. But again, this ignores the way that such a strategy defeats its own object – or merely substitutes a different form of hermeneutic closure – in so far as it effectively 'dissolves the authority of anything that tries to resist these systems' (Graff, p. 189).

This applies not only to Kermode's treatment of the issue but also to those various competing schools of post-structuralist, reader-response, or hermeneutic theory that elevate the notion of multiple meaning – or the 'plural' text – into a touchstone of aesthetic value. What these theories have in common is a kind of utopian mystification, a belief that any talk of interpretive 'truth' is *per se* an imposition of unwarranted authority and power, so that only by opening texts to all the multitude of possible senses and meanings can criticism work to challenge or subvert this closed economy of truth. This attitude finds its most seductive expression in a work like Roland Barthes's *S/Z*, a virtuoso demonstration of what commentary can achieve when released from all the irksome rules and constraints of a reading compliant with traditional interpretive norms.[2] It is likewise manifest in the writings of 'American deconstructionists' like Geoffrey Hartman, those for whom the line between 'creative' and 'critical' texts is at best a mere product of scholarly convention, an attempt to delegitimize any form of commentary that makes a point of 'crossing over' from the one to the other domain, and which thus constitutes a standing challenge to the orthodox division of realms.[3] To this way of thinking the most radical gesture available to critics is one that breaks down all the commonplace (institutional) distinctions between meaning and truth, text and commentary, 'literature' and 'criticism', or – in Kermode's case – narrative fiction and the various (equally fictive) methodologies that attempt to theorize the workings of narrative.

It is ironic, to say the least, that Spinoza should now be honoured as the thinker who first made way for these developments by arguing (in the context of scriptural exegesis) that meaning and truth were separate issues, so that interpreters could only produce all manner of harmful effects if they persisted in mixing them up. For Spinoza's point was exactly the reverse of what these present-day critics are arguing. That is to say, he saw nothing but multiplied error and confusion in the habit of 'accommodating' reason to faith, or adapting the requirements of rational critique to a sense of what the passage in question *ought* to mean according to some present (orthodox or other) interpretive consensus. This is where he differs most sharply with critics like Kermode, those for whom the single most important distinction is that between 'closed' and 'open' readings, or degrees of liberty along a scale of hermeneutic options running from the sheerly conformist to the downright heterodox. But no matter how extreme these localized points of disagreement, they are still conceived as taking place against a background of communal values and beliefs, an ongoing dialogue that sets the terms for meaningful interpretive debate. For Spinoza, on the contrary, truth was what resisted all such attempts to make sense of scripture through a sequence of endless hermeneutical revisions, a process of adjustment by which problematic passages could be brought into line with the needs of present understanding. Hence his attack on those over-subtle exegetes who suppose that 'we may explain the words of Scripture according to our preconceived opinions, twisting them about or reversing or completely changing the literal sense, however plain it may be' (*TPT*, P. 117). For the result of this practice, as Spinoza sees it, is to leave the field open

to interpreters – orthodox or otherwise – whose readings will be
based on nothing more than mere prejudice, either through their
habit of passive compliance with existing codes and conventions, or
conversely through their zeal to revise the established, canonical
sense of things in order to save doctrinal appearances. What is
lacking in both cases is any ground for the critique of scriptural
truth-claims – or orthodox beliefs of whatever kind – that would
not in the end come down to some version of the hermeneutic
circle, or the appeal to readerly 'foreknowledge' as an ultimate
horizon of interpretive method.

Leo Strauss makes this point with particular reference to Spinoza's quarrel with Maimonides on the question of revealed truth
versus rational critique. The latter's main task, as Spinoza conceives
it, is that of establishing

> what it is that the Scriptures do actually teach, so that the teachings
> of Scripture may be measured by the standards of objective truth,
> and by establishing this to arrive at a judgement of the truth of the
> Scriptures . . . [And this] requires in principle a separation of the
> criticism based *on* Scripture from the criticism *of* Scripture . . . In
> the first case the only standard is the text itself. In the second case,
> the only standard is reason itself.[4]

This passage makes it clear why Spinoza cannot be assimilated to
that line of hermeneutic thought which – on Kermode's understanding of the relevant prehistory – leads from the practice of a heterodox
scriptural exegesis to the present-day schools of 'strong revisionist'
secular criticism. These latter take it for granted that interpretation
is an activity concerned with meaning (not truth), and with meaning,
moreover, as a field of open-ended 'intertextual' codes and conventions where truth is nothing more than a technique of closure
imposed in the interests of preserving the canon, or maintaining
the existence of orthodox entities like the 'classic realist text'. For
Spinoza, conversely, there is no way of criticizing such arbitrary,
false or unwarranted truth-claims unless one can establish an alternative ground of appeal, a 'ground' in the strong (non-circular) sense
of providing rational justification for arguments that go not only
against the grain of orthodox belief, but also – at times – against
the manifest sense of the passage one is given to interpret.

For it is at this point that reading becomes a genuinely *critical*
activity, an active engagement with the meanings of scripture that
treats them not as tokens of God's revealed truth, but as fallible

signs adapted to the limits of human understanding under this or that set of contingent historical circumstances. In which case criticism cannot be confined – as it was for Maimonides and other more traditional exegetes – to the business of 'reconciling' reason and faith by requiring of the former a due subservience to the dictates of orthodox belief, and allowing only for such innovative turns in the reading of scripture as would prevent reason from getting into conflict with those same imperative truths. It is against this doctrine – one whose aim and effect are to subjugate reason to revelation – that Spinoza presents his whole battery of arguments in the *Theologico-Political Treatise*. Again, Leo Strauss puts his case with admirable force and concision, so I shall quote the relevant paragraph at length:

> Who then is to exericse this critique, if not the philosopher? First of all, the Biblical exegete. The opponents appeal to Scripture against reason. They demand that human reason, corrupted by the Fall, be subject to Scripture. This claim made by the opponents must, by reason of that claim itself, be measured by Scripture, and only by Scripture. Spinoza takes up this claim . . . His argument runs: according to the intent of supernatural revelation itself, it is needful to go back to the unadulterated, the literal meaning of Scripture. For what can we, of ourselves, know of matters which transcend the range of our intelligence? Every human interpretation is as such false and falsifying: mere figments of the human mind which set themselves up in the place of the pure word of God. In this, Spinoza's critique sets out to perform no other task than to re-establish the genuine authority of Scripture. By so doing, he seeks to limit the authority of Scripture to its own realm, and thus to make philosophy independent of the authority of Scripture.[5]

Clearly this passage would bear a good deal of elucidating comment. For present purposes, however, it is enough to point out that Spinoza rejects any curbs or limits placed upon the exercise of critical reason; that he is willing to acknowledge the truth-claims of religion only in so far as they bear upon matters of faith (as distinct from the interests of free rational enquiry); and that he is deeply suspicious of those super-subtle exegetes who attempt to reconcile these different modes of knowledge by abandoning the literal signification of scripture and offering their own ingenious glosses (or tropological 'swerves' from the manifest sense) by way of avoiding any clash between reason and faith. For it is reason's prerogative to raise questions about scripture which *can and should* be raised even where they constitute an argument for regarding scriptural truth-claims as in no way binding on the activity of rational thought.

For Spinoza, these questions extend into the areas of comparative philology, textual criticism, political history and what would nowadays be called the sociology of belief. They also involve a close attention to issues in the field of narrative poetics in so far as that discipline serves to indicate those problematic points where the 'truth' of scripture turns out to be a matter of fictive or 'imaginary' knowledge. But it can only fulfil such a purpose by respecting the distinction between meaning and truth, or those aspects of scripture that have to be *interpreted* in order to produce any kind of coherent sense, and those passages that are capable of reasoned exposition in light of 'adequate ideas'. Thus Spinoza very firmly rejects the kind of levelling pan-textualist view that regards all truths as products of interpretation, or all attempts to theorize narrative as reducing in the end to yet another form of narrative fiction. In fact this viewpoint is more closely related to the tradition of scriptural exegesis that Spinoza attacks in Maimonides and other proponents of a more 'hermeneutical' approach. That is to say, it starts out from the foregone conclusion that truth is what emerges from the ongoing dialogue of variant readings or interpretations, a dialogue that allows for new departures in the interest of maintaining narrative coherence, but which excludes any appeal to rational criteria outside its own privileged sphere of understanding.

Spinoza has three main objections to bring against this mainstream philosophy of textual exegesis. Firstly, it leaves no room for the *criticism* of scriptural texts, taking 'criticism' to mean something other – and more – than an endless production of ingenious new readings that never touch upon basic issues of validity and truth. Secondly, it places the interpreter beyond reach of effective counter-argument, since his or her reading can always claim access to a 'truth' that reveals itself only to those with the wisdom (or the requisite hermeneutic skills) to draw out the authentic meaning of scripture, a meaning necessarily opaque or invisible from the standpoint of mere human reason. And thirdly – in consequence – it works to promote a mystified state of understanding where readings acquire a certain spurious authority through the absence of enlightened critical reflection on their historically contingent origins. This is why Spinoza's critique of revelation (i.e. his attack on the idea of scripture as a source of divinely-sanctioned meaning and truth) goes along with a deep scepticism with regard to miracles, prophecy, supernatural interventions, and other such ruses adopted in compliance with the demands of popular prejudice. 'Wherefore so far as our understanding goes, those phenomena which we clearly and distinctly understand have much better right to be called works of God, and to be referred to the will of God, than those about which we are entirely ignorant, although they appeal powerfully to the imagination, and compel men's admiration' (*TPT*, p. 86). From which it follows that the belief in miracles, prophecy and suchlike superstitious items of faith can only be encouraged – or protected from rational criticism – by an attitude to scripture that disarms reason by subjecting it to the dictates of revealed religious truth.

On the face of it nothing could be further from the intentions of a present-day secularizing critic like Kermode. In fact he makes a point of *not* falling back onto notions of privileged hermeneutic access, or the idea that texts only yield up their secrets to an elect, self-authorized community of readers already in possession of the requisite truth. Kermode writes self-consciously as a latter-day 'outsider', one for whom the meaning of scriptural texts is matter for attentive close-reading, informed speculation, and momentary glimpses of that which must elude more orthodox or rule-bound exegetes. Thus there operates a kind of compensatory mechanism whereby the loss of absolute authority goes along with an increase in the freedom to discover new kinds of significance in the text. This is why Kermode so admires those commentators – like Austin Farrer – who managed to accommodate the requirements of belief to the interests of a modern, more sceptical or questioning sense of narrative possibility.[6] On the one hand, undeniably, Farrer's innovative reading of the Gospels 'related to his faith and his vocation', that is to say, his purpose of sustaining scriptural authority against the inroads of a wholesale secularizing drive that would find no room for such values. But on the other, that desire could only be satisfied 'by means familiar to all interpreters, [since] like the rest he sensed that despite, or perhaps because of, the puzzles, the discontinuities, the amazements of Mark . . . his text can be read as somehow hanging together'.[7] Kermode sees the *Gospel according to Saint Mark* as especially revealing in this regard since it offers such resistance to our commonplace ideas of narrative coherence and closure. Thus it calls forth a range of interpretive strategies which resemble those involved in the reception of modern or postmodern secular texts. What such works have in common is the failure (or refusal) to offer up their secrets to a straightforward reading premised on the normative values and assumptions of classic realist fiction. This is what chiefly interests Kermode about novelists like Conrad, Ford Madox Ford, or Thomas Pynchon: their capacity to tease interpretation almost out of thought by providing multiple cues and clues that defy all attempts to arrive at some ultimate meaning, some authoritative truth of the matter.[8] It is precisely by resisting our desire for narrative closure – for stories that satisfy the 'sense of an ending' in its orthodox, naive or stereotypical forms – that such novels hold out against the dangerous slide from *fiction* into *myth*, a process whose end-point can be seen all too plainly in the record of recent historical events.

So Kermode is far from wishing to be counted an 'insider' if this entails having access to meanings or truths that reveal themselves only to a privileged company of readers fit though few. Indeed, he comes out strongly against this exclusivist position by arguing that 'the classic' is *not*, as commonly supposed, a text that communicates some timeless quality, some universal value conserved from age to age in the keeping of an authorized (priestly or interpretive) elite.[9] Such ideas may have carried conviction at a time – roughly speaking, the period from the Holy Roman Empire to the epoch of high European classical culture – when questions of canonical status and right interpretation were closely bound up with an ethos of cultural imperialism that claimed to transcend mere contingencies of time and place. T. S. Eliot could still adopt this standpoint in essays like 'Tradition and the Individual Talent', where the masterworks of Western literary culture – from Homer and Virgil, through Dante to the modern (post-Renaissance) line of descent – were taken to compose an 'ideal order', a sense of unifying vision and purpose that could only be achieved by the putting-away of all short-term historical interests.[10] But that moment has now passed, according to Kermode, and along with it the idea of 'classic' literature as somehow existing in a timeless continuum, an 'imaginary museum' of meanings and values available to a few choice spirits. In its place we have a different sense of the classic, one that tends to value texts not so much for their high cultural status or their plenitude of meaning, but for that in them which holds out against every kind of authorized or self-assured hermeneutic grasp. 'To be blessedly fallible, to have the capacity to subvert manifest senses, is the mark of good enough readers and good enough texts.'[11] To this extent at least Kermode speaks for those others – for the wider community of non-elect, non-privileged readers – who find themselves excluded for whatever reason (religious, historical, or socio-cultural) from the charmed circle of interpretive foreknowledge.

Hence the strong preference nowadays – as he sees it – for texts that deny the comforting resort to notions of ultimate meaning or truth, and which instead place endless obstacles in the path of any reading that remains attached to such values. And this applies not only to a range of postmodernist secular fictions but also to a work like the Gospel of Mark, a narrative whose highly problematical nature now commends it to interpreters themselves bereft of all final assurances, all transcendental guarantees. In this Gospel, as Kermode reads it,

> [t]he story moves erratically, and not always forward; one thing follows another for no very evident reason. And a good deal of the story seems concerned with failure to understand the story. Then the whole thing ends with what might be thought the greatest awkwardness of all, or the greatest instance of reticence: the empty tomb and the terrified women going away.[12]

As compared with the other New Testament writings, Mark offers little of the easy satisfaction to be had from narratives that offer a well-shaped sequence of events, a range of believable 'characters' (or at any rate figures whose behaviour displays some degree of apparent motivational psychology), and – in more general terms – a feeling of assurance that the story 'hangs together' as an act of broadly truthful historical witness. In this sense it answers to the modern need for what Kermode calls 'clerkly scepticism', an attitude that stands roughly midway on the scale between a willing suspension of disbelief and a principled refusal to accept the claims of scripture at anything like face value. The great virtue of this attitude, according to Kermode, is that it saves us from going along with the process by which fictions are converted into myths, or allowed to acquire the kind of sacralized status – the authority of revealed truth – that places them beyond criticism. In which case it falls to the interpreter to maintain an awareness of narrative forms as open, provisional sense-making constructs, spaces where the reader should always be free (within certain 'institutional' limits) to elaborate new hypotheses in light of changing historical and social concerns.

So there is much in Kermode's treatment of this topic that would lead us to view him as a liberalizing critic, an exponent of 'clerkly scepticism' whose aim is to prevent interpretation from becoming the preserve of a narrow-minded orthodox elite. But again, there are aspects of his work that suggest a very different reading, one more alert to his deep fascination with narrative mysteries or 'secrets', meanings that emerge only through the exercise of skilled (even arcane) hermeneutical techniques. Thus it is ironic, as Jonathan Arac notes, that *The Genesis of Secrecy* should bear the dedication 'To Those Outside' (i.e. outside the circle of scholarly initiates), while also citing these words in the original Greek, a gesture which excludes at least a sizable number of Kermode's likely readership.[13] And this ambivalence extends to numerous passages in the book where he dwells on the inherently secretive character of all good stories, sacred or secular; on the fact that modern novelists (like the Gospel writers) often go out of their way to reserve understanding to those already 'in the know', and leave other readers to make what sense they can through the mists of ignorance and error. Thus

> [o]utsiders see but do not perceive. Insiders read and perceive, but always in a different sense. We glimpse the secrecy through the meshes of a text; this is divination, but what is divined is what is visible from our angle. It is a momentary radiance, delusive or not . . .[14]

There are several things worth remarking about the rhetoric – especially the rhetoric of viewpoint and pronominal reference – at work in this passage. Kermode's attitude of 'clerkly scepticism' comes across in his refusal to equate 'divination' with an access to ultimate truth; his insistence that what is 'visible' becomes so only from 'our angle' of vision, an angle that permits certain aspects of the text to be 'glimpsed' momentarily while others retain their obscure, secretive character. In which case it would seem – to adapt Paul de Man's idiom – that interpreters' moments of greatest potential insight are also, inseparably, the moments when they are prone to manifest a certain symptomatic 'blindness', a failure to perceive what motivates their own, necessarily partial and self-interested reading.

But there is another side to Kermode's rhetoric which suggests a rather different attitude, and one far removed from de Man's stance of rigorously undeceiving irony. For the 'we' in this passage is firmly aligned with the community of knowing insiders, those who 'read and perceive, but always in a different sense', a sense that distinguishes their kind of reading from the kind practised by other, less gifted individuals. Kermode is more than ready to concede the point that the 'radiance' thus achieved may turn out to be 'momentary', even 'delusive'; that interpreters can only go wrong when they claim to transcend the limits of contingent or timebound human understanding. But his language contrives to suggest just the opposite through its insistent play on these quasi-religious metaphors of vision, revelation, radiance, reading as a 'divinatory' activity, and so forth. Their effect is to complicate his attitude of 'clerkly scepticism' to the point where commentary begins to take on something very like its original function as a guardian and purveyor of sacred truths.

II

This is where Kermode parts company with Spinoza on the question of narrative understanding and its relation to the interests of critical theory. For Kermode – as also for postmodern thinkers like Lyotard and sceptical historiographers like Hayden White – there is a bottom line of argument in all the humanistic disciplines where theory has to recognize its own prior commitment to some kind of narrative sense-making enterprise, a commitment which cannot then be subject to further criticism, since it provides the very basis for the self-understanding of the discipline or theory in question. In short, all knowledge is knowledge arrived at *in and through* the various shapes of narrative awareness, whether these have to do with the authority of scripture, the 'sense of an ending' imposed by our models of time, history and secular change, or the way in which disciplines proceed against a background of agreed-upon values and assumptions which in turn derive their legitimizing force from a narrative concerned with such 'ultimate' matters as knowledge, progress, 'truth at the end of enquiry' and so forth. Most often one finds this case put forward by those who regard such talk as a hung-over sympton of the old 'Enlightenment' ethos, a sympton (it is argued) all the more regressive in so far as the truth-claims of enlightened reason were themselves just a version – a secular re-working – of religious doctrines whose authority they sought to overthrow. Hence the widespread 'narrative turn' across various present-day disciplines of thought, a turn that involves the rejection of truth-claims in whatever shape or form, the idea that all knowledge comes down to a species of fictive or story-telling interest, and the rejection of any 'meta-narrative' theory that would seek a more adequate critical account of the story as told up to now.

In fact, as I have suggested, there is a different way of reading this entire pre-history, one that takes us back to Spinoza and his writings on the topic of scriptural exegesis. For Spinoza, narrative understanding is inherently unreliable in so far as it rests on 'inadequate ideas' or 'knowledge of imagination'. That is to say, it can teach us something useful in the way of practical, historical and moral wisdom just so long as we don't then confuse it with the kind of knowledge derived from the exercise of critical reason. Thus:

> the truth of a historical narrative, however assured, cannot give us the knowledge nor consequently the love of God, for love of God springs from knowledge of Him, and knowledge of Him should be derived from general ideas, in themselves certain and known, so that the truth of a historical narrative is very far from being a necessary requisite for attaining our highest good. (*TPT*, p. 61)

By now it should be clear that, when Spinoza talks about 'God' and the 'love of God', his use of these terms cannot be taken as in any sense an orthodox profession of belief, or even as suggesting a residual attachment to Judaeo-Christian concepts and values. Rather, he deploys them partly as a means of avoiding any head-on collision with those values, and partly as a series of encoded statements which the reader can always reinterpret to yield a fully secularized account of knowledge, truth and the interests of rational critique. And it is here that Kermode gets the message wrong when he reads Spinoza as having launched the history of modern (post-theological) thought by severing the hitherto sacrosanct tie between 'meaning' and 'truth', and thus leaving interpreters free to practise a form of hermeneutic 'divination' unconstrained by the dictates of orthodox belief. For this practice leads back, as we have seen, to a version of the self-same doctrine that Spinoza set out to challenge: the idea of scripture as a source of revealed truths accessible to those (and only those) in a state of receptive grace.

What we have here, I think, is a failure to distinguish between two very different kinds or orders of truth-claim. On the one hand 'truth' may be conceived in the traditional (Platonic or Christian) sense, as resulting from an inward revelation vouchsafed to some few select minds or spirits. It is Spinoza's main argument against excessive reliance on the witness of scriptural narrative that it tends to promote just such a mystified version of truth, since the scriptures (including the New Testament parables) are often couched in obscure, cryptic or allegorical terms which give little hold for rational understanding. (For Kermode, by contrast, it is these passages that present interpretation with its greatest challenge, and which thus give rise to the subtlest, most rewarding forms of revisionist commentary.) This is why Spinoza perceives a close relation between belief in the authenticity of biblical narrative – in the truth of those events supposedly set down under guidance of divine inspiration – and belief in miracles, prophecies, and other such happenings that run directly counter to natural law and reason alike. In other words, the inability to distinguish true ideas from fictive, inadequate or 'imaginary' notions is one that gives rise to all variety of credulous or downright superstitious attitudes. Spinoza allows that there may have been times – periods of crisis, civil discord, threats to the sense of Jewish national identity – when the Old Testament prophets were justified in exploiting such beliefs with the object of enforcing obedience to the law. But this could only be a matter of short-term strategic necessity, and surely not in any sense a model for subsequent (more enlightened or rational) communities of knowledge.

Hence Spinoza's first rule of adequate understanding: 'to distinguish and separate the true idea from other perceptions, and to keep the mind from confusing with true ideas those which are false, fictitious, and doubtful' (*OIU*, p. 18). And from this precept it follows that the knowledge attained *directly or naively* through narrative representation is not to be confused with the knowledge that derives from a *reasoned critique* of such first-order narrative beliefs. It can thus be argued that Spinoza's philosophy amounts to a point-for-point reversal of the programme announced by postmodern sceptics (and, less stridently, by thinkers like Kermode who see no exit from the hermeneutic hall of mirrors). 'While leaving such persons in their error', Spinoza writes,

> we will take care to derive from our argument with them a truth serviceable for our purpose, namely, that the mind, in paying attention to a thing hypothetical or false, so as to meditate upon it and understand it . . . will readily discover its falsity; and if the thing hypothetical be in its nature true . . . the mind will proceed with an uninterrupted series of apt conclusions; in the same way as it would at once discover (as we showed just now) the absurdity of a false hypothesis, and of the conclusions drawn from it. (*OIU*, p. 23)

I have already suggested how Spinoza's line of argument with regard to the difference between 'false', 'fictitious', and 'true' ideas anticipates the work of those modern theorists – notably Althusser and Macherey – who have likewise sought to differentiate the realms of 'ideology', 'literature', and 'science'. For their enterprise rests on a similar conviction: that theory is capable of providing a knowledge that doesn't reduce to just another form of narrative understanding or inescapable complicity with the fictions it seeks to interpret. Macherey makes the point with specific reference to Spinoza, and by way of arguing against those critics (in this case Roland Barthes, but the same might be said of Kermode) who fail to perceive the essential distinction between narrative and critical discourse.

> Fiction is not *truer* than illusion; indeed, it cannot usurp the place of knowledge. But it can set illusion in motion by penetrating its insufficiency, by transforming our relationship to ideology . . . Fiction deceives us in so far as it is feigned; but this is not a primary act of deception because it is aimed at one even more profound, exposing it, helping to release us from it.[15]

This is why it is wrong – a determinate misreading – to treat Spinoza as belonging to the line of hermeneutic thinkers for whom epistemological questions of truth and falsehood were banished altogether from the realm of textual or narrative understanding. He adopts this standpoint only with regard to that particular form of confusion which mistakes the *unwarranted* truth-claims of scripture – prophecies, miracles and the like – for items of veridical belief. Here indeed, as Kermode argues, Spinoza holds it necessary to give imagination its due and not follow the line of those commentators (like Maimonides) who create all kinds of sophistical error by striving to accommodate reason to faith. But this applies only to passages that resist the best efforts of enlightened commentary, or which cannot be construed in accordance with the standards of rational consistency and truth. And even here, Spinoza thinks, it is the commentator's task *not* to treat such passages as bearing a mystical, allegorical or revelatory import beyond reach of further analysis, but – on the contrary – to ask what precisely were the socio-historical conditions that caused them to be couched in a manner so resistant to the interests of rational comprehension.

So Spinoza is very far from adopting the viewpoint attributed to him by Kermode. Nor can he be read as in any way endorsing the current trend toward theories of narrative that end up by making narrative itself the limiting condition – or horizon of intelligibility

– within which theory has to operate. On the contrary: Spinoza lays it down as a first precept of scriptural exegesis that any passage (or narrative episode) so obscure as to defeat rational understanding must *therefore* be accounted either a product of ancient superstition (in which case one can offer a causal explanation in socio-historical terms), or an illusion brought about by 'inadequate ideas' which must likewise be examined in light of their contingent causes. 'For many things are narrated in Scripture as real, and were believed to be real, which were in fact only symbolical and imaginary' (*TPT*, p. 93). The force of the word 'only' here is to insist that such passages shouldn't be regarded as matter for 'deep' hermeneutical treatment, or as offering up their meaning only to those for whom scripture is a vessel of revealed truth. Rather, they require the kind of critical exegesis that begins by asking what *reasons* may have prompted some particular narrative diversion or oblique form of words, and which ends – when the rational explanations run out – by adducing various *causal* factors that presumably lay beyond the author's knowing grasp. In this respect Spinoza anticipates the argument of present-day moral philosophers who see human acts and motives as falling under two different kinds of description: on the one hand those that can best be explained as following from some rational-deliberative process of thought, and on the other those that bear witness to causes that the agent could scarcely have acknowledged, at least while continuing to act or think in that way.[16] And he applies the same criteria when discussing problematic passages of Old and New Testatment scripture. What is distinctive about Spinoza's treatment of such passages – and what sets it apart from the modern hermeneutic approach – is that he carries this double-aspect theory across into the textual-interpretive domain, and makes of it an argument against any appeal to truths of a mystical, revealed or transcendent character, truths of which no adequate account could be given in rational or causal terms.

Of course it might be argued (and we have seen several commentators who take this line) that Book V of the *Ethics* is the point at which Spinoza does give way to irrationalist talk of 'intuitive knowledge', 'eternal ideas', the 'intellectual love of God', and other such high-toned mystical claims. But there is, as I have suggested, a stronger case for regarding his use of those terms as a convenient – or at that time more acceptable – means of asserting what amounted to a consistent theory of knowledge based on the claims of critical reason as the final arbiter of truth and falsehood. Thus

Stuart Hampshire: '[Spinoza's] is an interesting, not implausible, account of freedom of mind, as the detachment from causes in the common order of nature, a detachment that lasts while self-critical thinking lasts'.[17] And Errol E. Harris argues to similar effect in a passage that I have cited once already, but which seems to me the single most convincing statement of the case for Book V as by no means given over to a mystical or irrationalist set of truth-claims. What Spinoza is here proposing is a theory of mind as that attribute which, in Harris's words,

> transcends time and space in the sense that time and space are *for* it
> and it is not *in* them . . . The human mind is thus both finite and
> potentially infinite, both the idea of a finite mode of Extension (and
> thus itself a finite mode of Thought) and, nevertheless, in being idea,
> capable of adequate knowledge of the total scheme of things. It is
> thereby self-transcendent and eternal.[18]

So it is possible, at least, to construe Book V as a more 'metaphysical' re-statement of views that Spinoza had argued previously with regard to the sufficiency of critical reason and the non-availability of revealed (religious) truths that somehow transcended the limits of rational comprehension. In other words, the most *consistent* reading of Spinoza is that which places him squarely in the line of demystifying rationalist thinkers. And this reading goes against Kermode's view of him as a signal precursor of modern hermeneutics, itself conceived as a form of semi-secularized textual 'divination' still closely tied to its formative background in the history of scriptural exegesis.

This book has argued for a different understanding of Spinoza's role in the history of thought that led up to the current complex of debates in literary theory and criticism. Most importantly, he stands in the line of those thinkers – albeit a very mixed company, from Althusser and Macherey to Empson, Derrida, and de Man – who have offered various reasons for *not* treating literature as exempt from the cognitive interests that characterize other kinds of truth-seeking discourse. The principal cause of confusion here is the belief that prevails among post-structuralists, postmodernists, and others of a kindred (anti-Enlightenment) persuasion: namely, that any talk of 'truth' – in whatever disciplinary or cultural context – must always involve a covert appeal to some ultimate, transcendent source of meaning and value, an appeal whose authority can only derive from a mystified ('metaphysical') ground of all knowledge. To some extent, no doubt, this confusion has been reinforced by a widespread misreading of what Derrida has to say about 'logocentrism' or the so-called Western 'metaphysics of presence', terms which are commonly taken to signify a repressive regime of old-fashioned ideas about language, truth and reality which can now be 'deconstructed' – once and for all – by pointing up their blindspots of rhetorical implication. That this is a travesty of Derrida's arguments should be clear to anyone who has read his work and not relied on the usual handful of slogans taken out of context. In fact he makes a point of insisting *firstly* that standards of truth and right reading are integral to the deconstructive enterprise, and *secondly* that any notion of escaping logocentrism – of jumping outside it, so to speak, 'with both feet' – is yet another form of inverted metaphysical thinking, and one that is destined to fall straight back into the most naive of pre-critical assumptions.[19]

So it is not just a matter of unmasking all truth-claims as complicitous with a sovereign 'metaphysics of presence' that runs all the way, as Terry Eagleton put it, 'from Plato to Nato'.[20] If this were the only message of Derrida's work – as it is for many of his literary-critical disciples – then deconstruction would amount to little more than a series of elegant (though rather tedious) variations on a well-worn theme. What is distinctive about Derrida's writing is the extreme analytical rigour with which he draws out the elements of textual resistance – the antinomies or unstable binary oppositions – that tend to undermine this classical (ultimately Christian and Platonist) economy of truth. And in order to do so he operates always with a strict regard for those other kinds of truth-claim that regulate the critical reading of texts and which are simply indispensable to any project whose aim is to question that otherwise seamless metaphysical enclosure. For the alternative, as we have seen with Kermode, is to introduce a radical disjunction between questions of meaning and questions of truth, such that understanding becomes in the end a kind of brooding on sacred mysteries, and none the less so for maintaining an outlook of 'clerkly scepticism' that professes to oppose all forms of orthodox doctrinal adherence. It is for this reason that Derrida so often insists – most forcefully in his latest response to John Searle – that deconstruction is far from abandoning the standards of 'serious' philosophical debate.[21] These standards are those of argumentative rigour, fidelity to the text (in this case J. L. Austin's *How To Do Things With Words*), and a willingness not to let one's own prejudices – or the dictates of consensual wisdom – prevent one from perceiving problematic details that go strongly against the interpretive grain.[22] What makes this a particularly apt example from our point of view is that it shows Derrida contesting one, highly generalized and purportedly self-evident order of truth-claim – the priority of 'authentic' over 'inauthentic' speech-acts, as theorized by Searle – yet doing so precisely through the claim to present a more adequate, meticulous, and *truthful* reading of crucial passages in Austin's text. Moreover, these are passages that Searle can be shown to have ignored, misread or reconstrued in favour of his own, confidently orthodox approach. In short, deconstruction derives all its critical force from the way that it questions certain kinds of mystified truth-claim while yet subscribing to the highest standards of argumentative rigour and respect for the protocols of textual close-reading. If this fact goes unnoticed by opponents like Searle it is equally lost upon those who embrace deconstruction as a licence for dispensing with every last notion of truth, validity, and reason.

The point is best made in a passage by de Man, responding to the widespread mistaken belief that a deconstructive reading can find no room for epistemological questions (or values of truth and falsehood). It all depends, de Man writes,

> on how one 'understands' the relationship between truth and understanding. Understanding is not a version of one single and universal Truth that would exist as an essence, a hypostasis. The truth of a text is a much more empirical and literal event. What makes a reading more or less true is simply the predictability, the necessity of its occurrence, regardless of the reader's or of the author's wishes . . . It depends, in other words, on the rigor of the reading as an argument. Reading is an argument (which is not necessarily the same as a polemic) because it has to go against the grain of what one would want to happen in the name of what has to happen: this is the same as saying that understanding is an epistemological event prior to being an ethical or aesthetic value. This does not mean that there can be a true reading, but that no reading is conceivable in which the question of its truth or falsehood is not primarily involved.[23]

This passage connects with a number of crucial arguments in de Man's late writing. Among them is the topic of 'aesthetic ideology', that turn toward a certain mystified discourse of meaning and value that de Man saw as having taken hold in the tradition of German idealist philosophy after Kant, and as still exerting a powerful – though unrecognized – influence on present-day critical thought. In fact his chief concern in these essays was to show just how and where Kant had been misread by those subsequent thinkers – notably Schiller – who promoted the idea of aesthetic understanding to a role far beyond anything envisaged in the Kantian scheme of faculties.[24] For Kant, it was essential that the various forms and modalities of knowledge – pure and practical reason, theoretical understanding, aesthetic judgement – be assigned each to its own proper sphere, its place within the overall 'architectonic' of human knowledge in general.

This is not to say that the aesthetic in Kant is confined to matters of artistic taste with no bearing on the other (cognitive or ethical) dimensions. Indeed, it provides the only possible means of bridging the otherwise unbridgeable gulf between (on the one hand) concepts of understanding and phenomenal intuitions, and (on the other) knowledge arrived at through this synthesizing power, and knowledge belonging to the realm of 'supersensible' or ethico-religious and political ideas. This is why the 'transcendental aesthetic' occupies such a prominent place in the first *Critique*, as well as emerging – in various oblique or analogical forms – wherever Kant comes up against the problem of explaining how the faculties coexist in a relationship defined by their differences one from another. It is also why the notion of aesthetic experience comes to play such a pivotal role in post-Kantian attempts to find a way beyond those troubling antinomies. For at this point there develops a philosophy of art – very broadly conceived – which treats it as a kind of emancipating promise, a domain where sensuous intuitions might at last be *fully reconciled* with cognitive interests, thus offering a glimpse of that perfected utopian condition that Kant was unable to envisage, mainly on account of his express determination that aesthetic understanding *not* be confused with the orders of pure and practical reason. De Man sees this as the single most seductive and dangerous form of transcendental illusion. Thus he argues that the impulse to 'aestheticize politics' is one that may indeed start out (as in Schiller) with the wish for a better, more harmonious relation between the various faculties of human knowledge and experience, but which can easily end – and here he offers some striking examples – with the resort to a wholesale irrationalist mystique whose effect is to *enforce* that desired state of balance, most often by appealing to some dubious source of revealed authority and truth.[25]

So the critique of aesthetic ideology in de Man has implications that extend far beyond the realm of aesthetics or of art-criticism as commonly understood.[26] It has to do with the way that such ideas have been pressed – whether knowingly or not – into the service of a quasi-religious ontology of art, language and aesthetic value, a tradition that de Man traces back to its origins in Schiller's misreading of Kant, and forward to its bad apotheosis in the writings that Heidegger produced during the period of Nazi cultural hegemony. This is why, as he argues, 'the link between literature (as art), epistemology, and ethics is the burden of aesthetic theory at least since Kant' (*RT*, p. 25). And moreover: 'it is because we teach literature as an aesthetic function that we can move so easily from literature to its apparent prolongation in the spheres of self-knowledge, of religion, and of politics' (ibid). De Man's late writings are best understood as a persistent – even obsessive – attempt to uncover the sources of this deep-laid confusion and show just how widespread its influence has been among present-day critics and theorists. The effect is most clearly visible in that line of high Romantic argument – from Schiller to M. H. Abrams – where poetry figures as a uniquely privileged mode of understanding, a language that somehow transcends the limitations of commonplace (rational or prosaic) thought, and which does so precisely by virtue of its power to reconcile the Kantian antinomies of mind and nature, subject and object, concepts of understanding and sensuous perceptions. Here it takes hold through the frequent appeal to certain canonized values and ideas – 'organic form', vividness of perception, the 'defamiliarizing' power of poetic language, its capacity (in Abrams' words) to 'manifest a transaction between subject and object in which the thought incorporates and makes explicit what was already implicit in the outer scene' – which de Man sees as nothing more than a species of seductive aesthetic mystification. What makes the interpreters so prone to fall in with these and other such delusory beliefs is their readiness to accept romantic poetry *at its own valuation*, that is to say, its self-image as a source of revealed or visionary truths, truths to which we can only have access through those privileged figures of thought (like metaphor and symbol) which are taken as its highest, most characteristic achievement. Thus for Abrams it is an item of critical faith – as well as a touchstone of value for distinguishing the 'greater romantic lyric' – that in such poetry 'nature is made thought and thought nature, both by their sustained interaction and by their seamless metaphorical continuity'.[27]

To de Man's way of thinking, on the contrary, such passages

only show how completely these critics have internalized the dictates
of a potent 'aesthetic ideology', a doctrine that blinds them to the
ontological *difference* between language and nature, or the error
involved in all such attempts to assimilate poetry to the order of
natural, organic, or spontaneous life-forms. And this confusion
turns up just as frequently in other schools of criticism, including
some (like reader-response theory, *Rezeptionsaesthetik*, and various
latterday offshoots of the formalist approach) which might appear
to have little or nothing in common with the high-Romantic line of
descent. What unites them at a deeper level – so de Man argues –
is the tendency to treat literary works as somehow analogous with
forms and processes in the natural world, or as yielding up their
meaning in the same way that objects acquire salience in the field
of visual perception.

One example is of particular interest here since it shows how this
turn toward phenomenalist models of literary perception goes along
with a form of historical thinking where aesthetic values and categories are often in play. The critic in question is Hans-Robert Jauss,
whose project involves nothing less than the aim to synthesize
poetics and literary history – or the so-called 'intrinsic' and 'extrin-
sic' modes of approach – through a detailed account of the various
contexts, the constitutive 'horizons' of intelligibility, that make up
the relevant historical 'background' for deciding which structural
aspects of the work have assumed particular significance at any
given time.[28] The end-result of this process, so Jauss believes, will
be to overcome a whole series of bad antinomies (synchronic *versus*
diachronic models; formalist close-reading *versus* historical method;
structural *versus* socio-cultural analysis) and to demonstrate that in
fact these approaches must be seen as strictly interdependent, since
questions of meaning, structure and style can only receive an
adequate treatment when viewed against the background of a certain
reception-history. For it will then become possible to account *both*
for those distinctive features that characterize the literary work *and*
for the fact that such features have acquired different kinds or
degrees of prominence – even, at times, a whole different aspect –
in accordance with changes in the dominant mode of aesthetic and
cultural perception.

What de Man remarks chiefly about Jauss's programme is the
prevalence of metaphors drawn from the lexicon of visual and tactile
experience. Thus structural features are *perceived* as *standing out*
against a *background* or *horizon* of interpretive norms which in turn

allow works to achieve that effect of *foregrounding* (or aesthetic *concretization*) which the Formalists regarded as the hallmark of poetic language. And this effect comes about, furthermore, through poetry's power to make strange (or 'defamiliarize') our commonplace, prosaic habits of perception, habits that afflict us with the lethargy of custom and whose hold can only be shaken by exposure to these and similar devices. But once again – as with Abrams – this argument comes down to a form of phenomenalist reduction, a blindness to those complicating factors in language (notably the tension between logic, grammar and rhetoric) which cannot be accounted for by any model that derives its terms of analysis from the order of sensuous or phenomenal cognition. For Jauss, in short, 'the condensation of literary history and structural analysis occurs by way of the category of the aesthetic and depends for its possibility on the stability of this concept' (*RT*, p. 64). And it is here that Jauss's method joins up with all those other variations on the same basic theme – from Schiller to the New Criticism – which take it for granted that poetry is a special kind of language, one that gives access to truths beyond reach of mere rational understanding, either on account of its rhetorical structures ('paradox', 'irony' etc.), or because it enjoys a peculiarly close and 'organic' relation to the realm of natural or sensuous experience.

In *Blindness and Insight* de Man finds one or another version of this belief at work across just about the entire range of modern literary-critical thinking. And in the later essays – especially those assembled for his posthumous collection *The Resistance to Theory* – this argument takes on a more sharply diagnostic and at times admonitory tone. This is why he asserts it as a general truth, as against Jauss, that 'all the obstacles to understanding . . . belong specifically to language rather than to the phenomenal world; consequently, the expectation that they could be mastered by analogy with processes that stem from the psychology of perception is by no means certain' (*RT*, p. 62). For if de Man finds criticism dangerously prone to these forms of aesthetic mystification, he is equally convinced that rhetorical close-reading can work to undo such effects, or at least to show how they always take rise from some specific moment of error or self-induced interpretive 'blindness'. And this applies even in the case of those readers, like the New Critics, whose attentiveness to nuances of language and style was sufficient – on occasion – to contest or subvert their larger programmatic claims, especially their belief in the talismanic virtues of 'organic form', of the poem as 'verbal icon', and other such delusory aestheticist ideas. Thus it may always turn out, in de Man's words, that 'mere reading . . . prior to any theory, is able to transform critical discourse in a manner that would appear deeply subversive to those who think of the teaching of literature as a substitute for the teaching of theology, ethics, psychology, or intellectual history' (*RT*, p. 24). What gives 'mere reading' this transformative power is precisely the *resistance* that language puts up to any form of wholesale aestheticizing creed or premature escape into the 'hermeneutic circle' of naturalized organicist metaphors.

III

I can anticipate several objections that might be raised to my treatment of Spinoza as a signal precursor of these and related issues in recent critical theory. One – the most obvious – is that Spinoza had nothing to say about aesthetics, let alone about 'aesthetic ideology'; that he was writing, after all, at a time long before that term entered the discourse of philosophy (with Baumgarten), and then received its further elaboration at the hands of Kant, Schiller, Hegel and others.[29] In fact there is no evidence from Spinoza's writing that he took the least interest in art or its relation to matters of philosophical concern. But really this objection is beside the point since, as I have argued, the role of aesthetics after Kant was to act as a focus for problematical issues in the theory of knowledge and representation which go back well beyond the invention of 'aesthetics' as a quasi-autonomous field of study. On the one hand it can be shown – as comes out very clearly in de Man's reading of Pascal – that there is a deep continuity between the discourse of seventeenth-century rationalist metaphysics and the kinds of question that later philosophers addressed in terms of aesthetic understanding. On the other, those subsequent modes of address may themselves conceal a certain will to avoid more pressing or troublesome issues, as when Schiller thinks to resolve the antinomies of Kantian thought by having recourse to a notion of 'aesthetic education' which opens the way to all manner of mystified beliefs.[30] In short, one could argue that the entire post-Kantian discourse on aesthetics has served as an alibi, a means of shifting attention from problems in the nature of knowledge and truth which would otherwise remain – as de Man thinks they do remain for Kant – incapable of ever achieving resolution at the level of reflective understanding. For it is simply not the case, he writes, that aesthetics has succeeded 'in its admirable ambition to unite cognition, desire and morality in one single synthetic judgement' (*RT*, p. 25). The idea that such a synthesis could or should occur is itself a product of that same 'aesthetic ideology' that begins with Schiller's misreading of Kant and continues in the routine statements and assumptions of mainstream Romantic scholarship.

My point is that Spinoza not only raises these questions but raises them in a sharply insistent form which as yet finds no room for the convenient escape-route represented by the discourse of aesthetic values. And this is nowhere more apparent than in Spinoza's dealing with *fiction* as a determinate mode of knowledge, a mode that stands (so to speak) half-way between truth and falsehood, since it involves untruths that are knowingly entertained as such, rather than mistaken for adequate ideas. As we have seen, it is this aspect of Spinoza's thinking that led Althusser and Macherey to propose a new point of departure for Marxist 'theoretical practice', an approach that would respect the relative autonomy attained by various levels of cultural production, and thus avoid the reductionist error that treated them indifferently as so many forms of ideological 'false consciousness'. What is crucial here – and what links their project to de Man's critique of aesthetic values – is the insistence that questions of truth and falsehood not be overridden by a mystified appeal to some alternative realm of aesthetic understanding where such questions are effectively ruled out of court. 'Literature is fiction', de Man writes, 'not because it somehow refuses to acknowledge "reality", but because it is not *a priori* certain that language functions according to principles which are those, or which are *like* those, of the phenomenal world' (*RT*, p. 11). And again (this time from the essay on Jauss): 'the aesthetic is, by definition, a seductive notion that appeals to the pleasure principle, a eudaimonic judgement that can displace and conceal values of truth and falsehood likely to be more resilient to desire than values of pleasure and pain' (*RT*, p. 64).

There are two main points to be made in this connection, both leading back to the Spinozist account of how fiction stands in relation to truths of reason (or 'adequate ideas'). Firstly, it is wrong – a kind of category-mistake – to regard fictive statements as belonging to an order of uniquely privileged aesthetic understanding where standards of truth and falsehood simply don't apply. This error comes about through a failure to perceive the more complex

three-term relationship between truth (or science), fiction (or literary
form), and falsehood (or the realm of commonsense, naturalized
ideological belief which fiction *reworks* into narrative structures that
reveal various blindspots, aporias, or moments of internal self-
contradiction). Macherey puts the case as follows in a passage that
argues strongly against any move to treat literature as a realm of
mere 'illusion', or a discourse that lends itself unresistingly to the
purposes of ideological obfuscation.

> On this side or on that of the distinction between true and false is
> the text, a dense fabric which obeys its own logic (stylistics ought to
> be part of this logic). Notice in passing that once we have thus
> mapped out the site of the literary discourse it becomes difficult to
> describe the work of the writer as a mystification which produces a
> pure illusion. If there is no line dividing true and false, how could
> we detect any deception, except in relation to another truth – the
> truth of a world or an intention outside the text, and which has no
> jurisdiction over the text? If it is truly constitutive, the illusion that
> hides in, or contains, the text could not thus be isolated and reduced.
> Far from being opposed to a reality on the basis of which it would
> play a very precarious game, this illusion must have a certain reality
> of its own.[31]

So fiction is not to be regarded – as it has been so often by
aestheticizing critics and philosophers, from Schiller on down – as
a realm of illusory meanings and appearances that none the less
constitute their own, special kind of truth, a truth unbeholden to
normative standards of consistency, logic or 'adequate ideas'. Rather
it exists at a certain remove from both 'science' on the one hand
and 'ideology' on the other, since it is precisely in and through the
distancing effect of fictional forms – their capacity to reveal gaps and
contradictions in their own ideological project – that criticism is
able to articulate a knowledge of the real (material) conditions that
produced this oblique mode of truth-telling discourse.

It is here that Macherey's approach to these questions converges
with de Man's on a number of crucial points. Both see nothing but
error and delusion in the idea that literature must somehow be
exempt from all rational sense-making standards (or values of truth
and falsehood). Both make this point in direct opposition to an
idealist (or metaphysical) philosophy of art which locates the highest
levels of creative achievement in a realm of self-confirming aesthetic
values – 'organic form', the poem as 'verbal icon', 'concrete universal' and so forth – which then serve as a pretext for avoiding any

question as to the *social and material* factors bound up with the work of literary production. And finally, they both – though de Man more emphatically – equate this powerful mystifying drive with a tendency to ignore the ontological difference between language (as a realm of signifying structures irreducible to the order of intuitive or phenomenal self-evidence) and reality (or the naturalized, 'commonsense' view of reality) as that which presents itself directly to the senses without any intervening process of linguistic mediation. This is why, in de Man's words, although 'it is by no means an established fact that aesthetic values and literary structures are incompatible', nevertheless 'their compatibility, or lack of it, has to remain an open question', so that 'the manner in which the teaching of literature, since its beginning in the later nineteenth century, has foreclosed the question is unsound, even if motivated by the best of intentions' (*RT*, p. 25). For the effect of this premature conflation of realms is to exclude the possibility that language itself – or language as the unstable force-field of relations between logic, grammar and rhetoric – might offer resistance to the various forms of uncritical or naturalized perception that derive their considerable power from precisely such delusive totalizing metaphors.

It is essentially the same point that Macherey is making when he argues against the kind of critical approach that would seek out the 'truth' of a literary text as if that truth were finally revealed at the point where all narrative contrivances dropped away and the meaning at last stood plain to view. In which case, Macherey writes,

> the true and sincere story would gradually abolish its own contours, proclaim its own redundance, suggest that its linear progress was an avoidable detour. The object, hitherto concealed beneath the folds of the narration, would appear, after the delay required for the fulfilment of the text, at the merest glance. (Macherey, p. 18)

Such criticism falls into the same kind of error that de Man attributes to 'aesthetic ideology' in its various forms and guises. That is to say, it involves the reduction of literature – narrative fictions for Macherey, rhetorical structures for de Man – to an order of revealed or self-evident truth that marks the end-point of critical enquiry, and which thus rules out any detailed analysis of the modes and conditions of textual production that characterize literary discourse. Furthermore, as Macherey remarks,

[t]his was precisely what Spinoza defined, in the appendix to the first volume of his *Ethics*, as the confusion of causes and effects. In like fashion, the critic begins from the model, ignoring the fact that the enigmatic narrative gives the solution and the problem in inextricable simultaneity. (p. 18)

One could develop this point by comparing the pages of closely-worked commentary in *Allegories of Reading* where de Man takes a lead from Nietzsche's diagnosis of the same root confusion, i.e. the metaleptic reversal of cause and effect which allows us to ignore the sheer contingency of events (whether factual or textual events) in pursuit of some ideal, imaginary order of meaning, history, and truth.[32] But my immediate purpose in citing these passages from Macherey and de Man is to remark on their common allegiance to a Spinozist theory of knowledge, an allegiance that Macherey signals very clearly, here and elsewhere, but which remains unspoken – and so far unrecognized – in de Man's writings. I have already argued this case at some length with regard to his essay on Husserl. What emerged there was the close relationship between issues of interpretive truth and error – as revealed through a reading of the prejudicial blindspots in Husserl's project – and those questions of a wider political or socio-historical import which arose at the point where textual analysis led on inescapably to a form of applied *Ideologiekritik*. It seems to me that Spinoza's ideas have been crucial for these present-day developments in critical theory, and none the less so for his rarely having figured expressly in the widespread debate about deconstruction and its various philosophical antecedents.

At this stage it is worth recalling the passage from Althusser and Balibar that I cited in chapter 1, since they offer what amounts to a point-for-point endorsement of the case I have presented thus far. Spinoza was the first thinker to have raised

> the problem of *reading* and, in consequence, of *writing* . . . also the first to have proposed both a theory of history and a philosophy of the opacity of the immediate. With him, for the first time ever, a man held together in this way the essence of reading and the essence of history in a theory of the difference between the imaginary and the true.[33]

It was on the basis of these Spinozist categories, they argue, that Marx was able to achieve his most significant theoretical advance, a distinction between 'science' and 'ideology' which avoided the

errors of reductionist thought while maintaining the material speci-
ficity of discourse at its various levels of production. And this break
was in turn made possible by what they describe as 'the dissipation
of the *religious* myth of reading', that is to say, the move against
hermeneutic models which located the truth of the text in some
realm of deep symbolic meaning, a realm to which readers could
only have access through divine revelation, intuitive foreknowledge,
or other such privileged points of entry. This is why – as I have
argued – Spinoza stands firmly apart from the long tradition of
exegetical thought which began with the attempt to 'accommodate'
Old and New Testament scriptural texts, and whose latest variant
(in a half-way secularizing critic like Kermode) still bears the signs
of its religious origin. What disappears from view in this reading
of Spinoza is his principled refusal to entertain truth-claims other
than those arrived at by subjecting scripture to a rigorous critique
of its grounding suppositions, especially where these went against
the dictates of logic, consistency, or plain good sense.

We are now better placed to understand the connection that
Althusser and Balibar make between Spinoza's theory of *language*
(or 'writing and reading') and his signal contribution to Marxist
debate about the nature and modalities of *historical* knowledge. This
connection has to do with his threefold argument: (1) that our grasp
of historical events is necessarily partial and timebound (i.e. that it
belongs to the realm of *experientia vaga*, or inadequate and confused
ideas); (2) that this condition also applies to any knowledge attained
through language, since verbal signs – written or spoken – are
likewise subject to all manner of change collocations or random
associative linkage, and are thus inherently suspect from the standpoint of reason; and (3) that the mind's only recourse against these
sources of error is to grasp the conditions that brought them about
– the historical, causal, or linguistic factors – and thereby achieve
the kind of rational grasp that converts 'passive' into 'active' understanding. And it is here that questions of writing and reading
acquire a special salience in Spinoza's work, along with the related
topic of fictive or 'feigned' utterances, those that occupy a third
domain of knowledge situated (so to speak) *between* truth and
falsehood, and which therefore – as Althusser and Macherey argue
– cannot be assigned to some separate realm of non-cognitive or
purely 'aesthetic' values. Thus fiction gives access to 'adequate
ideas' in so far as it reworks, deconstructs or estranges the materials
of commonsense (ideological) perception, or the forms under which

experience presents itself to a mind held captive by 'knowledge of imagination'. In Spinoza's words: 'in proportion as the mind's understanding is smaller, and its experience multiplex, so will its power of coining fictions be larger, whereas, as its understanding increases, its capacity for entertaining fictitious ideas becomes less' (*OIU*, p. 23). The most important point here is that Spinoza – like Althusser and Macherey – insists on treating fiction as a determinate mode of knowledge, admittedly a partial or 'mutilated' mode, but one that has its own distinctive role to play in the process of arriving at adequate ideas.

For it is precisely by way of such mediating discourses – those that take rise from the 'multiplex' nature of phenomenal experience, but which also involve a distancing effect whereby that experience is cast into a different, more articulate (and often contradictory) form – that criticism is enabled to locate the various errors or blindspots of commonsense belief. And this can only come about to the extent that fictions (whether 'literary' fictions or imaginary ideas) are treated with a view to distinguishing their various levels of co-implicated truth and falsehood. By means of such analyusis, Spinoza argues, we can discipline the mind to perceive more clearly where reason has erred in attributing truth to some plausible fictive idea, or where fiction has flouted its own immanent laws (of consistency, non-contradiction, or existence in some logically 'possible world') by falling into manifest absurdity. Thus:

> I call a thing IMPOSSIBLE, when its existence would imply a contradiction; NECESSARY, when its non-existence would imply a contradiction; POSSIBLE, when neither its existence nor its non-existence imply a contradiction, but when the necessity or impossibility of its nature depends on causes unknown to us, while we feign that it exists. (*OIU*, p. 19).

Of course one should bear it in mind that when Spinoza talks about 'feigning' or 'fictions' he is using those terms in a sense – and an intellectual context – far removed from present-day debates in literary theory. The context is that of Cartesian rationalism, and the sense has more to do with ideas or mental representations than with anything in the nature of a narrative or story-telling discourse. Hence Spinoza's catalogue of typical fictive entities: 'trees speaking, men instantly turned into stones, ghosts appearing in mirrors, something issuing from nothing, even gods changed into beasts, and men, and infinite other absurdities of the same kind' (*OIU*, p.

22). These all serve to illustrate Spinoza's point: that there do exist certain imaginary ideas – like that of the centaur, then as now a great favourite among philosophers – whose chimerical character by no means prevents us from conceiving them as lively impressions in the mind. But they also display what might be called a latent narrative dimension, a background of more or less mythical events (metamorphoses, apparitions, creations *ex nihilo* and so forth) which involve at least the rudiments of a sequential plot-structure. This is one reason why Macherey is able to develop the Spinozist theory of knowledge into a version of Marxist *Ideologiekritik* whose categories are also – indispensably – those of narrative representation.

But in fact this ambivalence is there already in Spinoza's writing, as we have seen with those passages in the *Ethics* that aim at a knowledge of 'eternal ideas' (or a wisdom achieved *sub specie aeternitatis*), but which none the less involve an implicit appeal to temporal or historical conditions. And it is hardly surprising that this should be the case, given the fact of his own deep engagement with Dutch political events in the mid-century crisis years, and with the way that issues in the realm of scriptural interpretation could be seen to bear directly on questions of national sovereignty and legitimate rule. In short, Spinoza's writings are best regarded as a sustained mediation on the powers and limits of historical understanding, one that inevitably goes by way of narrative models and metaphors, though *not* – and this is the crucial point – with the upshot of reducing all such knowledge to just another form of fictive imposition on the inchoate materials of memory or record. For it is Spinoza's chief contention – taken up by Althusser and Macherey – that there is a difference between the kind of naturalized, common-sense narrative grasp that arises in response to the pressures of contingent historical events, and the capacity of reason (or theoretical understanding) to criticize those first-order narrative constructs from the standpoint of a more adequate conceptual knowledge. This is where Spinoza and his present-day disciples part company with postmodernist gurus like Baudrillard or neo-pragmatist adepts like Rorty and Fish. For these latter, any such argument can only be a product of the old (now obsolete) Enlightenment paradigm that separated questions of theory and truth from questions of presently-acceptable consensus belief. So on their view it is mistaken – just a form of high theoreticist delusion – to imagine that criticism could ever achieve a knowledge that somehow broke with the story-telling interests, the legitimizing myths or forms of narrative representation (whether fictive or avowedly factual) that characterize a given consensual status quo.

This difference is brought out most strikingly in the following passage from Macherey's essay on Jules Verne, a passage that again points back to Spinoza as its chief theoretical source. 'The interest of Verne's work', he writes,

> lies in the fact that, through the unity of its project – a unity borrowed from a certain ideological coherence, or incoherence – and by the means which inform this project (or fail in this enterprise), by specifically literary means, it reveals the *limits*, and to some extent the *conditions* of this ideological coherence, which is necessarily built upon a discord in the historical reality, and upon a discord between this historical reality and its *dominant* representation. (Macherey, p. 238)

And this argument connects in turn with the Spinozist principle that fictions should be treated as mixed or inherently 'multiplex' forms of knowledge, on the one hand bearing witness to the limiting conditions of their own (experiential or historically situated) character, while on the other making possible a reasoned account of the causes (or the structures of ideological misrecognition) that determined the particular form taken by this or that fictional project. At which point we return to the question of 'aesthetic ideology', as theorized in de Man's late essays. For it can now be seen that the aesthetic figures (for Spinoza and Macherey alike) as precisely the source of those mystified values and beliefs that result from confusing the two distinct orders of *phenomenal cognition* and *intelligible form*. In Spinozist terms, it is an 'error of imagination' brought about by the failure to grasp how fictions differ from straightforward falsehoods by virtue of their *not* laying claim to a truth which would simply collapse the distinction between sensuous impressions and adequate knowledge. What gives rise to 'complete deception', as Spinoza puts it, is the fact that 'certain things, presented to the imagination, also exist in the understanding', which means that 'so long as we do not separate that which is distinct from that which is confused, certainty, or the true idea, becomes mixed with indistinct ideas' (*OIU*, p. 29). And for Macherey this same confusion results when literary critics typically mistake the 'truth' of a work for the knowledge it gives of a reality that somehow preexists its own process of elaboration in narrative or textual form. The truth in question may be identified either with the author's wishes, desires, intentions etc., or with an order of real-world circumstances and events that would then stand as an objective index of the work's truth-telling value. Most often – as Catherine Belsey has noted – these ideas are run together in the doctrine of 'expressive realism', or the notion that authorial sincerity is enough to somehow guarantee such veridical qualities.[34] And criticism can only adopt this standpoint in so far as it treats the literary text as an object for aesthetic contemplation, a work whose meaning (or whose ultimate truth) must at last be brought to light through a mode of intuitive or 'deep' hermeneutical insight.

Macherey sees this as a thoroughgoing *mystification* of the critical process. It is an error that begins with the setting-up of 'literature' as a privileged aesthetic domain, and which then gives rise to an endlessly proliferating mass of commentaries, critiques, appreciative essays, scholarly articles and so forth whose sole aim is to restore the text to its original condition of pristine intelligibility. In which case criticism would finally efface itself in the presence of revealed truth, or 'culminat[e] in its own abolition when it is reassimilated into an unmodified, merely interpreted reality' (Macherey, p. 6). But this is to ignore what he regards as the single most decisive argument against all such interpretive methods: namely, their failure to remark the essential distinction between *literature* as a specific (and necessarily partial) mode of representing certain knowledge-effects, and *criticism* as a discourse that aims to produce a more adequate (theoretically articulated) knowledge of exactly those effects. Thus we are faced with a choice, as Macherey presents it:

either literary criticism is an art, completely determined by the pre-existence of a domain, the literary works, and finally reunited with them in the discovery of their truth, and as such it has no autonomous existence; or, it is a certain form of knowledge, and has an object, which is not a given but a product of literary criticism. (Macherey, p. 7)

The first option leads to a mystified understanding of literature and criticism alike, since both are thus consigned to a realm of aesthetic ideology where cognitive interests (or values of truth and falsehood) can have no legitimate place. The second points beyond this self-enclosed realm of interpretive foreknowledge, but only on condition that criticism not delude itself with notions of privileged hermeneutic access. In Macherey's words:

[k]nowledge is not the discovery or reconstruction of a latent meaning, forgotten or concealed. It is something newly raised up, an addition to the reality from which it begins. *Remember that the idea of a circle is not itself circular and does not depend on the existence of actual circles.* Remember that the emergence of thought institutes a certain distance and separation, thus circumscribing the domain of the real, rendering it finite as an object of knowledge. (Macherey, p. 6; italics added).

His use of the circle as an *exemplum* of the difference between ideas and phenomenal appearances is of course taken straight from Spinoza. It serves in both cases to warn against the errors that inevitably follow from any confusion of these two distinct realms, or any move to assimilate theoretical knowledge to the order of phenomenal sense-certainty. But Macherey is also using it to explain just what is wrong with literary-critical approaches that are premised on the notion of aesthetic understanding as a special mode of knowledge unique to the experience of literary texts. For this idea is nothing more than a piece of self-serving ideological baggage, a procedure invented for the purpose of sustaining one imaginary discourse ('literature'), and thereby reducing another (literary criticism) to a state of passive dependence on mystified values which it could otherwise work to subvert or deconstruct.

7 Why Spinoza Now? The Critique of Revelation Revisited

I

My main purpose in writing this book has been to redirect attention not only to Spinoza's work but also to those thinkers of a Spinozist persuasion – notably Althusser and Macherey – whose contributions have counted for little against the current tide of postmodern-pragmatist ideas. But it might be as well to bring these issues nearer home by asking what practical relevance they have in contexts beyond the fairly specialized preserve of literary-critical discourse.

The case of Salman Rushdie's novel *The Satanic Verses* is one that raises a number of pertinent questions about fictional truth and the status of literary texts in relation to forms of religious and political power.[1] Like Spinoza, Rushdie has had the courage to stand up against a resurgent fundamentalist movement whose authority rests on the appeal to scriptural warrant, and whose reading of scripture is clearly dictated by the struggle between rival claimants to the 'truth' as revealed through divine inspiration to a self-proclaimed pious elite. Like Spinoza again, he sets out to show how such movements come about; how the high priests and mystagogues are able to practise their craft by exploiting a range of 'imaginary' devices – prophecy, miracles, divine interventions, all manner of occult or supernatural 'proofs' – in order to win popular assent for doctrines that can scarcely withstand critical scrutiny. 'In despotic statecraft', Spinoza writes, 'the supreme and essential mystery [is] to hoodwink the subjects, and to mask the fear, which keeps them down, with the specious garb of religion' (*TPT*, p. 5). And again, lest anyone fail to take the point (or be tempted to apply it only to 'other' religions, those beyond the pale of Judaeo-Christian truth):

[t]he origin of superstition . . . affords us a clear reason for the fact
that it comes to all men naturally, though some refer its rise to a
dim notion of God, universal to mankind, and also tends to show,
that it is no less inconsistent and variable than other mental halluci-
nations and emotional impulses, and further that it can only be
maintained by hope, hatred, anger, and deceit; since it springs, not
from reason, but solely from the more powerful phases of emotion.
(*TPT*, p. 5)

As we have seen, Spinoza goes various ways around to break the
hold of such delusive beliefs, or – what he thinks should be sufficient
for the purpose – to show how they arise from errors of understanding which in turn have their cause in some particular context of
socio-political existence. On balance he considers the New Testament superior to the Old since (for instance) 'the long deductions
and arguments of Paul . . . are in nowise written from supernatural
revelation' (p. 159). But there can be little doubt that Spinoza
maintained a deep mistrust of *all* religious truth-claims, especially
where these took the form of an appeal to scriptural authority
backed up – as so often – by the threat of dire punishments (real
or imaginary) for anyone who challenged their presumptive self-
evidence.

However, there is a good deal more to be said about the parallel
between Spinoza's critique of religion and Rushdie's treatment of
Islamic fundamentalism in *The Satanic Verses*. Perhaps the most
extreme statement of the Spinozist case occurs in a passage from
the *Tractatus Theologico-Politicus* which effectively denies that scripture can contain any kind of sacred or authoritative truth since it
– like all language – is subject to a generalized relativity of sense
(or a process of historico-semantic drift) which might always have
erased the original meaning beyond hope of recovery. It is here that
Spinoza comes closest to the kind of all-embracing Nietzschean
scepticism that has characterized recent (post-structuralist) accounts
of language and representation. Thus:

[w]ords gain their meaning solely from their usage, and if they are
arranged according to their accepted signification so as to move those
who read them to devotion, they will become sacred, and the book
so written will be sacred also. But if their usage afterwards dies out
so that the words have no meaning, or the book becomes utterly
neglected, whether from unworthy motives, or because it is no longer
needed, then the words and the book will lose both their use and
their sanctity; lastly, if those same words be otherwise arranged, or
if their customary meaning becomes perverted into its opposite, then

both the words and the book containing them become, instead of sacred, impure and profane. (*TPT*, p. 167)

This passage can of course be read in light of Spinoza's argument elsewhere that the basic truths of scripture (i.e. those prerequisite to the 'intellectual love of God') are in no way dependent on the mere interpretation of fallible linguistic signs. Thus the exegetes go badly wrong – like Maimonides – when they twist the text this way and that, trying to square the manifest sense with some preconceived notion of its latent (allegorical) import. On this account scripture would be wholly redundant, at best a mixed bag of errors and truths (the latter in any case accessible to reason without such dubious assistance), and at worst a source of imaginary ideas which can only obscure and pervert such truths. But as we have seen, there is plentiful evidence in Spinoza's works – evidence which requires no very shrewd deconstructive reading to draw it out – that in fact philosophy, like every intellectual discipline, depends upon language as its only possible means of articulating truth-claims, advancing propositions, clarifying ideas and so forth. What the above passage would then be seen to warn against is the unreliability of *one particular kind* of language – namely, the language of scripture – as a source of genuine (rationally accountable) truth. And the reception-history of Spinoza's writings is surely proof enough that this is indeed how they have been understood, by religious opponents and free-thinking advocates alike.

One line of argument in the Rushdie affair has been to point out that this is after all a work of fiction – 'postmodernist' fiction at that – and should therefore not be judged (much less condemned) as if it were claiming any kind of factual, historical or truth-telling warrant.[2] Or again, to adopt an alternative idiom: *The Satanic Verses* belongs to the genre of so-called 'magical realism', a mode that typically mixes up the orders of verisimilitude and fantasy-projection to a stage where the reader loses all sense of where the one shades off into the other. From this point of view the whole controversy would seem just a species of egregious category-mistake, a confusion brought about by the failure to recognize that literary works are not in the business of arguing a case, reinterpreting history, or engaging in matters of doctrinal dispute. The Ayatollah and his fundamentalist disciples would then be seen as literal-minded readers – non-readers more often – who had attacked Rushdie's novel on the mistaken grounds *firstly* that it was a travesty of actual events in the life of the Prophet and the history of Islam, and *secondly* that it was preaching a set of irreligious or wickedly heterodox ideas at variance with everything their faith held sacred. So the best defence of Rushdie's book would be to point out its elaborately fictive construction – its not belonging to the 'language-game' of presenting truths, offering arguments, challenging scriptural witness etc. – and thus make it clear that the charges of apostasy were based on a gross misunderstanding.

This argument of course had the virtue of promising to soothe fundamentalist passions and afford at least the basis of a working truce in the current enflamed situation. Rushdie himself made the point in an open letter to Rajiv Gandhi protesting the fact that his novel had been banned by an act of government in India.

> The section of the book in question (and let's remember that the book isn't actually about Islam, but about migration, metamorphosis, divided selves, love, death, London and Bombay) deals with a prophet who is not called Muhammad living in a highly fantasticated city – made of sand, it dissolves when water falls upon it – in which he is surrounded by fictional followers, one of whom happens to bear my own first name. Moreover, this entire sequence happens in a dream, the fictional dream of a fictional character, an Indian movie-star, and one who is losing his mind, at that. How much further from history could one get?[3]

Clearly it is vital – not only for Rushdie but for many writers working under oppressive religious or political regimes – that this distinction be respected and that novels not be read as if they were straightforward statements of authorial opinion. And yet there is a sense in which one begs the whole question by adopting this stand-point, since it rests on principles that enjoy wide support in our own (liberal-humanist and relatively secularized) societies, but which would count for nothing with Rushdie's fundamentalist opponents. At their broadest these principles have to do with the separation of powers between church and state, the 'self-evident' democratic freedoms of thought and speech, and – closely related to these – the (again relative) autonomy of art as a form of expression exempt from certain otherwise normative juridical constraints. And it could further be argued that literary criticism has developed a more specialized version of the same basic attitude, one that progressively elaborates a whole range of concepts (aesthetic disinterest, the 'suspension of disbelief', ambiguity, paradox, the 'implied author', intertextuality and so forth) by way of backing up this claim for literature as a mode of utterance with its own *sui generis* standards of imaginative truth.[4]

These are some of the values invoked by Rushdie in the above-cited passage of self-justifying argument. It is a stance whose history in English criticism begins with Sidney's defence of poetry as a 'feigned' or fictive mode of utterance, one that could not be held to account – as Plato or the latter-day puritans would have it – as if poets were engaged in the same kind of language-game as philosophers, moralists, or historians.[5] This issue was confronted over again when the novel emerged as a distinctive genre in the early-to-mid eighteenth century. The main problem here was that prose-fiction, unlike poetry, lacked the more obvious formal markers of 'literary' status, and could thus all too easily be mistaken for factual or truth-telling discourse. Hence the various efforts – in the legislative sphere as well as among critics and commentators on the novel – to explain just how this distinction might be upheld and where exactly the line should be drawn between novels on the one hand and news reports, historical narratives, political tracts, or theological arguments on the other.[6] This can best be understood in Habermasian terms as an aspect of the progressive separating-out or specialization of discursive regimes that gave rise to the modern 'public sphere' of differential validity-claims, with literature enjoying a large measure of autonomy *vis-à-vis* those other forms of knowledge. And there is, as we have seen, some reason for regarding Spinoza as the first philosopher to have worked out this distinction in detail, thus resisting the tendency to confuse matters of revealed or authoritative truth with fictive or imaginary modes of representation. This is why Kermode and other critics – Tzvetan Todorov among them[7] – can take it as Spinoza's chief contribution to the history of secular interpretive thought that he managed to liberate the practice of textual hermeneutics from its erstwhile bondage to the dictates of orthodox belief. And it would surely be wrong to underrate this achievement at a time when such enlightened values are increasingly under siege, not only from resurgent fundamentalist creeds but also in the work of postmodernist thinkers like Foucault, Lyotard and Baudrillard who reject that whole history as just another form of oppressive, self-legitimizing power/knowledge. As against this view it is important to remember that the very possibility of open debate on such questions is a freedom that was won in large part through the efforts – very often the reviled and persecuted efforts – of writers who claimed an imaginative licence to satirize the truth-claims of religion.

Graham Swift makes this point – echoing Rushdie's own position – when he writes of *The Satanic Verses* that 'a work of literature is *more* than free expression. It is creative expression, which does not argue, state, or assert, so much as make. A novel exists, *lives* in the minds of its readers, as no statement or assertion can'.[8] And Carlos Fuentes offers what is perhaps the most eloquent defence of this kind by invoking the example of Mikhail Bakhtin, 'probably the greatest theorist of the novel in our century', and 'one whose life, in a way, is as exemplary as his books'. It is worth citing his remarks at some length since they state the case for imaginative freedom – and for the novel as our last, best hope of such freedom – while following Bakhtin in his pinpoint diagnosis of the pressures that make for conformity, dogmatism, and other forms of oppressive 'monological' discourse. Thus, according to Fuentes,

> Rushdie's work perfectly fits the Bakhtinian contention that ours is an age of competitive languages. The novel is the privileged arena where languages in conflict can meet, bringing together, in tension and dialogue, not only opposing characters, but also different historical ages, social levels, civilizations and other dawning realities of human life . . . But this is precisely what the Ayatollahs of this world cannot suffer. For the Ayatollahs reality is dogmatically defined once and for all in a sacred text. But a sacred text is, by definition, a completed and exclusive text. You can add nothing to it. It does not converse with anyone . . . It offers a perfect refuge for the insecure who then, having the protection of a dogmatic text over their heads, proceed to excommunicate those whose security lies in the search for truth . . . When we all understood everything, the epic was possible. But not fiction. The novel is born from the fact that we do not understand one another any longer, because unitary, orthodox language has broken down. Impose a unitary language: you kill the novel, but you also kill society.[9]

It is no coincidence that this coupling of Rushdie and Bakhtin goes by way of several interconnected themes – persecution, liberty of thought, the closed or 'monological' character of religious discourse – that were first brought together in Spinoza's critique of revelation. In fact one could argue that Spinoza belongs very much in the company of those novelists, poets, satirists and other such 'literary' figures whose work had the effect – at least in the long run – of securing vital new freedoms, at first for their own (henceforth recognizably distinctive) kind of writing, then in the realms of philosophy, politics, theology, and other such contested domains.

To this extent Kermode would be justified in his claim that Spinoza more or less invented the practice of secular hermeneutics, a practice which could only come into being with the challenge to canonical, self-authorized versions of scriptural truth.

But one must also recall Spinoza's argument – taken up by theorists like Althusser and Macherey – that fictions cannot be treated on a level with falsehoods or consigned to a realm of non-cognitive 'aesthetic' value where questions of truth and error simply don't arise. For it is precisely by virtue of what Spinoza terms the mixed or 'multiplex' character of fictive discourse – its power to clarify confused ideas by subjecting them to a different, more rigorous or undeceiving order of narrative representation – that criticism is enabled to perceive the blindspots, the errors of 'commonsense' belief or ideology, that would otherwise pass for truth. This is simply a more 'philosophical' way of making the point that novels can effectively *argue a case* and, what is more, give rise to counter-arguments which take fiction seriously for just that reason. And this applies not only to obvious instances – the *roman à thèse*, political novels, works like *Caleb Williams, Hard Times, The Roads to Freedom* or other such overtly didactic fictions – but also to texts whose design on the reader is much less palpable, but which none the less provoke a whole range of attitudinal responses, from straightforward endorsement to downright angry rejection. The latter alternative is one that rarely figures in the discourse of academic criticism, since here – as we have seen – there is a countervailing tendency to elevate issues of aesthetic worth above questions of argumentative warrant. But one still finds notable exceptions to this rule, among them Macherey, de Man, Empson, and others (like Gerald Graff) who have held out against the widespread aestheticizing drift. What unites these thinkers across otherwise considerable differences of view is the conviction, firstly, that fictive works make statements (or involve propositional attitudes); secondly, that criticism should not seek refuge in a realm of sacrosanct 'literary' values; and thirdly, that one can indeed *argue* with texts on a range of issues – philosophical, political, or socio-historical – which do inescapably lead on to questions of truth and falsehood.

For the move to dissociate literature from truth-claims of any kind is one that can only trivialize fiction, or reduce it to the level of a pure, self-occupied play with narrative codes and conventions that could have no possible bearing on matters of real-world practical concern. Significantly, it is a move that is made more often by *theorists* of the postmodern – by literary critics, sympathetic or hostile – than by novelists (for instance Kurt Vonnegut, Angela Carter, E. L. Doctorow and Rushdie himself) who apparently see no problem about combining on the one hand a commitment to various forms of experimental, postmodern, or defamiliarizing technique, and on the other a continuing (if intermittent) use of the documentary-realist mode. What characterizes their work – and Rushdie's in particular – is a constant intertwining of fictive and factual (or imaginary and truth-conditional) discourse which deliberately eschews such ready-made distinctions and asks us to conceive of alternative realities perceptibly akin to our own, but differing from it in certain crucial respects. To this extent they are working in the same area as modal logicians and 'possible worlds' theorists, those who seek to establish the rules or constraints that regulate the transfer of properties, individuals, and events from one such world to another.[10] It would then be a question for the literary critic just how far 'realism' – or the realist effect – is a product of the 'trans-world identity' that holds between features that turn out to be invariant across these otherwise disparate realms. One of them (the world we do in fact inhabit) would enjoy a greater or lesser degree of ontological privilege depending on the analytic framework adopted, or on the analyst's willingness to accept some version of 'modal realism' that treated all worlds as equally compossible, and therefore as *actually existing* so far as we can tell from our own (commonsense or this-worldly) standpoint.[11]

My purpose in these last few pages has been, once again, to challenge the idea that fictional texts have nothing to do with values of truth and falsehood, or with issues that arise more obviously in relation to other kinds of writing (historical, political, philosophical and so forth). It may also help to explain what is less than satisfactory about that line of defence in the Rushdie case which takes it for granted that fictions are somehow totally exempt from the commonplace requirements of truth-telling discourse. Of course this idea has a long prehistory, from Plato (who considered it a downright scandal) to those subsequent apologists for poetry and fiction, from Sidney to Shelley, Arnold, I. A. Richards and the New Critics, all of whom took the view that literature offered a *different* sort of 'truth', one that involved an appeal to values – of imagination, creativity, 'emotive' meaning, ambiguity, paradox etc. – which were simply irreducible to the standards of straightforward veridical utterance. And the upshot of such arguments, especially when joined to the interests of post-Kantian idealist thought, was to produce what I have called – following de Man – the discourse of present-day 'aesthetic ideology'. Hence the widely-held view – announced most emphatically by Eliot and Richards, and taken up by Kermode in *The Genesis of Secrecy* – that modern science had brought about a complete severance between cognitive interests and imaginative values, so that (in Richards's words) we were left with no choice but to 'cut our pseudo-statements free from belief, and yet retain them, in this released state, as the main instruments by which we order our attitudes to one another and to the world'.[12] In which case clearly the Islamic fundamentalists have got it wrong, not to mention a long succession of priests and commissars who have likewise ignored the essential difference between fictive and other modes of discourse.

Returning to Spinoza is one way of grasping what is at stake in this controversy over *The Satanic Verses*. For Spinoza, it is unthinkable that fiction should be treated as belonging to a realm quite apart from the interests of reason and truth, a realm of 'pseudo-statements' (or – as Richards would have it – equilibrated 'impulses' or 'attitudes') where the only operative standard of value is the pragmatist appeal to what is 'good in the way of belief'. On the contrary: fiction is a contested zone *between* truth and falsehood where 'adequate ideas' are mixed (but not inextricably mixed) with imaginary, erroneous, metaphorical, analogical and other such illusory knowledge-effects. Thus, according to Macherey: 'fiction, not to be confused with illusion, is the substitute for, if not the equivalent of, knowledge. A theory of literary production must show us what the text "knows", how it "knows"' (Macherey, p. 64). It is therefore the task of theory (or criticism) to explain just how – by what structural constraints specific to the nature of narrative form – fiction is enabled to reveal the limits of its own 'imaginary' presuppositions. And this follows directly from the Spinozist principle that errors of understanding (or 'ideas of imagination') are *not* mere mistakes to be put down to some localized aberration on the part of this or that individual thinker. Rather, they always take rise from the chain of 'multiplex' concatenated causes and effects which reason is presently unable to perceive owing to the limits placed upon it by prevailing forms of consensus belief, whether religious or socio-political in origin.

So fictions are allied to falsehoods in the sense that they offer imaginary solutions to unreal problems, problems that only come about through effects of ideological misrecognition. But they can also point the way toward genuine knowledge (or 'adequate ideas') in so far as reason reflects on their causes and thereby achieves a more perspicuous grasp of the conditions that produced them in the first place. And to Spinoza's way of thinking the chief cause of error is religion, or those forms of religious belief whose authority rests on the denial of reason and the resort to doctrines of revealed truth, scriptural warrant, divine inspiration and the like. The strongest statement of this case – along with its social and moral implications – is to be found in the following distinctly premonitory passage:

> Wholly repugnant to the general freedom are such devices as enthralling men's minds with prejudices, forcing their judgment, or employing any of the weapons of quasi-religious sedition; indeed, such seditions only spring up, when law enters the domain of speculative thought, and opinions are put on trial and condemned on the same footing as crimes, while those who defend and follow them are sacrificed, not to public safety, but to their opponents' hatred and cruelty. If deeds only could be made the grounds of criminal charges, and words were always allowed to pass free, such seditions would be divested of every semblance of justification, and would be separated from mere controversies by a hard and fast line (*TPT*, pp. 5–6)'

It is clear that when Spinoza uses the word 'sedition' he is not thinking of popular upheavals like those which had finally secured independence for the Dutch States General after years of violent colonial repression by the Spanish authorities and Catholic Church. The main threat now was from those various dissident factions that were grouping around the Calvinist interest on the one hand and on the other the revived monarchist pretensions identified with the House of Orange.[13] From both quarters came a challenge to the federal republic – to its values of religious tolerance, multi-racial coexistence, and freedom of thought and conscience – which Spinoza viewed with growing apprehension as one who had enjoyed at least some measure of these hard-won benefits.

What is most striking about the above-quoted passage is the connection it makes between religious fanaticism, based on the prejudiced or dogmatic reading of scripture, and those forms of repressive state power that take hold when 'law enters the domain of speculative thought'. This latter formulation anticipates Kant in its emphasis on the need to keep politics apart from religion, and also its requirement that the state authorities not overstep their rightful sphere of jurisdiction by seeking to legislate in matters of conscience, belief or 'speculative' reason.[14] Worst of all, in Spinoza's view, is the situation that arises when law becomes the instrument of sectarian religious interests, and when freedom of thought is thus curtailed in the name of revealed scriptural truth. And indeed, Spinoza writes, one can see such motives plainly at work in the procedures adopted by these adept purveyors of a false and self-serving wisdom; notably their habit of 'laying down beforehand, as a foundation for the study and the true interpretation of Scripture, the principle that it is in every passage true and divine' (*TPT*, p. 8). It was precisely in order to combat these dangerous tendencies that Spinoza, in the *Tractatus*, 'determined to examine the Bible afresh in a careful, impartial, and unfettered spirit, making no assumptions concerning it, and attributing to it no doctrines, which I do not find clearly therein set down' (p. 8). And his principal means to this end was the detailed examination of dubious passages where the issue was raised, not only of their truth or falsehood, but also of the mediating role played by *fictions* – or 'imaginary' ideas of various sorts – in the process of securing popular assent to doctrines whose ultimate validity (or lack of it) could only be established through the exericse of 'unfettered' critical reason. At the end of which process, Spinoza reports, 'I was able to conclude, that the authority of the prophets has weight only in matters of morality [i.e., in so far as it bears upon the conduct of civil and domestic life], and that their speculative doctrines affect us little' (*TPT*, p. 8). In short, the upshot of Spinoza's researches was to deny any authority to scripture beyond that of *either* reiterating truths self-evident to reason, or revealing those blindspots of error and prejudice that resulted historically from the limiting conditions of knowledge *sub specie durationis*. And this left little room – on whichever reckoning – for scripture as a source of 'adequate ideas', or of truths unavailable to any but a small, self-authorized interpretive elite.

In the case of Rushdie's novel there is clearly no question of assessing the book's arguments as if these were proffered in the form of a treatise explicitly intended to undermine the truth-claims of scriptural revelation. To this extent at least we are constrained to read fiction as belonging to a language-game (or mode of discourse) that differs from those of historical, philosophical, theoretical or other kinds of non-fictive writing. And of course this applies all the more when the work is one that self-consciously exploits a whole range of 'postmodern' narrative techniques (multiple viewpoint, dream-sequences, pronominal ambiguities, self-embedding episodic structures, *style indirecte libre* and so forth), thus producing a constant uncertainty about where to draw the line – if any such exists – between historical and fictive orders of discourse, or again, between authorial statements uttered (seemingly) *in propria persona* and ideas 'in the mind' of this or that imaginary 'character'. Thus in Lyotard's view there is a need – even a duty – to respect these distinctions within and between the various 'phrase-regimens', or orders of discursive practice. For it is only by allowing them to differ in regard to the applicable standards of validity, truth, or justice in any given case that one can prevent some currently prestigious language-game – some ultimate 'truth' of (say) science, philosophy, or dogmatic religion – from exerting a monopolistic claim to legislate in matters beyond its proper remit.

> Incommensurability, in the sense of the heterogeneity of phrase regimens and of the impossibility of subjecting them to a single law (except by neutralizing them), also marks the relation between either cognitives or prescriptives and interrogatives, performatives, exclamatives . . . For each of these regimens, there corresponds a mode of presenting a universe, and one mode is not translatable into another.[15]

To this list he might have added the further category of fictive utterances, those which – in Austin's parlance – exploit the conventions of first-order 'natural' speech-act implicature, but do so in a context where the standard (constative) requirements are lifted so that values of truth and falsehood simply don't apply.[16]

However, there are problems with any such attempt to set fiction apart from other kinds of discourse by reason of its not fulfilling the conditions of 'authentic' speech-act performance. These problems are already manifest in Austin's text, although they seem to have passed pretty much unnoticed until Derrida pointed them out in an essay of extraordinary subtlety and force.[17] One could also heed the lesson of critical theorists like Mary Louise Pratt, starting out from various plausible ideas of what constitutes a literary work, and coming round to the verdict that no such formal criteria exist, since 'literature' remains an open or 'essentially contested' category, one that gets applied to dfifferent kinds of text – or to different aspects of a given text – according to current evaluative notions.[18] But the main weakness with Pratt's line of argument is that it leads her to conclude – along with neo-pragmatists like Fish – that literature just *is* what we make of it in keeping with this or that set of readerly conventions. From which it would follow that literary texts can lay no claim to cognitive or truth-telling status, since it is precisely by the act of *suspending* such demands – setting them aside as misjudged or inappropriate – that we 'recognize' literature (or adopt the kind of attitude required to make sense of it in light of prevailing literary-critical norms). And there is a similar problem about Lyotard's argument with regard to the sheer multiplicity of 'phrase regimens' and the need to keep one of them – the cognitive order – from imposing its requirements, so to speak, across the board and thus depriving the others of their right to exist each one as a discourse *sui generis* with its own internal standards of justice or truth. For here again the question arises as to what could possibly count as a valid assertion in *any* of these speech-act genres – fiction, philosophy and criticism included – if their claims are to be treated as wholly 'incommensurable', and therefore as standing beyond reach of assessment on any but their own, self-authorizing grounds.

One great virtue of Spinoza's philosophy is that it helps us to see why thought is not condemned to this prison-house of endlessly circular reasoning. For Spinoza, the distinction between truth and error is one that can and must be maintained despite all the melancholy evidence to date that error has a hold upon human minds that may resist the best efforts of rational critique. And it is especially in the realm of fiction – the border-zone where 'inadequate ideas' are reworked into a different, more complex and articulated form – that theory is best placed to understand the effects of imaginary misrecognition. This is why a novel like *The Satanic Verses* has a power to convince – and also to antagonize – beyond what might be expected according to the current postmodernist wisdom. Rushdie himself takes exactly this line in an interview conducted at a time (mid-September, 1988) when the hate-campaign had begun to build up but had not yet assumed such lethal proportions.

> I guess some people might get upset because it is not reverent, but the point is a serious attempt to write about religion and revelation from the point of view of a secular person. I think that's a perfectly legitimate exercise. Besides, Muhammad is a very interesting figure. He's the only prophet who exists even remotely within history. He is the only one about whom there is some half-established more-or-less factual historical information. That makes him a human being and doubly interesting.[19]

For in the reading of fiction we are constantly engaged in that process of adjudicating different orders of truth-claim which Spinoza presents as the only means toward a better, more enlightened understanding. That is to say, the chief interest of critical thought is to see where the text reveals more than it can say, or where the need to make sense of recalcitrant details imposes a reading counter to received or canonical ideas of what the text ought to mean.

This argument receives its strongest theoretical elaboration at the hands of those critics (like Macherey) who have adopted an overtly Spinozist approach in the reading of literary works. Elsewhere it figures as a tacit but none the less crucial set of enabling assumptions, as with Terry Eagleton's widely influential reworking of Althusserian concepts and categories.[20] But it is also presupposed by *any* methodology – whether Marxist, deconstructionist, feminist, soiological or even (as I have argued) New Historicist – which operates on the principle that criticism can produce a knowledge of the text beyond what is given at the level of straightforward self-evidence or 'commonsense' belief. And to this extent one could claim that all the most significant developments in modern critical theory have their origin (knowingly or not) in Spinoza's way of treating the co-implicated orders of truth, falsehood, error, and fiction. Above all, they take for granted his basic premise with regard to the latter: that fictive ideas (or imaginary representations) are potentially a source of genuine knowledge in so far as they allow for a critical undertaking that seeks to distinguish those various orders and articulate the structural relations between them.

Macherey makes this point in the following passage, taking aim at what he calls the 'interpretive fallacy', or the notion that truth is what resides somehow hidden at the heart of the literary work, so that criticism must seek to uncover that truth through subtle techniques of hermeneutic commentary. As we have seen, this assumption runs deep in many schools of modern critical thought, to the point where (ironically) Kermode can regard it as deriving from Spinoza's exegetical writings. For Macherey, on the contrary, 'truth is not there in the work, like a nut in its shell; paradoxically, it is both interior and absent. If this were not the case, we would have to concede that the work was actually *unknowable*, miraculous and mysterious, and that criticism was futile' (Macherey, p. 77). And he then goes on to elaborate his reasons for rejecting this mystified and quasi-theological version of the commentator's task. In Macherey's words:

[t]he object of critical knowledge is not spontaneously available; it has first to be constructed into a cognitive object – not replaced by an ideal and abstract model, but internally displaced so as to reveal its rationality . . . Thus we must go beyond the work and explain it, must say what it does not and could not say: just as the triangle remains silent over the sum of its angles . . . Rejecting the mythology of comprehension, explanation recognizes the necessity that determines the work but which does not culminate in a *meaning*. It is not a question of confronting the work with some external truth: rather than passing a normative judgement, we identify the class of truth which constitutes the work and determines its meaning. (Pp. 77–8)

Macherey's pointed use of the geometrical idea – precisely an *idea* and not an image or metaphor, as the context of argument makes plain – is one sure sign that this passage takes its bearings from the Spinozist doctrine of knowledge and truth. But the intellectual debt goes much further than that, as can be seen from the way it develops Spinoza's distinction between 'spontaneous' (i.e. phenomenal or sensuous) cognition and knowledge arrived at through a reasoned critique of such first-order natural experience. And it is on this basis that Macherey rejects the 'interpretive fallacy' or 'mythology of comprehension'. For in the end these versions of the hermeneutic quest betray their origin in a theocentric model which identifies meaning with the access to truth through a form of inward revelation.

II

This is why the Rushdie affair raises issues that cannot be conveniently shunted aside by protesting that fiction has nothing to do with matters of doctrinal import or the truth-claims of revealed religion. Critics who take this accommodating line – no doubt with the best of placatory intentions – are ignoring the close relationship that exists between the critique of scriptural authority advanced by secularizing thinkers like Spinoza and the undeceiving virtues of fictive representation when directed against the forces of bigotry, superstition, and religious or political intolerance. Marina Warner makes this point most effectively in the following rejoinder to Rushdie's fundamentalist opponents. What has chiefly aroused their indignation, she writes,

is the idea that the Devil managed to interpolate verses into the Koran. Erasmus came into conflict with the Church becase he found that the original canonical translations of the New Testament had

not been accurate . . . Of course Salman Rushdie never cast himself
in any way as a learned commentator on the authenticity of the
Koran, in the Erasmian sense, but the crisis has given his levity, his
satire, a new, momentous seriousness, and its lessons should be built
on, to make an appeal to moderate thinkers within Islam, who are
able to entertain the possibility of historicist and textual analysis of
the Koran.[21]

In this respect *The Satanic Verses* asks to be read in much the
same way as works like Voltaire's *Candide* or Shelley's *Prometheus
Unbound*, writings whose sheer *argumentative* force – and whose
power to provoke extreme forms of hostile response – was scarcely
the less for the fact of their adopting a fictive, poetic, or 'imaginary'
form. Shelley provides the most interesting case for comparison
here since he read, admired (and even translated) Spinoza, as well
as publishing his own, much-reviled essay 'The Necessity of
Atheism' and also, in his poetry, presenting what amounted to a
full-scale Spinozist attack on the values of institutionalized Christian
belief, albeit in the guise of a counter-mythology decked out with
various arcane – mostly neo-Platonist – allegorical devices.[22] These
latter did nothing to obscure the central message: that religion had
lent itself all too easily to the interests of an orthodox elite whose
power derived partly from the joint machinations of church and
state, and partly from the sway of superstitious belief over minds
held captive by 'confused' or 'imaginary' ideas. Certainly few readers
– sympathetic or otherwise – would have failed to perceive that the
prose tract and the poetry were equally a part of Shelley's campaign
against the truth-claims of revealed religion.

In 'The Necessity of Atheism' Shelley also looks to Spinoza for
support in his argument that freedom of conscience is an absolute
right – and religious persecution an unmitigated evil – because,
quite simply, *beliefs are not volitional*, arising as they do from a
multitude of causes, some of which elude our conscious grasp while
others form a basis of principled (rational) conviction. In neither
case they can be altered by an act of will in obedience to this or
that form of doctrinal compulsion. Such beliefs may be confused
and contradictory, characterized by a 'passive' or unwitting relation
to the causes that brought them about. Or they may involve the
kind of 'active' self-knowledge that comes of striving to grasp
those causes – thus leaving no room for delusions of free-will or
autonomous agency and choice – but which grasps them from the
standpoint that Spinoza identifies with true philosophical wisdom.

And this latter brings benefits that need not involve any form of 'metaphysical' doctrine, as emerges from a passage cited by Kenneth Blackwell in his recent study *The Spinozistic Ethics of Bertrand Russell*. The point is best made by giving both Russell's remarks (from his 1912 book *The Problems of Philosophy*) and Blackwell's interspersed commentary on them.

> The value of philosophy, in addition to an intrinsic interest in its study, Russell holds, is to be found in 'its effects on the lives of those who study it'. One effect lies in the student's having to face uncertainty: 'The man who has no tincture of philosophy goes through life imprisoned in the prejudices derived from common sense . . . the world tends to become definite, finite, obvious, common objects rouse no questions, and unfamiliar possibilites are contemptuously rejected. Philosophy, by suggesting 'many possibilities which enlarge our thoughts and free them from the tyranny of custom', removes 'the somewhat arrogant dogmatism of those who have never travelled in the region of liberating doubt' . . . These statements express the Spinozistic aspect of Russell's theory of self-enlargement. Both hold that it is through the pursuit of knowledge that we escape the bondage of passive emotions (in Spinoza's case) or instinctive desires (Russell's).[23]

This passage is of special interest for several reasons. First, it shows how a radical empiricist like Russell – one, moreover, who professed atheistical views very much in the Shelleyan line of descent – can yet find reason to regard Spinoza as having offered a good (philosophically valid) account of the relation between belief, knowledge, and the interests of human wellbeing. Second, it is very firm in making the point that 'self-enlargement' is a process of freeing oneself from 'the bondage of passive emotions'; that these latter come about through the hold on our minds of unexamined values and prejudices; and that the only way to shake off such 'arrogant dogmatism' is to follow something closely akin to the Spinozist way of 'adequate ideas'. And third – most relevant in the present context – is Russell's strong suggestion that this process will help to disabuse us of religious or other such mystified beliefs, those that trade partly on the 'tyranny of custom', and partly on the absence of that 'liberating doubt' which promotes intellectual tolerance and progressive social values.

This book has argued that current debates in literary theory are one major forum where Spinoza's ideas are still very actively at work, though not without continued opposition from various quarters. The most important point on which these critics divide is the question whether literary works can be construed as advancing propositions, arguing a case, or involving knowledge-constitutive interests that are capable of reasoned assessment and critique. Empson's later writings are perhaps the most impressive example of a project that concerns itself both with questions in the realm of literary theory – giving rise to his arguments in *The Structure of Complex Words*[24] – and with broader issues of a moral, historical, and (above all) religious import. But it is wrong to suggest that these are separate interests since, as we have seen, Empson's defence of a truth-functional semantics applied to the language of poetry and fiction goes along with his aversion to Christian belief and his resolute attempts to make sense of literature on rationally accountable terms. In fact his entire critical production after *Milton's God* (1961) was devoted to arguing the case for various authors – Marlowe, Donne, Marvell, Coleridge, Joyce, Eliot, Yeats and others – as *either* the victims of neurotic guilt and conflict brought on by their accepting the full implications of Christian theology, *or* as having bravely resisted that 'appalling' doctrine, only to be kidnapped by neo-Christian interpreters in pursuit of some pious message or other.[25] My point is not to claim that these essays are all of them equally convincing, or that they represent a full-scale project of radically secularized hermeneutic thought growing directly out of Empson's historico-semantic researches in *Complex Words*. What they do help to show is the close relation that exists between a rationalist desire to demystify the sources of erroneous or confused belief, and an attitude to questions of literary meaning that refuses to fall back upon ideas of ambiguity, paradox, 'pseudo-statement', fictive licence or other such handy escape-routes.

It is no coincidence, therefore, that Empson's reading of Milton stands squarely in the line of left-romantic or radical revisionist accounts which begins with Blake's famous dictum (that Milton was 'of the Devil's party without knowing it'), and continues with Shelley's more elaborated version of the same antinomian thesis. Where Empson most emphatically rejoins this tradition is in arguing *firstly* that Milton's poetry has to do with doctrinal issues at the heart of Christian belief, and thus cannot be treated – as critics like C. S. Lewis would have it[26] – as 'great literature' but wildly heretical, and hence no problem from an orthodox theological standpoint; *secondly*, that the poem runs into all kinds of narrative complication in its effort to make good sense of the story and thereby justify God's ways to man; and *thirdly*, that we should at least give Milton due credit for the signs that his feelings revolted – at whatever 'unconscious' level – against the demands of this deeply offensive religious creed. In short, Empson comes out steadfastly against the kind of reading that treats literary works as belonging to a realm of 'imaginative' truths unaccountable to plain-prose reason or the standards of commonplace human decency. And this was why the New Critics found problems with Empson's work, admiring his extreme sophistication in the business of close-reading or verbal exegesis, but warning against his tendency to think that poems offered *arguments* or grounds for taking issue with their (supposed) argumentative claims. John Crowe Ransom articulates this feeling of unease when he writes that Empson takes poetry 'too seriously', and thus threatens to violate 'the law of its kind'.[27] And this habit went back to Empson's reading of Herbert in *Seven Types of Ambiguity*, a reading that not only teased out the paradoxes of Herbert's 'The Sacrifice', but which pushed them to the point of extracting a series of antinomies – logical contradictions – that seemed to impugn the very bases of Christian faith. For Ransom, in short, 'the metaphysical procedure was singularly like the theological, with a rather important difference: the poet was playful, while the theologian was in dead earnest'. And again: metaphysical poetry had to 'suggest theologies . . . to suggest them, or to imitate them; not to *be* them'.[28] Nothing could capture more precisely the distance that separates Empson's thinking from the currency, not only of the old New Criticism (with its marked 'neo-Christian' ethos), but also from those subsequent noncognitivist schools – hermeneutic, neo-pragmatist, postmodernist and so forth – which likewise drive a wedge between questions of meaning and values of truth and falsehood.

Jonathan Culler makes this point with admirable force in his book *Framing The Sign*.[29] Like Empson, he thinks it an alarming fact about recent (post-war) Anglo-American criticism that so much of this work is given over to a religious – or crypto-religious – set of doctrines and values, a tendency that is then passed off as just an aspect of our Christian 'cultural heritage', so that any serious attempt to question them is viewed as subversive, misguided, or somehow in bad taste. 'That this idea should be possible indicates just how far education has abandoned its historic tasks, of combating superstition, encouraging sceptical debate about competing religions and their claims or their myths, and fighting religious dogmatism and its political consequences' (Culler, p. 78). What is more, this falling-back into postures of religious conformism on the part of literary critics goes along with a widespread popular resurgence of fundamentalist belief among various creeds and denominations, a development that is all too clearly visible in the current Christian and Islamic revivalist campaigns. As Culler points out, this situation is doubly ironic in so far as the critique of dogmatic religion was a process initiated and carried through very largely on principles that derived from comparative philology, textual criticism, narrative poetics and other such fields of study. 'At the beginning of the eighteenth century, one might say without greatly oversimplifying, Protestants took the Bible to be the word of God; by the beginning of the twentieth century this belief was untenable in intellectual circles' (p. 79). Culler makes no mention of Spinoza's role in this history of thought, but it is reasonable to suppose – on all the evidence we have seen so far – that it would scarcely have taken the shape it did, or exerted such a powerful influence, had Spinoza not written the *Tractatus Theologico-Politicus*.

Culler goes on to deplore the way that this critical tradition has been kept from view by the orthodox (or not-so-orthodox) pieties of present-day academic scholarship. Thus he notes that there has lately been a 'striking revival of interest in the sacred', not only on the part of those conformist 'neo-Christians' whom Empson singled out for attack, but also among the votaries of myth-criticism, psychoanalysis, narrative theory, hermeneutics, and even deconstruction (thus 'Geoffrey Hartman . . . jokingly proposes that literature departments should be rechristened 'Departments of Mystery Management'). In each case, so Culler argues, 'instead of leading the critique of dogmatic mythologies, literary criticism is contributing to the legitimation of religious discourse' (p. 79). To which he might have added the further observation that this process can only be helped along – or at any rate encounters no effective resistance – from those schools of postmodern neo-pragmatist thought that come out 'against theory', or against the whole tradition of enlightened rational critique. For here also it is no great distance from moderate, historically-informed versions of the relativist argument (i.e., that ideas of reason and truth are always in some degree culture-specific) to the adoption of a wholesale irrationalist creed that denounces such ideas as chimerical at best, and at worst as mere instruments of the will-to-power masquerading as pure, disinterested knowledge. And at this point – where Nietzsche is most often invoked – there is nothing to prevent the further slide into a form of mystical or mythopoeic thought whose strongest affinities (as Habermas argues)

are with doctrines evolved among right-wing opponents of Enlightenment thinking in the immediate post-Kantian period.[30]

It seems to me that Culler gets the emphasis right when he
argues that 'respect for religious values' – whether Christian, Jewish,
Islamic or whatever – shouldn't be interpreted as granting those
values a total exemption from critical scrutiny, or restoring them to
the kind of sacrosanct status that they once enjoyed as matters of
revealed truth. And he is likewise persuasive when he treats current
issues in the field of literary theory as variants of the characteristic
liberal dilemma: how to make allowance for the sheer variety of
creeds, ideologies, and belief-systems while reserving the right to
criticize any manifest failures *on their part* with respect to these same
(no doubt culture-specific) values of uncoerced rational debate.
What is crucial here is the distinction established by Spinoza (and
developed by Kant) between *matters of faith* where each individual
is at liberty to believe and profess as they wish, and *matters of reason*
or intellectual conscience where again there is (or should be) no
constraint under law, but where the rule is that this freedom not
be curtailed by any imposition of dogmatic beliefs. From this point
of view the liberal dilemma comes about through a basic confusion
of realms, a failure to grasp that one can indeed condemn ideologies
or religions for promoting narrow, intolerant or prejudicial behaviour without thereby setting up to judge them from one's own
(equally prejudiced and intolerant) standpoint. For this objection
would apply only if one's grounds for thus judging were a matter
of unargued belief or passive compliance with the dictates of an
absolute creed. But the whole point of the liberal distinction between
private and public realms is to prevent such unwarranted intrusions
of faith upon the freedoms of thought, conscience, and expression.

Now of course it may be argued – as it has been by various
parties to the debate over Rushdie's book – that liberalism itself
has a political agenda, a core-set of values and beliefs, and hence
shouldn't pose as some kind of neutral adjudicative discourse devoid
of such partisan interests. But, once again, this ignores what is
distinctive about liberal ideology: the fact that it can indeed be put
to such self-interested, partial, or prejudiced uses, yet still provide
a yardstick by which to measure these distortions of its own legitimizing claims. Thus – to take what is perhaps the most familiar
example – a document may be framed which has a good deal to say
(in good liberal fashion) about the 'rights of man', but which the
framers – and interpreters for a good while thereafter – choose to
understand as specifically excluding women and slaves. But one

should also remark the other side of this story: that the blindspots of prejudice do come to light in the end, albeit (most often) against considerable odds of entrenched self-interest and selective interpretation. And the reason why liberalism exhibits this self-correcting tendency – unlike more dogmatic ideologies and creeds – is the fact that its central terms (freedom, justice, equality) are themselves subject to critical reassessment in light of changing social ideas, and not tied down to some stipulative meaning in accordance with scriptural warrant, revealed truth, the natural order of society, or other such potent immobilizing myths. And this difference is basically what separates the parties in dispute over Rushdie's novel. As Mihir Bose puts it:

> All religions venerate their holy books, but Islam's attitude towards the Koran is of a unique and unbending reverence . . . Even among Christians who might be described as fundamentalists, it is accepted that a whole school of textual criticism has grown up, convincingly suggesting that human hands were involved in the making of the Bible. To a Moslem any such thought about the Koran would be blasphemous. In Islam, even today, there is simply no tradition of theological criticism or enquiry.[31]

On the one side are those who advocate an allegiance to truths beyond reach of critical assessment or reasoned debate. On the other are those – admittedly in a state of some confusion at present – whose appeal (or whose best possible ground of appeal) is to the interests of open discussion and enquiry into the values that sustain both their own and their opponents' argumentative positions. Any hint of ethnocentric smugness here should be amply dispelled by the occasional reminder – such as Empson provides – of just how long it took for courageous free-thinkers like Erasmus, Montaigne, Spinoza, or Voltaire to knock Christianity into some kind of civilized shape.

This is where literary theory comes in, as a discourse specialised in the adjudication of different orders of truth-claim. 'Above all', Culler writes,

> we should work to keep alive the critical, demythologizing force of contemporary theory – a force which a considerable number of critics are striving to capture and to divert to pious ends. *Down with the priests!* is an unlikely motto for literary studies these days, but we ought to ask why this is so and turn some of our analytical energies on our own relation to religious discourse and ideology – not as a theoretical investigation asking whether literary studies could ever

free itself from the theological weight of the hermeneutic tradition
or the idea of authority invested in a special text, but as a practical,
political way of challenging the authority of a potentially repressive
religious discourse and ensuring that we do not encourage respect
for it. (Culler, p. 81)

My only quarrel with this concerns Culler's suggestion that the two
kinds of knowledge – 'theoretical' and 'practical' – are somehow at
odds, or that the former involves an expense of intellectual effort
that might better be directed to 'practical' ends. In fact Culler's
book gives clear indications to the opposite effect, as for instance
by including a chapter on Empson – and specifically on *Complex
Words* – where he argues that issues of interpretive theory bear
directly on questions in the wider (socio-historical) realm of understanding.[32] It seems to me that this has been the central issue in
recent debates about the 'function of criticism' – or the purpose of
literary studies – at a time when such debates are unignorably
affected by the pressures of real-world political circumstance. One
point where those pressures can be felt to impinge is precisely on
the question – as Culler puts it – whether literary criticiam 'could
ever free itself from the theological weight of the hermeneutic
tradition or the idea of authority invested in a special text' (p. 81).
And this question is still a focus of lively controversy, as can be
seen when conservatives like Allan Bloom put their case for a return
to 'traditional values' and a canon of acknowledged 'great works'
to be taught at school and university level.[33]

What Bloom lays down – along with other proponents of the new
'core curriculum' thinking – is a vulgarized recourse to that idea of
'tradition' that grew up around the reading of scriptural texts,
and in particular the process of canon-formation through selective
treatment of the Old and New Testament sources. It is an exercise
that allows for various shades of traditionalist or revisionist attitude,
as we saw in the highly ambivalent case of Kermode's *The Genesis
of Secrecy*, where a desire to open up the classic to new (anti-
canonical) ways of reading went along with an attachment to narrative 'secrets' – or intimations of revealed truth – available only to
those with the requisite hermeneutic skills. Clearly there is all the
difference in the world between Kermode's style of subtle, endlessly
self-qualifying commentary on the name and nature of the classic,
and Bloom's much-touted media campaign based on the ritual
invocation of canonical 'values', and backed up by all manner of
crude rhetorical tricks, like his constant allusion to the forces

threatening 'our' cultural heritage. My point is not at all to lump them together in the same 'conservative' camp, but to remark how their differences on one question (the status of interpretive truth-claims and values) go along with their basic disagreement on another (the extent to which such claims can or should be reserved to the keeping of a small, self-authorized cultural elite). On both questions Bloom stands squarely with the guardians of sacrosanct 'tradition', viewing all attempts to challenge or revise that tradition as melancholy evidence that Western culture has entered a period of well-nigh terminal decline. For Kermode, on the contrary, this process of canonical challenge and revision is exactly what keeps the 'classic' alive, whatever the attractions – and he is certainly not inclined to underrate them – of claiming (on occasion) to occupy a privileged 'insider' role with regard to narrative mysteries and secrets.

It would perhaps be over-stating the case for me to argue – by way of resounding conclusion – that the current 'situation' of literary theory is one that can only be understood by going back to Spinoza and examining his role at a crucial point in its formative prehistory. Nevertheless I would hope to have convinced the reader that this is not, after all, such a far-fetched claim; that Spinoza was indeed the first thinker to raise certain questions that are still very much on the agenda of present-day critical debate. One aspect of his thinking that has been widely recognized in this connection – as by critics like Kermode – is Spinoza's separation of 'meaning' from 'truth', or textual hermeneutics from matters of doctrinal import. But we shall misunderstand what that achievement amounts to if we don't also see that Spinoza's rationalist principles – his effort to distinguish 'imaginary' or 'confused' from 'adequate' or truthful ideas – were carried across *at every point* into his treatment of issues in the textual-interpretive sphere. And the same applies to his attitude with regard to 'fictions' or 'feigned' ideas, those mixed modes of knowledge – as Spinoza defines them – which partake of imaginary attributes, but can also be subjected to rational critique, and hence become a source of improved understanding. I have argued that this doctrine – or some variant of it – subtends all those later movements in the history of criticism which treat literature as a mode of discourse giving access to truths beyond reach of commonsense (or 'ideological') belief. And it is here that critical theorists would do well to acquire at least some knowledge of Spinoza's work and its relation to what is now – all too clearly – revealed as the unfinished project of Enlightenment thought.

Notes

Rather than include a separate Bibliography I have used this section for the joint purpose of providing detailed references to works cited in the text and offering suggestions for further reading where appropriate. See also 'A Note on Texts' (pp. 19–20) for a full explanation of the system deployed in referring to Spinoza's works.

Author's Preface

1 See for instance Frederick Pollock, *Spinoza: his life and philosophy* (Kegan Paul, London, 1880); Lewis Samuel Feuer, *Spinoza and the Rise of Liberalism* (Beacon Press, Boston, 1958); Pieter Geyl, *The Revolt of the Netherlands* (Benn, London, 1958); K. H. D. Haley, *The Dutch in the Seventeenth Century* (Thames & Hudson, London, 1972); Jonathan Israel, *The Dutch Republic and the Hispanic World, 1606–1661* (Clarendon Press, Oxford, 1982); Geoffrey Parker, *The Dutch Revolt* (Penguin, Harmondsworth, 1985); Simon Schama, *The Embarrassment of Riches: an interpretation of Dutch Culture in the Golden Age* (Collins, London, 1987).

2 See Walter Kaufmann (ed. and trans.), *The Portable Nietzsche* (Viking, New York, 1964), p. 92. On the kinship between Spinoza and Nietzsche, see also Edwin Curley, *Behind the Geometrical Method: a reading of Spinoza's Ethics* (Princeton University Press, New Jersey, 1988).

3 Stuart Hampshire, 'Spinoza's Theory of Freedom', in Eugene Freeman & Maurice Mandelbaum (eds.), *Spinoza: essays in interpretation* (Open Court Publishers, Illinois, 1975), pp. 36–47; p. 47. See also Hampshire, *Spinoza* (Penguin, Har-

mondsworth, 1951); H. H. Joachim, *A Study of the Ethics of Spinoza* (Clarendon Press, Oxford, 1901); S. Paul Kashap, *Spinoza and Moral Freedom* (State University of New York Press, Albany, NY, 1987); H. A. Wolfson, *The Philosophy of Spinoza* (Harvard University Press, Cambridge, Mass., 1934); Edwin Curley, *Spinoza's Metaphysics: an essay in Interpretation* (Harvard University Press, Cambridge, Mass., 1969); R. J. Delahunty, *Spinoza* (Routledge & Kegan Paul, London, 1985); Henry Allison, *Benedict de Spinoza* (rev. edn., Yale University Press, New Haven, 1987).

4   Robert A. Duff, *Spinoza's Political and Ethical Philosophy* (Augustus M. Kelly, New York, 1903), p. 4. See also Etienne Balibar, *Spinoza et la politique* (Presses Universitaires de France, Paris, 1985) and Lucien Mugnier-Pollet, *La Philosophie politique de Spinoza* (Vrin, Paris, 1976).

5   Duff, *Spinoza's Political and Ethical Philosophy*, p. 4.

6   Gilles Deleuze, *Spinoza: practical philosophy*, trans. Robert Hurley (City Lights Books, San Francisco, 1988), p. 129.

7   See Gilles Deleuze and Félix Guattari, *Anti-Oedipus*, trans. Robert Hurley, Mark Seem, and Helen R. Lane (Viking, New York, 1977); also Deleuze and Guattari, *A Thousand Plateaus*, trans. Brian Massumi (University of Minnesota Press, Minneapolis, 1987). The best introduction to their work is Ronald Bogue, *Deleuze and Guattari* (Routledge, London, 1989).

8   See especially Louis Althusser, *For Marx*, trans. Ben Brewster (Allen Lane, London, 1969) and Pierre Macherey, *A Theory of Literary Production*, trans. Geoffrey Wall (Routledge & Kegan Paul, London, 1978). See also the passages relating to Spinoza in Althusser, *Eléments d'autocritique* (Hachette, Paris, 1974), translated as 'Elements of Self-Criticism', in Althusser, *Essays in Self-Criticism* (New Left Books, London, 1976), pp. 101–61.

9   Spinoza, *Principles of Descartes' Philosophy*, trans. H. H. Britan (Open Court Publishers, Illinois, 1977). Also to be found – with copious notes and supporting apparatus – in *The Collected Works of Spinoza*, ed. and trans. Edwin Curley (Princeton University Press, Princeton, NJ., 1985), pp. 221–346.

10   Schama, *The Embarrassment of Riches*, p. 62.

CHAPTER 1:   SPINOZA *VERSUS* HEGEL: THE ALTHUSSERIAN
MOMENT

1   See Samuel Taylor Coleridge, *Biographia Literaria*, vols I and
II, ed. James Edgell and W. Jackson Bate (Routledge & Kegan
Paul, London, 1983). Paul Hamilton has written well on this
chapter of intellectual history – on the English Romantics' debt
to Spinoza and their problems in handling such a heterodox
legacy – in his book *Coleridge's Poetics* (Basil Blackwell, Oxford,
1983).
2   Matthew Arnold, 'Spinoza and the Bible', in *Lectures and Essays
in Criticism*, ed. R. H. Super (University of Michigan Press,
Ann Arbor, 1973), pp. 158–82. See also on Spinoza, in the
same volume, 'The Bishop and the Philosopher' (pp. 40–55)
and 'Tractatus Theologico-Politicus' (pp. 56–64). Some contemporary responses to Arnold's admiring treatment of Spinoza
may be found (*via* the index) in *Matthew Arnold: the critical
heritage (Prose Writings)*, ed. Carl Dawson and John Pfor-
drescher (Routledge & Kegan Paul, London, 1979).
3   On this reception-history, see Frederick C. Beiser, *The Fate
of Reason: German Philosophy from Kant to Fichte* (Harvard
University Press, Cambridge, Mass., 1987); also F. C. Cople-
ston, 'Pantheism in Spinoza and the German Idealists', *Philosophy* (1946), pp. 42–56.
4   Stephen Greenblatt, 'Invisible Bullets: Renaissance authority
and its subversion', in *Political Shakespeare: new essays in cultural materialism*, ed. Jonathan Dollimore and Alan Sinfield
(Cornell University Press, Ithaca, NY, 1985), pp. 18–47. See
also Greenblatt, *Shakespearean Negotiations: the circulation of
social energy in renaissance England* (University of California
Press, Berkeley and Los Angeles, 1988), and – for a useful
(often critical) survey of the field – *The New Historicism*, ed.
H. Aram Veeser (Routledge, London, 1989).
5   Coleridge, *Biographia Literaria* vol. I, pp. 193–4.
6   Spinoza, *Principles of Descartes' Philosophy* (ref. Foreword, n.
9, above). See also F. Bouillier, *Histoire de la Philosophie Carté-
sienne* (2 vols., 1st pub. 1868, repr. Slatkine, Geneva, 1970);
E. J. Dijksterhuis et al., *Descartes et le Cartésianisme Hollandais*
(PUF, Paris, 1950); Edwin Curley, 'Descartes, Spinoza and
the Ethics of Belief', in Freeman and Mandelbaum, *Spinoza:
essays in interpretation*, pp. 159–89; Curley, 'Spinoza as an

Expositor of Descartes', in *Speculum Spinozanum*, ed. S. Hessing (Routledge & Kegan Paul, London, 1977), pp. 133–42.

7 On this topic see especially Leo Strauss, *Spinoza's Critique of Religion*, trans. E. M. Sinclair (Schocken Books, New York, 1965); also Richard H. Popkin, *The History of Scepticism from Erasmus to Spinoza* (University of California Press, Berkeley & Los Angeles, 1979).

8 See for instance Stanislaus Breton, *Politique, Religion, Écriture chez Spinoza* (Profac, Lyon, 1973); Breton, *Théologie et Politique* (Desclée, Paris, 1977); Sylvain Zac, *Spinoza et l'Interpretation de l'Écriture* (Presses Universitaires de France, Paris, 1965) and Zac, *Philosophie, Théologie, Politique dans l'oeuvre de Spinoza* (J. Vrin, Paris, 1979).

9 See Matthew Arnold, *Dissent and Dogma* and *Essays Religious and Mixed*, ed. R. H. Super (University of Michigan Press, Ann Arbor, 1968 and 1972).

10 Arnold, 'Dr Stanley's lectures on the Jewish Church', in *Lectures and Essays In Criticism*, pp. 65–82.

11 Jonathan Arac, *Critical Genealogies: historical situations for postmodern literary studies* (Columbia University Press, New York, 1987).

12 Matthew Arnold, 'The Study of Poetry', in *English Literature and Irish Politics*, ed. R. H. Super (University of Michigan Press, Ann Arbor, 1973), pp. 161–88.

13 See for instance Francis Mulhern, *The Moment of 'Scrutiny'* (New Left Books, London, 1979); Terry Eagleton, *The Function of Criticism: from The Spectator to post-structuralism* (Verso, London, 1984); Eagleton, 'The Rise of English', in *Literary Theory: an introduction* (Oxford: Bassil Blackwell, 1983), pp. 17–53; Terence Hawkes, *That Shakespheherian Rag: essays on a critical process* (Methuen, London, 1986); Chris Baldick, *The Social Mission of English Studies* (Oxford University Press, Oxford, 1983); Brian Doyle, *English and Englishness* (Routledge, London, 1989); and *Re-Reading English*, ed. Peter Widdowson (Methuen, London, 1981).

14 On the importance of this distinction between 'truth' and 'meaning' for the subsequent development of literary studies, see Tzvetan Todorov, *Literature and its Theorists: a personal view of twentieth-century criticism* (Routledge, London, 1987). See also Thomas C. Mark, *Spinoza's Theory of Truth* (Columbia University Press, New York, 1972). I discuss this topic at

much greater length in chapters 5 and 6.

15 Maimonides' best-known work is his *Guide for the Perplexed*, trans. Schlomo Pines (University of Chicago Press, Chicago, 1963). See also Maimonides, *Le livre de connaissance*, trans. V. Nikiprowetzsky and A. Zaoui (PUF, Paris, 1961). For a detailed account of Spinoza's quarrel with Maimonides, see Leo Strauss, *Spinoza's Critique of Religion*; also Leon Roth, *Spinoza, Descartes and Maimonides* (Clarendon Press, Oxford, 1924) and Geneviève Brykman, *La Judéité de Spinoza* (J. Vrin, Paris, 1972).

16 On this diversity of approaches to Spinoza's work, see particularly Leszek Kolakowski, 'The Two Eyes of Spinoza', in *Spinoza: a collection of critical essays*, ed. Marjorie Grene (Anchor/ Doubleday, New York, 1973), pp. 279–94. The standard reference-work (with entries up to 1940) is A. S. Oko, *The Spinoza Bibliography* (Hall, Boston, 1964). For a survey of more recent scholarship, see Jon Wetlesen, *A Spinoza Bibliography, 1940–1970* (Universiteitsforlaget, Oslo, 1971); Theo van der Werf and Heine S. C. Westerveen, *A Spinoza Bibliography, 1971–1983* (E. J. Brill, Leiden, 1984).

17 Immanuel Kant, *A Critique of Pure Reason*, trans. N. Kemp Smith (Macmillan, London, 1933).

18 See for instance Peter Dews, *Logics of Disintegration: post-structuralist thought and the claims of theory* (Verso, London, 1987); Irene E. Harvey, *Derrida and the Economy of Différance* (Indiana University Press, Bloomington, 1986); Christopher Norris, *Derrida* (Collins/Fontana, London, 1987); Rodolphe Gasché, *The Tain of the Mirror: Derrida and the philosophy of reflection* (Harvard University Press, Cambridge, Mass., 1986); John Llewelyn, *Derrida on the Threshold of Sense* (Macmillan, London, 1986); Stephen W. Melville, *Philosophy Beside Itself: on deconstruction and modernism* (University of Minnesota Press, Minneapolis, 1986); *Deconstruction and Philosophy: the texts of Jacques Derrida*, ed. John Sallis (University of Chicago Press, Chicago & London, 1987); David Wood, *The Deconstruction of Time* (Humanities Press, New Jersey, 1989).

19 One exception – a book that does take account of this recent 'metaphysical' turn in post-stucturalist thought – is Richard Harland, *Superstructuralism* (Routledge, London, 1987).

20 See especially Michel Foucault, *The Order of Things*, trans. Alan Sheridan-Smith (Tavistock, London, 1970); also Foucault, *The*

Archaeology of Knowledge, trans. Sheridan-Smith (Tavistock, London, 1972).

21 Louis Althusser and Etienne Balibar, *Reading Capital*, trans. Ben Brewster (New Left Books, London, 1970), p. 16.
22 Ibid, p. 102.
23 Georg Lukács, *History and Class-Consciousness*, trans. Rodney Livingstone (Merlin, London, 1971).
24 Althusser and Balibar, *Reading Capital*, pp. 188–9.
25 Ibid, p. 105.
26 See especially Louis Althusser, 'Ideology and Ideological State Apparatuses', in *'Lenin and Philosophy' and other essays*, trans. Ben Brewster (New Left Books, London, 1977), pp. 121–73.
27 See Althusser, 'Freud and Lacan', in *Lenin and Philosophy*, pp. 177–202.
28 Althusser, *Lenin And Philosophy*, p. 169.
29 Ibid, p. 164.
30 E. P. Thompson, 'The Poverty of Theory', in *'The Poverty of Theory' and other essays* (Merlin, London, 1978).
31 E. P. Thompson, *The Making of the English Working Classes* (Harmondsworth, Penguin, 1972). See also Perry Anderson's response to this critique in *Arguments Within English Marxism* (New Left Books, London, 1980). For discussion of some relevant issues from a Spinozist standpoint, see Edwin Curley, 'Experience in Spinoza's Theory of Knowledge', in Grene, *Spinoza: critical essays*, pp. 25–59.
32 Karl Marx and Frederick Engels, 'The Eighteenth Brumaire of Louis Bonaparte', in Marx and Engels, *Collected Works*, vol. XI (Lawrence & Wishart, London, 1979), pp. 99–197; p. 103.
33 See for instance Donald Davidson, *Essays on Actions and Events* (Clarendon Press, Oxford, 1980).
34 Pierre Macherey, *Hegel ou Spinoza?* (Maspero, Paris, 1979), p. 79 [this and following passages trans. CN]
35 Ibid, p. 85.
36 Ibid, p. 260.
37 Ibid, p. 259.
38 Ibid, p. 76.
39 Although Leo Strauss (*Persecution and the Art of Writing* [Greenwood Press, New York, 1973] puts the case for such a reading of Spinoza and other philosophers who had to cope with various forms of religious or political censorship.
40 Jonathan Bennett, *A Study of Spinoza's Ethics* (Cambridge

University Press, Cambridge, 1984), p. 320.
41 Errol E. Harris, 'Spinoza's Theory of Human Immortality', in *Spinoza: essays in interpretation*, ed. Eugene Freeman and Maurice Mandelbaum (Open Court Publishers, Illinois, 1975), pp. 245–62; p. 260. See also H. F. Hallett, *Aeternitas: a Spinozistic study* (Clarendon Press, Oxford, 1930); C. L. Hardin, 'Spinoza on Immortality and Time', in *Spinoza: new perspectives*, ed. Robert W. Shahan and J. I. Biro (University of Oklahoma Press, Norman, Okl., 1978), pp. 129–38; and M. Kneale, 'Eternity and Sempiternity', in *Spinoza: a collection of critical essays*, ed. Grene, pp. 227–40.
42 See for instance P. F. Strawson, *Individuals: an essay in descriptive metaphysics* (Methuen, London, 1964).
43 Gregory Elliot, *Althusser: the detour of theory* (Verso, London, 1987). See also Perry Anderson, *Arguments Within English Marxism*; Anderson, *In The Tracks of Historical Materialism* (Verso, London, 1983); Alex Callinicos, *Is There a Future for Marxism?* (Humanities Press, New Jersey, 1982); Ted Benton, *The Rise and Fall of Structural Marxism* (New Left Books, London, 1984); Norman Geras, 'Althusser's Marxism: an assessment', in *Western Marxism: a critical reader*, ed. New Left Review (NLB, London, 1977), pp. 232–72; Fredric Jameson, *The Political Unconscious: narrative as a socially symbolic act* (Methuen, London, 1981); James H. Kavanagh, 'Marxism's Althusser: toward a politics of literary theory', *Diacritics*, Vol. XII (Spring, 1982), pp. 25–33; Michael Kelly, *Modern French Marxism* (Johns Hopkins University Press, Baltimore, 1982); Steven Smith, *Reading Althusser: an essay on structural Marxism* (Cornell University Press, Ithaca, NY, 1984).
44 Paul Hamilton, review of Richard Harland, *Superstructuralism* in *Textual Practice*, vol. III, No. 2 (Summer, 1989), pp. 259–63; p. 261.
45 See especially Michel Foucault, *Power/Knowledge: selected interviews and other writings, 1972–1977* (Harvester Press, Brighton, 1980) and *The Foucault Reader*, ed. Paul Rabinow (Pantheon, New York, 1985).
46 See for instance Foucault, *The History of Sexuality*, vol. I, trans. Robert Hurley (Pantheon, New York, 1978).
47 Roland Barthes, *The Pleasure of the Text*, trans. Richard Miller (Jonathan Cape, London, 1976).
48 Roland Barthes, *Camera Lucida*, trans. Richard Miller (Jonathan Cape, London, 1983).

49 See especially the essays collected in *Image-Music-Text*, trans. Stephen Heath (Fontana, London, 1977). Mary Wiseman's book *The Ecstasies of Roland Barthes* (Routledge, London, 1989) is of particular interest here since it focuses on the late writings and treats them from a broadly philosophical viewpoint.

CHAPTER 2 OF TRUTH AND ERROR IN A SPINOZIST SENSE: DELEUZE, DERRIDA, DE MAN

1 Gilles Deleuze and Félix Guattari, *Anti-Oedipus*, trans. Robert Hurley, Mark Seem, and Helen R. Lane (Viking, New York, 1977). See also Ronald Bogue, *Deleuze and Guattari* (Routledge, London, 1989).
2 Gilles Deleuze and Félix Guattari, *A Thousand Plateaus: capitalism and schizophrenia*, trans. Brian Massumi (University of Minnesota Press, Minneapolis, 1987).
3 Ibid, p. 153.
4 See Frederick C. Beiser, *The Fate of Reason: German philosophy from Kant to Fichte* (Harvard University Press, Cambridge, Mass., 1987) for a detailed account of these debates.
5 Louis Althusser and Etienne Balibar, *Reading Captial*, trans. Ben Brewster (New Left Books, London, 1970), p. 40.
6 Gilles Deleuze, *Spinoza: practical philosophy*, trans. Robert Hurley (City Lights Books, San Francisco, 1988), p. 129. See also Deleuze, *Spinoza et le problème de l'expression* (Minuit, Paris, 1968).
7 Efraim Shmueli, 'The Geometrical Method, Personal Caution, and the Ideal of Tolerance', in *Spinoza: new perspectives*, ed. Shahan and Biro, pp. 197–215; p. 209.
8 Ibid, p. 209.
9 Ibid, pp. 213–14.
10 On this affinity between Spinoza and Nietzsche, see also Edwin Curley, *Behind the Geometrical Method: a reading of Spinoza's Ethics* (Princeton University Press, New Jersey, 1988).
11 Gilles Deleuze, *Spinoza: practical philosophy*, p. 28.
12 Ibid, pp. 123–4.
13 David Savan, 'Spinoza and Language', in *Studies in Spinoza: critical and interpretive essays*, ed. S. Paul Kashap (University

of California Press, Berkeley & Los Angeles, 1972), pp. 236–48; p. 239. For a treatment of related issues in language, epistemology and the history of ideas, see Ian Hacking, *Why Does Language Matter to Philosophy?* (Cambridge University Press, Cambridge, 1975).

14 See for instance Jacques Derrida, *Speech and Phenomena and other essays on Husserl's theory of signs*, trans. David B. Allison (Northwestern University Press, Evanston, Ill., 1973); *Of Grammatology*, trans. Gayatri C. Spivak (Johns Hopkins University Press, Baltimore, 1976); *Margins of Philosophy*, trans. Alan Bass (University of Chicago Press, Chicago, 1982); *Dissemination*, trans. Barbara Johnson (University of Chicago Press, Chicago, 1981).

15 Derrida, 'Plato's Pharmacy' and 'The double Session', in *Dissemination*, pp. 61–171 and 173–285.

16 See Derrida, *Of Grammatology* and 'Signature Event Context', *Glyph*, Vol. I (Johns Hopkins University Press, Baltimore, 1977), pp. 172–97.

17 Derrida, *Edmund Husserl's 'Origin of Geometry': an introduction*, trans. John P. Leavey (Nicholas Hays, Stony Brook, New York, 1978).

18 Ibid, p. 29.

19 See especially Derrida, *Of Grammatology*.

20 David Savan, 'Spinoza and Language', p. 239.

21 Shmueli, 'Geometrical Method, Personal Caution, and the Ideal of Tolerance'.

22 G. H. R. Parkinson, 'Language and Knowledge in Spinoza', in *Spinoza: a collection of critical essays*, ed. Marjorie Grene (Anchor/Doubleday, New York, 1973), pp. 73–100; p. 93. See also Parkinson, *Spinoza's Theory of Knowledge* (Clarendon Press, Oxford, 1953) and '"Truth is its Own Standard": aspects of Spinoza's theory of truth', in *Spinoza: new perspectives*, eds. Shahan and Biro, pp. 35–55.

23 Ludwig Wittgenstein, *Tractatus Logico-Philosophicus*, trans. D. F. Pears and B. F. McGuinness (Routledge & Kegan Paul, London, 1962).

24 Cited by Parkinson, 'Language and Knowledge in Spinoza', p. 98.

25 Jonathan Bennett, *A Study of Spinoza's Ethics* (Cambridge University Press, Cambridge, 1984), p. 366. Further references given by page-number in the text.

26 See especially Edmund Husserl, *The Crisis of the European Sciences and Transcendental Phenomenology*, trans. D. Carr (Northwestern University Press, Evanston, Ill., 1970).

27 Rudolf Bernet, 'On Derrida's "Introduction" to Husserl's *Origin of Geometry*', in *Derrida and Deconstruction*, ed. Hugh J. Silverman (Routledge, London, 1989), pp. 139–53; p. 146.

28 See for instance Jacques Derrida, 'The Principle of Reason: the university in the eyes of its pupils', trans. Catherine Porter and Edward P. Morris, *Diacritics* 13, no. 3 (Fall, 1983), pp. 3–20; 'Of an Apocalyptic Tone Recently Adopted in Philosophy', trans. John P. Leavey, *The Oxford Literary Review* 6, no. 2 (1984), pp. 3–37; 'Parergon', in *The Truth in Painting*, trans. Geoff Bennington and Ian McLeod (University of Chicago Press, 1987), pp. 15–147.

29 Rodolphe Gasché, *The Tain of the Mirror: Derrida and the philosophy of reflection* (Harvard University Press, Cambridge, Mass., 1986).

30 Bernet, 'On Derrida's "Introduction" to Husserl', p. 148.

31 Leszek Kolakowski, 'The Two Eyes of Spinoza', in *Spinoza: a collection of critical essays*, ed. Marjorie Grene, pp. 279–94; p. 293.

32 See also Edmund Husserl, *Cartesian Meditations: an introduction to phenomenology*, trans. D. Cairns (The Hague, Nijhoff, 1969).

33 Paul de Man, 'Crisis and Criticism', in *Blindness and Insight: essays in the rhetoric of contemporary criticism* (Methuen, London, 1983), pp. 3–19. All further references given as *BI* with page-number in the text.

34 See Bernet, 'On Derrida's "Introduction" to Husserl', for a fuller account of Husserl's work during this period and its relation to historical events in the pre-war years.

35 Georg Lukács, *The Destruction of Reason* (Merlin, London, 1980).

36 See especially Paul de Man, *Allegories of Reading: figural language in Rousseau, Nietzsche, Rilke, and Proust* (Yale University Press, New Haven, 1979).

37 De Man refers mainly to Lévi-Strauss's *Le Cru et le Cuit* (Plon, Paris, 1964). Trans. by John and Doreen Weightman as *The Raw and the Cooked* (Harper & Row, New York, 1969). For another deconstructive reading of Lévi-Strauss – albeit from a somewhat different standpoint – see Jacques Derrida, 'Structure, Sign, and Play in the Discourse of the Human Sciences',

in *Writing and Difference*, trans. Alan Bass (Routledge & Kegan Paul, London, 1978), pp. 278–93.

38 Paul de Man, 'Heidegger's Exegeses of Hölderlin', in *Blindness and Insight*, pp. 246–66. All further references given as *BI* with page-number in the text.

39 See Norris, *Paul de Man: deconstruction and the critique of aesthetic ideology* (Routledge, New York & London, 1988).

40 See Paul de Man, *Wartime Journalism, 1939–1943*, eds. Werner Hamacher, Neil Hertz, and Thomas Keenan (University of Nebraska Press, Lincoln, Nebraska & London, 1988); also the companion volume *Responses: on Paul de man's wartime journalism*, eds. Hamacher, Hertz and Keenan (Nebraska, 1989).

41 Lewis Samuel Feuer, *Spinoza and the Rise of Liberalism* (Beacon Press, Boston, 1958), p. 90.

42 Paul Wienpahl, *The Radical Spinoza* (New York University Press, New York, 1979), p. 46.

43 See for instance Arne Naess, *Freedom, Emotion and Self-Subsistence* (Universiteits Forlaget, Oslo, 1975) and Naess, 'Through Spinoza to Mahayana Buddhism or through Mahayana Buddhism to Spinoza', in *Spinoza's Philosophy of Man: proceedings of the Scandinavian Spinoza symposium, 1977* (Universiteits Forlaget, Oslo, 1978), pp. 136–58; also James Daniel Collins, *Spinoza on Nature* (Southern Illinois University Press, Carbondale, 1984); George Sessions, 'Spinoza and Ecophilosophy', *Ecophilosophy: an informal newsletter*, no. 1 (April, 1976), pp. 1–5.

44 See Donald Davidson, *Inquiries into Truth and Interpretation* (Clarendon Press, Oxford, 1984).

CHAPTER 3 LANGUAGE, TRUTH AND HISTORICAL UNDERSTANDING

1 Gottlob Frege, 'On Sense and Reference', in *Translations from the Philosophical Writings of Gottlob Frege*, ed. P. Geach and M. Black (Basil Blackwell, Oxford, 1952), pp. 56–78.

2 W. V. O. Quine, 'Two Dogmas of Empiricism', in *From a Logical Point of View* (Harvard University Press, Cambridge, Mass., 1969), pp. 20–46.

3 See Richard Rorty, *Philosophy and the Mirror of Nature* (Basil Blackwell, Oxford, 1980); *Consequences Of Pragmatism*

(University of Minnesota Press, Minneapolis, 1982); *Contingency, Irony, and Solidarity* (Cambridge University Press, Cambridge, 1989).
4 See especially Foucault, *Language, Counter-Memory, Practice: selected interviews and other writings*, trans. Donald F. Bouchard and Sherry Simon (Cornell University Press, Ithaca, NY, 1977).
5 See Benjamin Lee Whorf, *Language, Thought and Reality: selected writings*, ed. J. B. Carroll (MIT Press, Cambridge, Mass., 1956).
6 See for instance Quine, *Word and Object* (Harvard University Press, Cambridge, Mass., 1960).
7 Donald Davidson, 'On the Very Idea of a Conceptual Scheme', in *Inquiries into Truth and Interpretation* (Clarendon Press, Oxford, 1984), pp. 183–98. All further references to this volume given by page-number only in the text. On Davidson's work in this area, see Ernest LePore (ed.), *Truth and Interpretation: essays on the philosophy of Donald Davidson* (Basil Blackwell, Oxford, 1986); Bjørn T. Ramberg, *Donald Davidson's Philosophy of Language: an introduction* (Basil Blackwell, Oxford, 1989); Christopher Norris, 'Reading Donald Davidson: truth, meaning and right interpretation', in Norris, *Deconstruction and the Interests of Theory* (Pinter Publishers, London & University of Oklahoma Press, Norman, Okl., 1988), pp. 59–83.
8 Rorty, *Philosophy and the Mirror of Nature*, pp. 261–2.
9 S. Pradhan, 'Minimalist Semantics: Davidson and Derrida on meaning, use, and convention', *Diacritics* 16 (Spring, 1986), pp. 66–77.
10 See especially Jacques Derrida, 'Signature Event Context', *Glyph*, Vol. I (Johns Hopkins University Press, Baltimore, 1977), pp. 172–97; also 'Limited Inc abc', *Glyph* 2, (1977), pp. 162–254.
11 See the essays collected in Stanley Fish, *Doing What Comes Naturally: change, rhetoric, and the practice of theory in literary and legal studies* (Oxford University Press, Oxford, 1989).
12 Fish develops this line of argument in the following essays, all reprinted in *Doing What Comes Naturally*: 'Consequences' (pp. 315–41); 'Anti-Foundationalism, Theory-Hope, and the Teaching of Composition' (342–55); 'Dennis Martinez and the Uses of Theory' (372–98); 'Critical Self-Consciousness, or Can We

Know What We Are Doing? (436–67).

13 See Fish, 'Consequences'.

14 Fish, 'Dennis Martinez and the Uses of Theory', p. 380.

15 E. D. Hirsch, *Validity in Interpretation* (Yale University Press, New Haven, 1967). For a more extreme statement of Hirsch's basic position, see P. D. Juhl, *Interpretation: an essay in the philosophy of literary criticism* (Princeton University Press, Princeton, NJ., 1980).

16 See Fish, 'Consequences', and the various responses brought together in W. J. T. Mitchell (ed.), *Against Theory: literary theory and the new pragmatism* (Chicago University Press, Chicago, 1985). See also my discussion of the issues raised by this current neo-pragmatist movement of thought in Norris, *Deconstruction and the Interests of Theory*.

17 See especially Paul de Man, *The Resistance to Theory* (University of Minnesota Press, Minneapolis, 1986).

18 See for instance Steven Knapp and Walter Benn Michaels, 'Against Theory', *Critical Inquiry* 8 (1982), pp. 723–42 and 'Against Theory 2', *Critical Inquiry* 14 (1987), pp. 49–68. The most sophisticated statement of the pragmatist case – though one that, to my mind, raises all the same problems – can be found in Barbara Herrnstein Smith, *Contingencies of Value: alternative perspectives for critical theory* (Harvard University Press, Cambridge, Mass., 1988).

19 Richard Rorty, *Philosophy and the Mirror of Nature*.

20 Gilles Deleuze and Félix Guattari, *A Thousand Plateaus*, trans. Brian Massumi (University of Minnesota Press, Minneapolis, 1987), p. 154.

21 Jacques Derrida, 'Cogito and the History of Madness', in *Writing And Difference*, trans. Alan Bass (Routledge & Kegan Paul, London, 1978), pp. 31–63. All further references given by CHM and page-number in the text. This essay is a reading of Foucault's *Folie et déraison: Histoire de la Folie à l'age classique* (Paris, Plon, 1961). See also roy Boyne, *Foucault and Derrida: the other side of reason* (London: Unwin Hyman, 1990).

22 See for instance John R. Searle, 'Reiterating the Differences', *Glyph* 1 (Johns Hopkins University Press, Baltimore, 1977), pp. 198–208 and Jürgen Habermas, *The Philosophical Discourse of Modernity: twelve lectures*, trans. Frederick Lawrence (Polity Press, Cambridge, 1987).

23 Jacques Derrida, 'Afterword: toward an ethic of discussion',

in *Limited Inc*, 2nd edn. (Northwestern University Press, Evanston, Ill., 1989), pp. 111–160; p. 146.

24 In Habermas, *The Philosophical Discourse of Modernity*.

25 Derrida, 'Afterword', p. 157.

26 Christopher Norris, 'Deconstruction, Postmodernism and Philosophy: Habermas on Derrida', *Praxis International* 8 no. 4 (1989), pp. 426–46.

27 Paul de Man, *The Resistance to Theory*. All further references given by *RT* and page-number in the text.

28 Paul de Man, 'Pascal's Allegory of Persuasion', in *Allegory and Representation*, ed. Stephen J. Greenblatt (Johns Hopkins University Press, Baltimore, 1981), pp. 1–25.

29 This line of argument is most fully developed in Stanley Fish, *Is There a Text in this Class? The authority of interpretive communities* (Harvard University Press, Cambridge, Mass., 1980).

30 De Man, 'Pascal's Allegory of Persuasion'. All further references given by PAP and page-number in the text.

31 Jonathan Bennett, *A Study of Spinoza's Ethics* (Cambridge University Press, Cambridge, 1984), p. 114.

32 Alan Donagan, *Spinoza* (Harvester/Wheatsheaf, London and New York, 1988).

33 See the essays collected in H. Aram Veeser (ed.), *The New Historicism* (Routledge, New York and London, 1989). These issues are treated in a wider philosophical context by Robert d'Amico, *Historicism and Knowledge* (Routledge, New York & London, 1989).

34 See for instance Stephen Greenblatt, *Renaissance Self-Fashioning: from More to Shakespeare* (University of Chicago Press, Chicago, 1984) and *Shakespearean Negotiations: the circulation of social energy in Renaissance England* (University of California Press, Berkeley & Los Angeles, 1988).

35 For some representative work of this kind, see Catherine Belsey, *The Subject of Tragedy: identity and difference in Renaissance drama* (Methuen, London, 1985); Catherine Belsey, *John Milton: language, gender, power* (Basil Blackwell, Oxford, 1988); Jonathan Dollimore, *Radical Tragedy: religion, ideology and power in the drama of Shakespeare and his contemporaries* (Harvester Press, Brighton, 1985); *Political Shakespeare: new essays in cultural materialism*, ed. Jonathan Dollimore and Alan Sinfield (Manchester University Press, Manchester, 1985); Francis Barker, *The Tremulous Private Body: essays on subjection*

(Methuen, London, 1984); *Alternative Shakespeares*, ed. John Drakakis (Methuen, London, 1985); Malcolm Evans, *Signifying Nothing: truths's true contents in Shakespeare's text* (Harvester, Brighton, 1986); Terence Hawkes, *That Shakespeherian Rag*; Peter Hulme, *Colonial Encounters: Europe and the native Caribbean* (Methuen, London, 1986); Peter Stallybrass and Allon White, *The Politics and Poetics of Transgression* (Methuen, London, 1986). Antony Easthope offers a useful survey of these and related developments in *British Post-Structuralism* (Routledge, London, 1988).

36 Terry Eagleton, *Criticism and Ideology* (New Left Books, London, 1976), p. 101.
37 See especially Foucault, *Language, Counter-Memory, Practice* (op. cit.).
38 Louis Althusser, *'Lenin and Philosophy' and other essays*, trans. Ben Brewster (New Left Books, London, 1971), p. 164.
39 Ibid, p. 164.

CHAPTER 4   THE CLAIM OF REASON: SPINOZA AS A LEFT-CARTESIAN

1 Alan Donagan, *Spinoza* (Harvester/Wheatsheaf, London and New York, 1988), pp. 8–11. Further references given by page-number in the text.
2 On the intellectual and socio-political context of seventeenth-century Dutch liberal thought, see R. Colie, *Light and Enlightenment* (Cambridge University Press, Cambridge, 1958); Lewis Samuel Feuer, *Spinoza and the Rise of Liberalism* (Beacon Press, Boston, 1957); Pieter Geyl, *The Revolt of the Netherlands* (Benn, London, 1958); K. H. D. Haley, *The Dutch in the Seventeenth Century* (Thames & Hudson, London, 1972); Simon Schama, *The Embarrassment of Riches: an interpretation of Dutch culture in the Golden Age* (Collins, London, 1987).
3 Jacques Derrida, 'Afterword: toward an ethic of discussion', in *Limited Inc*, 2nd edn. (Northwestern University Press, 1989), pp. 111–60.
4 Stanley Fish, *Surprised by Sin* (Macmillan, New York, 1967); *Self-Consuming Artifacts: the experience of seventeenth-century literature* (University of California Press, Berkeley and Los Angeles, 1972). Jonathan Culler has also noted this tacit conti-

nuity in Fish's work, despite the appearance of a radical shift of ground. See Culler, *The Pursuit of Signs* (Routledge & Kegan Paul, London, 1981). For a shrewd brief account of Fish's work, see William Ray, *Literary Meaning: from phenomenology to deconstruction* (Basil Blackwell, Oxford, 1984), pp. 152–69.

5   See for instance Cleanth Brooks, *The Well-Wrought Urn* (Harvest Books, New York, 1947) and W. K. Wimsatt, *The Verbal Icon* (University of Kentucky Press, Lexington, Ky., 1954).

6   Stanley Fish, *Is there a Text in this Class?*

7   Pierre Macherey, *A Theory of Literary Production*, trans. Geoffrey Wall (Routledge & Kegan Paul, London, 1978), pp. 63–4. One might compare this passage and others like it in Macherey with the account of Spinozist epistemology given in Don Garratt, 'Truth and Ideas of Imagination in the *Tractatus de Intellectus Emendatione*', *Studia Spinozana*, no. 2 (1986), pp. 61–92. See also Thomas C. Mark, 'Truth and Adequacy in Spinozistic Ideas', in *Spinoza: new perspectives*, ed. Robert W. Shahan and J. I. Biro (University of Oklahoma Press, Norman, Okl., 1978), pp. 11–34.

8   Robert A. Duff, *Spinoza's Political and Ethical Philosophy* (Augustus M. Kelley, New York, 1903, repr. 1970), p. 5.

9   Michael Walzer, 'The Politics of Michel Foucault', in *Foucault: a critical reader*, ed. David Couzens Hoy (Basil Blackwell, Oxford, 1986), pp. 51–68.

10 Gilles Deleuze, *Spinoza: practical philosophy*, trans. Robert Hurley (City Lights Books, San Francisco, 1988), pp. 28–9.

11 Ibid, p. 94.

12 Ibid, p. 95.

13 Ibid, p. 106.

14 Robert J. McShea, *The Political Philosophy of Spinoza* (Columbia University Press, New York, 1968), pp. 180–81. I have drawn upon McShea's translation of certain passages in the *Political Treatise* where his rendering seemed preferable to other versions.

15 Ludwig Feuerbach, *The Essence of Christianity* (Harper & Row, New York, 1965). See also *The Fiery Brook: selected writings of Ludwig Feuerbach*, ed. Zawar Hanfi (Anchor, New York, 1972).

16 Karl Marx, 'Theses on Feuerbach', in *Early Writings* (Penguin, Harmondsworth, 1977).

17 Jacques Derrida, *The Ear of the Other: texts and discussions*, trans. & ed. Christie V. McDonald, Claude Levesque and Peggy Kamuf (Schocken Books, New York, 1985), p. 32. For a commentary on this text, see Christopher Norris, 'Deconstruction Against Itself: Derrida and Nietzsche', *Diacritics* 16, no. 4 (Winter, 1986), pp. 61–69.

18 Edwin Curley, *Behind the Geometrical Method: a reading of Spinoza's Ethics* (Princeton University Press, New Jersey, 1988), p. 130.

19 Ibid, p. 129.

20 David Bidney, *The Psychology and Ethics of Spinoza* (Russell & Russell, New York, 1962), p. 283; cited by McShea, p. 53.

21 Feuer, *Spinoza and the Rise of Liberalism*. All further references given by author-name and page-number in the text.

22 On Jan de Witt and the left-Cartesian connection, see also Schama, *The Embarrassment of Riches*, and Haley, *The Dutch in the Seventeenth Century* (op. cit.); also Shmueli, 'The Geometrical Method, Personal Caution, and the Ideal of Tolerance'.

23 See Harry A. Wolfson, 'Behind the Geometrical Method', in *Spinoza: a collection of critical essays*, ed. Marjorie Grene, pp. 3–24. This essay is drawn from Wolfson's *The Philosophy Of Spinoza* (2 vols.: Schocken Books, New York, repr. 1969), which remains a standard source of biographical information and interpretive commentary.

24 Spinoza, *Principles of Descartes' Philosophy*, trans. H. H. Britan (Open Court Publishers, New York, 1977).

25 See especially Jürgen Habermas, *Communication and the Evolution of Society*, trans. Thomas McCarthy (Heinemann, London, 1979) and *The Theory of Communicative Action* 1, trans. Thomas McCarthy (London, Heinemann, 1984).

26 Habermas, *The Philosophical Discourse of Modernity: twelve lectures*, trans. Frederick Lawrence (Polity Press, Cambridge, 1987).

27 See for instance Stephen Greenblatt, 'Invisible Bullets: renaissance authority and its subversion', in *Political Shakespeare: new essays in cultural materialism*, ed. Jonathan Dollimore and Alan Sinfield (University of Manchester Press, Manchester, 1985), pp. 18–47.

28 See Immanuel Kant, *Political Writings*, ed. Hans Reiss (Cambridge University Press, Cambridge, 1970). For a succinct

(often brilliant) commentary on the Kantian 'tribunal' of reason and its various modalities of judgement, see Gilles Deleuze, *Kant's Critical Philosophy: the doctrine of the faculties*, trans. Hugh Tomlinson and Barbara Habberjam (Athlone Press, London, 1984). It would be interesting (but beyond the scope of this book) to make a detailed comparison of Deleuze's and Lyotard's arguments with regard to Kant's so-called 'Fourth Critique', i.e. his late writings on politics, history, and the prospects for enlightened social change.

29 Jean-François Lyotard, *The Differend: phrases in dispute*, trans. Georges Van Den Abbeele (Manchester University Press, Manchester, 1988). See also David Carroll, *Paraaesthetics: Foucault, Lyotard, Derrida* (Methuen, London, 1987).

30 Ibid, pp. 179–80.

31 See especially Christopher Hill, *Milton and the English Revolution* (Faber, London, 1977); also W. R. Parker, *Milton* (2 vols., Clarendon Press, Oxford, 1968) and Andrew Milner, *John Milton and the English Revolution: a study in the sociology of literature* (Macmillan, London, 1981). Catherine Belsey (*John Milton*, op. cit.) offers a reading in the jointly post-structuralist and cultural-materialist mode which raises many of the issues I am addressing in this book.

CHAPTER 5   FROM SCRIPTURAL HERMENEUTICS TO SECULAR
CRITIQUE

1 Barbara Johnson, *The Critical Difference: essays in the contemporary rhetoric of reading* (Johns Hopkins University Press, Baltimore, 1980), p. xii.

2 See Kant, *Political Writings*, ed. Hans Reiss (Cambridge University Press, Cambridge, 1970).

3 Kant, *Critique of Aesthetic Judgement*, trans. J. C. Meredith (Clarendon Press, Oxford, 1911). Among recent commentaries, see for instance Lyotard, *The Differend*; Lyotard, *The Postmodern Condition: a report on knowledge*, trans. Geoff Bennington and Brian Massumi (Manchester University Press, Manchester, 1984); Meaghan Morris, 'Postmodernity and Lyotard's Sublime', in *The Pirate's Fiancée* (Verso, London, 1988), pp. 223–39; Jacques Derrida, 'Parergon', in *The Truth in Painting*, trans. Geoff Bennington and Ian McLeod (University of

Chicago Press, Chicago, 1987), pp. 15–147; Derrida, 'Econom-
imesis', trans. Richard Klein (*Diacritics* 11, no. 2 (Summer,
1981), pp. 3–25; Paul de Man, 'Phenomenality and Materiality
in Kant', in *Hermeneutics: questions and prospects*, eds. Gary
Shapiro and Alan Sica (University of Massachusetts Press,
Amherst, 1984), pp. 121–44; de Man, 'Hegel on the Sublime',
in *Displacement: Derrida and after*, ed. Mark Krupnik (Indiana
University Press, Bloomington, Ind., 1983), pp. 139–53; David
Carroll, *Paraaesthetics: Foucault, Lyotard, Derrida* (Methuen,
London, 1987); Paul Hamilton, *Coleridge's Poetics* (Basil
Blackwell, Oxford, 1983), pp. 47–57.

4   Lyotard, *The Differend*, p. 165. See also Lyotard, 'Sensus
Communis', trans. Marian Hobson and Geoff Bennington,
Paragraph 11 no. 1 (March, 1988), pp. 1–23.

5   See Kant, *The Conflict of the Faculties*, trans. & ed. Mary J.
Gregor (Abaris Books, New York, 1979); also Deleuze, *Kant's
Critical Philosophy* and Jacques Derrida, 'Mochlos, ou le conflit
des facultés', *Philosophie*, no. 2 (1984), pp. 21–53.

6   Lyotard, *The Differend*, p. 166.

7   See Jürgen Habermas, *The Theory of Communicative Action* 1,
trans. Thomas McCarthy (Heinemann, London, 1984).

8   See Michael Walzer, *Spheres of Justice* (Basil Blackwell, Oxford,
1983) and *Interpretation and Social Criticism* (Harvard University
Press, Cambridge, Mass., 1987).

9   See my discussion of these various claims and counter-claims
in Norris, 'Narrative Theory or Theory-as-Narrative: the politics of post-modern reason', *The Contest of Faculties: philosophy
and theory after deconstruction* (Methuen, London, 1985), pp.
19–46.

10   Jürgen Habermas, *Knowledge and Human Interests*, trans Jeremy J. Shapiro (Heinemann, London, 1972).

11   For a spirited rendition of the case against Habermas from
a Lacanian/post-structuralist standpoint, see Rainer Nägele,
'Freud, Habermas, and the Dialectic of Enlightenment', *New
German Critique*, no. 22 (1981), pp. 41–62 and Nägele, 'The
Provocation of Jacques Lacan', *New German Critique*, no. 16
(1979), pp. 5–29. These issues receive their most comprehen-
sive treatment to date – albeit one with its own distinctly
'Frankfurt' philosophical orientation – in Manfred Frank, *What
Is Neostructuralism?*, trans. Sabine Wilke and Richard Gray
(University of Minnesota Press, Minneapolis, 1989). See also

Gillian Rose, *Dialectic of Nihilism: post-structuralism and law* (Basil Blackwell, Oxford, 1984); Peter Dews, *Logics of Disintegration: post-structuralist thought and the claims of theory* (Verso, London, 1987); and David Macey, *Lacan In Contexts* (Verso, London, 1989), esp. chapter 4, 'Philosophy and Post-Philosophy', pp. 75–120.

12   Michel Foucault, *Madness and Civilization: a history of insanity in the age of reason*, trans. Richard Howard (Pantheon, New York, 1965).

13   Gilles Deleuze, *Spinoza: practical philosophy*, p. 18.

14   Ibid, p. 19.

15   Johnson, *The Critical Difference*, p. xii.

16   Leo Strauss, *Persecution and the Art of Writing* (Greenwood Press, New York, 1973).

17   Frank Kermode, *The Genesis of Secrecy* (Harvard University Press, Cambridge, Mass., 1979).

18   See Kermode, *The Classic* (Faber & Faber, London, 1975).

19   See especially Roland Barthes, *S/Z*, trans. Richard Miller (Jonathan Cape, London, 1975); Barthes, 'From Work to Text', in *Image-Music-Text*, trans. Stephen Heath (Fontana, London, 1977); also Catherine Belsey, *Critical Practice* (Methuen, London, 1980) and Colin MacCabe, *James Joyce and the 'Revolution of the Word'* (Macmillan, London, 1978).

20   On this topic see also A. C. Charity, *Events and their Afterlife: the dialectics of Christian typology in the Bible and in Dante* (Cambridge University Press, Cambridge, 1966).

21   Kermode, *The Genesis of Secrecy*, p. 119.

22   Ibid, p. 119.

23   See for instance the chapter on Kermode in Jonathan Arac, *Critical Genealogies: historical situations for postmodern literary studies* (Columbia University Press, New York, 1987).

24   See Harold Bloom, *Agon: towards a theory of revisionism* (Oxford University Press, New York, 1982); *The Anxiety of Influence* (O.U.P., New York, 1973); *Kabbalah and Criticism* (Continuum, New York, 1975); *Poetry and Repression: revisionism from Blake to Stevens* (Yale University Press, New Haven, 1976). The best introduction to this body of work is Peter de Bolla, *Harold Bloom: towards historical rhetorics* (Routledge, London, 1988).

25   Jürgen Habermas, 'Summation and Response', cited in David Held, *Introduction to Critical Theory: Horkheimer to Habermas*

(Hutchinson, London, 1980), p. 314.

26   Ibid, p. 315.

27   Kermode, *The Genesis of Secrecy*, p. 119.

28   Leo Strauss, *Spinoza's Critique of Religion*, trans. E. M. Sinclair (Schocken Books, New York, 1965), p. 262.

29   See Hans-Georg Gadamer, *Truth And Method*, trans. Garrett Barden and John Cumming (Sheed & Ward, London, 1975) and Gadamer, *Philosophical Hermeneutics*, trans. David E. Linge (University of California Press, Berkeley and Los Angeles, 1977).

30   T. S. Eliot, *For Lancelot Andrewes* (Faber & Faber, London, 1928).

31   See for instance Geoffrey Hartman and Sanford Budick (eds.), *Midrash And Literature* (Yale University Press, New Haven, 1986); also Hartman, *Criticism In The Wilderness: the study of literature today* (Yale U. P., New Haven, 1980) and *Saving The Text: literature/Derrida/philosophy* (Johns Hopkins University Press, Baltimore, 1981).

32   W. K. Wimsatt, *The Verbal Icon: studies in the meaning of poetry* (University of Kentucky Press, Lexington, Ky., 1954).

33   Cleanth Brooks *The Well-Wrought Urn* (Harcourt Brace, New York, 1947).

34   See the chapter on Marvell in Brooks, *The Well-Wrought Urn* (op. cit.).

35   See Eliot's two essays 'Milton' (1936) and 'Milton' (1947), in *On Poetry and Poets* (Faber & Faber, London, 1957).

36   F. R. Leavis, 'Milton's Verse', in *Revaluation: tradition and development in English Poetry* (Penguin, London, 1964), pp. 42–61.

37   William Empson, *The Structure of Complex Words* (Chatto & Windus, London, 1951); also Empson, *Seven Types of Ambiguity* (Chatto & Windus, London, 1930; repr. Penguin, Harmondsworth, 1961 and Hogarth Press, London, 1987).

38   Cleanth Brooks, *The Well-Wrought Urn*, p. 198.

39   Empson, review of T. S. Eliot, 'George Herbert', *New Statesman* (4 January 1963), p. 18.

40   Jürgen Habermas, *The Philosophical Discourse of Modernity: twelve lectures*, trans. Frederick Lawrence (Polity Press, Cambridge, 1987), p. 209.

41   See Norris, 'Deconstruction, Postmodernism and Philosophy:

Habermas on Derrida', *Praxis International* 8, no. 4 (1989), pp. 426–46.

42 Gerald Graff, *Poetic Statement and Critical Dogma* (Northwestern University Press, Evanston, Ill., 1970).

43 Graff, *Literature Against Itself: literary ideas in modern society* (University of Chicago Press, Chicago, 1979), p. 179.

44 Ibid, p. 163.

45 Ibid, pp. 1–2.

46 Hayden White, *Metahistory* (Johns Hopkins University Press, Baltimore, 1973); *Tropics of Discourse* (Johns Hopkins, Baltimore, 1978); *The Content of the Form* (Johns Hopkins, Baltimore, 1988). See also Stephen Bann, *The Clothing of Clio: a study of the representation of history in nineteenth-century Britain and France* (Cambridge University Press, Cambridge, 1983) and Peter Gay, *Style in History* (Jonathan Cape, London, 1974).

CHAPTER 6   FICTION, PHILOSOPHY AND THE WAY OF IDEAS

1 Frank Kermode, *The Sense of an Ending* (Oxford University Press, New York, 1967).

2 Roland Barthes, *S/Z*, trans. Richard Miller (Jonathan Cape, London, 1975).

3 See especially Geoffrey Hartman, *Criticism in the Wilderness*.

4 Leo Strauss, *Spinoza's Critique of Religion*, p. 114. See also Norman O. Brown, 'Philosophy and Prophecy: Spinoza's Hermeneutics', *Political Theory* 14 (1986), pp. 195–213 and Berel Lang, 'The Politics of Interpretation: Spinoza's modernist turn', *Review of Metaphysics* 43 no. 2 (1989), pp. 327–56.

5 Ibid, pp. 113–4.

6 See for instance Austin Farrer, *Faith and Speculation: an essay in philosophical theology* (repr. T. and T. Clark, London, 1988).

7 Kermode, *The Genesis of Secrecy*, p. 73.

8 See also Kermode, *Essays on Fiction, 1971–82* (Routledge & Kegan Paul, London, 1983).

9 Kermode, *The Classic*.

10 T. S. Eliot, 'Tradition and the Individual Talent', in *Selected Essays* (Faber & Faber, London, 1964).

11 Kermode, *The Genesis of Secrecy*, p. 98

12 Ibid, p. 69.

13 Arac, *Critical Genealogies*.

14 Kermode, *The Genesis of Secrecy*, p. 144.
15 Pierre Macherey, *A Theory of Literary Production*, trans. Geoffrey Wall (Routledge & Kegan Paul, London, 1978), p. 64.
16 See for instance Donald Davidson, *Essays on Actions and Events* (Clarendon Press, Oxford, 1980).
17 Stuart Hampshire, 'Spinoza's Theory of Freedom', in *Spinoza: essays in interpretation*, eds. Eugene Freeman and Maurice Mandelbaum (Open Court Publishers, Illinois, 1975), pp. 36–47; p. 47.
18 Errol E. Harris, 'Spinoza's Theory of Human Immortality', in Freeman and Mandelbaum, *Spinoza: essays in interpretation*, pp. 245–62; p. 261.
19 Jacques Derrida, 'The Double Session', in *Dissemination*, trans. Barbara Johnson (Athlone Press, London, 1981), pp. 173–285; p. 207.
20 See Terry Eagleton, 'Frère Jacques: the politics of deconstruction', in *Against The Grain: selected essays* (Verso, London, 1986), pp. 79–87.
21 Jacques Derrida 'Afterword: toward an ethics of discussion', in *Limited Inc* (2nd edn., Northwestern University Press, Evanston, Ill., 1989), pp. 111–60.
22 For a similar argument (much indebted to de Man) see J. Hillis Miller, *The Ethics of Reading* (Columbia University Press, New York, 1987); also Geoffrey Galt Harpham's remarkably original and stimulating book *The Ascetic Imperative in Culture and Criticism* (University of Chicago Press, Chicago, 1988).
23 Paul de Man, Preface to Carol Jacobs, *The Dissimulating Harmony* (Johns Hopkins University Press, Baltimore, 1978), p. xi.
24 Among other late essays by de Man with a bearing on this topic, see especially 'Aesthetic Formalization: Kleist's *Über das Marionettentheater*, in de Man, *The Rhetoric of Romanticism* (Columbia University Press, New York, 1984), pp. 263–90; 'Phenomenality and Materiality in Kant', in *Hermeneutics: questions and prospects*, ed. Gary Shapiro and Alan Sica (University of Massachusetts Press, Amherst, Mass., 1984), pp. 121–44; and 'Sign and Symbol in Hegel's *Aesthetics*', *Critical Inquiry* 8, no. 4. (1982), pp. 761–75. See also *Reading de Man Reading*, ed. Wlad Godzich and Lindsay Waters (University of Minnesota Press, Minneapolis, 1988) for a number of articles dealing with the topic of deconstruction and aesthetic ideology.
25 De Man, 'Aesthetic Formalization'.

26 This argument has been taken up by Michael Sprinker in a book that convincingly articulates the claims of Althusserian Marxism with those of deconstructive or rhetorical close-reading as practised by de Man. See Sprinker, *Imaginary Relations: aesthetics and ideology in the theory of historical materialism* (Verso, London, 1987). See also Michael Ryan, *Marxism and Deconstruction: a critical articulation* (Johns Hopkins University Press, Baltimore, 1982).

27 M. H. Abrams, 'Structure and Style in the Greater Romantic Lyric', in *From Sensibility to Romanticism*, ed. F. W. Hillis and H. Bloom (Oxford University Press, New York, 1965), pp. 530–59.

28 Paul de Man, 'Reading and History', in *The Resistance to Theory* (University of Minnesota Press, Minneapolis, 1986), pp. 54–72. All further references given by *RT* and page-number in the text. This essay was first published as the Introduction to Hans Robert Jauss, *Toward an Aesthetics of Reception*, trans. Timothy Bahti (University of Minnesota Press, Minneapolis, 1982), pp. vii–25.

29 For a useful brief account of this tradition, its philosophical sources and wider influence, see William K. Wimsatt and Cleanth Brooks, *Literary Criticism: a short history*, vol III, *Romantic Criticism* (Routledge & Kegan Paul, 1957). See also René Wellek, *A History of Modern Criticism, 1750–1950*, vols I and II, *The Later Eighteenth Century* and *The Romantic Age* (Yale University Press, 1955).

30 De Man, 'Aesthetic Formalization' and 'Phenomenality and Materiality in Kant'.

31 Macherey, *A Theory of Literary Production*, p. 56. Further references given by page-number in the text.

32 Paul de Man, *Allegories Of Reading: figural language in Rousseau, Nietzsche, Rilke, and Proust* (Yale University Press, New Haven, 1979), pp. 79–131.

33 Louis Althusser and Etienne Balibar, *Reading Capital*, trans. Ben Brewster (New Left Books, London, 1970), p. 16.

34 Catherine Belsey, *Critical Practice* (Methuen, London, 1980).

CHAPTER 7   WHY SPINOZA NOW? THE CRITIQUE OF
REVELATION REVISITED

1   Salman Rushdie, *The Satanic Verses* (Viking Books, New York
and London, 1988).

2   See various contributors to *The Rushdie File*, eds. Lisa Appi-
gnanesi and Sara Maitland (Fourth Estate, London, 1989).

3   'Salman Rushdie writes to Rajiv Gandhi', in *The Rushdie File*,
pp. 42–5; p. 44.

4   For an account of this historical process, see Jürgen Habermas,
Strukturwandel der Öffentlichkeit (Luchterhand, Neuwied,
1962); also, from a more sharply diagnostic or oppositional
standpoint, Oskar Negt and Alexander Kluge, *Öffentlichkeit
und Erfahrung: zur Organisationsanalyse von bürgerlicher und
proletärischer Öffentlichkeit* (Suhrkamp, Frankfurt-am-Main,
1972); Peter Uwe Hohendahl, *The Institution of Criticism*
(Cornell University Press, Ithaca, NY, 1982) and Terry Eagleton, *The Function of Criticism: from The Spectator to post-structuralism* (Verso, London, 1984).

5   Sir Philip Sidney, 'A Defence of Poetry', in *Miscellaneous Prose
of Sir Philip Sidney*, ed. Katherine Duncan-Jones and Jan Van
Dorsten (Clarendon Press, Oxford, 1973), pp. 71–121.

6   See especially Lennard J. Davis, *Factual Fictions: origins of the
English novel* (Columbia University Press, New York, 1983);
also Michael McKeon, *The Origins of the English Novel,
1600–1740* (Johns Hopkins University Press, Baltimore, 1987).

7   Tzvetan Todorov, *Literature and its Theorists* (Routledge, London, 1987).

8   Graham Swift, 'Understanding the Place of Literature in Society', in *The Rushdie File*, p. 219.

9   Carlos Fuentes, 'Worlds Apart', ibid, pp. 245–9; pp. 245–6.

10   See especially Thomas Pavel, *Fictional Worlds* (Harvard University Press, Cambridge, Mass., 1987).

11   This issue has been much debated among modal logicians. See
David Lewis, *On The Plurality of Worlds* (Basil Blackwell,
Oxford, 1986) for a provocative statement of the realist case.

12   I. A. Richards, *Science And Poetry* (W. W. Norton, New York,
1926), p. 72. Cited by Graff in *Literature Against Itself*, p. 148.

13   See Feuer, *Spinoza and the Rise of Liberalism*.

14   See Kant, *The Conflict of the Faculties*, trans. and ed. Mary J.
Gregor (Abaris Books, New York, 1979).

15 Lyotard, *The Differend*, p. 128.
16 See J. L. Austin, *How To Do Things With Words* (Oxford University Press, London, 1963).
17 Jacques Derrida, 'Signature Event Context'.
18 Mary Louise Pratt, *Toward a Speech-Act Theory of Literary Discourse* (Indiana University Press, Bloomington, Ind., 1977).
19 Rushdie, interview with Shrabani Basu, in *The Rushdie File*, p. 41.
20 Terry Eagleton, *Criticism and Ideology* (New Left Books, London, 1976).
21 Marina Warner, contribution to *The Rushdie File*, pp. 208–11; p. 210.
22 See *Shelley's Prose, or The Trumpet of a Prophecy*, ed. David Lee Clark (University of New Mexico Press, Alberquerque, 1954). Spinoza's influence can be seen most clearly in the following essays, notes and fragments: 'The Necessity of Atheism' (pp. 37–9); 'Necessity! Thou mother of the world' (note to line from 'Queen Mab', 109–12); 'A Refutation of Deism' (118–37); 'A Fragment on Miracles' (143–4); 'Essay on Christianity' (196–214); 'A Philosophical View of Reform' (229–61).
23 Kenneth Blackwell, *The Spinozistic Ethics of Bertrand Russell* (Allen & Unwin, London, 1985), p. 148; citing passages from Bertrand Russell, *The Problems of Philosophy* (1912, repr. Oxford University Press, New York, 1959), pp. 156–7.
24 William Empson, *The Structure of Complex Words* (Chatto & Windus, London, 1951).
25 See Empson, *Milton's God* (Chatto & Windus, London, 1961); *Using Biography* (Chatto & Windus, London, 1984); *Essays on Shakespeare* (Cambridge University Press, Cambridge, 1986); *Argufying*, ed. John Haffenden (Chatto & Windus, London, 1987); *Faustus and the Censor* (Basil Blackwell, Oxford, 1987).
26 C. S. Lewis, *A Preface to Paradise Lost* (Oxford University Press, London, 1942).
27 John Crowe Ransom, 'Mr Empson's Muddles', *Southern Review* 4 (1938/9), pp. 322–39.
28 Ibid, p. 334.
29 Jonathan Culler, *Framing The Sign: criticism and its institutions* (Basil Blackwell, Oxford, 1988). All further references given by page-number in the text.

30 See Habermas, *The Philosophical Discourse of Modernity* (op. cit.).
31 Mihir Bose, contribution to *The Rushdie File* (op. cit.), pp. 114–7; p. 115.
32 Culler, 'Empson's Complex Words', in *Framing The Sign*, pp. 85–95. See also Christopher Norris, *William Empson and the Philosophy of Literary Criticism* (Athlone Press, London, 1978).
33 Allan Bloom, *The Closing of the American Mind* (Simon & Shuster, New York, 1987). For a cogent critique of Bloom's arguments, see the review of his book by Dan Latimer, *Textual Practice* 2, no. 2 (Summer, 1988), pp. 280–89.

POSTSCRIPT

As this book went to press I received a copy of Yirmiyahu Yovel's impressive two-volume study *Spinoza and Other Heretics* (Princeton University Press, Princeton N.J., 1989). Volume one ('The Marrano of Reason') sets out to reconstruct the intellectual and cultural background of Spinoza's thought, in particular the attitude of free-thinking rational scepticism adopted by Jewish intellectuals who had officially 'converted' to Christianity under threat of persecution in Spain and Portugal, but whose longer-term response took the form of a cryptic and ambivalent questioning of all religious truth claims. Volume two ('The Adventures of Immanence') carries the story forward from Spinoza to those subsequent thinkers – among them Kant, Hegel, Heine, Marx, Nietzsche and Freud – whose work continues in the same tradition of secularizing immanent critique. This is clearly a notable contribution to Spinoza scholarship and one that – quite apart from its own distinctive merits – provides a useful complement to my own focus on episodes in the latter reception-history.

Christopher Norris: A Selected Bibliography 1974–1989

Compiled by Holly Henry and Brenda O'Boyle

1974

1 'Charles Ives: American Pioneer', *Music and Musicians* 23 (October) pp. 36–40.
2 'Elgar', *Music and Musicians* 22 (March), pp. 30–1.
3 'Havergal Brian', *Music and Musicians* 22, pp. 24–5.
4 'Stockhausen', *Music and Musicians* 22 (July), pp. 32–3.
5 'Les Plaisirs des Clercs: Barthes's latest writing', *The British Journal of Aesthetics* 14, pp. 250–7.
6 'The Modern Age', *Tempo*, no. 111 (December) pp. 36–9 (Review of *The Oxford History of Music, Vol. X*).
7 'On the Experimental Front', *Music and Musicians* 23 (November), pp. 24–5 (Review of *Experimental Music* by Michael Nyman).
8 'The String Quartets of Shostakovich', *Music and Musicians* 24 (December) pp. 26–30.

1975

9 'Adventures of Phenomenology', *Radical Philosophy*, no. 11, pp. 42–4 (Merleau-Ponty).
10 'Aesthetics and Criticism', *Music and Musicians*, vol. 23 (July) pp. 28–30.
11 'Ansermet on Music', *Composer* 55, pp. 27–30.
12 'Charles Ives', *Music and Musicians* 23 (March), pp. 26–7.
13 'Fact and Fiction', *Critical Quarterly* 17, pp. 282–4.

14   'Haydn's Quartets', *Music and Musicians* 23 (January), pp. 30–2.
15   'Introduction to Stockhausen', *Music and Musicians* 23 (June), pp. 33–4.
16   'Havergal Brian', *Tempo*, no. 115 (December) pp. 45–6.
17   'The Influence of Tempo on the Appreciation of Music', *Literature, Music, Fine Arts* 8, pp. 239–41.
18   'Martinu', *Music and Musicians* 24 (November), pp. 32–3.
19   'Marxism and the Philosophy of Language', *Radical Philosophy*, no. 10, pp. 36–8.
20   'Modern Poetry and the Idea of Language', *The British Journal of Aesthetics* 15, pp. 373–5. (review of book by Gerald L. Bruns).
21   'Music and Pure Thought: Outline of a Study', *The British Journal of Aesthetics* 15, pp. 50–8.
22   'Richard Stoker', *Music and Musicians* 23 (February) pp. 16–20.
23   'Stravinsky', *Music and Musicians* 24 (November), pp. 34–5.
24   'Thomas Mann and Music', *Music and Musicians* 23 (June) pp. 26–8, 30.
25   'Western Traditions', *Music and Musicians* 24, pp. 38–9.

1976

26   'Ansermet on Music: A Forgotten Masterpiece', *Composer*, nos. 55 & 56, pp. 27–30 & 25–8.
27   'Ernst Bloch: On Philosophy and Music', *Philosophy and History* 9, pp. 32–40.
28   'Music and Politics', *Music and Musicians* 24 (August) pp. 24–6.
29   'A Common Sky', *Mind* 85, pp. 312–15 (A. D. Nuttall).
30   'Joyce's Returningties', *Books and Bookmen* 21, no. 5 (February), pp. 22–3.
31   'Humanism in the English Novel', *Books and Bookmen* 21, no. 9 (June), pp. 46–8.
32   'Eliot and Sartre', *Books and Bookmen* 21 (September), pp. 35–7.
33   'Expression in Movement and the Arts', *The British Journal of Aesthetics* 16, pp. 180–2, (David Best).
34   'Letters of Thomas Mann and Hermann Hesse', *Books and Bookmen* 21, no. 8 (May), pp. 32–4.

35 'Marxism and the Novel', *Books and Bookmen* 22, nos. 1 & 2, pp. 52–3, 59–60 (Review of *Myths of Power* by Terry Eagleton and *The English Novel from Dickens to Lawrence* by R. Williams).

36 'Philosophy of Modern Music', *Philosophy and History* 9, pp. 178–82 (T. W. Adorno).

37 'Porgy and Bess', *Tempo*, no. 118 (September) pp. 30–1.

38 'William Empson: The Man and His Work', *Critical Quarterly*, vol. 18, pp. 90–6.

39 Review of *Philosophy and the Novel* by Peter Jones, *The British Journal of Aesthetics* 16, pp. 90–3.

40 'Portrait in Depth', *Books and Bookmen* 21, nos. 10 & 11 (July and August) pp. 48–51, 54–7 (Review of *The Exile of James Joyce* by Hélène Cixous).

41 'The Prophet's Mantle', *Books and Bookmen* 22, no. 3, pp. 44–6 (Review of *Thought, Words and Creativity* by F. R. Leavis).

42 'Sense and Structuralism', *Essays in Criticism* 26, pp. 268–73 (Review of *Structuralist Poetics* by Jonathan Culler).

43 'What Language?', *Music and Musicians*, vol. 24 (August), pp. 29–30 (Review of *The Language of Modern Music* by Robert Fink and Robert Ricci).

1977

44 'Charles Rosen', *Music and Musicians* 25, pp. 30–2, 34 (Interview).

45 'Essays on Bartok', *Music and Musicians* 25, no. 1 (September), pp. 39–41.

46 Review of *Adorno and Krenek: an exchange of letters* by W. Rogge (ed.), *Philosophy and History* 10, pp. 47–51.

47 'The Apprentice Years', *Books and Bookmen* 22, no. 8, pp. 56–7 (Review of *Sibelius Vol. I* by Erik Tawastsjerna).

48 Review of *British Music Now* by L. Foreman, *Composer* 59, pp. 44–5.

49 'Counterfeit Realism', *Books and Bookmen* 22 (April), pp. 62–3 (Review of *The Alteration* by Kingsley Amis).

50 'Elective Biographies', *Books and Bookmen* 22, pp. 21–2 (Review of *The Poet's Self and the Poem* by Eric Heller).

51 'Heads Together', *Books and Bookmen* 22, pp. 51–2 (Review of *English Poetry* by Alan Sinfield).

52   'History and Reason', *Books and Bookmen* 22, nos. 9, 10 &
      11, pp. 44–6, 51–2, 49–51 (Review of *Critique of Dialectical
      Reason* by Sartre).

53   Review of *Language, Truth and Poetry* by G. D. Martin, *Mind*,
      86, pp. 617–20.

54   Review of *Luigi Nono: Texte und Studien zur seiner Musik* by
      J. Stenzl (ed.), *Literature, Music, Fine Arts* 10, pp. 102–6.

55   Review of *Music and the Brain* by M. Critchley and R. Henson,
      Composer 60, p. 31.

56   Review of *Treemonisha* by S. Joplin, *Tempo* 120, pp. 37–8
      (record review).

1978

57   *William Empson and the Philosophy of Literary Criticism*,
      (London: Athlone Press) x, 222 pp.

58   'John Michael East talks to Christopher Norris', *Composer*,
      no. 62, pp. 13–15, 17–20.

59   'Instinct for Drama', *Records and Recording* 21, pp. 22–3.

60   'Laura Riding's *The Telling*: language, poetry, and neutral
      style', *Language and Style* 11, pp. 137–45.

61   'Methods and Meanings', *Books and Bookmen* 23, no. 6, pp.
      42–4.

62   'Music and Philosophy', *Records and Recording* 21, pp. 18–19.

63   'Sociology of Music', *Records and Recording* 21, no. 10 (July),
      pp. 98–100.

64   'Schoenberg: Life, World and Work', no. 11 (August), *Records and Recording* 21, pp. 104–6.

65   'Sense and Structuralism', *Books and Bookmen* 24, pp. 28–31.

66   'Theory of Language and the Language of Literature', *Journal
      of Literary Semantics* 7, pp. 90–8.

67   'T. W. Adorno: the sociological writings', *Philosophy and
      History*, 11, pp. 123–6.

68   'After Babel', *Philosophy and Literature* 1, pp. 107–17 (George
      Steiner).

69   Review of *Art and Knowledge* by J. Chiari, *The British Journal
      of Aesthetics* 18, pp. 89–91.

70   'Roland Barthes: the view from here', *Critical Quarterly* 20,
      pp. 27–43.

71   'Jacques Derrida's *Grammatology*', *PN Review* 6, pp. 38–40.

72   Review of *Einführung in die Moderne Musik, 1900–1950* by S.

Borris, *Literature, Music, Fine Arts* 11, no. 2, pp. 123–6.

73 Review of *The Fate of Reading and Other Essays* by G. Hartman, *Language and Style* 11, no. 4, pp. 261–4.

74 Review of *Marxism and Form* and *The Prison House of Language* by Frederic Jameson, *Language and Style* 11, pp. 59–62.

75 Review of *Inquiries into the Fundamentals of Aesthetics* by S. Morawski, *The British Journal of Aesthetics* 18, pp. 35–7.

76 Review of *Janacek's Tragic Operas* by M. Ewans, *Composer* 63, pp. 29–31.

77 'Maître Sans Marteau', *Books and Bookmen* 23, no. 2, pp. 42–3 (Review of *Boulez: Composer, Conductor, Enigma* by Joan Peyser).

78 'New Presbyters, Old Priests', *Books and Bookmen* 23, nos. 4–5, pp. 26–8, 57–8 (Review of *Milton and The English Revolution* by Christopher Hill).

79 'Overhauling Modern Poetics', *Books and Bookmen* 23, no. 7 (April), pp. 21–3 (Review of *Structure and Society in Literary History* by Robert Weimann).

80 Review of *Tolstoy's Major Fiction* by E. Wasiolek, *Philosophy and Literature* 2, no. 2, pp. 267–9.

1979

81 'The Limits of Deconstructive Discourse', *Lettera* 18, pp. 218–26.

82 'Love Among the Structuralists', *Poetry Nation Review* 6, pp. 60–1.

83 'Woolf and Feminism', *Books and Bookmen* 24, no. 12 (September), pp. 63–4.

84 Review of *At the Pillars of Hercules* by Clive James, *Books and Bookmen*, vol. 24, no. 8 (May), pp. 24–5.

85 'Authentic Contemplation', *The Literary Review* 5, pp. 15–16 (Review of *Reflection, Time and the Novel* by Angel Medina).

86 'Critical Beginnings', *The Literary Review* 5, pp. 11–12 (Edward Said).

87 'Heroic Emblems', *Poetry Nation Review* 6, pp. 59–60 (Ian Hamilton Finlay).

88 'Types of Ambiguity: Shakespeare's Sonnets', *Essays in Criticism* 28, no. 3, pp. 245–53 (Review of *Shakespeare's Sonnets* by S. Booth).

1980

89   'Harold Bloom: a poetics of reconstruction', *The British Journal of Aesthetics* 20, no. 1, pp. 84–93.
90   'Criticism: a liberal charter', *The Literary Review*, 11, pp. 24–5 (Wayne Booth).
91   'De Man's Allegories of Reading', *The Literary Review* 16, pp. 44–6.
92   'Deconstruction and the Limits of Sense', *Essays in Criticism* 30, no. 4, pp. 281–92.
93   'Nietzsche: Being and Thinking', *The Literary Review* 16, no. 24, pp. 28–9.
94   'Poetries: their media and ends', *Yearbook of English Studies* 10, pp. 356–7 (on I. A. Richards).
95   'Slay What You Mean: Derrida's Nietzsche', *Quarto* 6, pp. 16–17.
96   Review of *James Joyce and the Revolution of the Word* by C. MacCabe, *Etudes Irlandaises*, no. 5, pp. 314–15.
97   'The Margins of Meaning', *The Cambridge Quarterly* 9, no. 3, pp. 280–4 (Review of *Spurs: Nietzsche's Styles* by Jacques Derrida).
98   'The Polymetaphorical Mailman', *Times Literary Supplement*, no. 4032, p. 761 (Review of *The Postcard: From Socrates to Freud and Beyond* by Jacques Derrida).
99   Review of *Poetic Artifice: A Theory of 20th Century Poetry* by V. Forrest-Thomson, *The British Journal of Aesthetics* 20, pp. 275–8.
100   'Gittings on Hardy', *The Literary Review* 26, pp. 40–1.
101   'Wrestling with Deconstructors', *Critical Quarterly* 20, pp. 57–62 (Review of *Literature Against Itself* by G. Graff).
102   'Clerkly Skepticism', *Essays in Criticism* 30, no. 1, pp. 84–93 (Review of *The Genesis of Secrecy: An Interpretation of Biblical Narrative* by Frank Kermode).
103   Review of *The Structure of Literary Understanding* by S. H. Olsen, *The British Journal of Aesthetics* 20, no. 1, pp. 82–4.

1981

104   'Deconstruction and Criticism', *Notes and Queries* 28, no. 4, pp. 376–8.
105   'Derrida at Yale: the deconstructive moment in modernist

poetics', *Philosophy and Literature* 4, no. 2, pp. 242–56.

106 'Derrida's *Positions*', *The British Journal of Aesthetics* 21, no. 4, pp. 372–5.

107 Review of *Beyond the Letter: a philosophical inquiry into ambiguity, vagueness, and metaphor* by I. Scheffler and *Metaphor and Thought* by A. Ortony (ed.), *Mind* 90, pp. 448–52.

108 Review of *Critical Practice* by C. Belsey, *The British Journal of Aesthetics* 20, pp. 275–8.

109 Review of *Formalism and Marxism*, by T. Bennett, *Modern Language Review* 76, pp. 143–6.

110 'Hardy's Letters', *Literary Review*, no. 35, pp. 18–20.

111 'Lacan: the talking cure', *Literary Review*, no. 32, pp. 16–17.

112 Review of *Linguistic Perspectives on Literature* by Ching, Haley, and Lunsford and *The Reader in the Text: Essays on Audience and Interpretation*, Suleiman and Crosman (eds.), *Modern Language Review* 76, pp. 906–9.

113 'On Difficulty', *Modern Language Review* 76, pp. 138–9 (Review of *On Difficulty and Other Essays* by George Steiner).

114 Review of *Politics and Letters: Interviews with the New Left Review* by Raymond Williams, *Critical Quarterly* 23, no. 4, pp. 87–90.

115 Review of *Pouvoirs de l'Horreur: An Essay on Abjection* by Julia Kristeva, *French Studies* 35, no. 4, pp. 492–3.

116 'The Verbalization of Violence', *Times Literary Supplement*, no. 4097, p. 1170 (Review of *The Origin of Language: A Formal Theory of Representation* by E. Gans).

1982

117 *Deconstruction: theory and practice* (London: Methuen) xiii, 157 pp. Translated into Japanese (Tokyo: UNI Agency Inc., 1985); and into Hebrew (Tel Aviv, 1988). 2nd Edn., revised and expanded, forthcoming 1991.

118 (Ed.), *Shostakovich: the man and his music* (London: Lawrence and Wishart) 233 pp.

119 'Between Marx and Nietzsche: the prospects for critical theory', *Journal of Literary Semantics* 10, no. 2, pp. 104–15.

120 'Deconstruction', 'Linguistics', 'Sociolinguistics', 'Structuralism', *What's What in the 1980's*, ed. Christopher Pick (London: Europa Publications) pp. 84–5, 194–5, 326–7, 346–8.

121   'The Great Illusion', *Performance*, no. 7, pp. 76–7 (Roland Barthes).

122   Review of *In The Arresting Eye: the rhetoric of imagism* by J. T. Gage, *The British Journal of Aesthetics* 22, no. 2, pp. 184–7.

123   Review of *Interpretation: An Essay on the Philosophy of Literary Criticism* by P. D. Juhl, *Modern Language Review* 77, pp. 130–2.

124   Review of *On the Margins of Discourse: The Relationship of Literature to Language* by B. H. Smith, *Modern Language Review* 77, pp. 136–7.

125   'Openness', *Essays in Criticism* 32, no. 1, pp. 89–93 (Review of *After the New Criticism* by Frank Lentricchia).

126   'School Prospectus', *Times Literary Supplement*, no. 4132, p. 628 (Review of *Modern Literary Theory – A Comparative Introduction* by A. Jefferson and D. Robey, eds.).

127   Review of *The Sign in Music and Literature* by W. Steiner, *The British Journal of Aesthetics* 22, no. 4, pp. 371–3.

128   'Transindividually Speaking', *Times Literary Supplement*, no. 4114, p. 144 (Review of *Lucien Goldmann: An Introduction* by M. Evans).

129   Review of *Working with Structuralism: Essays and Reviews on 19th & 20th Century Literature* by David Lodge, *Essays in Criticism*, 32, no. 4. pp. 369–74.

1983

130   *The Deconstructive Turn: essays in the rhetoric of philosophy* (London: Methuen) 201 pp. Japanese translation forthcoming 1990.

131   'Fictions of Authority: Narrative and Viewpoint in Kierkegaard's Writing', *The Southern Review* 16, no. 1, pp. 174–90. Reprinted in *Criticism* 25, no. 2, pp. 87–107. Reprinted and translated into Danish in *Kredsen* 51, no. 2, pp. 51–72 (1986).

132   'Image and Parable: Readings of Walter Benjamin', *Philosophy and Literature* 7, no. 1, pp. 15–31. Reprinted and translated into Japanese in *Modern Ideas* (Tokyo, 1985) pp. 96–118.

133   'Marxist or Utopian? – The Philosophy of Ernst Bloch', *Literature and History* 9, no. 2, pp. 240–5.

134   'That the Truest Philosophy is the Most Feigning: Austin on the Margins of Literature', *Renaissance and Modern Studies* 27, pp. 102–23.

135 'Transcendent Fictions: Imaginary Discourse in Descartes and Husserl', *Bradford Occasional Papers* 4, pp. 1–36. Reprinted in *Comparative Criticism*, ed. E. S. Shaffer (Cambridge: Cambridge University Press, 1985) pp. 25–47.

136 Review of *Against Criticism* by Ian McGilchrist, *Modern Language Review* 78, pp. 89–92.

137 Review of *Camera Lucida* by Roland Barthes, *Critical Quarterly*, 25, no. 1, pp. 88–91.

138 Review of *Comparative Criticism: a yearbook, vols. 2 & 3*, ed. E. S. Shaffer, *Modern Language Review* 78, pp. 375–7.

139 Review of *The Critical Difference: Essays in the Rhetoric of Contemporary Reading* by Barbara Johnson, *Modern Language Review* 78, pp. 381–3.

140 Review of *Essays in Modern Stylistics*, ed. Donald C. Freeman *Poetry Nation Review* 9, no. 6, pp. 61–2.

141 Review of *Four Critics: Croce, Valéry, Lukács, and Ingarden* by René Wellek, *Modern Language Review* 78, pp, 634–5.

142 Review of *Introduction to Poetics* by Tzvetan Todorov, *Modern Language Review* 78, pp. 636–7.

143 Review of *Marxism and Deconstruction: a critical articulation* by Michael Ryan, *Times Literary Supplement*, no. 4162, p. 6.

144 'Mortal Scripts', *London Review of Books* 5, no. 7, pp. 20–3.

145 Review of *Nature and Language* by Ralf Norrman and Jon Haarberg, *Modern Language Review* 78, pp. 395–7.

146 Review of *Philosophy and Fiction: Essays in Literary Aesthetics* by Peter Lamarque, *Times Literary Supplement*, no. 4199, p. 1024.

147 'From Plato to Nato', *London Review of Books* 5, no. 12, pp. 21–4.

148 Review of *Semiotics and Interpretation* by Robert Scholes, *Philosophy and Literature* 7, no. 2, pp. 278–9.

149 Review of *Reading Relations: A Dialectical Text/Book* by Bernard Sharratt, *Modern Language Review* 78, pp. 640–2.

150 Review of *Semiotics and Thematics in Hermeneutics* by T. K. Seung, *Times Literary Supplement*, no. 4173, p. 304.

151 Review of *System and Structure: Essays in Communication and Exchange* by Anthony Wilden, *Language and Style* 16, no. 1, pp. 107–9.

152 Review of *Untying the Text: A Post-structuralist Reader*, ed. Robert Young, *Modern Language Review* 78, pp. 383–5.

1984

153   (Ed.), *Inside the Myth: George Orwell – Views From the Left* (London: Lawrence and Wishart) 288 pp.

154   'Aesthetics and Politics: Reading Roger Scruton', *Southern Review* 17, no. 3, pp. 215–26.

155   'Beyond Textualism', *London Review of Books* 6, no. 1. pp. 16–18.

156   'Deconstruction and "Ordinary Language"': Speech *versus* Writing in the Text of Philosophy', *Indian Journal of Applied Linguistics* 10, pp. 107–24.

157   'Deconstruction, Naming and Necessity: Some Logical Options', *Journal of Literary Semantics* 13, no. 3, pp. 159–80.

158   'On Marxist Deconstruction: Prospects and Problems', *Southern Review* 17, no. 2, pp. 203–11.

159   'Philosophy as a Kind of Narrative: Rorty on Postmodern Liberal Culture', *enclitic* 7, pp. 144–59.

160   'Saving Deconstruction from the Pragmatists', *Meridian* 3, pp. 120–9. Reprinted as 'Philosophy, Theory and the "Contest of Faculties": Saving Deconstruction from the Pragmatists', *Journal of Literary Criticism* 1, no. 2, pp. 37–51; reprinted in Rajnath (ed.), *Deconstruction: a critique* (London: Macmillan, 1989) pp. 105–22.

161   'Some Versions of Rhetoric: Empson and de Man', *Genre*, vol. 7, pp. 191–214. Reprinted in *Rhetoric and Form*, ed. Robert Davis and Ronald Schleifer (Norman: Oklahoma University Press, 1985).

162   'Intimacy Regained', *Times Literary Supplement*, no. 4251, p. 1058 (Review of *Roland Barthes: The Professor of Desire* by S. Ungar).

163   'Justified Margins', *Southern Humanities Review* 18, pp. 289–98 (Review of *Margins of Philosophy* by Jacques Derrida).

164   Review of *The Pursuit of Signs: Semiotics, Literature, Deconstruction* by Jonathan Culler, *Modern Language Review* 79, pp. 388–90.

165   Review of *Reading Deconstruction/Deconstructive Reading* by G. Douglas Atkins, *Times Literary Supplement*, no. 4230, p. 470.

166   'Robert C. Elliott and the Literary Persona', *Yearbook of English Studies* 14, pp, 287–90.

167   'Some Versions of Narrative', *London Review of Books* 6, nos. 14/15, pp. 14–16.

1985

168 *The Contest of Faculties: Philosophy and Theory after Deconstruction* (London: Methuen) 247 pp.

169 'Dialectics and Difference: On the Politics of Deconstruction', *Southern Humanities Review* 19, no. 2, pp. 159–69.

170 'The Importance of Empson: The Criticism', *Essays in Criticism* 35, pp. 25–44.

171 'The Insistence of the Letter: Textuality and Metaphor in Wittgenstein's Later Philosophy', translated into Japanese in *Modern Ideas* (Tokyo) (December) pp. 118–39.

172 'The Politics of Theory', *PN Review* 7, no. 4, pp. 56–9.

173 'Post-Structuralist Shakespeare: Text and Ideology' in *Alternative Shakespeares*, ed. John Drakakis (London: Methuen) pp. 47–66.

174 'Reason, Rhetoric, Theory: Empson and de Man', *Raritan* 5, no. 1, pp. 89–106.

175 'Sense, Reference, and Logic: A Critique of Post-Structuralist Reason', *Journal of Literary Semantics* 14, no. 2, pp. 98–120.

176 'Suspended Sentences: Textual Theory and the Law', *The Southern Review* 18, no. 2, pp. 123–41.

177 Review of *Applied Grammatology: Pedagogy from Jacques Derrida to Joseph Beuys* by Gregory Ulmer, *Times Literary Supplement*, no. 4276, p. 295.

178 Review of *The Function of Criticism* by Terry Eagleton, *Southern Humanities Review* 19, no. 3, pp. 286–7.

179 Review of *Literary Criticism and Philosophy*, ed. J. P. Strelka *Modern Language Review* 80, pp. 398–400.

180 'Questions of Method: Greimas's Structural Semantics', *Journal of Literary Semantics* 19, no. 3, pp. 186–94.

181 'Reading as a Woman', *London Review of Books* 7, no. 6, pp. 8–11.

182 Review of *René Wellek* by M. Bucco and *R. P. Blackmur* by G. J. Pannick, *Modern Language Review* 80, pp. 138–9.

183 Review of *Teaching the Text* by Bryson and Kappeler (eds.), *Southern Humanities Review* 19, pp. 95–6.

184 'Textual Theory at the Bar of Reason', *London Review of Books* 7, no. 4, pp. 17–20.

185 Review of *Using Biography* by William Empson, *Southern Humanities Review* 19, no. 3, pp. 285–6.

1986

186 'Home Thoughts from Abroad: Derrida, Austin, and the Oxford Connection', *Philosophy and Literature* 10, no. 1, pp. 1–25. Reprinted in *Imagining France: Studies in Anglo-French Cultural Relations*, ed. Ceri Crossley and Ian Small (London: Macmillan, 1988) pp. 210–35.

187 Introduction, *Figuring Lacan: Criticism and the Cultural Unconscious* by Juliet MacCannell (London: Croom Helm) pp. vii–x.

188 'Jeremy Bentham', 'Jacques Lacan', 'C. K. Ogden', 'Structuralism and Post-Structuralism' in Sebeok, Thomas A. (ed.), *Encyclopedic Dictionary of Semiotics* (Amsterdam: Mouton de Gruyter) pp. 78–80, 422–4, 644–7, 986–91.

189 'Misreading the Signs', *Meridian* 5, pp. 84–8.

190 'On Derrida's "Apocalyptic Tone": Textual Politics and the Principle of Reason', *Southern Review* 19, no.1, pp. 13–30.

191 'Semiotics in Great Britain' in *The Semiotic Sphere*, ed. Thomas Sebeok and Jean Umiker-Sebeok (New York: Plenum Press) pp. 229–51.

192 Review of *Samuel Beckett and the Meaning of Being* by L. S. Butler, *Southern Humanities Review* 20, no. 3, pp. 268–9.

193 Review of *Beyond Metaphysics: The Hermeneutic Circle in Contemporary Continental Philosophy* by John Llewelyn, *Philosophical Books* 27, no. 4, pp. 225–9.

194 Review of *The Craft of Criticism* by Alan Rodway, *Modern Language Review* 81, pp. 429–31.

195 Review of *Does Deconstruction Make Any Difference?* by Michael Fischer, *Essays in Poetics* 11, no. 1, pp. 88–95.

196 Review of *The Ear of the Other: Texts and Discussions* by Jacques Derrida, *Diacritics* 16, no. 4, pp. 61–9.

197 Review of *Essays on the Philosophy of Music* by E. Bloch, *Composer*, no. 88, pp. 20–3.

198 Review of *The Leavises – Recollections and Impressions* by D. Thompson, *Southern Humanities Review* 20, no. 3, pp. 269–70.

199 'Names', *The London Review of Books* 8, no. 3, pp. 10–12 (Review of *Signsponge* by Jacques Derrida).

200 Review-essay on *The Rhetoric of Romanticism* by Paul de Man, *Southern Humanities Review* 20, no. 1, pp. 53–69.

201 Review of *Reconstructing Literature* by L. Lerner, *Southern Humanities Review* 20, no. 3, pp. 270–1.

202 Review of *The Rhythms of English Poetry* by Derek Attridge, *Southern Humanities Review* 20, no. 2, pp. 173–4.
203 'Semiotics Right and Left', *London Review of Books* 8, no. 6, pp. 16–18.
204 'Whose Game is it Anyway? or The Politics of Postmodernism', *Southern Review* 19, no.3, pp. 334–43 (Review of *Just Gaming* by J. F. Lyotard and J. L. Thébaud).
205 Review of *Wittgenstein and Derrida* by Henry Staten, *Comparative Literature* 38, no. 4, pp. 350–9.

1987

206 *Jacques Derrida* (London: Fontana and Cambridge, Mass.: Harvard University Press) 271 pp. Japanese and Russian translations forthcoming, 1990 and 1991.
207 (Ed. with Richard Machin), *Post-Structuralist Readings of English Poetry* (Cambridge: Cambridge University Press) x, 406 pp.
208 'Against a New Pragmatism: Law, Deconstruction and the Interests of Theory', *Southern Humanities Review* 21, no. 4, pp. 301–26.
209 'Against Postmodernism: Derrida, Kant and Nuclear Politics', *Paragraph* 9, pp. 1–30.
210 'Allegories of Disenchantment: Poetry and Politics in de Man's Early Essays' *Southern Review* 20, no. 3, pp. 215–39.
211 'Derrida, On Reflection', *New Formations* 1, no. 3, pp. 139–51.
212 Introduction, *A. J. Greimas and the Nature of Meaning* by Ronald Schleifer (London: Croom Helm) pp. iii–xix.
213 Introduction, *Christopher Caudwell* by Robert Sullivan (London: Croom Helm) pp. 1–5.
214 'Orwell Revisited: Democracy and Nuclear Politics', *The Age Monthly Review* (Melbourne) 7, no. 7, pp. 4–6.
215 'Paul de Man's Past', *London Review of Books* 10, no. 3, pp. 7–11.
216 'Philosophy as *Not* Just a "Kind of Writing": Derrida and the Claim of Reason', *Meridian* 6, no. 1, pp. 3–14. Dutch translation in *Restant* 15, no. 4, pp. 211–27; reprinted in *Redrawing the Lines: Analytical Philosophy, Deconstruction, and Literary Theory*, ed. Reed Way Dasenbrock (Minneapolis: University of Minnesota Press) pp. 189–203.

217 'Pope Among the Formalists: Textual Politics in "The Rape of the Lock"', in *Post-Structuralist Readings of English Poetry*, (Cambridge: Cambridge University Press) pp. 134–61.

218 'The Politics of Style and the Fate of Reading', *Southern Humanities Review* 21, no. 1, pp. 49–64 (Review of *Easy Pieces* by G. Hartman).

219 'The Rhetoric of Remembrance: Derrida on de Man', *Textual Practice* 1, no. 2, pp. 154–68.

220 Review of *Derrida and the Economy of Differance* by Irene Harvey, *Criticism* 29, no. 3, pp. 393–403.

221 'Dissonant Activity', *Times Literary Supplement*, no. 4392, p. 606. (Music Review of *Lady Macbeth of Mtsensk* by Shostakovich).

222 'Thinking the Unthought', *Times Literary Supplement*, no. 4420, pp. 407–8 (Review of *Glassary* by J. P. Leavey et al; *Glas* by Jacques Derrida; and *The Tain of the Mirror: Derrida and the Philosophy of Reflection* by R. Gasché).

1988

223 *Paul de Man: Deconstruction and the Critique of Aesthetic Ideology* (New York and London: Routledge) 218 pp.

224 (With Ian Whitehouse) 'The Rhetoric of Deterrence', in *Styles of Discourse*, ed. Nikolas Coupland (London: Croom Helm) pp. 293–322.

225 Editor's Introduction, *F. R. Leavis* by Michael Bell (London: Routledge) pp. viii–xviii.

226 'Feminist Criticism' and 'Formalism' in *The Cambridge Guide to Literature in English*, ed. Ian Ousby (Cambridge: Cambridge University Press) pp. 347–8, 361.

227 'Law, Deconstruction and the Resistance to Theory', *Journal of Law and Society* 15, pp. 166–87.

228 'Paul de Man and the Critique of Aesthetic Ideology', *AUMLA* (Journal of the Australasian Universities Language & Literature Association), no. 69, pp. 3–47. Reprinted in *Genius: The History of an Idea*, ed. Penelope Murray (Oxford: Basil Blackwell) pp. 141–65.

229 'Philosophy and Literary Theory: The Work of Donald Davidson', *Textual Practice* 2, No. 2, pp. 219–29.

230 'Postmodernizing History: Right-Wing Revisionism and the Uses of Theory' *Southern Review* 21, no. 2, pp. 123–40.

231 'Reading Donald Davidson: Truth, Meaning and Right Interpretation', in *Analytic Aesthetics*, ed. Richard Shusterman (Oxford: Basil Blackwell) pp. 97–122.

232 'Remembering Paul de Man: A Review Article', *Prose Studies* 11, pp. 90–100.

233 'Utopian Deconstruction: Ernst Bloch, Paul de Man and the Politics of Music', *Paragraph* 11, no. 1, pp. 24–57. Reprinted in *Deconstruction in Contemporary Criticism*, ed. A. C. Sukla (Calcutta: Rupa & Co.) pp. 183–220.

234 Review of *Difference in Translation*, ed. Joseph F. Graham, *Comparative Literature* 40, pp. 52–8.

1989

235 *Deconstruction and the Interests of Theory* (London: Pinter Publishers; Norman: Oklahoma University Press) 250 pp.

236 (with Andrew Benjamin) *What is Deconstruction?* (London: Academy Editions) 56 pp. Translated into French and German (Academy Editions, forthcoming 1991).

237 (Ed.) *Music and the Politics of Culture* (London: Lawrence & Wishart) 356 pp.

238 'Deconstruction, Postmodernism and Philosophy: Habermas on Derrida', *Praxis International* 8, (January) pp. 426–46.

239 'Jacques Derrida in Discussion with Christopher Norris', *Architectural Design* 59, nos. 1–2, pp. 7–11. Reprinted in *Deconstruction: Omnibus Volume* (London: Academy Editions) pp. 71–5.

240 'Derrida's Verité', *Comparative Criticism* 11, pp. 235–51.

241 'The Ethics of Reading and the Limits of Irony: Kierkegaard Among the Postmodernists', *Southern Humanities Review* 23, pp. 1–35. Reprinted in *Kierkegaard, Poet of Existence*, ed. Birgit Bertung (Copenhagen: C. A. Reitzel) pp. 89–107.

242 Review of *Language, Music, and the Sign: a study in aesthetics, poetics and poetic practice from Collins to Coleridge* by Kevin Barry, *Ideas And Production*, no. 11, pp. 107–18.

243 'Lost in the Funhouse: Baudrillard and the Politics of Postmodernism', *Textual Practice* 3, no. 3, pp. 360–87.

244 Review of *Electric Language: a philosophical study of word-processing* by Michael Heim, *Comparative Literature* 41, No. 3, pp. 270–77.

The following works by Christopher Norris are cited in the Introduction:

William Empson and the Philosophy of Literary Criticism (1978) (WE)
Deconstruction: theory and practice (1982) (DTP)
Jacques Derrida (1987) (D)
Paul de Man: Deconstruction and the Critique of Aesthetic Ideology (1988) (PDM)
Deconstruction and the Interests of Theory (1989) (DIT)

Index

Printed in the United States
17027LVS00006B/56

9 780631 175575